A Handbook of

EMPLOYEE REWARD
MANAGEMENT
AND PRACTICE

A Handbook of

EMPLOYEE REWARD MANAGEMENT AND PRACTICE

2ND EDITION

Michael Armstrong

KOGAN
PAGE

London and Philadelphia

Publisher's note

Every possible effort has been made to ensure that the information contained in this book is accurate at the time of going to press, and the publishers and author cannot accept responsibility for any errors or omissions, however caused. No responsibility for loss or damage occasioned to any person acting, or refraining from action, as a result of the material in this publication can be accepted by the editor, the publisher or any of the authors.

First published in Great Britain and the United States in 2005 by Kogan Page Limited
Second edition 2007

120 Pentonville Road
London N1 9JN
United Kingdom
www.kogan-page.co.uk

525 South 4th Street, #241
Philadelphia PA 19147
USA

© Michael Armstrong and Tina Stephens, 2005
© Michael Armstrong, 2007

ISBN-10 0 7494 4962 4
ISBN-13 978 0 7494 4962 9

British Library Cataloguing-in-Publication Data

A CIP record for this book is available from the British Library.

Library of Congress Cataloging-in-Publication Data

Armstrong, Michael, 1928–
   A handbook of employee reward management and practice / Michael Armstrong. – 2nd ed.
      p. cm.
   ISBN-13:   978-0-7494-4962-9
   ISBN-10:   0-7494-4962-4
 1. Incentives in industry. 2. Employee motivation. I. Title.
   HF5549.5.I5A668 2007
   658.3'142–dc22
                                                    2006039560

Typeset by JS Typesetting Ltd, Porthcawl, Mid Glamorgan
Printed and bound in Great Britain by Bell & Bain, Glasgow

Contents

Preface

This is a practical handbook designed to provide guidance on the approaches that can be adopted in developing and managing reward strategies, policies and processes. It is aligned to the professional standards of the Chartered Institute of Personnel and Development for employee reward. The plan of the book is shown in Figure 0.1.

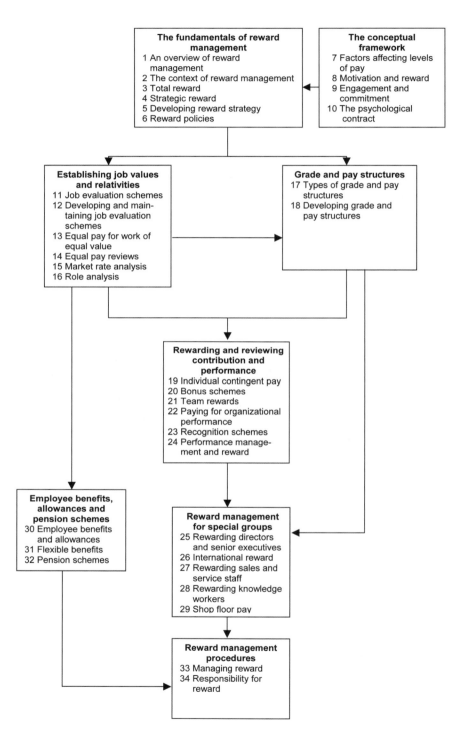

Figure 0.1 Plan of the book

Part 1

The fundamentals of reward management

1

Reward management: an overview

This chapter starts with an introductory discussion of the concept of reward management and its aims. This is followed by an assessment of how these aims can be achieved,
a description of the elements of a reward system and an analysis of the factors that
affect reward management. The chapter concludes with a survey of developments in
reward management.

REWARD MANAGEMENT DEFINED

Reward management deals with the strategies, policies and processes required to ensure
that the contribution of people to the organization is recognized by both financial and
non-financial means. It is about the design, implementation and maintenance of reward
systems (reward processes, practices and procedures), which aim to meet the needs of
both the organization and its stakeholders. The overall objective is to reward people
fairly, equitably and consistently in accordance with their value to the organization in
order to further the achievement of the organization's strategic goals.

Reward management is not just about pay and employee benefits. It is equally
concerned with non-financial rewards such as recognition, learning and development
opportunities and increased job responsibility.

THE AIMS OF REWARD MANAGEMENT

The aims of reward management are to:

- reward people according to the value they create;
- align reward practices with business goals *and* with employee values and needs;
- reward the right things to convey the right message about what is important in terms of behaviours and outcomes;
- help to attract and retain the high-quality people the organization needs;
- motivate people and obtain their engagement and commitment;
- develop a high-performance culture.

ACHIEVING THE AIMS

The aims of reward management are achieved by developing and implementing strategies, policies, processes and practices that are founded on a philosophy, operate in accordance with the principles of distributive and natural justice, function fairly, equitably, consistently and transparently, are aligned to the business strategy, fit the context and culture of the organization, are fit for purpose and help to develop a high-performance culture.

Reward philosophy

Reward management is based on a well-articulated philosophy – a set of beliefs and guiding principles that are consistent with the values of the organization and help to enact them. The philosophy recognizes that, if human resource management (HRM) is about investing in human capital from which a reasonable return is required, then it is proper to reward people differentially according to their contribution (ie the return on investment they generate).

The philosophy of reward management also recognizes that it must be strategic in the sense that it addresses longer-term issues relating to how people should be valued for what they do and what they achieve. Reward strategies and the processes that are required to implement them have to flow from the business strategy.

Reward management adopts a 'total reward' approach, which emphasizes the importance of considering all aspects of reward as a coherent whole that is linked to other HR initiatives designed to achieve the motivation, commitment, engagement and development of employees. This requires the integration of reward strategies with other HRM strategies, including talent management and human resource development. Reward management is an integral part of an HRM approach to managing people.

Distributive justice

As defined by Leventhal (1), distributive justice refers to how rewards are provided to people. They will feel that they have been treated justly if they believe that the rewards have been distributed in accordance with the value of their contribution, that they receive what was promised to them and that they get what they need.

Procedural justice

Procedural justice refers to the ways in which managerial decisions are made and reward policies are put into practice. The five factors that affect perceptions of procedural justice as identified by Tyler and Bies (2) are:

1. The viewpoint of employees is given proper consideration.
2. Personal bias towards employees is suppressed.
3. The criteria for decisions are applied consistently to all employees.
4. Employees are provided with early feedback about the outcome of decisions.
5. Employees are provided with adequate explanations of why decisions have been made.

Fairness

A fair reward system is one that operates in accordance with the principles of distributive and procedural justice. It also conforms to the 'felt-fair' principle formulated by Eliot Jaques (3). This states that pay systems will be fair if they are felt to be fair. The assumptions underpinning the theory are that:

● there is an unrecognized standard of fair payment for any level of work;
● unconscious knowledge of the standard is shared among the population at work;
● pay must match the level of work and the capacity of the individual to do it;
● people should not receive less pay than they deserve by comparison with their fellow workers.

This felt-fair principle has passed into the common language of those involved in reward management. It is sometimes used as the final arbiter of how a job should be graded, possibly overriding the conclusions reached by an analytical job evaluation exercise (the so-called 'felt-fair test'). Such tests are in danger of simply reproducing existing prejudices about relative job values.

Equity

Equity is achieved when people are rewarded appropriately in relation to others within the organization. Equitable reward processes ensure that relativities between jobs are measured as objectively as possible and that equal pay is provided for work of equal value.

Consistency

A consistent approach to reward management means that decisions on pay do not vary arbitrarily – without due cause – between different people or at different times. They do not deviate irrationally from what would generally be regarded as fair and equitable.

Transparency

Transparency exists when people understand how reward processes function and how they are affected by them. The reasons for pay decisions are explained at the time they are made. Employees have a voice in the development of reward policies and practices.

Strategic alignment

The strategic alignment of reward practices ensures that reward initiatives are planned by reference to the requirements of the business strategy and are designed to support the achievement of business goals.

Contextual and culture fit

The design of reward processes should be governed by the context (the characteristics of the organization, its business strategy and the type of employees) and the organization's culture (its values and behavioural norms). Account should be taken of good practice elsewhere, but this should not be regarded as best practice, ie universally applicable. Best fit is more important than best practice.

Fit for purpose

The formulation of reward strategy and the design of the reward system should be based on an understanding of the objectives of reward management and should be developed to achieve that purpose.

Developing a high-performance culture

A high-performance culture is one in which people are aware of the need to perform well and behave accordingly in order to meet or exceed expectations. Employees will be engaged in their work and committed to the organization. Such a culture embraces a number of interrelated processes that together make an impact on the performance of the organization through its people in such areas as productivity, quality, levels of customer service, growth, profits and, ultimately in profit-making firms, the delivery of increased shareholder value. In our more heavily service- and knowledge-based economy, employees have become the most important determinant of organizational success.

Lloyds TSB has produced the following definition of what they mean by a high-performance organization:

- People know what's expected of them – they are clear about their goals and accountabilities.
- They have the skills and competencies to achieve their goals.
- High performance is recognized and rewarded accordingly.
- People feel that their job is worth doing, and that there's a strong fit between the job and their capabilities.
- Managers act as supportive leaders and coaches, providing regular feedback, performance reviews and development.
- A pool of talent ensures a continuous supply of high performers in key roles.
- There's a climate of trust and teamwork, aimed at delivering a distinctive service to the customer.

A high-performance culture can be developed by taking into account characteristics such as those listed above and applying an integrated set of processes, of which reward is an important part. Besides reward, the processes will include those concerned with resourcing and talent management (ensuring that the organization has the high-performing people it needs), learning and development, performance management, the enhancement of the working environment (for example, work design and work/life balance) and communication.

THE REWARD SYSTEM

The approaches to achieving the aims of reward management as described above are incorporated in the reward system of an organization. This consists of:

- *Reward strategies*, which set out what the organization intends to do in the longer term to develop and implement reward policies, practices, processes and procedures that will further the achievement of its business goals. For example, an organization may have a strategy to maintain competitive rates of pay.
- *Reward policies*, which set guidelines for decision making and action. For example, an organization may have a policy that sets the levels of pay in the organization compared with median market rates.
- *Reward practices*, which consist of the grade and pay structures, techniques such as job evaluation, and schemes such as contingent pay used to implement reward strategy and policy. For example, the policy on pay levels will lead to the practice of collecting and analysing market rate data, and making pay adjustments that reflect market rates of increase.
- *Reward processes*, which consist of the ways in which policies are implemented and practices carried out, for example the way in which the outcomes of surveys are applied and how managers manage the pay adjustment and review process.
- *Reward procedures*, which are operated in order to maintain the system and to ensure that it operates efficiently and flexibly and provides value for money. For example, a procedure will be used for conducting the annual pay review.

ELEMENTS OF A REWARD SYSTEM

The elements of a reward system and the interrelationships between them are shown in Figure 1.1. A brief description of each element follows.

Business strategy

The starting point of the reward system is the business strategy of the organization. This identifies the business drivers and sets out the business goals. The drivers are unique to any organization but will often include items such as high performance, profitability, productivity, innovation, customer service, quality, price/cost leadership and the need to satisfy stakeholders – investors, shareholders, employees and, in local authorities, elected representatives.

Reward strategy and policy

The reward strategy flows from an analysis of the business drivers. The question is: 'How can these be supported by reward in order to achieve the goals of the business?' The reward strategy will define longer-term intentions in such areas as pay structures, contingent pay, employee benefits, steps to increase engagement and commitment and adopting a total reward approach.

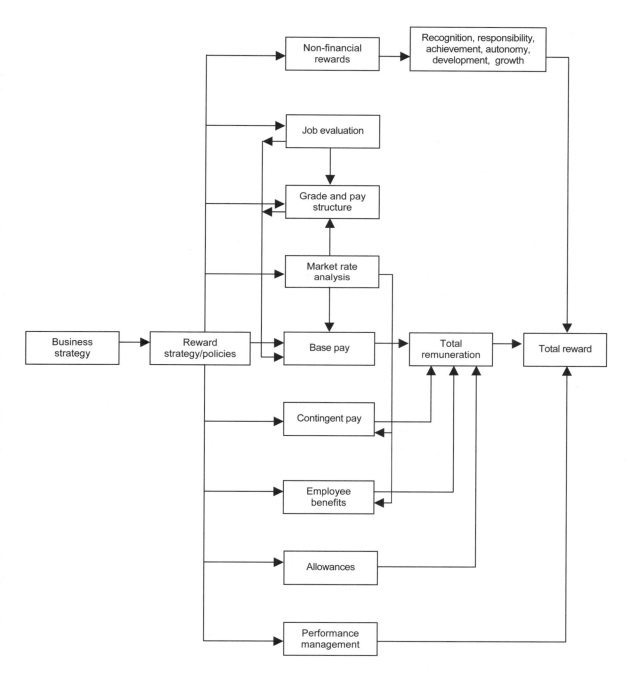

Figure 1.1   Reward system elements and interrelationships

Reward policy will cover such matters as levels of pay, achieving equal pay, approaches to contingent pay, the use of job evaluation and market surveys and flexing benefits.

Base or basic pay

The base rate is the amount of pay (the fixed salary or wage) that constitutes the rate for the job. It may be varied according to the grade of the job or, for shop floor workers, the level of skill required.

Base pay will be influenced by internal and external relativities. The internal relativities may be measured by some form of job evaluation. External relativities (going rates) are assessed by tracking market rates. Alternatively, levels of pay may be agreed through collective bargaining with trade unions or by reaching individual agreements.

Base pay may be expressed as an annual, weekly or hourly rate. This is sometimes referred to as a time rate system of payment. Contingent pay or allowances as described later may be added to base pay. The rate may be adjusted to reflect increases in the cost of living or market rates by the organization unilaterally or by agreement with a trade union.

Contingent pay

Additional financial rewards may be provided that are related to performance, competence, contribution, skill or experience. These are referred to as 'contingent pay'. Contingent payments may be added to base pay, ie 'consolidated'. If such payments are not consolidated (ie paid as cash bonuses) they are described as 'variable pay'. Contingent pay schemes are described in Chapters 19 to 22.

Employee benefits

Employee benefits include pensions, sick pay, insurance cover, company cars and a number of other 'perks'. They consist of elements of remuneration additional to the various forms of cash pay and also include provisions for employees that are not strictly remuneration, such as annual holidays (see Chapters 30 to 32).

Allowances

Allowances are paid in addition to basic pay for special circumstances (eg living in London) or features of employment (eg working unsocial hours). They may be determined unilaterally by the organization but they are often the subject of negotiation. The main types of allowances are location allowances, overtime payments, shift payments, working conditions allowances and stand-by or call-out allowances made to those who have to be available to come in to work when required.

Total earnings

Total earnings (financial rewards) consist of the value of all cash payments (base pay, contingent pay and allowances, ie total earnings).

Total remuneration

Total remuneration consists of the financial rewards represented by total earnings plus the value of the benefits received by employees.

Job evaluation

Job evaluation is a systematic process for defining the relative worth or size of within an organization in order to establish internal relativities and pr basis for designing an equitable grade structure, grading jobs in the managing relativities. It does not determine the level of pay dir can be analytical or non-analytical. It is based on the analys leads to the production of job descriptions or role profi in Chapters 11 and 12.

Market rate analysis

Market rate analysis is the proc for comparable jobs to inf on pay structures. A r compare with ex described in Chap

Grade and pay stru

Jobs may be placed in structure, pay is influenc provide scope for pay prog. service. Alternatively, a 'spo no provision is made for pay j structures are described in Chap

Performance management

Performance management processes (see Chapter 24) define individual perform-ance and contribution expectations, assess performance against those expectations, provide for regular constructive feedback, and result in agreed plans for performance improvement, learning and personal development. They are a means of providing non-financial motivation and may also inform contingent pay decisions.

Non-financial rewards

Non-financial rewards do not involve any direct payments and often arise from the work itself, for example achievement, autonomy, recognition, scope to use and develop skills, training, career development opportunities and high-quality leadership.

Total reward

Total reward is the combination of financial and non-financial rewards available to employees (see Chapter 3).

FACTORS AFFECTING REWARD MANAGEMENT POLICY AND PRACTICE

d management policy and practice are subject to a number of influences. As
ized below, these consist of contextual factors arising from the internal and
nvironment and conceptual factors relating to theories and beliefs about
nagement, total reward, human capital management, the factors affecting
otivation, engagement, commitment and the psychological contract.

vironment

onment consists of the organization's culture and its business,
le, as considered in Chapter 2.

ent

environment are competitive pressure, globalization, and
d employment. These are also considered in Chapter 2.

Strategic management

Strategic reward (see Chapter 4) is an aspect of strategic management the purpose of which, as expressed by Rosabeth Moss Kanter (4), is to 'elicit the present actions for the future' and become 'action vehicles – integrating and institutionalizing mechanisms for change'. Strategic management has been defined by Pearce and Robinson (5) as 'the set of decisions and actions resulting in the formulation and implementation of strategies designed to achieve the objectives of an organization'.

However, strategic management in reality is not necessarily a formal, well-articulated and linear process. Strategies may be formulated as they are used, and Mintzberg (6) has emphasized that strategy emerges over time in response to evolving situations. He believes that business strategy is best regarded as a 'pattern in a stream of activities'. This applies equally to reward strategy.

Total reward

Total reward policies as discussed in Chapter 3 provide for a holistic approach to be adopted to reward management, which ensures that all aspects of reward are treated as a coherent portfolio of policies and practices.

Human capital management

Human capital management (HCM) is concerned with obtaining, analysing and reporting on data, which informs the direction of value-adding people management strategic, investment and operational decisions at corporate level and at the level of front-line management. An HCM approach to reward management will assemble data on the effectiveness of reward management policies but in a more advanced form will attempt to assess the impact of remuneration policies on people and the business, thus informing strategic plans.

The factors affecting levels of pay

The factors affecting levels of pay considered in Chapter 7 influence pay decisions regarding the rate for the job, market rates and pay reviews.

Motivation

Motivation theory as described in Chapter 8 is important as a guide to the use of contingent pay and the non-financial elements of total reward.

Engagement and commitment

The concepts of job engagement and organizational commitment also provide guidance on total reward policies and contingent pay (see Chapter 9).

The psychological contract

It is necessary to understand what the psychological contract is and its significance when formulating and implementing reward policy as a key aspect of relationships with employees (see Chapter 10).

THE DEVELOPMENT OF REWARD MANAGEMENT

The development of the concept of reward management and the reward system as described above has taken place over a number of years. An analysis of the overall developments is given in Figure 1.2.

The contributions of the more influential commentators (mainly US) to these developments are summarized below.

Strategic pay (Lawler)

Lawler (7) emphasized that when developing reward policies it is necessary to think and act strategically about reward. Reward policies should take account of the organization's goals, values and culture and of the challenges of a more competitive global economy. New pay helps to develop the individual and organizational behaviour that a company needs if its business goals are to be met. Pay policies and practices must flow from the overall strategy and they can help to emphasize important objectives such as customer satisfaction and retention and product or service quality.

The new pay (Schuster and Zingheim)

Lawler's concept of the new pay was developed by Schuster and Zingheim (8), who described its fundamental principles as follows:

- Total compensation programmes should be designed to reward results and behaviour consistent with the key goals of the organization.
- Pay can be a positive force for organizational change.
- The major thrust of new pay is in introducing variable (at risk) pay.
- The new pay emphasis is on team as well as individual rewards, with employees sharing financially in the organization's success.

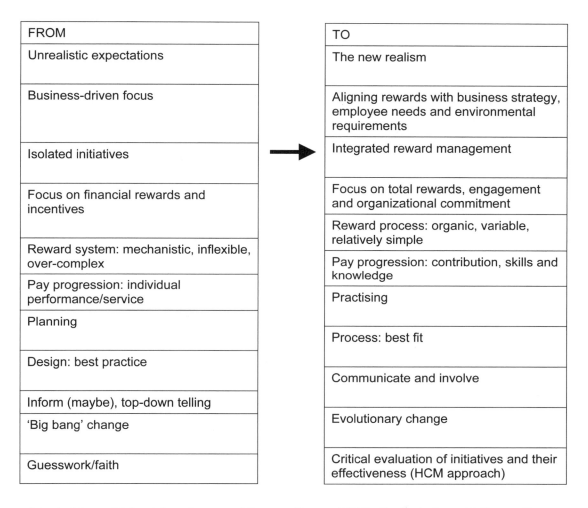

FROM	TO
Unrealistic expectations	The new realism
Business-driven focus	Aligning rewards with business strategy, employee needs and environmental requirements
Isolated initiatives	Integrated reward management
Focus on financial rewards and incentives	Focus on total rewards, engagement and organizational commitment
Reward system: mechanistic, inflexible, over-complex	Reward process: organic, variable, relatively simple
Pay progression: individual performance/service	Pay progression: contribution, skills and knowledge
Planning	Practising
Design: best practice	Process: best fit
Inform (maybe), top-down telling	Communicate and involve
'Big bang' change	Evolutionary change
Guesswork/faith	Critical evaluation of initiatives and their effectiveness (HCM approach)

Adapted from: Michael Armstrong and Duncan Brown (2006) *Strategic Reward*, Kogan Page, London

Figure 1.2   Overall developments in reward management

● Pay is an employee relations issue – employees have the right to determine whether the values, culture and reward systems of the organization match their own.

But Lawler (9) later emphasized that the 'new pay' ideology should be regarded as a conceptual approach to payment rather than a list of prescriptions, pointing out that: 'The new pay is not a set of compensation practices at all, but rather a way of thinking about reward systems in a complex organization... The new pay does not necessarily mean implementing new reward practices or abandoning traditional ones; it means identifying pay practices that enhance the organization's strategic effectiveness.'

Dynamic pay (Flannery, Hofrichter and Platten)

Flannery, Hofrichter and Platten (10) expounded the concept of 'dynamic pay' and suggested that the nine principles that support a successful pay strategy are:

1. Align compensation with the organization's culture, values and strategic business goals.
2. Link compensation to the other changes.
3. Time the compensation programme to best support other change initiatives.
4. Integrate pay with other people processes.
5. Democratize the pay process.
6. Demystify compensation.
7. Measure results.
8. Refine. Refine again. Refine some more.
9. Be selective. Don't take to heart everything you hear or read about pay.

Pay people right (Zingheim and Schuster)

Zingheim and Schuster (11) have laid down the following six principles for 'paying people right':

1. Create a positive and 'natural' reward experience.
2. Align rewards with business goals to achieve 'a win–win partnership'.
3. Extend people's 'line of sight' between effort and outcome, motivating 'smart working' over simply expending extra effort.
4. Integrate reward with strategic aims and the kind of contribution desired.
5. Reward individual ongoing (input) value to the organization with base pay.
6. Reward results (outputs) with variable pay.

The new realism (Armstrong and Brown)

The US writers referred to above created the belief that reward management was a major lever for change, even the main lever. This view was tempered by Armstrong and Brown (12), who wrote:

> Models of pay popularized in the 1980s and 1990s are not necessarily regarded as appropriate or workable in the 21st century. The belief that reward can be a leading driver of, rather than a contributor to, cultural change is not accepted in the UK so readily as it used to be. Mark Thompson at Oxford University writes that, 'Managing reward is often a job of short-term damage limitation, not the strategic lever for change that appears so seductive in the writing of American commentators' [13]. The dream of all-powerful strategic reward, of the Tom Cruise *Top Gun* style reward managers described by Schuster and Zingheim [8] has been subjected to a reality check.

Armstrong and Brown (14) have suggested the following approach to reward strategy, which more realistically fits the UK scene. This has the following characteristics:

- appreciating that a good strategy is one that works and therefore focusing on implementation programmes;
- 'planning with implementation in mind' – recognizing during the design process that plans have to be converted into reality and taking steps to anticipate the problems involved;
- aligning reward strategies with the business and HR strategies;
- ensuring that reward strategy fits the culture and characteristics of the organization, meets business needs and takes account of individual needs and preferences;
- being aware of good practice elsewhere but not being seduced by the notion that it is best practice, ie universally applicable and easily replicated;
- paying more attention to using strategic reward initiatives to support the engagement and commitment of people so that they are motivated and productive, rather than focusing on the mechanics of new reward 'fads';
- bearing in mind that the development and implementation of reward strategy is an evolutionary process – it is about doing things better at a manageable pace rather than extraordinary new developments;
- providing 'flexibility within a framework', ie developing a flexible approach to the reward of different people but always within a framework that provides for consistent treatment;
- appreciating that implementing reward strategy will require a comprehensive change management programme;

- recognizing the importance of the part played by line managers in implementing reward strategy and the need to ensure that they are committed and have the necessary skills;
- paying close and continuous attention to communicating with employees and involving them in the development as well as the implementation of reward strategy;
- being absolutely clear about the objectives of the strategy and resolute about evaluating its effectiveness.

REFERENCES

1   Leventhal, GS (1980) What should be done with equity theory?, in *Social Exchange: Advances in theory and research*, ed GK Gergen, MS Greenberg and RH Willis, Plenum, New York

2   Tyler, TR and Bies, RJ (1990) Beyond formal procedures: the interpersonal context of procedural justice, in *Applied Social Psychology and Organizational Settings*, ed JS Carrol, Lawrence Erlbaum, Hillsdale, NJ

3   Jaques, E (1961) *Equitable Payment*, Heinemann, London

4   Kanter, RM (1984) *The Change Masters*, Allen & Unwin, London

5   Pearce, JA and Robinson, RB (1988) *Strategic Management: Strategy formulation and implementation*, Irwin, Georgetown, Ontario

6   Mintzberg, H (1987) Crafting strategy, *Harvard Business Review*, July/August, pp 66–74

7   Lawler, EE (1990) *Strategic Pay*, Jossey-Bass, San Francisco

8   Schuster, JR and Zingheim, PK (1992) *The New Pay*, Lexington Books, New York

9   Lawler, EE (1995) The new pay: a strategic approach, *Compensation and Benefits Review*, November

10 Flannery, TP, Hofrichter, DA and Platten, PE (1996) *People, Performance, and Pay*, Free Press, New York

11 Zingheim, P and Schuster, JR (2000) *Pay People Right! Breakthrough strategies to create great companies*, Jossey-Bass, San Francisco

12 Armstrong, M and Brown, D (2005) Reward strategies and trends in the United Kingdom: the land of diverse and pragmatic dreams, *Compensation and Benefits Review*, July, pp 155–63

13 Thompson, M (1998) Trust and reward, in *Trust, Motivation and Commitment: A reader*, ed SJ Perkins and St J Sandringham, pp 66–71, Strategic Remuneration Research Centre, Faringdon

14 Armstrong, M and Brown, D (2006) *Strategic Reward*, Kogan Page, London

2

The context of reward management

Reward management takes place within the context of the internal (corporate) and external environments. These can exert considerable influence on reward strategy and policies as described in this chapter. Reward policies cannot be considered, designed or operated independently of their context. The approach to reward between organizations differs considerably and there are no universally effective or ineffective reward practices. The diversity of people working in highly varied organizations and settings explains why this is the case.

One of the recurring themes in this book is the importance of best fit rather than best practice. Best fit is what organizations have to strive for when formulating reward strategies, although, to a degree, 'fit' can be forced upon them by the circumstances in which they operate and the type of people they employ.

THE INTERNAL ENVIRONMENT

Reward policy and practice will be affected by the characteristics of the organization with regard to its purpose, products and services, processes, sector (private, public, voluntary or not-for-profit) and, importantly, culture, which is influenced by all the other characteristics.

Corporate culture

The culture of the organization can make a significant impact on reward management policy and practice. Corporate or organizational culture consists of shared values, norms, attitudes and assumptions, which influence the way people act and the way things get done. It is significant because it is rooted in deeply held beliefs and reflects what has worked in the past. A positive culture can work for an organization by creating an environment conducive to performance improvement, the management of change and a sense of identity and unity of purpose. It can help to shape behaviour by giving guidance on what is expected. The wrong culture can work against an organization by erecting barriers that prevent the attainment of reward strategic objectives. These barriers include resistance to change and lack of commitment.

In reward management, the most important aspect of culture that needs to be taken into account is the core values of the organization. Values are expressed in beliefs as to what is best for the organization and what sort of behaviour is desirable. The 'value set' of an organization may be recognized only at top level, or it may be shared throughout the firm, so that the enterprise can be described as 'value-driven'. The stronger the values the more they will affect behaviour. Values are concerned with such matters as care and consideration for people, the belief that employees should be treated as stakeholders, employee involvement, equity in the treatment of employees, equal opportunity, care for customers, innovation, quality, social responsibility and teamwork.

These values may influence policies in such areas as performance management, paying for contribution, resolving the often competing pressures for internal equity and external competitiveness, the equity and 'transparency' of reward arrangements and the extent to which employees are involved in the development of reward processes and structures. They should be taken into account in determining the criteria to be used in reviewing performance and rewarding people for their contribution. The research into performance management conducted by the CIPD in 2003/04 (1) found that many organizations were aiming to become 'value-driven' and were using their performance management processes to achieve that purpose, thus ensuring that their espoused values became 'values in use'.

Tesco has a widespread recognition scheme applying to all staff, including the directors. Values Awards are designed to recognize staff for living the Tesco values, which are:

- No one tries harder for customers.
- Understand customers better than anyone.
- Be energetic, be innovative and be first for customers.

- Use our strengths to deliver unbeatable value to our customers.
- Look after our people so they can look after our customers.
- Treat people how we like to be treated.
- There's one Tesco Team.
- Trust and respect each other.
- Strive to do our very best.
- Give support to each other and praise more than criticize.
- Ask more than tell and share knowledge so that it can be used.
- Enjoy work, celebrate success and learn from experience.

The awards are non-financial, taking the form of a blue badge for anyone who receives four Values Awards and a gold badge for anyone with seven Values Awards. Thus these non-financial rewards are being used as part of a clear strategy to inculcate the corporate values and culture, which create the context for high performance in the organization.

The B&Q 'work ethic' is set out in Table 2.1.

The four core values at Centrica are: 1) think team; 2) have respect; 3) listen and share; and 4) deliver results. Their reward system is designed to set a clear line of sight from business strategy to individual objectives using a balanced scorecard approach. The focus is on: what is expected – 'delivering results'; and how it is delivered – the ability to understand and manage behaviour within the context of the organization.

The Progression, Performance and Pay framework at Norwich Union Insurance is underpinned by their brand values: Progressive, Shared Benefit and Integrity. Xansa's recognition scheme aims to recognize and celebrate exceptional achievement that demonstrates the company's values in operation.

The business of the organization

The business of the organization – manufacturing, profit-making service, not-for-profit services, public sector services, education – will govern its ethos and therefore core values. It will influence the type of people it employs and the degree to which it is subject to turbulence and change. All these factors will contribute to the reward strategy. For example, in the public and voluntary sector the tradition of paying service-related increments rather than progressing pay according to performance or contribution dies hard, although successive governments have driven the adoption of performance pay in the Civil Service.

Table 2.1 The B&Q 'work ethic'

We work hard	Winning through hard work We're well rewarded A job worth doing Real job satisfaction
The B&Q family	Belonging Supporting and encouraging each other Real teamwork Fun to be with
Total involvement	Know where B&Q is heading Know where I fit in My voice is heard My contribution is valued I can grow
Proud to be here	Proud of B&Q Proud of our success Proud of my store Pride in my team Pride in my personal growth Proud of my career Proud to be a professional in my current job and future career Proud to grow, to be well rewarded and recognized and to make an impact
We can do	Drive, energy and passion Focused on achieving Individual and team rewards Lead and not follow

Technology

The technology of a business exerts a major influence on the internal environment – how work is organized, managed and carried out. The introduction of new technology may result in considerable changes to systems and processes. Different skills are required; new methods of working and therefore reward are developed. The result may be an extension of the skills base of the organization and its employees, including the use of knowledge and expertise, and multiskilling (ensuring that people have a range of skills that enable them to work flexibly on a variety of tasks, often within a teamworking environment). Traditional piecework pay systems in manufacturing industry have been replaced by higher fixed pay and rewards focused on quality and employee teamwork.

People

The type of people employed and therefore the approach to reward will clearly be dependent on the type of business and its technology, for example the growing importance of 'knowledge workers'. But what has become increasingly recognized by management is that 'people make the difference' and that unique competitive advantage is achieved by having better people who are capable of doing better things than those in other businesses. The aim is to acquire, develop, motivate and retain people who possess distinctive capabilities (competencies) that arise from the nature of the firm's activities and relationships. As Nicki Demby, formerly Performance and Reward Director at Diageo, observed to e-reward (2): 'It is our people who deliver our performance, which is why "release the potential of every employee" is at the heart of our growth strategy. Alongside what we deliver, every bit as important is *how* we deliver. Our people are judged against global leadership capabilities: edge, emotional energy, ideas, people performance, and living the values.'

Business strategy

Where the business is going (the business strategy) determines where reward should go (the reward strategy). Integrating reward and business strategies means combining them as a whole so they contribute effectively to achieving the mission or purpose of the organization. The process of linking strategies is the best way of achieving vertical integration, or 'internal fit', in the sense that business and reward strategies are in harmony. As described in Chapter 5, it is necessary to see that reward goals are aligned with business goals and reward strategies are defined in a way that spells out how they will contribute to the achievement of the business plan.

Business strategies change and as Nicki Demby, remarked: 'This is a key issue. This changes reward strategy.' Put simply, she said, 'Your organization's fundamental purpose may be revised. Major long-term goals in terms of outcomes and achievement of performance objectives may change. As a result, what your organization has to be good at doing to fulfil its mission and achieve its strategic goals will need refining.'

Nicki Demby pointed out that:

> Whenever you change your business strategy and/or your HR strategy, your reward strategy may need to respond. We are just getting to grips with the profound and detailed implications of a shift in our business strategy in the last two or three years. What Diageo calls its Organization and People Strategy has also necessarily been given greater clarity. It provides direction to our talent, operational effectiveness and performance and reward agendas.

The company's underlying thinking here is that the people strategy is not for the human resource function to own but is the responsibility of the whole organization, hence the title Organization and People Strategy.

The employees' point of view

Reward management policies should take account of the aspirations, expectations and needs of employees as stakeholders in the organization. Consideration has also to be given to the needs or views of other stakeholders, especially owners in the private sector and governments, local authorities and trustees elsewhere.

Employee involvement is crucial to the development of reward policies and programmes. The wishes of employees need to be ascertained. Their comments on existing practices should be listened to and acted upon. They should be involved in the development of new reward processes, for example job evaluation, performance management and contingent pay. They should continue to be involved in the implementation and evaluation of these processes.

THE EXTERNAL ENVIRONMENT

The external environment in the shape of globalization, increased competition, government interventions, the industrial relations scene and the characteristics of the organization's sector can all influence reward policies and practices.

Globalization

As Ulrich (3) has pointed out, globalization requires organizations to move people, ideas, products and information around the world to meet local needs. Traditionally, discussions of international reward strategies and practices have tended to focus on an elite of expatriate workers, sourced from headquarter locations and rewarded in isolation from local country staff. We are now seeing a more diverse and complex pattern emerging, requiring a much more strategic approach, as described in Chapter 26.

Employment trends

An increasing demand for skills and qualifications is taking place, especially for managerial and professional workers, knowledge workers, customer service staff, technical and office staff and skilled manual workers. This, coupled with the skill shortages associated with low levels of unemployment, influences reward strategies designed to attract and retain people.

Demographic trends

One of the most important factors that reward and HR strategies have to address for the future is demographic change. Birth rates throughout the developed world have been falling in recent decades, and this has been paralleled by declining mortality rates and increasing longevity. Just as traditional labour pools are shrinking, traditional reward practices and mindsets have been encouraging a further reduction in employment, with early retirement through defined benefit pensions arrangements in the 1990s helping to explain falls in the average age of retirement for both men and women. The UK faces a long-term pensions 'crisis' as the ratio of the retired to the working population increases. In individual companies such as British Airways and BAe Systems, this has produced major deficits in traditional defined benefits pensions plans, which represent a significant proportion of the market value of the firm. Industrial action in public and private sectors has resulted from employers trying to change pension arrangements to address these deficits. As Armstrong and Brown (4) emphasize: 'Resourcing and reward strategies which are heavily focused on either recruiting young "dynamic" staff and getting rid of "old" employees at a fixed retirement date or before; or the opportunistic poaching of staff with the requisite skills and experience from competitors, are therefore becoming increasingly outdated and undesirable from both an employer and national perspective.'

Rates of pay in the marketplace

The external environment exerts a major influence on rates of pay and pay reviews within organizations. Market or going-rate levels and movements have to be taken into account by organizations if they want their pay to be competitive. Some organizations are affected by national agreements with trade unions.

UK employment legislation

The following pieces of UK legislation directly or indirectly affect pay policies and practices:

- The Equal Pay Act 1970 and the Equal Pay (Amendment) Regulations 1983 provide that pay differences are allowable only if the reason for them is not related to the sex of the job holder. The Employment Act 2002 provides for the use of equal pay questionnaires. Equal pay legislation is described in Chapter 13.
- The Employment Equality (Age) Regulations, 2006, state that service-related pay is only permitted for a maximum of five years.
- The National Minimum Wage Act 1998 provides workers in the UK with a level of pay below which their wages must not fall. The government prescribes by regulation the minimum wage.
- The Working Time Regulations 1998 provide *inter alia* for a limit of 48 hours on average weekly working time, which an individual worker may voluntarily agree to exceed, and a minimum of four weeks' paid annual leave subject to a 13-week qualifying period.
- The Data Protection Act 1998 provides *inter alia* that employees are entitled to make a formal request to access information on the personal data held on them and the uses to which this will be put, and have the right: 1) to be provided as a matter of course with certain information about any data relating to them (the exceptions are those relating to confidential references, management forecasting and planning and negotiating positions); and 2) to access any purely automated decision-making process, relating for example to work performance, that might affect them.
- The Transfer of Undertakings (Protection of Employment) Regulations 1981 (TUPE) provide that when a business or part of a business is transferred the workers in that business automatically transfer into the employment of the transferee together with their existing terms and conditions of employment (except for pensions) intact and with their accrued periods of continuous service.
- The Financial Services Act 1986 places restrictions on the provision of financial advice to employees. Only those who are directly authorized by one of the regulatory organizations or professional bodies are permitted to give detailed financial advice on investments.

The industrial relations scene

The trade unions influence reward practices at national level through national pay negotiations, pronouncements on such issues as the pay of top executives, and exerting pressure to achieve equal pay. They produce policies and advice for their members on such matters as:

- the use of job evaluation (they are in favour of analytical schemes while emphasizing the need for involvement in their design);
- pay structures (they tend to be against broad-banded structures);
- contingent pay (they are universally hostile to it, preferring the traditional service-related incremental scales);
- protection policies (they accept limited periods but want these to be four or five years);
- the use of equal pay audits and questionnaires;
- employee benefits and pension schemes (they object to the move towards defined contribution schemes).

In general, they also provide advice and support on conducting pay negotiations at local level, involvement practices and the conduct of appeals.

Locally, at organizational or establishment levels, trade union representatives echo their national policies. They increasingly demand transparency in pay policies and practices and the right to be involved in developing new systems or revising existing ones. They will request membership of project steering groups and task forces and demand that no changes are made without their consent.

The national government scene

The Cabinet Office develops policy guidelines for implementation by government departments and agencies, although departments and, especially, agencies have some freedom to develop their own pay structures.

The pay modernization agenda of the government consists of the following elements:

- simplified grading structures based on job evaluation;
- harmonized scales for different groups of staff;
- new integrated bargaining structures;
- national pay spines;
- equality proofing in pay, progression and promotion;
- single-status terms and conditions;
- harmonizing the length of the working week;
- shortening scales to aid retention;

- aiding skilled people to stay in the front line;
- introducing a target rate for the job.

The local government scene

In 2003 the Office of the Deputy Prime Minister and the Local Government Employers' Association (5) developed a pay and workforce strategy for local government. Their two main recommendations were: 1) move from pay structures with a large number of narrow grades that do not reflect real differences in job size or levels of responsibility to broader, more flexible ranges that permit authorities to respond to local market pressures or to reward exceptional employee contribution; and 2) encourage the introduction of pay systems that align with service priorities and seek to motivate staff through a balanced assessment of the competence and contribution of employees to replace the traditional system based on time served.

The voluntary and not-for-profit sectors

The voluntary and not-for-profit sectors are very diverse and it is difficult to detect any general trends in the development of pay systems. Most of the big charities have traditionally adopted public sector schemes with pay spines consisting of service-related incremental scales. In recent years, however, a number of the larger charities and housing associations have introduced broad-banded structures and some form of contribution pay. In two examples (the Peabody Trust and the Shaw Trust) the contribution pay scheme has involved an arrangement of four or five steps to a target rate or reference point with progression based on competence. Above the target rate, bonuses are given for special achievements, which can be consolidated if the high level of achievement is sustained.

IMPACT OF THE ENVIRONMENT

Tough competition in the marketplace means that organizations are developing an 'employment value proposition'. Lloyds TSB provides a good example of how a very large financial sector business dealt with this issue.

Lloyds TSB is operating in a rapidly changing business environment, with ever-increasing consumerism and the harsh challenges of a competitive world market. Customers have a multitude of choices in today's financial services industry. The company is perpetually under pressure to improve quality, keep a lid on costs and reduce process times to meet customers' expectations and keep the organization ahead of the competition. Lloyds TSB needs to offer the highest standards of service if it is to remain customers' first choice. To achieve this, the bank realizes it must offer employment policies that will attract and retain the best people from the widest possible pool of applicants.

In the past, the 'big four' banks dominated the financial services sector. This meant that employees could generally be sure of a job for life, and there was little or no turnover of staff. People were sometimes paid (and promoted) according to their grade and length of service, rather than ability or performance. Today, the marketplace is full of competition from new entrants, and all financial services companies are competing for good-quality staff.

Lloyds TSB recognizes that it is people – rather than finance or technology – who make the difference. Operating in a vastly different employment environment in which there is intense competition for a pool of increasingly skilled people, employees really are the primary sustainable source of competitive advantage in the modern service-based economy. Compensation and benefits not only account for about half of the bank's £3.5 billion per annum operating costs, but, for better or worse, it is people – their intellects, creativity, scarce skills, commitment and leadership – who are central to business success.

A key question emerging from the new strategic orientation to reward at Lloyds TSB concerned the need to redefine the organization's performance culture. Put simply, what would this low-inflation environment mean for the pay-for-performance system introduced in 1989? Was it sustainable? Lloyds TSB decided it most certainly was not.

Salary budgets of around 3 per cent or at most 4 per cent offer little or no opportunity to differentiate between high-flyers and poor performers. Moreover, with almost a third of Lloyds TSB employees already paid above the market, the company was faced with the prospect of informing some employees that they were unlikely to receive a pay rise during forthcoming annual reviews.

As Tim Fevyer, Senior Manager, Compensation and Benefits, Lloyds TSB, points out, this required a complete change of mindset amongst employees. In essence, managing this process was about changing employees' expectations. Rather than a focus on movements in the cost of living, Lloyds TSB's emphasis is now very much on the market. 'If the market has not moved, our market indicators might not move', says Tim Fevyer. This represented a far-reaching cultural change for Lloyds TSB. If an employee's salary is going to increase, it is either because he or she is growing in terms of competencies, skills and performance or because the market has changed. Tim Fevyer sums it up:

> Previously the deal was 'I've been here so I'll get an increase' or 'I've been here and I've done a good job so I'll get a good increase'. Actually, now our philosophy is that

you are paid to do a good job, and if you are paid the right rate you only get more if you are contributing more or because the market has moved. Otherwise you are being paid the right price.

REFERENCES

1 Armstrong, M and Baron, A (2004) *Managing Performance: Performance management in action*, Chartered Institute of Personnel and Development, London
2 e-reward (2003–06) *Reward Case Studies*, e-reward.co.uk, Stockport
3 Ulrich, D (1997) *Human Resource Champions*, Harvard Business School Press, Boston, MA
4 Armstrong, M and Brown, D (2006) *Strategic Reward*, Kogan Page, London
5 Office of the Deputy Prime Minister and the Local Government Employers' Association (2003) *Pay and Workforce Strategy for Local Government*, Office of the Deputy Prime Minister/Local Government Employers' Association, London

3

Total reward

The concept of total reward is exerting considerable influence on reward strategies. This chapter begins by defining what it means. The importance of the concept is then explained and the chapter continues with an analysis of the components of total reward. It concludes with a description of how a total reward approach to reward management can be developed.

TOTAL REWARD DEFINED

As defined by Manus and Graham (1), total reward 'includes all types of rewards – indirect as well as direct, and intrinsic as well as extrinsic'. All aspects of reward, namely base pay, contingent pay, employee benefits and non-financial rewards, which include intrinsic rewards from the work itself, are linked together and treated as an integrated and coherent whole. Total reward combines the impact of the two major categories of reward (as illustrated in Figure 3.1): 1) *transactional rewards* – tangible rewards arising from transactions between the employer and employees concerning pay and benefits; and 2) *relational rewards* – intangible rewards concerned with learning and development and the work experience.

A total reward approach is holistic, reliance is not placed on one or two reward mechanisms operating in isolation, and account is taken of every way in which people can be rewarded and obtain satisfaction through their work. The aim is to maximize the combined impact of a wide range of reward initiatives on motivation, commitment

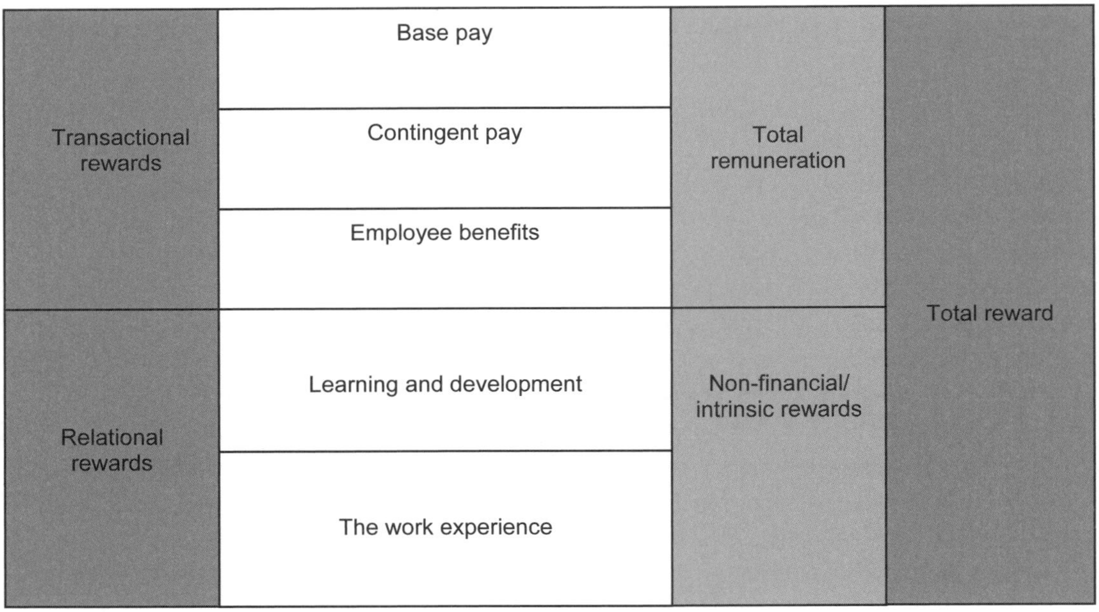

Transactional rewards	Base pay	Total remuneration	Total reward
	Contingent pay		
	Employee benefits		
Relational rewards	Learning and development	Non-financial/ intrinsic rewards	
	The work experience		

Figure 3.1 The components of total reward

and job engagement. As Sandra O'Neal (2) has explained: 'Total reward embraces everything that employees value in the employment relationship.'

An equally wide definition of total reward is offered by WorldatWork (3), who state that total rewards are 'all of the employer's available tools that may be used to attract, retain, motivate and satisfy employees'. Paul Thompson (4) suggests that: 'Definitions of total reward typically encompass not only traditional, quantifiable elements like salary, variable pay and benefits, but also more intangible non-cash elements such as scope to achieve and exercise responsibility, career opportunities, learning and development, the intrinsic motivation provided by the work itself and the quality of working life provided by the organization.'

The conceptual basis of total rewards is that of configuration or 'bundling', so that different reward processes are interrelated, complementary and mutually reinforcing. Total reward strategies are vertically integrated with business strategies, but they are also horizontally integrated with other HR strategies to achieve internal consistency.

THE SIGNIFICANCE OF TOTAL REWARD

Essentially, the notion of total reward says that there is more to rewarding people than throwing money at them.

For Sandra O'Neal (2), a total reward strategy is critical to addressing the issues created by recruitment and retention as well as providing a means of influencing behaviour: 'It can help create a work experience that meets the needs of employees and encourages them to contribute extra effort, by developing a deal that addresses a broad range of issues and by spending reward dollars where they will be most effective in addressing workers' shifting values.'

Perhaps the most powerful argument for a total rewards approach was produced by Pfeffer (5):

> Creating a fun, challenging, and empowered work environment in which individuals are able to use their abilities to do meaningful jobs for which they are shown appreciation is likely to be a more certain way to enhance motivation and performance – even though creating such an environment may be more difficult and take more time than simply turning the reward lever.

BENEFITS OF TOTAL REWARD

The benefits of a total reward approach are:

- *Greater impact* – the combined effect of the different types of rewards will make a deeper and longer-lasting impact on the motivation and commitment of people.
- *Enhancing the employment relationship* – the employment relationship created by a total rewards approach makes the maximum use of relational as well as transactional rewards and will therefore appeal more to individuals.
- *Flexibility to meet individual needs* – as pointed out by Bloom and Milkovich (6): 'Relational rewards may bind individuals more strongly to the organization because they can answer those special individual needs.'
- *Winning the war for talent* – relational rewards help to deliver a positive psychological contract and this can serve as a differentiator in the recruitment market, which is much more difficult to replicate than individual pay practices. The organization can become an 'employer of choice' and 'a great place to work', thus attracting and retaining the talented people it needs.

MODEL OF TOTAL REWARD

A model of total reward developed by Towers Perrin (7) is shown in Figure 3.2.

The upper two quadrants – pay and benefits – represent *transactional rewards*. These are financial in nature and are essential to recruit and retain staff but can be easily copied by competitors. By contrast, the *relational (non-financial) rewards* produced by the lower two quadrants are essential to enhancing the value of the upper two quadrants and they are less easy to imitate by competitors. The real power, as Thompson (4) states, comes when organizations combine relational and transactional rewards.

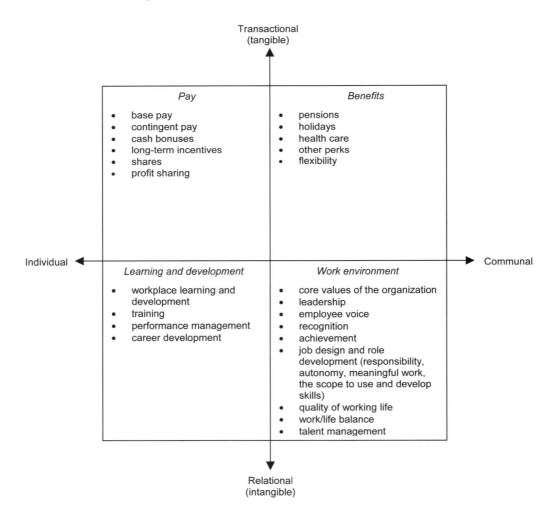

Figure 3.2 Model of total reward

RELATIONAL REWARDS

Consideration is given below to the main areas of relational or non-financial rewards as set out in the lower quadrants of Figure 3.2.

Learning and development

Workplace learning

The workplace itself as an environment for learning can reward people by offering them opportunities to develop their skills and therefore their employability. Learning can be intentional and planned, aimed at training employees by supporting, structuring and monitoring their learning on the job. But, significantly, learning is an everyday part of the job. People develop skills, knowledge and understanding through dealing with the challenges posed by their work. This can be described as continuous learning, and line managers can be encouraged and trained to enhance this process.

Training

The provision of systematic and planned instruction and development activities to promote learning can enable employees continually to upgrade their skills and progressively develop their careers. Many people now regard access to training as a key element in the overall reward package. The availability of learning opportunities, the selection of individuals for high-prestige training courses and programmes and the emphasis placed by the organization on the acquisition of new skills as well as the enhancement of existing ones can all act as powerful motivators. This is particularly important in delayered organizations where upward growth through promotion is restricted but people can still develop laterally.

Performance management

Performance management processes are a powerful means of providing relational rewards. They can be the basis for developing a positive psychological contract by clarifying the mutual expectations of managers and their staff. Motivation can be provided by feedback. Performance reviews can inform personal development planning, thus encouraging self-managed learning with the support as required of the manager and the organization.

Career development

Alderfer (8) emphasized the importance of the chance to grow as a means of rewarding people and therefore motivating them. He wrote: 'Satisfaction of growth needs depends on a person finding the opportunity to be what he is most fully and to become what he can.' The organization can offer this opportunity by providing people with a sequence of experience and training that will equip them for whatever level of responsibility they have the ability to reach. Talented individuals can be given the guidance and encouragement they need to fulfil their potential and achieve a successful career in tune with their abilities and aspirations. Paths can be defined that will map out how people can be rewarded by progressing their careers. Rewarding people through career development is associated with the process of talent management, which deals with the recruitment and retention of talented people and their career progression but is also associated with providing rewards through the working environment.

Work environment

Core values of the organization

The significance of the core values of an organization as a basis for creating a rewarding work environment was identified by the research conducted by John Purcell and his colleagues at Bath University (9). The most successful companies had what the researchers called 'the big idea'. They had a clear vision and a set of integrated values, which were embedded, enduring, collective, measured and managed. They were concerned with sustaining performance and flexibility. Clear evidence existed between positive attitudes towards HR policies and practices, levels of satisfaction, motivation and commitment, and operational performance.

Leadership

Leaders play a vital role in reward management. They exist to get things done through people, ensuring that the task is achieved but also building and maintaining constructive and supportive relationships between themselves and members of their team and between the people within the group. They are there to motivate people and to obtain engaged performance. Leaders are the source of many relational rewards such as recognition through feedback, scope to carry out meaningful work and exercise responsibility and the opportunity to grow through workplace learning and training. They are crucial to the success of performance management processes and may make or strongly influence contingent pay decisions.

Employee voice

As defined by Peter Boxall and John Purcell (10), 'Employee voice is the term increasingly used to cover a whole variety of processes and structures which enable, and sometimes empower employees, directly and indirectly, to contribute to decision-making in the firm.' Having a voice in the affairs of the firm is rewarding because it recognizes the contribution people can make to the success of the organization or their team.

Employees can have a voice as an aspect of the normal working relationships between them and their managers and this is linked closely to the other relational reward factors inherent in those relationships, concerning recognition, achievement and responsibility. But the organization, through its policies for involvement, can provide motivation and increase commitment by putting people into situations where their views can be expressed, listened to and acted upon.

Recognition

Recognition is one of the most powerful methods of rewarding people. They need to know not only how well they have achieved their objectives or carried out their work but also that their achievements are appreciated. Recognition needs are linked to the esteem needs in Maslow's (11) hierarchy of needs. These are defined by Maslow as the need to have a stable, firmly based, high evaluation of oneself (self-esteem) and to have the respect of others (prestige). These needs are classified into two subsidiary sets: first, 'the desire for achievement, for adequacy, for confidence in the face of the world, and for independence and freedom', and second, 'the desire for reputation or status defined as respect or esteem from other people, and manifested by recognition, attention, importance or appreciation'.

Recognition can be provided by positive and immediate feedback from managers and colleagues that acknowledges individual and team contributions. It is also provided by managers who listen to and act upon the suggestions of their team members. Other actions that provide recognition include promotion, allocation to a high-profile project, and enlargement of the job to provide scope for more interesting and rewarding work.

There are other forms of recognition such as public 'applause', status symbols of one kind or another, sabbaticals, treats, trips abroad and long-service awards, all of which can function as rewards. But they must be used with care. One person's recognition implies an element of non-recognition to others, and the consequences of having winners and losers need to be carefully managed. Recognition schemes are examined more thoroughly in Chapter 23.

Financial rewards, especially achievement bonuses awarded immediately after the event, are clearly symbols of recognition to which are attached tangible benefits, and this is an important way in which mutually reinforcing systems of financial and non-financial rewards can operate.

Achievement

The need to achieve applies in varying degrees to all people in all jobs, although the level at which it operates will depend on the orientation of the individual and the scope provided by the work to fulfil a need for achievement. People feel rewarded and motivated if they have the scope to achieve as well as being recognized for the achievement. University researchers, for example, want to enhance their reputation as well as making a significant contribution to their institution's research rating.

If achievement motivation is high it will result in discretionary behaviour. As defined by Purcell *et al* (9), 'Discretionary behaviour refers to the choices that people make about how they carry out their work and the amount of effort, care, innovation and productive behaviour they display. It is the difference between people just doing a job and people doing a great job.' Self-discretionary or self-motivated behaviour occurs when people take control of situations or relationships, direct the course of events, create and seize opportunities, enjoy challenge, react swiftly and positively to new circumstances and relationships, and generally 'make things happen'. People who are driven by the need to achieve are likely to be proactive, to seek opportunities and to insist on recognition. Those whose orientations are not as strongly defined can be helped to satisfy possibly latent achievement needs by being given the scope and encouragement to develop and use their abilities productively. Achievement motivation can be increased by organizations through processes and systems such as job design and performance management.

Job design and role development

Job design has two aims: first, to meet the needs of the organization for operational efficiency, quality of product or service and productivity; and second, to reward individuals by satisfying their needs for meaningful work that provides for interest, challenge and accomplishment. However, job design is not a static process. The roles people play at work develop as they respond to opportunities and changing demands, acquiring new skills and developing competencies. Managers and members of their teams have to work together to achieve mutual understanding of expectations as they change and to ensure that the role continues to provide intrinsic motivation from the work itself (the most powerful form of motivation). Ed Lawler (12) has suggested that, to be intrinsically motivating, roles should have the following characteristics:

- *Feedback* – individuals must receive meaningful feedback about their perform-ance, preferably by evaluating their own performance and defining the feedback. This implies that they should ideally work on a complete process or product or a significant part of it that can be seen as a whole.
- *Use of abilities* – the role must be perceived by individuals as requiring them to use abilities they value to perform it effectively.
- *Self-control (autonomy)* – individuals must feel that they have a high degree of self-control over setting their own goals and defining the paths to these goals.

To develop rewarding jobs and roles, attention should be given to the following five principles set out by Robertson and Smith (13), which expand on the points made by Lawler:

1. *Influence skill variety*, providing opportunities for people to do several tasks and to combine tasks.
2. *Influence task identity*, combining tasks to form natural work units.
3. *Influence task significance*, forming natural work groups and informing people of the importance of their work.
4. *Influence autonomy*, giving people responsibility for determining their own working systems and making their own decisions.
5. *Influence feedback*, opening and using feedback channels.

Quality of working life

Rewards can be provided by the working environment if it improves the quality of working life. This is a matter of how the work is organized and the type of facilities provided as well as the design of the job or role. For example, research workers may feel well rewarded when they have excellent laboratory or other facilities that they can use to deliver exciting results.

Work/life balance

Work/life balance policies can reward people by recognizing their needs outside work by, for example, providing more flexible working arrangements and making it clear that people will not be rewarded simply because they stay on after normal finishing time. It's what they deliver that counts, not how long they work.

Talent management

Talent management is about ensuring that the organization attracts, retains, motivates and develops the talented people it needs. It is associated with a number of other relational reward processes such as designing jobs and developing roles that give people opportunities to apply and grow their skills and provide them with autonomy, interest and challenge. It is also concerned with creating a working environment in which work processes and facilities enable rewarding (in the broadest sense) jobs and roles to be designed and developed.

Talent management also means developing reward processes and a working environment that ensure that the organization is one for which people want to work – an 'employer of choice'. There is a desire to join the organization and, once there, to want to stay. Employees are committed to the organization and engaged in the work they do. On the basis of their longitudinal research in 12 companies, Purcell *et al* (9) concluded that:

> What seems to be happening is that successful firms are able to meet people's needs both for a good job and to work 'in a great place'. They create good work and a conducive working environment. In this way they become an 'employer of choice'. People will want to work there because their individual needs are met – for a good job with prospects linked to training, appraisal and working with a good boss who listens and gives some autonomy but helps with coaching and guidance.

Becoming an employer of choice starts with developing the image of the organization so that it is recognized as one that achieves results, delivers quality products and services, behaves ethically and provides good conditions of employment. Organizations with a clear vision and a set of integrated and enacted values are likely to project themselves as being rewarding to work for.

DEVELOPING A TOTAL REWARD APPROACH

The transactional and tangible elements of total reward (financial rewards) are quite clear cut. It may not be easy to make them work well but, as explained in later chapters of this book, it is not too difficult to decide on what needs to be done. There are plenty of guidelines available to help in selecting the approach and to indicate the means available for the design and implementation of tangible reward processes.

Relational or non-financial rewards are more difficult. By definition, they are intangible. Their provision may depend on top management providing the lead by developing what John Purcell and his colleagues (9) call 'the big idea'.

The organization can contribute by communicating the values, giving employees a voice, setting up performance management processes, instituting formal recognition schemes and taking steps to improve work/life balance. A conscious effort can be made to 'bundle' reward and HR practices together, for example developing career family structures where the emphasis is on mapping career paths rather than providing a pay structure.

The organization can ensure that line managers appreciate the importance of using relational rewards – exercising effective leadership, giving feedback, recognizing achievement and providing meaningful work. Ultimately, relational rewards are in the hands of line managers, and what the organization must do is to ensure as far as possible that they understand the significance of this aspect of their work and are given the training and guidance needed to acquire the skills to do it well.

APPROACHES TO TOTAL REWARD

Approaches to total reward adopted by a number of organizations are summarized below. See also Chapter 28 for a description of the total reward policies of Bristol-Myers Squibb, Elan Computers and GlaxoSmithKline.

Camelot

At Camelot total reward is an important element in the move to align people with the organization's goals.

Centrica

As defined for Centrica employees the total reward approach integrates many diverse elements: *financial rewards* like base pay, contingent or variable pay, share ownership and employee benefits; and *non-financial rewards* such as the work environment, including recognition, quality of working life considerations, the opportunity to learn and develop skills and work/life policies. It concentrates overall on developing reward management as a strategic, innovative and integrative process that is designed to meet the evolving needs of the organization and the people it employs.

Benefits of total reward

The company believes that a total reward programme offers substantial benefits. These include:

- improving employees' perception of the value of their reward package;
- increased organizational performance through greater workforce commitment and motivation;
- improved recruitment, arising from a quantified total employment package;
- supporting the objective of becoming an 'employer of choice';
- promoting flexibility in pay delivery;
- reallocating reward to match individual employee needs;
- helping manage costs and maximize the return on the investment in HR;
- mixing extrinsic and intrinsic rewards to encourage employees' discretionary effort.

Problems

However, Centrica was aware that there were formidable stumbling blocks in delivering their reward strategy, which they had to overcome, including the following:

- Developing total reward is time-consuming – it took 10 months to plan and implement.
- It is easier to believe that total reward strategy is a good thing than to put it into practice.
- Implementation and management require full support from the management team – they are not something done by HR to the business.
- The cost of some intangible rewards is not quantifiable, and hence it is difficult to make a business case.

Financial Services Authority (FSA)

Total reward policy at the FSA emphasizes the rewards that arise from the intrinsic interest and importance of the work itself and the opportunities for development it provides. It comprises:

- a unique insight into the full breadth of financial services;
- the chance to contribute first-hand to the financial well-being of millions of UK consumers and to the health of the financial markets;
- outstanding technical and business skills development;
- access to a range of career development opportunities, including the ability to specialize or do a broad range of interesting jobs;
- a competitive overall remuneration package including a market-leading flexible benefits system.

The FSA was one of the first organizations in the UK public sector to adopt a total reward approach. It helped the organization to integrate the very different terms and conditions that existed in its many predecessor regulatory bodies and offers considerable choice in benefits to employees.

Lands' End

At Lands' End the focus is on total reward rather than just pay. The company tries to help people understand the value of their entire reward package – both financial and non-financial rewards. This is because, says Mark Harris, the Employee Services Director, 'although pay is important it is not decisive in motivating people to continuously improve their performance' and 'no one ever left a good job because a competitor was offering an extra day's holiday'. Instead, Lands' End concentrates on rewards that recognize the whole person, namely the experience of being appreciated and valued. Everyone wants to be great, Mark Harris says, and 'it is our job to make that happen'. The total reward strategy consists of seven key strands:

1. *Financial rewards.* Traditional rewards – such as base pay and benefits – remain important fundamentals that companies must get right in order to compete for and retain key talent. Pay rates are pitched at or slightly above the median for the location and benefits are more generous than its rivals.
2. *Career development.* There is a strong emphasis on developing all employees at Lands' End. Many people now high in the ranks of the organization have worked their way up from some of the lowest-level jobs. The whole ethos is to encourage everyone to develop as far as they are able using on-the-job training and cross-training
3. *Pride.* This is one of the key elements of how Lands' End motivates its staff. The company seeks to engender a strong sense of pride in employees as to what the business stands for and the extent to which it delivers. Whether it succeeds or not is measured by the company's score in the 'Great Place to Work' survey.

    The thinking behind why the company wants to inspire staff is straightforward: employees' willingness to do that little bit extra is the difference between a good experience for customers and a poor one. Lands' End reckons that the reason its staff are willing to go the extra mile is because of their sense of pride in what the organization stands for: quality, service and value.
4. *Appreciation.* Lands' End favours the term 'appreciation' over 'recognition', since it thinks the latter suggests something tangible. It prefers to look for any and every opportunity to demonstrate its real appreciation of what staff do. The company tries to show its appreciation by promoting six dimensions of employee well-being:

- physical;
- emotional;
- intellectual;
- social;
- spiritual;
- occupational.

5. *Make work challenging and fun.* Where jobs are repetitive or less challenging, it is particularly important to provide some challenge and fun. Lands' End believes that, if it isn't possible to give people a choice as to the type of work they do, they can be given a choice as to how they do it.

6. *Leader relations.* For Lands' End the quality of the relationship between manager and employee is the biggest motivational factor at work, and has more influence on job satisfaction than anything else.

7. *Involvement.* Mark Harris believes that 'Involvement shows respect for others, it adds emphasis to our view that everyone is important and there are few motivational things better than being able to influence and shape the way in which you do your own job or how the company operates.'

Lloyds TSB

At Lloyds TSB the emphasis is on creating a 'compelling employment offer' – one that is individually focused, tailored to employees' needs and interests, and more in tune with the expectations of a diverse workforce. By concentrating on monetary rewards it is all too easy to overlook ways of succeeding that rivals cannot readily copy. But with competitive pressures so strong, the need for Lloyds TSB to differentiate its reward package from that of other financial services employers has never been more intense. The bank decided that what really gives employers the edge as they struggle to woo and retain scarce talent is appealing to the beliefs, personal values and lifestyle choices of today's employees. Its total reward package, replete with one of the biggest flexible benefits schemes in the UK and a new share incentive plan, seeks to integrate all aspects of the work experience so that prominence is given not only to remuneration but also to less tangible rewards.

Nationwide

Paul Bissell, Senior Manager – Rewards at Nationwide, defines their approach to total reward as follows: 'A mixture of pay elements, with a defined cash value, benefits which have an intrinsic value, a positive and enjoyable work environment and opportunities for learning and development, all designed to make Nationwide an employer of choice.'

Nationwide are the highest-rated large employer in the *Sunday Times* Best Company to Work For listing of 2005.

Norwich Union Insurance

Progression, Performance and Pay is the name given to Norwich Union Insurance's total reward strategy. It comprises four main elements:

1. *reward* – salary and benefits, variable pay, all-employee share option plan and incentive awards;
2. *career framework* – meaningful job content and career opportunities;
3. *performance* – challenging work, recognition and brand-supporting behaviours;
4. *development* – learning opportunities and personal development.

Royal Bank of Scotland

The bank's reward policies are designed to ensure that RBS is recognized as an 'employer of choice'. While the design of individual pay programmes is easily replicated, the way in which total reward programmes are integrated with other practices is often idiosyncratic and linked to organization-specific factors. Individual practices can be borrowed by rivals, but copying this unique 'organizational personality' – the positive environment and employment relationship – is much more difficult. The value of total reward programmes, in contrast to standardized packages, lies in creating programmes that are suited to the needs of the organization and are rooted in an understanding of what optimizes employee satisfaction. They encourage employers to look at more imaginative ways to reward their people. They are much more likely to create and sustain competitive advantage as they make the organization distinctive.

The Royal Bank of Scotland states that: 'Our approach to total reward focuses on the overall content and value of the pay and benefits package and how this supports the needs of our staff and the Group as a whole. Put another way, it's the value of everything staff get in return for working for the bank.'

Pay is just one element of the RBS reward package, and the compensation team is keen to ensure that staff understand that it is their total package that is significant rather than individual elements within it. The concept is sold as a series of events, and a desk calendar given to each staff member identifies one, or more, significant total reward event in nine of the 12 months.

An important element of the RBS approach to total reward is the use of a concept that the bank calls ValueAccount, which is made up of basic pay for non-managerial staff and basic plus the benefits funding for managers. This distinction is made because managerial pay is market-driven and includes entitlement to a company car and private medical insurance. The benefits element has been turned into a fixed percentage whereby salary is 90.9 per cent of the ValueAccount and the benefits spend is 10 per cent of 90.9 per cent, that is, 9.09 per cent. Pensions, profit-share payments, bonuses and so on are all based on the basic pay element rather than the ValueAccount.

Each June staff receive a personal reward statement. This sets out the value of the key elements of the total reward package and the available flexible benefits. Staff are also given a total reward desk calendar to reinforce the message about the unique employment offer.

TURNING RHETORIC INTO REALITY

The rhetoric of the total reward concept is compelling. The reality of total reward – making it work – is much more difficult. It requires a lot of effort on the part of top managers and line managers, with the determined encouragement and guidance of HR. The issues to be dealt with are:

1. *Putting the whole package together* – it is relatively easy to decide on the financial elements of total reward but much more difficult to ensure that the non-financial elements – recognition, opportunity to grow and develop and the work environment – are dealt with specifically so that a coherent whole emerges. It is necessary to establish priorities. To start with, it is advisable to ensure that the financial rewards package is appropriate. Typically, designers of total reward processes give the next priority to the development of recognition schemes which are specifically concerned with ensuring that people are valued. Other elements of total reward, for example opportunitues for growth, and the work environment, are just as important and should be tackled as aspects of the HR strategy. However, it is necessary to ensure that they are conceived, presented and perceived as part of the total reward strategy as well as desireable developments in their own right.
2. *Communicating the total reward approach to employees* – it is too easy to produce vague, generalizes aspirations which are too easily dismissed as management hyperbole. Total reward policies need to be explained in meaningful language which clearly indicates how people will benefit.
3. *Making the business case to top management* – it is fairly easy to convince management that some form of financial incentive or bonus scheme is desirable – it is in line with their experience and values. It is much more difficult to persuade them that, for example, a formal recognition scheme or programmes for developing a learning culture will pay off. Hard evidence may be difficult to obtain but it is essential to be explicit about how the business will benefit.

4. *Getting line managers on board* – line managers have a vital role to play. It is essential to make huge efforts to persuade, encourage, guide and educate them on their responsibility for total reward.

REFERENCES

1   Manus, TM and Graham, MD (2003) *Creating a Total Rewards Strategy*, American Management Association, New York
2   O'Neal, S (1998) The phenomenon of total rewards, *ACA Journal*, **7** (3), pp 18–23
3   WorldatWork (2000) *Total Rewards: From strategy to implementation*, WorldatWork, Scottsdale, AZ
4   Thompson, P (2002) *Total Reward*, Chartered Institute of Personnel and Development, London
5   Pfeffer, J (1998) *The Human Equation: Building profits by putting people first*, Harvard Business School Press, Boston, MA
6   Bloom, M and Milkovich, GT (1998) Rethinking international compensation, *Compensation and Benefits Review*, April, pp 17–27
7   Towers Perrin (2005) *Reconnecting with Employees: Quantifying the value of engaging your workforce*, Towers Perrin, London
8   Alderfer, C (1972) *Existence, Relatedness and Growth*, Free Press, New York
9   Purcell, J *et al* (2003) *People and Performance: How people management impacts on organisational performance*, Chartered Institute of Personnel and Development, London
10 Boxall, P and Purcell, J (2003) *Strategic Human Resource Management*, Palgrave Macmillan, Basingstoke
11 Maslow, A (1954) *Motivation and Personality*, Harper & Row, New York
12 Lawler, EE (1969) Job design and employee motivation, *Personnel Psychology*, 22, pp 426–35
13 Robertson, IT and Smith, M (1985) *Motivation and Job Design*, IPM, London

4

Strategic reward

STRATEGIC REWARD MANAGEMENT DEFINED

Strategic reward management is an approach to the development and implementation over the longer term of reward strategies and the guiding principles that underpin them. As described by Armstrong and Brown (1):

> It provides answers to two basic questions: first, where do we want our reward practices to be in a few years' time? and second how do we intend to get there? It therefore deals with both ends and means. As an end it describes a vision of what reward processes will look like in a few years' time. As a means, it shows how it is expected that the vision will be realized.

Strategic reward can be described as an attitude of mind – a belief in the need to plan ahead and make the plans happen.

The aim of strategic reward is to create total reward processes that are based on beliefs about what the organization values and wants to achieve. It does this by aligning reward practices with both business goals and employee values. As Duncan Brown (2) emphasizes, the 'alignment of your reward practices with employee values and needs is every bit as important as alignment with business goals, and critical to the realisation of the latter'.

THE RATIONALE FOR STRATEGIC REWARD

In the words of Duncan Brown (2), strategic reward 'is ultimately a way of thinking that you can apply to any reward issue arising in your organization, to see how you can create value from it'. More specifically, there are four arguments for adopting a strategic approach to reward management:

1. You must have some idea where you are going, or how do you know how to get there, and how do you know that you have arrived (if you ever do)?
2. As Cox and Purcell (3) explain, 'the real benefit in reward strategies lies in complex linkages with other human resource management policies and practices'. Isn't this a good reason for developing a reward strategic framework that indicates how reward processes will be aligned to HR processes so that they are coherent and mutually supportive?
3. There can be a positive relationship between rewards, in the broadest sense, and performance, so shouldn't we think about how we can strengthen that link?
4. Pay costs in most organizations are by far the largest item of expense – they can be 60 per cent and often much more in labour-intensive organizations – so doesn't it make sense to think about how they should be managed and invested in the longer term?

GUIDING PRINCIPLES

Strategic reward management is based on a set of beliefs and guiding principles that are consistent with the values of the organization and help to enact them. They define the approach an organization takes to dealing with reward, are the basis for reward policies, and provide guidelines for the actions contained in the reward strategy. Guiding principles should incorporate or be influenced by general beliefs about fairness, equity, consistency and transparency. Reward strategies in the past have sometimes focused exclusively on business needs and alignment. Yet unless employees see and experience fairness and equity in their rewards, the strategy is unlikely to be delivered in practice. Typical guiding principles are set out below and examples are given in Chapter 5.

Overall reward management principles

● Align reward strategies with the business and HR strategy.

- Align reward policies with the culture of the organization and use them to underpin that culture and, as required, help to change it.
- Reward people according to what the organization values and is prepared to pay for.
- Value employees according to their competence and contribution.
- Aim to achieve equity, fairness and consistency in the operation of reward policies and practices.
- Ensure that reward processes are transparent and that staff are treated as stakeholders.
- Adopt an integrative approach that ensures that no innovations take place and no practices are changed without considering how they relate to other aspects of human resource management so that they can become mutually supportive.
- Provide managers with the authority and skills needed to use rewards to help achieve their goals, but ensure that they are given the training, guidance and continuing support required to develop and use these skills well.
- Remember that reward policies and practices express what the organization values and is prepared to pay for – they are driven by the need to reward the right things to convey the right message about what is important.
- Concentrate overall on developing reward management as a strategic, innovative and integrative process designed to meet the evolving needs of the organization and the people who contribute to its success.

Designing grade and pay structures

- The design should take place within the context of articulated reward strategies, which should be integrated with the corporate and HR strategies of the organization.
- The design should be based on a thorough analysis of the needs of the organization and of its employees.
- Stakeholders should be involved in the design of the structure.
- The structure should be based on an analytical form of job evaluation.
- The structure should provide for pay progression in accordance with agreed principles and policies.
- Performance management processes should be developed that, if required, will inform decisions on pay progression as well, importantly, as providing guidance on continuous development.
- Equal value considerations should be at the forefront of the design process.
- It should be remembered that grade structures can and should provide valuable information on career ladders as the basis for career planning.

- The cost implications of a new structure should be evaluated.
- The introduction of new pay structures will probably involve considerable changes, which may create major concerns amongst those affected by them – close attention will therefore have to be given to how such change should be managed when designing and implementing the structure.

Pay progression principles

Pay progression policy and practices should:

- ensure that people are valued and rewarded fairly according to their contribution;
- provide rewards for those skills and behaviours that support the future success of the individual and the organization, not just immediate past results;
- deliver a clear message to staff on what the organization believes to be important in terms of performance (results) and behaviour;
- adopt a fair, consistent and transparent approach to measuring and assessing performance and competence, which is based on agreed expectations and success criteria;
- ensure that as far as possible judgements on performance and contribution are based on evidence, not opinion;
- recognize that performance may be a function of effective teamwork as well as individual effort;
- be developed in consultation with those concerned – managers, employees and union representatives;
- be communicated to staff so that they understand the operation of the process, the part they and their managers play and its impact on them;
- devolve the maximum amount of responsibility to managers in operating the system but provide safeguards to ensure that fair and consistent decisions are made within the framework of policies and guidelines, including budgets;
- provide training and guidance for managers on the system and their role in operating it.

Job evaluation principles

The pay and grade structure should be designed and managed with the aid of a system of job evaluation that should:

- enable fair, equitable, consistent and transparent judgements to be made about the relative value or size of jobs;

- help in the management of job relativities and in making decisions on the grading of posts;
- provide guidance on the design and maintenance of rational and orderly grade and pay structures;
- be analytical in the sense that judgements on the size of jobs are based on an analysis of the key factors in terms of job demands and working arrangements that affect relative values – the scheme should be thorough in analysis and capable of impartial implementation;
- have been equality-proofed;
- ensure that the factors used in the scheme cover the whole range of jobs to be evaluated without favouring any particular type of job or occupation and without discriminating on the grounds of gender or for any other reason;
- ensure that any weighting contained in the scheme is justified and non-discriminatory;
- provide the basis for ensuring that equal pay for work of equal value is achieved, including the data required to conduct equal pay reviews;
- ensure that the processes used for evaluating jobs are conducted fairly and openly and involve those affected;
- be communicated to staff so that they understand how it operates;
- only be introduced if those involved receive thorough training in its operation;
- contain provision for appeals against job gradings resulting from job evaluation;
- be reviewed regularly to ensure that it is operating effectively.

THE CONCEPT OF REWARD STRATEGY

The concept of reward strategy is generally agreed to be a good thing, and why this is the case is explained below. But this view is not translated to any great extent into formal strategies. IRS (4) noted on the basis of their 2006 survey that: 'Again our results indicate more talk of reward strategies but little action… 45.4 per cent of respondents said that their organization's overall reward strategy would be important in the next 12 months, but only 17.9 per cent had a written strategy.'

Reward strategy defined

Reward strategy is a business-focused description of what the organization wants to do about reward in the next few years and how it intends to do it. The aim is to provide the organization with a sense of purpose and direction in delivering reward programmes that support the achievement of business goals and meet the needs of stakeholders. It generally starts with a review of the current reward arrangements and situation, then a definition of the desired future state, and the development of reward initiatives and activities to close the gap between the two.

Reward strategy provides a sense of purpose and direction, a pathway that links the needs of the business and its people with the reward policies and practices of the organization and thereby communicates and explains these practices. It constitutes a framework for developing and putting into effect reward policies, practices and processes that ensure that people are rewarded for doing the things that increase the likelihood of the organization's business goals being achieved.

Characteristics of reward strategy

As Helen Murlis (5) points out: 'Reward strategy will be characterized by diversity and conditioned both by the legacy of the past and the realities of the future.' All reward strategies are different, just as all organizations are different. Of course, similar aspects of reward will be covered in the strategies of different organizations but they will be treated differently in accordance with variations in their contexts, business strategies and cultures. But the reality of reward strategy is that it is not such a clear-cut process as some believe. It evolves, it changes and it has sometimes to be reactive rather than proactive.

The content of reward strategy

Reward strategy often has to be a balancing act, because of potentially conflicting goals. For example, it may be necessary to reconcile the competing claims of being externally competitive *and* internally equitable – paying a specialist more money to reflect market rate pressures may disrupt internal relativities.

At one end of the scale, a reward strategy may simply address a single major issue, for example the need to develop a performance culture by introducing a new or more effective form of contingent pay.

When Glaxo Wellcome and SmithKline Beecham merged to form GlaxoSmithKline (100,000 employees worldwide) the organization adopted a new approach to reward that embodied the new GSK 'spirit' of entrepreneurship, innovation and performance. This stresses pay for performance and increases the proportion of pay 'at risk'.

B&Q switched from a fairly traditional pay scheme to a total reward system because of a desire for better strategic alignment of reward programmes with its business objectives in a labour market environment of increasing diversity and changing social values.

PricewaterhouseCoopers considers itself engaged in the 'war for talent'. It recruits hundreds of graduates each year, and seeks to attract the best. The average age of the firm's employees is only 27, so its attitude to reward is pitched towards the aspirations and needs of this age group in the sense that younger workers are likely to demand fulfilling careers, excellent development and competitive pay as well as work/life balance. To meet its employees' requirements, PwC has therefore adopted a total reward policy – replete with a competitive reward package, flexible benefits, genuine work/life choices, flexible working and a strong emphasis on personal development, advancement and recognition.

At the other end, a reward strategy can be a much more comprehensive affair, covering a number of aspects of reward, possibly under the overarching objective of developing a total reward approach. Examples are given below.

Airbus

The aims of the reward strategy developed by Airbus are to introduce an element of performance into the pay of all employees, to ensure that its rates are competitive with the external labour market and to deal with any anomalies caused by previous rigidities, such as grade drift brought about by people having to be promoted to a higher grade to receive additional pay.

British Telecommunications

The reward strategy at British Telecommunications (BT) indicates the general direction in which it is thought reward management at BT should go, with an emphasis on adopting a more holistic, total reward approach. It states: 'Use the full range of rewards (salary, bonus, benefits and recognition) to recruit and retain the best people, and to encourage and reward achievement where actions and behaviours are consistent with the BT values.'

Centrica

At Centrica, following the merger between British Gas and Enron, the aim of the reward strategy was to:

- establish a link between pay and performance;
- align pay with the market;
- boost team working and the creation of a single Centrica culture, rather than have the two cultures of British Gas Trading and Enron;

- create a single Centrica Business Services employment contract instead of the two that then existed.

The Children's Society

The Children's Society defined its overarching reward strategy as follows: 'We intend to develop reward systems which will support our mission and corporate objectives. We will move towards processes which:

- recognise contribution;
- are transparent;
- are owned by line managers and staff;
- reinforce leadership, accountability, team working and innovation;
- are market sensitive but not market led;
- are flexible and fair.'

COLT Telecom

The reward strategy of COLT Telecom is expressed as follows:

- Base salaries should be determined generally by position against median market, but always taking account of personal performance and contribution to business success.
- At the senior level there will be greater emphasis on the variable portion of the total package including bonus potential and the opportunity to participate in share programmes.
- Internal equity is sought by working to ensure that the overall compensation package reflects the value and contribution of each job, in relation to other jobs in the organization across Europe through the introduction of COLT job levels.
- Increases to base salary and variable pay will always be related to the company's ability to pay. Compensation must be affordable by the business in relation to its business success and equitable to its employees, customers and shareholders.

Diageo

The overall objective of the reward strategy at Diageo is to 'release the potential of every employee to deliver Diageo's performance goals'. The role of the reward strategy comprises five key elements:

1. *Support and enable the talent agenda.* 'Our role in reward is to help to provide the talent the business needs, at the right time, in the right place and for the right price', says Nicki Demby, Diageo's former Performance and Reward Director. 'This means developing reward processes and plans that will hire the best talent, keep it and develop it. We simply can't buy all the talent that we need to take the organization into its future. We need to grow our own.'

2. *Provide clear principles to enable decision making in the business.* By developing clear principles, Diageo hopes that, when line managers are faced with choices, the right decisions will be more obvious. 'Less demand will be placed on reward 'experts' in the business, who can spend more of their time on value creating enhancements to our processes.'

3. *Align the reward approach with Diageo business strategy.* The success of the reward strategy depends heavily on developing appropriate performance measures in incentives, the cost-effective delivery of reward and consistent processes.

4. *Enable every employee to understand why they get paid what they get paid.* 'We need to have a big push on communication', admits Nicki Demby. 'People do not necessarily understand what they are paid and how we perform. The connection between performance and reward needs to become visceral. As a formal part of each business review, we are telling people the impact the performance of their business is likely to have on their pay. It helps people to make the connections between the business decisions that they make and the likely personal impact.'

5. *Have a customer service ethic that results in great execution.* The reward team's ethic is now based on a much greater orientation towards the needs of employees – its internal customers. 'This demands great planning, great communication and great execution', says Nicki Demby.

Friends Provident

The rationale behind the development of a reward strategy at Friends Provident was the need to:

- match salaries directly to the market;
- give line managers greater accountability for staff salaries and career progression;
- increase the flexibility of pay arrangements at business unit level;
- facilitate a real and fundamental top-down change in corporate culture;
- reward the best performers by paying salaries above the market rate;
- manage salary costs;
- encourage greater accountability by staff for development of their own competencies.

Lloyds TSB

The emphasis at Lloyds TSB is on creating a 'compelling employment offer' – one that is more individually focused, tailored to employees' needs and interests, and more in tune with the expectations of a diverse workforce.

Nationwide

At Nationwide the organizational redesign of the reward system emerged from the company's desire to:

● respond to occupational and labour market pressures;
● encourage more flexible working practices;
● streamline operations;
● improve customer service;
● increase skills.

Norwich Union Insurance

The Norwich Union Insurance strategic reward framework is shown in Figure 4.1.

Tesco

Tesco's overall reward strategy is to:

● be on the right side of the competition on total reward, with the reward package being above the median;
● focus on making reward investment deliver more rather than reducing the size of the pot;
● reinvest to ensure that every element of reward adds value to the business and is valued by staff;
● build a simplified, global pay and grading system that enables mobility and flexibility and supports the values that are critical to future business growth;
● ensure the affordability of the reward package is sustainable, and use Tesco's buying power to deliver as much unbeatable value to staff as to customers;
● focus on rewarding staff for their contribution in a way that enables them to benefit directly from the success they help to create;
● ensure more transparency so that the reward package offered by the company is fully understood and valued.

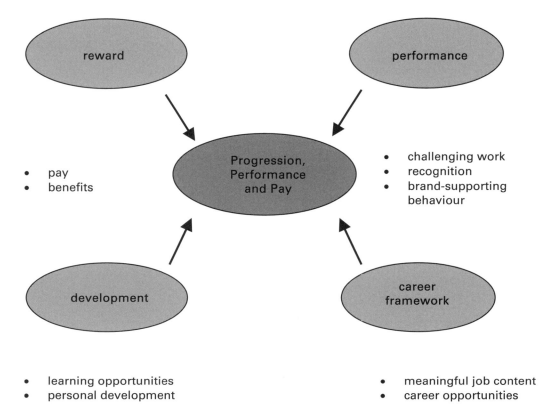

Figure 4.1 The Norwich Union Insurance Progression, Performance and Pay framework

The structure of reward strategy

Reward strategies are diverse and so is the structure used by different organizations to define and present them. Some reward strategies are more complex than others but in one form or other their structure will contain:

1. *A declaration of intent* – the proposed reward developments.
2. *A rationale* – the reasons why the proposals are being made. The rationale makes out the business case for the proposals, indicating how they will meet business needs and setting out the costs and the benefits. It also refers to any people issues that need to be addressed and how the strategy will deal with them. It includes a clear statement of the objectives of the strategy and the criteria for success.
3. *A definition of guiding principles* – the values that it is believed should be adopted in formulating and implementing the strategy.

4.   *A plan* – how, when and by whom the reward initiatives will be implemented. The plan indicates what steps have to be taken and allows for resource constraints and the need for communications, involvement and training. The priorities attached to each element of the strategy are indicated and a timetable for implementation drawn up.

Criteria for an effective reward strategy

As suggested by Clive Wright (6) the five criteria against which a reward strategy should be judged are that it:

1.   defines broad objectives;
2.   is a framework against which decisions on reward can be made;
3.   is long-term;
4.   is flexible enough to change when circumstances require;
5.   has clearly planned goals based on business objectives.

REFERENCES

1   Armstrong, M and Brown, D (2006) *Strategic Reward*, Kogan Page, London
2   Brown, D (2001) *Reward Strategies: From intent to impact*, Chartered Institute of Personnel and Development, London
3   Cox, A and Purcell, J (1998) Searching for leverage: pay systems, trust, motivation and commitment in SMEs, in *Trust, Motivation and Commitment*, ed SJ Perkins and St J Sandringham, Strategic Remuneration Research Centre, Faringdon
4   IRS (2006) Making the most of reward, *IRS Pay and Benefits Bulletin*, 19 May, pp 27–31
5   Murlis, H (1996) *Pay at the Crossroads*, Institute of Personnel and Development, London
6   Wright, C (2005) Reward strategy, *Reward Management Manual*, Chartered Institute of Personnel and Development, London

5

Developing and implementing reward strategy

This chapter deals with how to develop reward strategies. It starts with a discussion of general considerations, which is followed by a description of the sequence of development activities including an analysis of what needs to be done to assess strategic business needs and achieve vertical and horizontal alignment. The chapter is completed with a description of approaches to implementation.

GENERAL CONSIDERATIONS

The basic considerations that should be taken into account when reviewing and rethinking existing rewards, as set out by Armstrong and Brown (1), are discussed below.

Focus on the context

It's a matter of what works within the context of the organization, rather than the 'next big thing'. Will Astill, Reward Manager of B&Q, explains the thinking behind their reward review: 'An overriding theme running through our review was on the desirability of adopting a strategic approach. It wasn't a case of "let's follow the best practice", nor were we lured into adopting the latest fads and fashions. Taking what someone has done before will not push you ahead of rivals.'

Tim Fevyer, Senior Manager, Compensation and Benefits at Lloyds TSB, has a similar message: 'We need to get away from adopting new initiative after new initiative and move away from a culture of "flavour of the month".'

It's about evolution not revolution

Reward professionals rarely start with a clean sheet. They have to take note, and keep taking note, of changes in organizational requirements, which happen all the time. They must track emerging trends and modify their views accordingly, as long as they do not leap too hastily on the latest bandwagon. They have to ensure that reward strategy can be implemented at a pace the organization can manage and people can deal with. The fundamental change in culture often inherent in such projects takes a lot of time – and trouble – to achieve.

It is helpful to define reward strategy formally for the record and as a basis for planning and communication. But this should be regarded as no more than a piece of paper that can be modified when needs change – as they will – and not a tablet of stone. Reward strategy, like business strategy, may be formulated and reformulated as it is used. In the words of Mintzberg (2), it may emerge over time in response to evolving situations, to become a 'pattern in a stream of activities'.

Manage the balance

A reward strategy can include all sorts of things. But you have to get the balance right, paying attention to the initiatives that are most needed and are most likely to make a difference. You have to establish priorities, reflect realities and make the right strategic choices. If you try to do too much too soon or go too far and too fast in one direction you will run into trouble. For example, it is necessary to balance the often competing claims of pay flexibility against cost control, the devolution of reward responsibilities down the organization against consistency across it, internal equity against external competitiveness, and individual incentives against teamwork.

Keep it simple

Over-complexity is the bane of reward management. It complicates implementation, puts off the people affected, hampers effective communication and makes the life of line managers difficult. The history of reward management is littered with examples of 'the light that failed' – over-engineered and ambitious plans that did not work.

Think implementation

No reward initiative should be planned without thinking about how it is going to be implemented, what problems might arise and how they will be dealt with. It is particularly important to consider the part that will be played by line managers in implementation and whether they are up to the task. It is also necessary to consider the reactions of people generally – the extent to which they might resist change and what can be done about it. Change management has to be planned; it won't work if it takes place on an ad hoc basis after the event.

THE REWARD STRATEGY DEVELOPMENT SEQUENCE

The sequence of steps required to develop reward strategy is shown in Figure 5.1.

Analysis of current reward arrangements

The starting point is an analysis of the current reward arrangements. These can be considered under the headings of the existing reward strategy and its different financial and non-financial elements. The analysis should be conducted with stakeholders such as senior management, line managers and employees. The views of employees can also be sought by means of opinion surveys.

The following frameworks for this analysis can be used:

● reward strategy – the level of achievement against criteria, (Figure 5.2, page 64);
● the effectiveness of present reward arrangements (Figure 5.3, page 65);
● a reward gap analysis (Figure 5.4, pages 66–67);
● an employee opinion survey (Figure 5.5, pages 68–69);
● an analysis of the internal environment (Figure 5.6, pages 70–71).

Examples of analyses

An example of the analysis of the reward system is provided by B&Q. This included:

● a full audit of the current reward investment and its focus;
● consideration of the existing use of bonus schemes;
● examination of pay-for-performance arrangements;
● the current provision of financial and non-financial rewards;
● the findings of 20 focus groups comprising people from different levels of B&Q and different divisions.

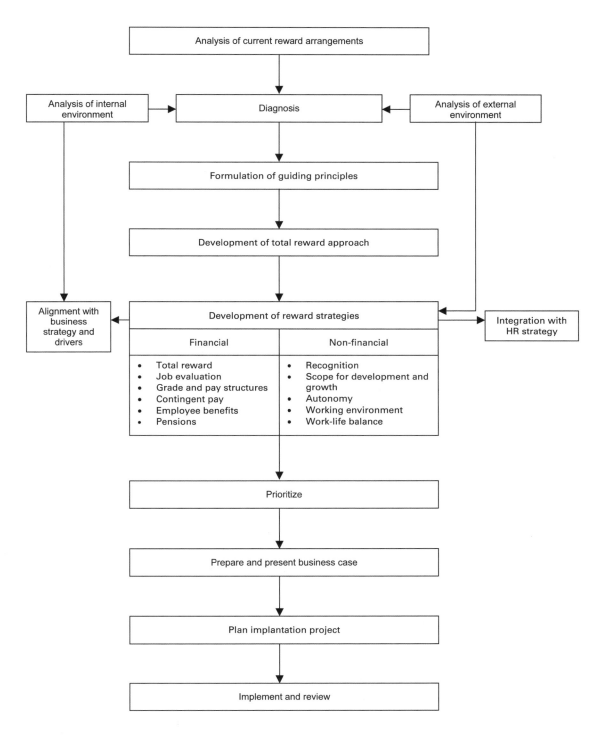

Figure 5.1 The reward strategy development sequence

Criteria	Level of achievement (✓)			
	In full	Mostly	Partly	Not at all
Defines broad objectives				
Is a framework against which decisions on reward can be made				
Is long-term				
Is flexible enough to change when circumstances require				
Has clearly planned goals based on business objectives				

Figure 5.2 Analysis of reward strategy

The opinions of employees about reward can be sought through a survey, as in the following examples.

At Camelot in 2000, the annual employee survey made it clear that staff were concerned about the lack of fairness and transparency in reward. Employees were uncertain how their pay was determined or what they could do to influence their salaries. The company decided to overhaul completely its approach to reward, and in 2001 internal consultation established a new set of reward principles and agreement that a new pay system would:

● be transparent and consistently applied;
● provide a clear link between pay and performance;
● encourage and recognize high performance;
● be clearly aligned with Camelot's values and business strategy.

At Elan Computers, when employees were asked what benefits they knew about, what benefits they wanted, and what they thought about their current benefits package:

● 68 per cent said they wanted the package to be reviewed;
● 35 per cent said they did not understand what they were eligible for;
● 43 per cent said they were too busy to take much interest.

There was a general view that people wanted more benefits, but that was mostly because they did not understand what they had at the time.

	Statement	Fully agree	Partly agree	Partly disagree	Fully disagree
1	We have well-defined and understood reward guiding principles.				
2	Our reward system effectively enhances the engagement of people.				
3	We implement our policy on levels of pay compared with market rates.				
4	We pay insufficient attention to non-financial rewards.				
5	We are satisfied with our methods of deciding on internal relativities.				
6	There is an unacceptable incidence of grade drift (unjustified upgradings).				
7	We are vulnerable to an equal pay claim.				
8	Our rates of pay are uncompetitive.				
9	We do not have adequate data on market rates.				
10	We have too many grades in our pay structure.				
11	Our grade structure is too complex.				
12	People are fairly rewarded according to their contribution.				
13	Our reward system does not succeed in motivating people.				
14	We get value for money from our reward system.				
15	Our performance management processes work well.				
16	We have an excellent and competitive range of employee benefits.				
17	There is room for more choice by employees on benefits.				
18	We spend too much on employee benefits.				
19	Our pension scheme is too expensive.				
20	Our employees fully understand the value of the reward they get.				

Figure 5.3   Analysis of reward system effectiveness

What should be happening	What is happening	What needs to be done
1 A total reward approach is adopted that emphasizes the significance of both financial and non-financial rewards.		
2 Reward policies and practices are developed within the framework of a well-articulated strategy that is designed to support the achievement of business objectives and meet the needs of stakeholders.		
3 A job evaluation scheme is used that properly reflects the values of the organization, is up to date with regard to the jobs it covers and is non-discriminatory.		
4 Equal pay issues are given serious attention. This includes the conduct of equal pay reviews that lead to action.		
5 Market rates are tracked carefully so that a competitive pay structure exists that contributes to the attraction and retention of high-quality people.		
6 Grade and pay structures are based on job evaluation and market rate analysis, are appropriate to the characteristics and needs of the organization and its employees, facilitate the management of relativities, provide scope for rewarding contribution, clarify reward and career opportunities, are constructed logically, operate transparently and are easy to manage and maintain.		
7 Contingent pay schemes reward contribution fairly and consistently, support the motivation of staff and the development of a performance culture, deliver the right messages about the values of the organization, contain a clear 'line of sight' between contribution and reward and are cost-effective.		
8 Performance management processes contribute to performance improvement, people development and the management of expectations, operate effectively throughout the organization and are supported by line managers and staff.		
9 Employee benefits and pension schemes meet the needs of stakeholders and are cost-effective.		
10 A flexible benefits approach is adopted.		
11 Reward management procedures exist that ensure that reward processes are managed effectively and that costs are controlled.		
12 Appropriate use is made of computers (software and spreadsheets) to assist in the process of reward management.		
13 Reward management aims and arrangements are transparent and communicated well to staff.		
14 Surveys are used to assess the opinions of staff about reward, and action is taken on the outcomes.		
15 An appropriate amount of responsibility for reward is devolved to line managers.		

Figure 5.4 A reward gap analysis

16 Line managers are capable of carrying out their devolved responsibilities well.		
17 Steps are taken to train line managers and provide them with support and guidance as required.		
18 HR has the knowledge and skills to provide the required reward management advice and services and to guide and support line managers.		
19 Overall, reward management developments take account of the need to achieve affordability and to demonstrate that they are cost-effective.		
20 Steps are taken to evaluate the effectiveness of reward management processes and to ensure that they reflect changing needs.		

Figure 5.4 *Continued*

A decision was taken by Elan to rebrand the existing benefit package and deliver it differently. The company wanted the new arrangements to be accessible and flexible, so an online system that employees could access whenever it suited them was chosen.

At Dell Computers the conclusions reached from their analysis were as follows:

- *What is the mix of factors that shape the Dell experience?*
  See Figure 5.7 (page 71).
- *What characteristics do we look for in our people?*
- customer orientation;
- drive for results/passion for winning;
- personal accountability;
- team players;
- flexible – high tolerance for ambiguity;
- high integrity.
- *What do the people we want, want?*
- individualized reward;
- partake in the company's success;
- career advancement;
- flexibility;
- responsibility;
- opportunity to socialize.

	I believe that:	Strongly agree	Inclined to agree	Neither agree nor disagree	Inclined to disagree	Strongly disagree
	REWARD OPINION SURVEY					
	Please place a tick in the box that most closely fits your opinion					
1	My pay adequately rewards me for my contribution.					
2	The pay system is clear and easy to understand.					
3	It is right for staff to be rewarded according to their contribution.					
4	The basis upon which my pay is determined is fair.					
5	I am paid fairly compared to other jobs in the organization.					
6	Rates of pay in the organization are not consistent with levels of responsibility.					
7	My rate of pay compares favourably with rates paid outside the organization.					
8	My pay does not reflect my performance.					
9	The current pay system encourages better performance.					
10	The pay system badly needs to be reviewed.					
11	I am clear about the standards of performance I am expected to achieve.					
12	I do not understand the competence levels I am expected to reach.					
13	The performance management scheme is helpful.					
14	I receive good feedback from my manager on my performance.					
15	My manager is not really interested in carrying out my performance review.					
16	I am motivated by my performance review meeting.					
17	The process of setting objectives and reviewing achievements is fair.					
18	The assessment of my performance by my manager is objective and fair.					
19	Performance management does not help me to improve my performance.					
20	Performance management clearly indicates areas where I can learn more about how to do my job.					

Figure 5.5   A reward opinion survey

The rewards philosophy that emerged from this analysis at Dell computers was:

- Dell targets average base pay at the market median, but this doesn't mean that everyone is paid in the middle of the market.
- Variable pay programmes (short-term, sales and long-term incentives) allow total pay to rise above the market median where performance is strong.
- Pay and benefits are continually reviewed in line with market movement, employee feedback and business impact.

Analysis of external environment

Dave Ulrich (3) has written that what happens inside an organization must be linked to what happens outside. The main features of the external environment that influence reward strategy are competitive pressures, globalization, changes in demographics and employment, legal developments and pay levels and trends in the marketplace. These were analysed in Chapter 2. A framework for analysing the external environment is provided in Figure 5.8 (page 72).

An example is provided by B&Q of an analysis of the external environment. This included:

- an examination of the changing labour market;
- a literature review of employers' responses to emerging employment trends and how competitors reward staff;
- an analysis of the HR and reward strategies typically adopted by high-performing organizations;
- a survey of 50 high-performing people in a sample of 20 high-performing organizations examining what these staff need in the reward package;
- two commissioned surveys of 200 people each to examine external perceptions of B&Q as an employer;
- a benchmarking exercise using retail industry salary surveys.

Diagnosis

Analysis is followed by diagnosis. Note the distinction. These processes are often confused. Analysis is about *what* is happening; diagnosis is concerned with finding out *why* it is happening. These are related but separate activities. A framework for diagnosis leading to action is given in Figure 5.9.

An example of a diagnostic framework prepared for a large local authority is shown in Figure 5.10.

Question	Response	Implications for reward strategy
What are the espoused values of the organization?		
What evidence is there that these values are used in the everyday life of the organization?		
What are the factors that shape the experience of working for our organization?		
What are the implications of the type of business we are in and its technology or method of operation on our reward strategy?		
What characteristics do we look for in our people?		
What do the people we want, want?		

Figure 5.6 Analysis of internal environment

What are the key objectives of our business strategy?		
What are the main drivers of success in our business?		

Figure 5.6 *Continued*

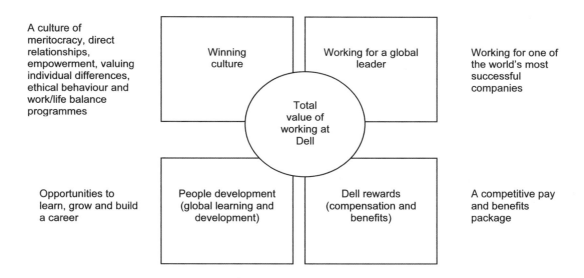

A culture of meritocracy, direct relationships, empowerment, valuing individual differences, ethical behaviour and work/life balance programmes

Winning culture

Working for a global leader

Working for one of the world's most successful companies

Total value of working at Dell

Opportunities to learn, grow and build a career

People development (global learning and development)

Dell rewards (compensation and benefits)

A competitive pay and benefits package

Figure 5.7 The unique mix of factors that shape the Dell work experience

External factor	Impact on HR policy and practice	Impact on reward strategy
Competitive pressures		
Globalization		
Employment and demographic trends		
Legislation		
Market rates of pay and trends		

Figure 5.8 External environment analysis framework

Issues identified by analysis	Reasons for issues	Action proposed to deal with issue

Figure 5.9 Diagnostic framework

Issue	Diagnosis of cause	Proposed action
Pay levels are not keeping pace with market rates.	The intelligence available on market rates is inadequate and pay levels have been allowed to slip.	Continually monitor market rates and take steps to ensure that pay levels are competitive in line with market relativities policy.
Performance management is well established but it is not being used effectively as a means of improving corporate performance.	Performance management tends to focus only on short-term issues of individual performance and does not address the wider need to develop a performance culture.	Review operation of performance management processes to ensure that they support the development of a performance culture by clarifying what individuals and teams are expected to do to improve organizational performance.
Unacceptable grade drift is taking place.	The job evaluation scheme has decayed and is being manipulated.	Develop a new computer-assisted job evaluation scheme.
Difficult to ensure that consistent and appropriate grading decisions are made. Too much grade drift.	Too many narrow grades (16).	Design new broad-graded structure (8–10 grades) supported by new job evaluation scheme.

Figure 5.10 Example of reward diagnosis in a local authority

Formulation of guiding principles

A set of guiding principles is important as a means of planning the development of reward strategy and practice. They can be used to monitor the impact of the implemented strategy. The principles should be developed in consultation with stakeholders to ensure acceptance and understanding. Use can be made of surveys, workshops and focus groups. Examples of guiding principles in other organizations as provided below can be helpful but every effort should be made to think through what is right for the organization and not slavishly adopt other people's ideas. The approach should not be too directive.

BT

The five key principles of the reward framework at BT are:

1. *Clarity* – the reward framework brings transparency to the way people are rewarded for their contribution to the business. The same role profiles (within the same job families) now apply right across BT, and command the same published salary ranges. People know exactly where they stand.
2. *External focus* – the way BT rewards and recognizes people must conform to the market in which it operates. Under the new reward framework, salary ranges are aligned with the going rate for equivalent jobs across a range of comparable organizations, geographies and skill sets. This will ensure BT remains competitive and able to recruit and retain the people it needs.
3. *Focus on roles* – a person's place in the organization should be valued by the work the person does – not by where he or she sits in a hierarchy. The new reward framework has replaced grades with job families, which represent a group of similar roles in a similar field of activity. A large number of operational managers from across the business have helped to define a structure that reflects the roles individuals actually do, not historical grades.
4. *Reward for performance* – people who perform well will earn higher rewards than people who don't. Reward decisions are now based on capability in role and proven contribution through achievement of objectives. People should be clear about why they earn what they do.
5. *Choice* – not all BT managers currently have a choice over how they receive their rewards. In keeping with BT's position as a highly innovative company and employer, the new framework will offer an increased choice over the benefits people receive as part of their total reward package. This approach ensures that everyone knows exactly where he or she stands in relation to the market, and in relation to his or her performance.

COLT Telecom

COLT's reward philosophy states that:

- COLT believes that talented and motivated people make a difference; talented people put the company ahead of the competition and deliver the results on which the success of COLT is built. COLT seeks to offer a compensation and benefits package that rewards people for their contribution to the success of the company and ensures that external market competitiveness and internal relativities are taken into account.
- The *reward mix* is designed to promote a performance culture that underpins the company business strategy. Reward is geared to driving exceptional effort through the variable elements of the total package whilst maintaining flexibility, simplicity and equity within the guiding principles of driving discretionary effort, rewarding employee contribution and encouraging employees to behave like owners.
- The *compensation package* includes cash and non-cash payments as well as fixed and variable elements. The ability to have an impact on shareholder value influences the mix of the total reward package, with a greater emphasis on variable pay (bonus, share incentive and share ownership schemes) for those at the senior level within the company.
- *Base salaries* are benchmarked regularly across Europe against other telecommunication operators, the high-tech sector and other appropriate industries.
- The *performance management* system ensures that performance is assessed and used to differentiate achievement among employees at all levels, thus driving discretionary effort. The bonus scheme rewards individual performance against a mix of company and individual objectives and contribution to overall company performance.
- The company believes in encouraging an ownership mindset, so *share option* schemes offer employees a stake in the organization, which will allow them to share in the company's success over the medium and long term. COLT offers voluntary, all-employee share participation schemes in the countries where it is possible to do so. Management can participate in performance-related option schemes, and it is expected that those with greater opportunities to influence directly the success of the business will have a larger proportion of shareholding within their total reward package.
- *Benefits* are designed to be market-competitive whilst protecting both employees and the company. They comply with local legislation, are tax-effective and take into account social security benefits in all the countries within which COLT operates.

Lloyds TSB

The guiding reward strategy principles at Lloyds TSB are:

- Basic pay is linked to the market.
- Benefits are market-driven and individually focused.
- Pay decisions are devolved to line managers.
- Pay reflects individual contribution in a high-performance organization.
- Pay complies with equal pay principles.
- Variable pay is linked to performance.
- Wealth creation and share ownership are encouraged.
- Reward and HR practices are managed in an integrated way.

Tesco

The guiding principles in Tesco are:

- Tesco will provide an innovative reward package that is valued by staff and communicated brilliantly to reinforce the benefits of working for Tesco.
- Reward investment will be linked to company performance so that staff share in the success they create and, by going the extra mile, receive above-average reward compared to local competitors.
- All parts of the total reward investment will add value to the business and reinforce Tesco's core purpose, goals and values.

Developing total rewards

The steps required to develop total rewards are:

1. Be clear about what the concept means and how it can benefit the organization as a foundation for its reward strategy.
2. Convince top management that a total reward approach of this nature will benefit the organization in significant ways, eg recruitment and retention, motivation, commitment and job engagement, and talent management.
3. Define the components of total reward in terms of pay, benefits, learning and development, and the work environment.
4. Analyse the present arrangements for total reward with regard to each of the components and decide where it is necessary to improve those arrangements.
5. Prepare a statement of how each of the relevant components can be developed and applied in the organization.

6. Communicate to staff details of the proposed total reward strategy and discuss with staff how a total reward approach will work and will benefit them.
7. As part of the reward strategy, plan and implement each of the total reward initiatives that have been agreed with management and staff.
8. Conduct training as required to improve the capability of line managers to play a major part in providing relational rewards.
9. Ensure that HR is there to provide encouragement and guidance and to see that the total reward programme coheres.
10. Monitor the progress made in introducing total reward so that action can be taken to deal with any problems.

The following method of analysing the total rewards strategy in an organization using the Towers Perrin model described in Chapter 3 is shown in Figure 5.11.

Groups of managers and/or staff can be asked to describe the current total rewards provision using this grid. They can then be asked to describe the improvements and changes in content and emphasis they would like to see to better support the business of the organization and make it a more rewarding and motivating place to work.

The current and required total reward strategy in a public sector organization, developed by this process with their top 50 managers working in groups, is shown in Figure 5.12.

Alignment with business strategy and business drivers

Reward strategy development involves ensuring so far as possible that there is vertical alignment or fit between the reward strategy and the business strategy. This means that the reward strategy has specifically to take account of business goals and be designed to support their achievement. The reward strategy must also take account of the business drivers of the organization – the factors that contribute to its success. Again, the reward strategy should aim to reinforce them.

The analysis of the internal environment should have identified the key features of the business strategy and what drives the business. The implications of these for reward strategy can be assessed using Figure 5.13.

Alignment with external trends

In devising reward strategy, account must be taken of external trends, especially those relating to competition, globalization, employment and demographics, employment legislation and market rate levels and movements. The impact of external trends can be analysed using the framework set out in Figure 5.8.

PAY	BENEFITS
• Now	• Now
• Future	• Future
LEARNING	**ENVIRONMENT**
• Now	• Now
• Future	• Future

Source: Michael Armstrong and Duncan Brown (2006) *Strategic Reward*, Kogan Page, London

Figure 5.11   Total reward analysis grid

Integration with HR strategy

Integration of reward strategy with HR strategy (horizontal fit) is desirable in order to ensure that the various HR and reward practices are linked together so that they are mutually supporting. This may mean identifying integrating practices such as the use of competency-based processes that impact on recruitment, training, performance management and reward or the design of career family grade and pay structures that map career paths. In particular it is necessary to explore how reward practices can support the recruitment and retention of high-quality staff, talent management and learning and development. A checklist of the links that can be made is given in Figure 5.14.

PAY	BENEFITS
Now	**Now**
• Secure	• Family friendly
• Below average	• Paternalistic
• 'One size fits all'	• Secure
Future	**Future**
• Aligned to business goals	• Individually tailored
• Market rates	• Flexibility
• Flexible	• Valued by employees
LEARNING	**ENVIRONMENT**
Now	**Now**
• Good learning opportunities	• Comfortable
• Spoon-fed	• Family
• Structures	• Formal
Future	**Future**
• More targeted training	• Challenging
• Focused on business goals	• Responsive
• Good opportunities as before	• Enjoyable

Source: Michael Armstrong and Duncan Brown (2006) *Strategic Reward*, Kogan Page, London

Figure 5.12   Current and required total reward strategy

Examples of vertical and horizontal alignment

The following examples of vertical and horizontal alignment are derived from case studies produced by e-reward (4):

- *B&Q* – summarize the alignment between their business and HR and reward strategies as shown in Figure 5.15.
- *GlaxoSmithKline* – here the business strategy is very different from that adopted by B&Q but, similarly, it is reinforced by the HR and reward strategies as shown in Figure 5.16.
- *Lands' End* – this mail-order clothing business regularly tops the best-places-to-work listings, and its HR and reward strategies are integral to its business strategy.

	Possible elements	Actual elements	Implications for reward strategy
Business strategy	• Growth – revenue/profit • Maximize shareholder value • Growth through acquisitions/mergers • Growth in production/servicing facilities • Product development • Market development • Price/cost leadership		
Business drivers	• Innovation • Maximize added value • Productivity • Customer service • Quality • Satisfy stakeholders – investors, shareholders, employees, elected representatives • Price/cost leadership		

Figure 5.13 Alignment with business strategy and drivers

HR strategy area	Reward strategy contribution
Resourcing	• Total reward approaches that help to make the organization a great place in which to work. • Competitive pay structures that help to attract and retain high-quality people.
Performance management	• Contingent pay schemes that contribute to the motivation and engagement of people. • Performance management processes that promote continuous improvement and encourage people to uphold core values.
Talent management	• Non-financial rewards such as recognition and opportunities for growth and development. • Policies that recognize talented people for their contribution. • Career-linked grade and pay structure, for example a career family structure.
Learning and development	• Performance management processes that identify learning needs and how they can be satisfied. • Career family structures that define career ladders in terms of knowledge and skill requirements.
Work environment	• Total reward approaches that emphasize the importance of enhancing the work environment. • Work/life balance policies.

Source: Michael Armstrong and Duncan Brown (2006) *Strategic Reward*, Kogan Page, London

Figure 5.14   Links between HR and reward strategy areas

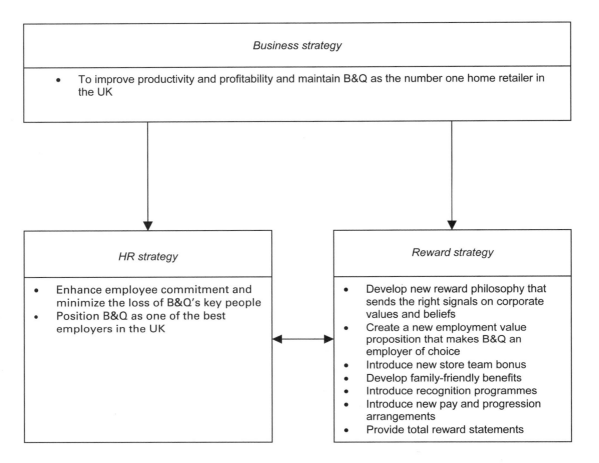

Figure 5.15   Integrated reward strategy at B&Q

Formulation of reward strategies

The first step is to consider in the light of the analysis and diagnosis possible strategies in each of the main areas. A framework for this purpose is provided in Figure 5.17.

Prioritization

It is necessary to prioritize the selected strategies bearing in mind the urgency of the need, the resources available, the benefits of achieving a quick win and the dangers of trying to do too much. Figure 5.18 can be used for this purpose.

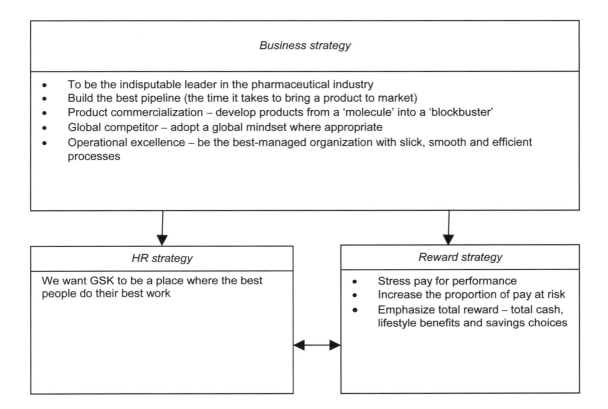

Figure 5.16   Integrated reward strategy at GlaxoSmithKline

Preparing the business case

It is essential to take care over preparing the business case for whatever strategy is proposed, and a checklist for this purpose is given in Figure 5.19.

IMPLEMENTATION

The development and implementation of a reward strategy often constitute a complex project, which has to be managed effectively. It will be much easier to do this if throughout the project the approach has been, in the words of Armstrong and Brown, 'to develop with implementation in mind'. Effective project management is essential, and a checklist is set out in Figure 5.20.

Strategy area		Examples of possible strategies	Yes ✓	No ✓	Modify
Financial	Total reward	Introduce total reward approach			
	Job evaluation	Develop new analytical scheme			
		Develop new non-analytical scheme			
		Modify existing scheme			
		Rely on analytical matching			
	Grade and pay structure	Reduce number of grades considerably (broad-grading)			
		Introduce broad-banding			
		Develop job or career family structure			
		Replace pay spine with broad-graded structure			
		Replace pay spine with job or career families			
	Contingent pay	Introduce performance-related pay (not pay spine)			
		Introduce contribution-related pay (not pay spine)			
		Introduce performance-related pay (pay spine)			
		Introduce contribution-related pay (pay spine)			
		Introduce variable pay (bonus) scheme			
	Employee benefits	Revise benefits provision			
		Introduce flexible benefits			
	Pensions	Change to defined contribution scheme			

Figure 5.17   Reward strategy formulation framework

	Recognition	Introduce formal recognition scheme			
Non-financial	Scope for development and growth	Improve learning and development programmes			
	Autonomy	Encourage, guide and train line managers to increase autonomy			
	Working environment	Develop 'great place to work' policies			
	Work/life balance	Introduce more comprehensive work/life balance policies			

Figure 5.17 *Continued*

A bar chart as shown in Figure 5.21 (based on an actual example) is a useful way of planning, illustrating and controlling the project. The illustrated chart does not cover the initial analysis, diagnosis and planning stage.

In addition, a clearer picture of the interdependencies can be presented in the form of a network as shown in Figure 5.22.

Implement and review – the BT approach

Kevin Brady, HR Director, Reward and Employee Relations at BT, commented to Paul Thompson of e-reward (4) that: 'Introducing the new reward framework represented a formidable challenge. It was a major exercise in change management. It certainly involved a lot of learning along the way.' He believes that it is necessary to remember the following seven key learning points for change when planning the implementation of reward strategy:

1. *Business sponsorship and ownership are key.* From the outset, BT's aim was to secure 'sponsorship and ownership' amongst senior people, a feeling that the change is something that they are happy to live with because they have been involved in its planning and introduction – it has become *their* change. But Kevin Brady admits that problems may arise in achieving sponsorship and the unwavering commitment by all concerned – these difficulties should never be underestimated.

Strategy area		Proposed strategy	Priority (1,2,3 etc)	Proposed programme	
				Start	Finish
Financial	Total reward				
	Job evaluation				
	Grade and pay structure				
	Contingent pay				
	Employee benefits				
	Pensions				
	Other				
Non-financial	Recognition				
	Scope for development and growth				
	Autonomy				
	Working environment				
	Work/life balance				
	Other				

Figure 5.18 Prioritization of strategy development

Have you:

- produced a convincing argument that the proposal will make a positive impact on key areas of the organization's operations, eg customer service levels, quality, shareholder value, productivity, income generation, innovation, skills development, talent management;

- proof that the innovation has already worked well within the organization (perhaps as a pilot scheme) or represents 'good practice' that is likely to be transferable to the organization;

- demonstrated that it can be implemented without too much trouble, for example not taking up a lot of managers' time, or not meeting with strong opposition from line managers, employees or trade unions (it is as well to check the likely reaction before launching a proposal);

- indicated that it will add to the reputation of the company by showing that it is a 'world-class' organization, ie what it does is as good as, if not better than, what is done by the world leaders in the sector in which the business operates (a promise that publicity will be achieved through articles in professional journals, press releases and conference presentations will help);

- shown that it will enhance the 'employer brand' of the company by making it a 'best place to work';

- ensured that the proposal is brief, to the point and well argued – it should take no more than five minutes to present orally and should be summarized in writing on the proverbial one side of one sheet of paper (supplementary details can be included in appendices)?

Figure 5.19   Business case checklist

The harsh reality for BT was that the degree of sponsorship that it thought it had achieved was not really there. 'If I'm brutally honest, it's easy to put across a very positive message about sponsorship – that people are doing all the right things and they're signed up to it and the CEO wants it', says Brady. 'But if people haven't got an active interest in the project and it's not their top priority, they don't realize what the impact is until way down the road. That's when they suddenly come back to you.'

Brady describes the process of organizational change management as a 'continual circle whereby you constantly need to go back to sponsors and reconfirm their responses and re-engage' with them. 'People will tell you they are happy with the project and they'll nod it through, but you actually need more than that. You have to keep going back and reinforcing the sponsorship and then you can stand up and be counted. It's only human nature. People were only too happy to delegate and say, "I'll let so-and-so design the structure for me and whatever they say goes." But then when we published the structure we'd get dozens of e-mails saying, "This is

Have you:

- specified the objectives of the project and the deliverables;

- defined who is to be responsible for directing and managing the project and the degree of authority he or she has;

- set out what should be done (activities), who does what and when it will be done;

- involved senior managers/heads of department as sponsors, to provide comment, guidance, support and encouragement;

- broken down the project into stages with defined starting and completion dates to produce the programme;

- clarified interdependencies;

- defined resource requirements – people, outside advisers, finance;

- defined methods of control, eg progress reports, meetings;

- ensured that everyone knows what is expected of them and has the briefing, guidance and resources required;

- seen that progress is monitored continuously against the plan as well as at formal meetings;

- ensured that corrective action is taken as required, for example amending timings, reallocating resources;

- evaluated progress and the end result against objectives and deliverables?

Figure 5.20   Project management checklist

nuts. I can't believe you've done this."' Above all, Brady thinks it is crucial to avoid the programme being tagged as just another HR or reward initiative, rather than as something that is owned by the organization as a whole. 'It's essential to get continued operational ownership of the programme. It's not about an HR project – it's about a fundamental shift in terms of the business. And it's a business-driven change initiative. We're trying to shift the culture of the business.'

2. *Don't underestimate resistance.* Kevin Brady believes that the level of resistance that may arise when reorganizing reward systems should never be underestimated,

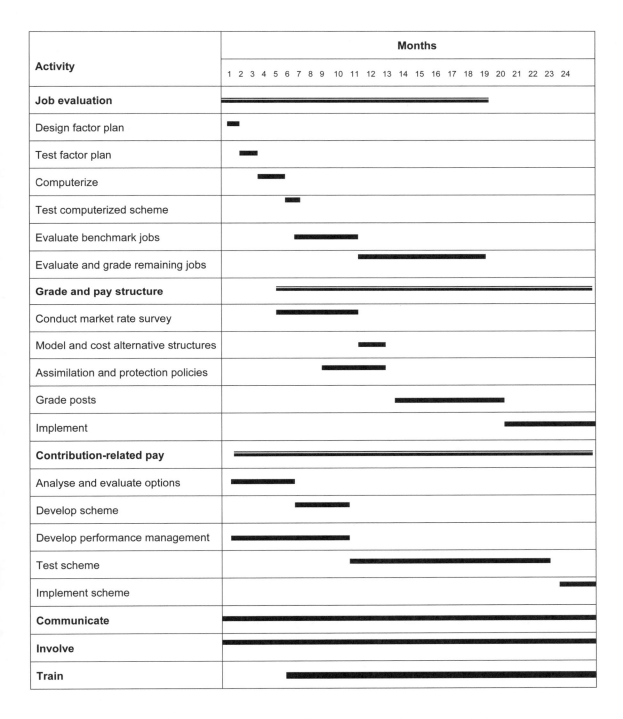

Figure 5.21 Reward strategy design and implementation control chart

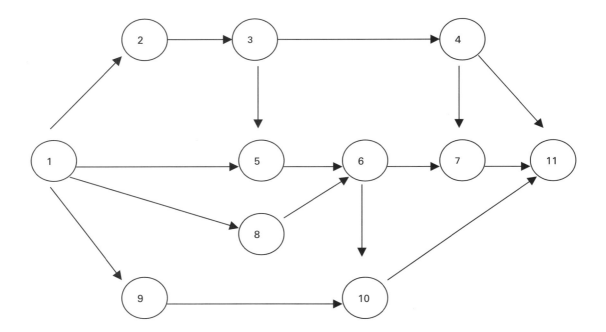

Index of activities

1 Develop strategy.
2 Design and test job evaluation scheme.
3 Evaluate benchmark jobs.
4 Evaluate remaining jobs.
5 Design grade structure.
6 Grade jobs.
7 Conduct market rate survey.
8 Attach pay ranges to grade structure.
9 Consider and assess contribution pay options.
10 Develop and test contribution pay scheme.
11 Implement.
The timing and responsibility for each activity would also be indicated.

Figure 5.22   A reward strategy development and implementation network

hence the importance he places on sponsorship, communication and training. 'I've had resistance from my own team, resistance from senior operations directors and resistance from the business', says Brady. Almost inevitably, changes in reward systems can be perceived by people as not only potentially hitting them where it hurts – in their pockets – but also undermining their status. They can be unsettled, unduly apprehensive and resist anything that alters an existing arrangement. This is an area of great interest to people, and their expectations must be managed. 'It's about being aware that, as you go into the change, not everyone is going to be happy with the change. Reward is such a sensitive area. Even little things that you believe to be beneficial, which you would think would convey a positive message, are not seen that way. In fact, we almost managed to snatch a defeat from the jaws of victory. People still perceived that they were losing status – because they previously had been entitled to a car and, although they were still going to get that car, someone doing the same job working alongside them wouldn't now receive a car. Therefore that was a slight on them.'

3. *Understand the internal dependencies on your current structure.* BT discovered that, when it scrapped its grading structure, which had been in place for 15 years, many of its systems and authority levels were grade-driven. As Brady explains: 'What tends to happen is that people build all the systems around grades, so in terms of sign-off levels we had something like 360 systems that still referred to the old grading structure. All of our operating systems that are embedded in the system are built around grade. All of our internal customer service systems have got grade in there. Finance systems are all driven off grade.' For the duration of the transitional period, BT decided that each individual employee would maintain his or her current grade. This was necessary to allow 'business-as-usual decisions' to be made and processes to operate, whilst appropriate systems work was carried out as part of a change to role-driven systems.

4. *Project management skills are critical.* BT reckons that the introduction of the new reward framework was one of the largest change management programmes of its kind in the UK. It was certainly the most ambitious and complex project that BT has ever undertaken. 'To be successful, your new reward programme should be implemented by means of a carefully planned and managed project to organize and shape work more effectively', says Brady. 'The normal rules of project management should apply. So you need to establish a steering committee, appoint sponsors from each line of the business, ensure that you have clear and agreed objectives, prepare a project plan with project milestones and clear change control processes. But, above all, with something on this scale and complexity with a huge number

of internal dependencies, you need a full-time, dedicated individual, trained in project management, who can manage all aspects of the project. In hindsight, our project management could have been better and we could have done things differently.'

5. *Cost can restrict speed of change.* All too often, huge amounts of money are spent devising and implementing new reward systems. But BT has developed its new reward structure without making a substantial financial investment. Clearly, if there is limited additional investment, in terms of increased pay and benefits, then the 'process of change can be impacted', says Brady. 'In our case, launching a new structure at the same time as a very tight annual review meant people blamed the structure rather than the commercial pressures. The project was broadly cost-neutral, whereas often a big reward change like this would be driven by a merger or something like that, and there's some money to smooth the way. We had a very limited amount of additional funding to do that.'

6. *Engage, engage, engage!* Kevin Brady believes that ownership and acceptance are much more likely if the maximum degree of engagement of all concerned is built into the entire change programme: 'Stop and talk to people; involve them in the implementation process; let them know their views are important. Involvement in the programme of introducing new reward systems is a key component of the change management process. It gives people the chance to raise and resolve their concerns and make suggestions about the form of the change and how it should be introduced. Employees should be given every opportunity to participate and contribute to the decision-making processes concerning the development of the new reward programme.' For BT, this was a matter of undertaking attitude surveys and involvement in focus groups – made up of representatives of all of the lines of business – along with briefings and roadshows. 'We did everything you can think of to make sure that people understood the message we were trying to get across', says Brady.

7. *Clear, consistent communications.* In Kevin Brady's view, an essential feature of any reward change programme is the very clear, effective and regular communication of aims, methods of operation and impact. Transparency is essential. His recommendations are these:
   - It is vital to reinforce your key principles through all communications. The importance of ensuring that communications are consistent cannot be over-emphasized, says Brady. 'We have tried to be more consistent about putting across what are the key reward principles for this part of the workforce. The core message has not really changed, but it has evolved as we have taken on board comments and developed it as we have gone along.'

- It is essential to communicate consistently and, wherever possible, use one signatory or one voice on communications. 'Lines-of-business CEOs fronted many of our reward communications. It's about them embedding that in their organization', says Brady.
- It is imperative to communicate to staff at every stage of the process – even in advance of launch – using one bank of collateral copy and images, without any 'reinvention'.
- Early engagement with trade unions and works councils, where appropriate, is important.
- 'Line HR is a priority for advance briefing and upskilling', says Brady. They must have a clear understanding of what the change is, why it is taking place and, importantly, how it affects employees. As part of this process, BT developed training programmes – for example, in role mapping – to ensure that everyone acquired the skills needed to manage the new processes and play a part in them. Brady is confident that BT's reward communications have become 'much crisper' as the implementation programme has progressed. 'Communication has improved immensely in terms of clarity. But the harsh reality is that all too often the feedback you get is along the lines of "you don't tell us enough". However, more recently, one of the positives is that people have told us that they were unsure why they had received the latest call, as there was nothing new in it. This means that the message is getting through. But you've got to reinforce continuously.' Without doubt, the introduction of job families at BT has constituted a major culture change. 'I think employees were saying that intellectually they get it, but emotionally they didn't. They were telling us that their grade had been taken away. People can find it difficult to accept that they have lost their old grade, which defined their status, and are now placed in a role which they may share with others who were previously in lower grades. That is why the process of communicating to staff generally and as individuals the rationale for job families is so important.'

Evaluating success at BT

It is always vital to specify the objectives and success criteria for reward strategies and changes, and to put some processes in place to assess how well your new systems and schemes are working. No thoroughgoing shift in reward is complete until you find out if it has worked. So far as possible, you should be able to demonstrate that it has made a difference. So how has BT measured the effectiveness of its new reward programme?

Kevin Brady outlines five key measures of success:

1. *Language of total reward.* Are people talking differently? Brady is confident that a 'total reward' mindset is gradually being established within BT, and people now recognize that there is more to their reward than just base pay. He reckons employees are increasingly focusing on the external market: 'People are talking more about the external market, whereas two years ago they might have been comparing their salaries with what someone in Retail received, or what someone in Wholesale gets. I think we have shifted the whole debate around reward forward. Are we fully there yet? No, but I don't think on a journey like this you change things overnight. This is a 5- or 10-year programme to change the culture. You are trying to change the perception of employees.'

2. *Clear impact on salary, bonus and make-up of package.* Is the mix of the reward package any different? In BT's case it has shifted, with increased levels of variable pay, which was a key requirement at the start of the project.

3. *Confidence in market data.* Acceptance by employees of the validity of the market data used to set salary ranges remains a source of concern, admits Brady. 'The view tends to be, "if it's not the right message for me personally, I don't believe the data".' But he points out that employee 'churn' is still well below external benchmark comparisons.

4. *Employee relations.* 'If you are in open warfare with your union, you'll have problems', warns Brady. BT says it worked closely with Connect, the main union, throughout the entire change project. 'We engaged them on almost a weekly basis. They were fully involved', says Brady.

5. *Cost neutrality.* Kevin Brady emphasized that 'The new reward framework is emphatically *not* about saving money – the factors which determine the annual budget will remain the same.' Nor is it designed to inject new funding. But it is about using that budget more effectively to ensure that BT can recruit and retain the people it needs by aligning reward more closely to performance and the external market.

REFERENCES

1 Armstrong, M and Brown, D (2006) *Strategic Reward*, Kogan Page, London

2 Mintzberg, H (1987) Crafting strategy, *Harvard Business Review*, July/August, pp 66–74

3   Ulrich, D (1998) A new mandate for human resources, *Harvard Business Review*, January/February, pp 124–34
4   e-reward (2003–05) *Reward Case Studies*, e-reward.co.uk, Stockport

6

Reward policies

This chapter covers: 1) the purpose of reward policies; 2) the headings under which policies may be defined; and 3) the approach to their formulation. Examples of reward policies are given at the end of the chapter.

THE PURPOSE OF REWARD POLICIES

Reward policies set specific guidelines for decision making and action. They indicate what the organization and its management are expected to do about managing reward and how they will behave in given circumstances when dealing with reward issues. They can be distinguished from guiding principles, which usually express a more generalized philosophy.

REWARD POLICY HEADINGS

Reward policies deal with:

- the level of rewards;
- the relative importance attached to external competitiveness and internal equity;
- the use of job evaluation;
- achieving equal pay;

- the approach to total reward;
- the scope for the use of contingent rewards related to performance, competence, contribution or skill;
- the role of line managers;
- transparency – the publication of information on reward structures and processes to employees;
- the assimilation of employees into new pay structures;
- the protection of the pay of employees affected by new pay structures;
- decisions on the rates of pay offered to staff on appointment or promotion.

Level of rewards

The policy on the level of rewards indicates whether the company is a high payer, is content to pay median or average rates of pay or even, exceptionally, accepts that it has to pay below the average. Pay policy, which is sometimes referred to as the 'pay stance' or 'pay posture' of a company, will depend on a number of factors. These include the extent to which the company demands high levels of performance from its employees, the degree to which there is competition for good-quality people, the traditional stance of the company, the organization culture, and whether or not it can or should afford to be a high payer. A firm may say that 'We will pay upper-quartile salaries because we want our staff to be upper-quartile performers.'

Policies on pay levels will also refer to differentials and the number of steps or grades that should exist in the pay hierarchy. This will be influenced by the structure of the company. In today's flatter organizations an extended or complex pay hierarchy may not be required on the grounds that it does not reflect the way in which work is organized and will constrain flexibility. Policies on the level of rewards also cover employee benefits – pensions, sick pay, health care, holidays and perks such as company cars.

Pay level policies are linked to policies on external competitiveness and internal equity.

External competitiveness versus internal equity

A policy needs to be formulated on the extent to which rewards are market-driven rather than equitable. This policy will be influenced by the culture and reward philosophies of the organization and the pressures on the business to obtain and keep high-quality staff. Any organizations that have to attract and retain staff who are much in demand and where market rates are therefore high may, to a degree, have to sacrifice their ideals (if they have them) of internal equity to the realism of the marketplace. They will provide 'market pay' and be 'market-driven'.

The pay management process must cope as best it can when the irresistible force of market pressures meets the immovable object of internal equity. There will always be some degree of tension in these circumstances and, while no solution will ever be simple or entirely satisfactory, there is one basic principle that can enhance the likelihood of success. That principle is to make explicit and fully identifiable the compromises with internal equity that are made and have to be made in response to market pressures.

The policy may indicate that market considerations will drive levels of pay in the organization. There are three ways in which this policy can be applied. The first is by having job family pay structures containing different 'market groups' that cover each 'family' of jobs where the basic kinds of activities are similar, eg marketing, finance or HR, but are carried out at different levels. The pay ranges in different job families will vary by reference to the market rates for the jobs in the family. Second, a broad-banded structure with only four or five grades may be used in which the rates of pay for individual or generic roles (ie similar jobs carried out by a number of people) are determined by reference to market rates, not job evaluation. Third, a spot rate structure may be used in which there are no pay ranges and the individual rates of pay are wholly related to market rates. Further information on these structures is given in Chapter 17.

Alternatively, it may be decided that there should be a common grade and pay structure (ie no special structures for market groups) so that the basic pay of all jobs in a grade is the same. Single broad-graded and career family structures come into this category (see Chapter 17). However, the use of market supplements or recruitment premiums may be allowed. These are additional payments to the rate for a job as determined by job evaluation (internal equity) that reflect market rates. The policy may lay down that these payments should be reviewed regularly and no longer offered if they are unnecessary. Market supplements for those who have them may not be withdrawn (they would not lose pay), but adjustments may be made to pay progression to bring their rates more into line with those for comparable jobs.

Market pay and market supplements can lead to gender inequalities if, as is often the case, men in comparable jobs are paid more generously than women. Equal pay case law has ruled that market pay and market supplements should be 'objectively justified', which means that there should be adequate evidence from a number of sources that pay levels need to be higher to maintain competitiveness. The requirement to produce objective justification should be included in the pay policy.

Use of job evaluation

Policy on the use of formal job evaluation procedures to determine internal relativities will depend on the policies on equal pay and internal equity referred to above. The policy may determine how a formal job evaluation should be used. The choice is between evaluating every job with the full scheme or allocating a support role to job evaluation, which, after the grade structure has been designed, is only used when gradings need to be validated or in special circumstances, which would need to be defined, eg for new jobs, for appeals against gradings or in equal pay reviews. Further details of how job evaluation can be used are given in Chapters 11 and 12.

Achieving equal pay

A policy is required on the degree to which equal pay considerations should drive the management of the reward system. The policy should also cover the use of equal pay reviews. This raises the important policy issue of the degree to which pay levels should be market-led, which would mean that the pay inequities that exist outside the organization would be reproduced inside it.

Total reward policy

A policy is required on the extent to which the organization wants to adopt a 'total reward' approach as described in Chapter 3. This will mean assessing the importance of the non-financial relational rewards and how they should complement the financial transactional rewards.

Contingent rewards

The policy will need to determine whether or not the organization wants to pay for performance, competence, contribution or skill and, if so, how much and under what circumstances. There may, for example, be a policy that bonuses should be paid for exceptional performance but that, to be significant, they should not be less than, say, 10 per cent of basic pay, while their upper limit should be restricted to 30 per cent or so of base pay. The policy may also indicate the approach to be used in relating pay to individual, team or organizational performance.

The role of line managers

Line managers play a crucial role in administering rewards, and the policy should recognize this. The extent to which the responsibility for rewards should be devolved to line managers is a policy decision. The aim may be to devolve it as far as possible, bearing in mind the need to ensure that other reward policy guidelines are followed and that consistent decisions are made across the organization by line managers. The policy may cover the level of decisions managers can make, the guidance that should be made available to them and how consistency will be achieved. The training required by line managers to increase their capacity to exercise judgements on reward and to conduct performance management reviews could also be covered by the policy.

Transparency

Traditionally, organizations in the private sector have kept information about pay policies secret. This is no longer a tenable position. Employees will only feel that the reward management processes of an organization are fair if they know what they are and how they are used to determine their level of pay and methods of pay progression. Lack of understanding breeds suspicion and hostility. One of the aims of reward management should be to enhance engagement and commitment, but there is no possibility of this being achieved if the organization is secretive about pay.

Without transparency, people will believe that the organization has something to hide, often with reason. There is no chance of building a satisfactory psychological contract unless the organization spells out its reward policies and practices. Transparency is achieved through involvement and communication.

Policies on pay decisions

Policies may be required on the extent to which the level of pay offered on appointment can exceed the minimum pay for the grade into which the individual will be allocated. It is also necessary to consider the policy on what promotion increases should be awarded.

Assimilation policies

The introduction of a new or considerably revised pay structure means that policies have to be developed on how existing employees should be assimilated into it. These policies cover where they should be placed in their new grades and what happens to them if their new grade and pay range mean that their existing rate is above or below the new scale for their job. Assimilation policies are dealt with in greater detail in Chapter 18.

Protection policies

A policy is needed on how employees whose pay is above the upper limit of their new grade after assimilation should be 'protected' or 'safeguarded'. It is usual to guarantee that employees in this position who have been 'red-circled' should not suffer an immediate reduction in pay. Thereafter, the policy lays down how quickly pay can and should be brought in line. Protection policies are dealt with in greater detail in Chapter 18.

DEVELOPING REWARD POLICIES

Reward policies should be developed by:

- referring to the list of policy issues and adding or subtracting items that appear to be most relevant, taking into account the structure, culture, management style and values of the organization, its reward philosophy and its business, HR and reward strategies;
- consulting with those concerned on what policy approach is likely to be most relevant to the business priorities of the organization and the needs of its employees – it is particularly important to consult on assimilation and protection policies, and trade unions are likely to insist that a formal agreement on these policies is reached after negotiation;
- ensuring that the policies are practical (implementable) and will provide the requisite level of guidance for decision and action;
- deciding on the amount of training and guidance that will be required to enable line managers and others to implement policies with an appropriate degree of consistency;
- communicating the policies to all affected by them – ideally, they should be expressed in writing and the communication process should include briefing groups to ensure that employees have the opportunity to seek clarification and make suggestions.

Reviewing policies

It needs to be re-emphasized that all aspects of reward management are dynamic and evolutionary. They cannot stand still. They must be continually reviewed and modified in line with changes in organization structures, strategic priorities, core values, processes, technologies and the new demands such changes make on people.

It is necessary therefore to review current reward policies at regular intervals to answer such questions as:

- Are they still relevant?
- Are they providing the level of guidance required?

- What problems, if any, are being met with in implementing them?
- Are there any new areas of reward policy that need to be covered?
- Does anyone (top managers, line managers, HR specialists, employees, union representatives) want them changed and, if so, how?

The review should be carried out by HR specialists or, possibly, outside consultants, working with a project team of staff and, importantly, their representatives (proper consultation is vital). The review should be based on an attitude survey supplemented by focus groups. The need to monitor reward policies regularly to identify the need for changes extends to all reward processes. It is a good idea to include a firm review date – one or two years ahead – following the introduction of any new reward system or structure. And this should not preclude earlier reviews if the necessity arises.

EXAMPLES OF REWARD POLICIES

Diageo

In accordance with policy guidelines issued from the centre to ensure that reward systems are fair and consistent across all Diageo's global operations:

- *Base salary* for all employees is based on practice in the relevant labour market.
- At least one of the performance criteria in *annual incentives* should be a profit measure. 'It may be possible to grow sales volume by cutting margins in the short term. However, this is unlikely to be a recipe for long-term sustainable profits growth. Ensuring that there is a profit measure in incentives makes sure that we stay focused on profitable growth', says Nicki Demby.
- The structure of *long-term incentives* – stock options and restricted stock – is globally consistent. 'They are regarded as a Diageo group resource, so we apply a consistent approach to the use of stock', says Nicki Demby.

A financial services company

At the heart of this company's approach to compensation philosophy is its market-led 'pay stance' or 'pay policy'. The ultimate aim is to continue to offer a 'highly competitive compensation package' to all of its employees. This package includes market-based competitive base pay and market-leading variable pay in the form of annual cash incentives and long-term incentives (for senior roles).

GlaxoSmithKline

The company's policy is to base pay rates on the median, but total cash can range from median to the 65th percentile for good performers.

Lands' End

Lands' End's reward policy is based on the idea that staff who are enjoying themselves, who are being supported and developed and who feel fulfilled and respected at work will provide the best service to customers. The advice of Mark Harris, Employee Services Director, is:

> Don't let the policy makers drive your culture. In a highly legislative environment, it would be easy to become very rule-driven to the detriment of individual circumstances. If you find yourself saying to someone, 'Sorry, we can't let you do that; it's our policy', then question if the policy is right. Make your policies as flexible as possible to allow managers to meet the needs of their people.

Lloyds TSB

Lloyds TSB recognizes that it has to compete for scarce skills in the labour market and has consequently adopted a much more market-driven pay policy. Within eight broader pay bands, the target salary for a competent person is aligned to functional market data, which relies on data collected for job families, while among the less senior levels increasing attention is paid to geographical considerations. Under a total reward policy all aspects of the work experience are recognized and prominence is given not only to remuneration but also to less tangible rewards.

Part 2

The conceptual framework

7

Factors affecting pay levels

Perhaps the most significant policy decisions that have to be made by those concerned with reward management are about levels of pay. In making these decisions it is necessary to be aware of the various factors that influence pay levels, including the key economic theories that explain those factors. The practical value of such awareness is that the parts to be played by job evaluation, labour market surveys and trade union negotiations in developing grade and pay structures, fixing pay levels and relativities and using market supplements or recruitment premiums will be understood and applied to produce equitable and competitive pay systems.

This chapter summarizes the main theoretical concepts drawn from the fields of labour economics and then deals with the factors influencing job values within organizations. Finally, conclusions are drawn on what these concepts and factors tell us about reward management.

ECONOMIC DETERMINANTS OF PAY

The following economic theories and concepts provide guidance on the factors that affect pay levels:

- the labour theory of value;
- the nature of the external and internal labour market;

- the economic 'laws' of supply and demand;
- human capital theory;
- efficiency wage theory;
- agency theory (also known as principal agent theory);
- the effort bargain.

The labour theory of value

In 1865 Karl Marx wrote in *Das Kapital* that the value of goods and services is determined by the amount of labour that goes into them. It is not the marketplace that sets prices. Thus the *content* of labour determines the *price* of labour. Mainstream economists have never accepted this concept and assert the primacy of supply and demand in the marketplace in setting prices of goods and services. However, as pointed out by Niels Nielsen (1), conventional job evaluation schemes are based on the labour theory of value in that they are only concerned with job *content* and ignore market rate pressures. They make no attempt to price jobs directly.

The labour market

Markets consist of buyers and sellers of goods. Too many buyers for a limited number of goods forces prices up and a surplus of goods beyond what buyers want forces prices down. The labour market is a market like any other market; it has buyers (employers) and sellers (employees). The price of labour is the rate of pay required to attract and retain people in organizations.

The efforts of these buyers and sellers to transact and establish an employment relationship constitutes a labour market. An external market may be local, national or international. It may be related to specific occupations, sectors or industries in any of these areas. It is within these markets that the economic determinants of pay levels operate, which include not only supply and demand factors (see below) but also the impact of inflationary pressures.

In any sizeable organization there is also an internal labour market. This is the market that exists when firms fill their vacancies from the ranks of existing employees. Pay levels and relativities in the internal market may differ significantly between firms in spite of general external market pressures. These arise particularly when long-term relationships are usual, even though these are becoming less common. Pay in the internal market will be affected by views on the intrinsic value of jobs and what individuals are worth on the basis of their expertise and contribution, irrespective of the market rate for their job. Pay progression related to length of service and an 'annuity' approach to pay increments (ie pay that goes up but does not come down, what economists call 'the sticky wage') may lead to higher internal rates. But the relationship between internal and external rates will also depend on policy decisions within the firm on its levels of pay generally compared with the 'going rate' in the external market.

Classical economic theory

Classical economic competitive theory states that pay levels are prices that in labour markets are determined by supply and demand considerations. Other things being equal, if there is a surplus of labour and supply exceeds the demand, pay levels go down; if there is a scarcity of labour and demand exceeds the supply, pay goes up. Pay stabilizes when demand equals supply at the 'market clearing' or 'market equilibrium' wage. This is sometimes known as the theory of equalizing differences. It was first stated by Adam Smith (2) over 200 years ago when he wrote that: 'The whole of the advantages and disadvantages of different employments and stock must, in the same neighbourhood, be either perfectly equal or continually tending to equality.'

As Elliott (3) has noted: 'Competitive theory predicts that the forces of supply in the market as a whole will determine the rates of pay within each firm. The relative pay of any two occupations in a single firm will be the mirror image of the relative pay of the same two occupations in the market as a whole.'

Classical theory, however, is based on the premises that 'other things are equal' and that a 'perfect market' for labour exists. In the real world, of course, other things are never equal. And there is no such thing as a universally perfect market, that is, one in which everyone knows what the going rate is and there are no monopolistic or other forces interfering with the normal processes of supply and demand. The existence of internal markets means that individual firms exercise a good deal of discretion about how much they pay and how much attention they give to external market pressures. Human capital theory as discussed in the next section also explains why individual rates of pay may be influenced by other forces besides supply and demand. And imperfections in the market exist because of poor information, lack of opportunity and immobility. They also arise when employers or trade unions exert pressures on pay levels or when governments intervene in normal pay determination processes.

Human capital theory

Human capital theory, as stated by Ehrenberg and Smith (4), 'conceptualizes workers as embodying a set of skills which can be "rented out" to employers. The knowledge and skills a worker has – which comes from education and training, including the training that experience brings – generate a certain *stock* of productive capital.'

For the employee, the expected returns on human capital investments are a higher level of earnings, greater job satisfaction and, at one time, but less so now, a belief that security in employment is assured. For the employer, the return on investment in human capital is expected to be the improvements in performance, productivity, flexibility and capacity to innovate that should result from enlarging the skill base and increasing levels of competence.

Efficiency wages theory

Efficiency wages theory proposes that firms will pay more than the market rate because they believe that high levels of pay will contribute to increases in productivity by motivating superior performance, attracting better candidates, reducing labour turnover and persuading workers that they are being treated fairly. This theory is also known as 'the economy of high wages'.

Organizations are using efficiency wages theory (although they will not call it that) when they formulate pay policies that place them as market leaders or at least above the average.

Agency theory

Agency theory, or principal agent theory, in its purest form recognizes that in most firms there is a separation between the owners (the principals) and the agents (the managers). However, the principals may not have complete control over their agents. The latter may therefore act in ways that are not fully revealed to their principals and that may not be in accordance with the wishes of those principals. This generates what economists call agency costs, which arise from the difference between what might have been earned if the principals had been the managers and the earnings achieved under the stewardship of the actual managers. To reduce these agency costs, the principals have to develop ways of monitoring and controlling the actions of their agents.

Agency theory as described above can be extended to the employment contract within firms. The employment relationship may be regarded as a contract between a principal (the employer) and an agent (the employee). The payment aspect of the contract is the method used by the principal to motivate the agent to perform work to the satisfaction of the employer. But according to this theory, the problem of ensuring that agents do what they are told remains. It is necessary to clear up ambiguities by setting objectives and monitoring performance to ensure that those objectives are achieved.

Agency theory also indicates that it is desirable to operate a system of incentives to motivate and reward acceptable behaviour. This process of 'incentive alignment' consists of paying for measurable results that are deemed to be in the best interests of the owners. Such incentive systems track outcomes in the shape of quantifiable indices of the firm's performance such as earnings per share rather than being concerned with the behaviour that led up to them. The theory is that, if the incentive schemes for top managers are designed properly, those managers will out of self-interest closely monitor performance throughout the organization.

Agency theory has been criticized by Gomez-Mejia and Balkin (5) as 'managerialist'. In other words, it looks at the employment relationship purely from the point of view of management and regards employees as objects to be motivated by carrot-and-stick methods. It is a dismal theory, which suggests that people cannot be trusted.

Agency theory is the basis of McGregor's (6) Theory X, in which he described the traditional assumptions of managers about people and work as follows: 'The average human being has an inherent dislike of work and will avoid it if he can. Because of this human characteristic of dislike of work, most people must be coerced, controlled, threatened with punishment to get them to put forth adequate effort towards the achievement of organizational objectives.'

McGregor, of course, advocated his much more optimistic Theory Y as an alternative approach. This states that: 'External control and the threat of punishment are not the only means for bringing about effort toward organizational objectives. Man will exercise self-direction and self-control in the service of objectives to which he is committed… Commitment to objectives is a function of the rewards associated with their achievement.'

The effort bargain

The concept of the effort bargain is referred to less frequently nowadays and it is not strictly an economic theory. But it has its uses as a further means of describing the employment relationship on pay matters. The concept states that the task of management is to assess what level and type of inducements it has to offer in return for the contribution it requires from its workforce.

The aim of workers is to strike a bargain about the relationship between what they regard as a reasonable contribution and what their employer is prepared to offer to elicit that contribution. This is termed the 'effort bargain' and is, in effect, an agreement that lays down the amount of work to be done for a rate of pay or wage rate, not just the hours to be worked. Explicitly or implicitly, all employees are in a bargaining situation with regard to pay. A system will not be accepted as effective and workable until it is recognized as fair and equitable by both parties and unless it is applied consistently.

FACTORS AFFECTING PAY LEVELS WITHIN ORGANIZATIONS

Within most organizations there are defined or generally understood pay levels for jobs. These are usually set out in the form of a pay structure, which may cover the whole organization or groups of related occupations (job families). There may be different structures at various levels, for example senior management, other staff and manual workers. In some organizations, however, the pay system is highly flexible and relatively unstructured. It may, for example, simply consist of individual rates for the various jobs (spot rates), which bear no apparent logical relationship to one another and are determined by management intuitively. Structures for manual workers may also consist of spot rates that are based on negotiations and custom and practice.

Where there are formal structures, pay levels and ranges may be determined by the processes of job evaluation, which assesses the relative internal worth of jobs (internal relativities), and market pricing, which assesses external relativities. The type of processes used and the degree to which they are formal and analytical or informal and intuitive will vary widely.

Individual rates of pay may be governed by the structure in the form of a fixed rate for the job or by movement in the form of fixed increments up a scale (a fixed increment is a predetermined addition to an individual's rate of pay that is related to service in the job). These may take place within a pay bracket with fixed minima and maxima in a graded structure or by progression through defined pay ranges in a pay spine (a series of incremental pay points extending from the lowest to the highest jobs covered by the structure within which pay ranges for the jobs in the hierarchy are established). Alternatively, pay progression within brackets or bands or within job family structures may vary according to individual performance, competence or contribution.

The level of pay of employees within organizations is affected by the economic factors mentioned above, which impact on the intrinsic value attached to the job, internal relativities, external relativities and the value of the person. It is also affected by the financial circumstances of the organization, the 'market stance' it adopts and trade union pressures.

Intrinsic value

The concept of intrinsic value is that jobs have value because of the impact they make on organizational results and by reference to the levels of responsibility and skill required to perform them. Increases in impact and these levels lead to higher rates of pay. This concept is in line with the labour theory of value and provides the theoretical base for job evaluation. However, as an explanation of the value attached to jobs it is limited because it ignores internal and external relativities.

Internal relativities

It can be argued that the value of anything is always relative to something else. This applies to jobs as well as commodities and services in general. Views on job values within organizations are based on perceptions of the worth of one job compared with others. This is the concept of internal equity, which is achieved when people are rewarded appropriately in relation to others according to the value of their contribution. The case for equal pay for work of equal value is based on the imperative to achieve internal equity.

External relativities

The rates of pay for jobs and people will be influenced by market rates in accordance with the policy of the organization on how it wants its pay levels to relate to market levels and the degree to which market forces impact on the amounts required to attract and retain the quality of people the organization needs. It is often claimed that 'a job is worth what the market says it is worth' and this belief leads to reliance on 'market pricing' to value jobs rather than on job evaluation to establish internal relativities. But Rosabeth Moss Kanter (7) has argued that this process is circular: 'We know what people are worth because that's what they cost in the job market, but we also know that what people cost in the job market is just what they're worth.'

However, no organization can ignore external relativities if it wants to compete successfully in the labour market, just as no organization can ignore internal relativities if it believes in equitable pay. The problem is reconciling the two, that is, attempting to achieve external competitiveness while maintaining internal equity. This is always difficult and often impossible.

The value of the person

Individuals are valued by organizations for four reasons: 1) the contribution they make to organizational success; 2) their skills and competences; 3) the experience they bring to their roles; and 4) their potential. People also have their own value in the marketplace – their 'market worth' – which has to be taken into account by employers in setting their rates of pay.

Financial circumstances of the organization

'Affordability' is an important concept in reward management. Pay systems must not cost more than the organization can afford, and this will influence the level of pay that can be offered to employees.

Pay stance

Policy decisions on an organization's pay stance – whether it should be a high, medium or even low payer – will depend partly upon what it can afford but will also be affected by the extent to which it believes that it must be competitive in the labour market.

Trade union pressures

Pay levels may be determined through collective bargaining with trade unions. They will want their members' pay to keep ahead of inflation, to match market rates and to reflect any increases in the prosperity of the business. The amount of pressure they can exert on pay levels will depend on the relative bargaining strengths of the employer and the union, and this will reflect the amount of power either party can exert in pay negotiations.

The minimum wage

Minimum wage legislation in the UK sets minimum rates of pay. In October 2006 the minimum wage for those aged 22 and above was £5.35 an hour. The amount is increased from time to time.

Summary: factors affecting pay levels

The factors affecting individual pay levels are summarized in Figure 7.1.

THE SIGNIFICANCE OF THE FACTORS AFFECTING PAY LEVELS

The factors affecting pay levels described above are significant because they exert a major influence on how organizations manage their pay. That is why it is important to take them into account when making pay decisions, as described below.

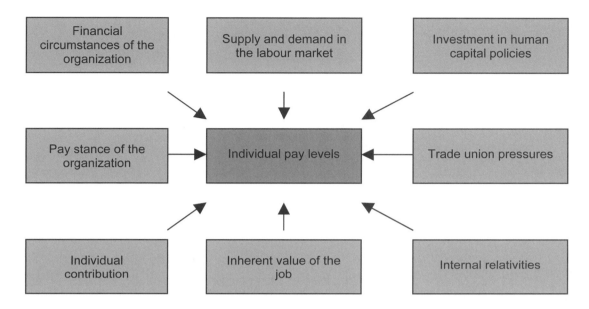

Figure 7.1 Factors affecting pay levels

The labour theory of value

The labour theory of value in effect provides the rationale for job content evaluation and the design of internally equitable grade structures. But it is necessary to take into account market rates through 'market pricing' based on market rate analysis to ensure that pay is competitive as well as equitable. The process is illustrated in Figure 7.2.

Classical economic theory

The significance of classical economic theory is that it focuses attention on external pressures and the perceived need for 'competitive pay', that is, pay that matches or exceeds market rates. Classical theory is used as a justification for 'market' pricing rather than job evaluation, concentrating on external competitiveness at the expense of internal equity.

External competitiveness versus internal equity

Organizations must understand the other factors besides market pressures that may affect pay levels, such as perceived needs for equity and for rewarding individual contribution and competence, long service and loyalty. This means appreciating that

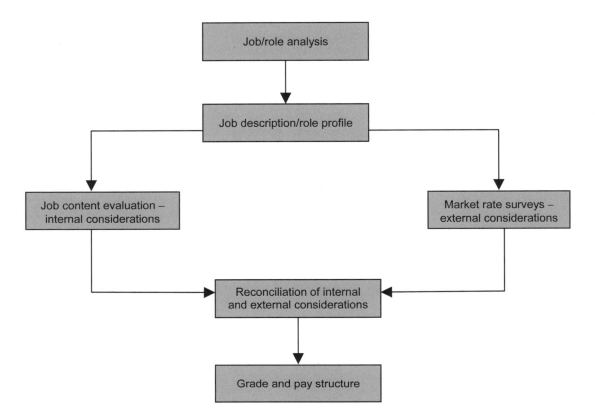

Figure 7.2 Developing a grade and pay structure

there will be tension between pay determination policies based on external comparisons (market pricing) and those focusing on internal relativities (job evaluation). The problem is always how to reconcile the often conflicting requirements for internal equity and external competitiveness. Organizations cannot ignore the former because, if they do, they will create unequal pay situations and dissatisfaction amongst employees. But they ignore the latter at their peril because, if they do, they may have problems in attracting and retaining quality employees. In any organizations relying on the external market, and this means most organizations, the need to be competitive may well prevail. The reconciliation process is often a balancing act involving the judicious use of market supplements or recruitment premiums to avoid permanently distorting internal relativities.

Labour markets

Organizations must be aware of the labour markets in which they are operating so that they can make appropriate decisions on pay levels in the light of market intelligence and policies on where they want to be in relation to the market.

Human capital theory

Organizations must appreciate the implication of human capital theory, which is that investment in people adds to their value to the firm. Individuals expect a return on their own investment, and firms recognize that the increased value of their employees should be rewarded. Human capital theory encourages the use of competence-related or skill-based pay as a method of reward. It also underpins the concept of individual market worth. This indicates that individuals have their own value in the marketplace, which they acquire and increase through investments by their employer and themselves in gaining extra expertise and competence through training, development and experience. The market worth of individuals may be considerably higher than the market rate of their jobs, and if they are not rewarded accordingly they may market their talents elsewhere.

Agency theory

Agency theory performs the useful function of directing attention to the ambiguities inherent in the employment relationship and to the importance of managing expectations. These aspects of reward are covered by the concepts of expectancy theory and the psychological contract as discussed in Chapters 8 and 10.

The effort bargain

The notion of an effort bargain highlights the fact that pay levels are subject to collective and individual negotiation. It also draws attention to the need for equity, fairness and consistency in reward systems.

APPLICATION OF THE FACTORS

Within organizations the main factors affecting individual levels of pay interrelate as shown in Figure 7.3.

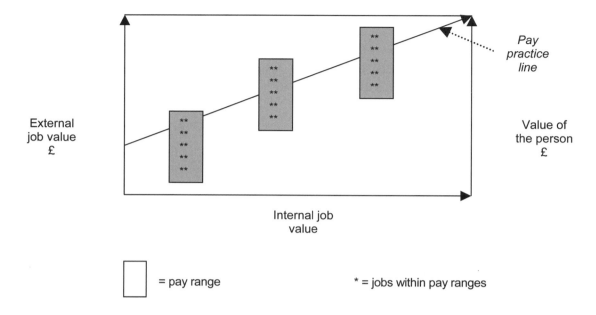

External
job value
£

Internal job
value

Value of
the person
£

Pay
practice
line

□ = pay range   * = jobs within pay ranges

Figure 7.3   Interrelation of factors affecting individual pay

REFERENCES

1   Nielsen, NH (2002) Job content evaluation techniques based on Marxian economics, *WorldatWork Journal*, **11** (2), pp 52–62
2   Smith, Adam (1776) *The Wealth of Nations*
3   Elliott, RF (1991) *Labor Economics*, McGraw-Hill, Maidenhead
4   Ehrenberg, RG and Smith, RS (1994) *Modern Labor Economics*, Harper Collins, New York
5   Gomez-Mejia, LR and Balkin, DB (1992) *Compensation, Organizational Strategy, and Firm Performance*, Southwestern Publishing, Cincinnati, OH
6   McGregor, D (1960) *The Human Side of Enterprise*, McGraw-Hill, New York
7   Kanter, RM (1989) *When Giants Learn to Dance*, Simon & Schuster, London

8

Motivation and reward

One of the most fundamental concerns of reward management is how high levels of performance can be achieved by motivating people. The development of a performance culture is a typical aim of reward strategy.

It is therefore necessary to understand the factors that motivate people and how, in the light of these factors, reward processes and practices can be developed that will enhance motivation, job engagement, commitment and positive discretionary behaviour. Motivation theories provide essential guidance on the practical steps required to develop effective reward systems (there is nothing so practical as a good theory). This chapter examines the process of motivation and those theories that most influence reward. The relationship between money and motivation is then considered, and the chapter ends with an analysis of how motivation theory can be put to good use. Approaches to achieving engagement and commitment are considered in Chapter 9.

THE PROCESS OF MOTIVATION

Motivation theory is concerned with what 'moves' people to do something – what influences people to behave in certain ways. It explains the factors that affect the effort that they put into their work, their levels of engagement and contribution and their discretionary behaviour.

Motivation defined

A motive is a reason for doing something – for moving in a certain direction. People are motivated when they expect that a course of action is likely to lead to the attainment of a goal – a valued reward that satisfies their particular needs. Well-motivated people are those with clearly defined goals who take action that they expect will achieve those goals.

How motivation works

A model of motivation based on reinforcement and needs theory as described later in this chapter is shown in Figure 8.1.

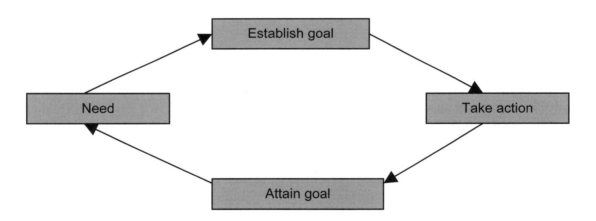

Figure 8.1   A motivation model

This model suggests that the process of motivation is initiated by the conscious or unconscious recognition of unsatisfied needs. These needs create wants, which are desires to achieve or attain something. Goals are then established that it is believed will satisfy these needs, and a behaviour pathway is selected that it is believed will achieve the goal. If the goal is achieved, the need is satisfied and the behaviour is likely to be repeated the next time a similar need emerges. If the goal is not achieved, the same action is less likely to be repeated. However, as some needs are satisfied new needs emerge and the process continues. As Maslow (1) says, it is unsatisfied needs that motivate behaviour.

But it can be argued that this deterministic model oversimplifies the motivation process and does not take sufficient account of the cognitive factors that influence motivation through the perceptions of individuals about what is important to them in their working environment.

Individual differences

Some common needs headings have been established by theorists such as Maslow (1) and Herzberg (2), and these are described later in this chapter. But it cannot be assumed that these are present at any moment to the same extent or even present at all in all the members of a population such as the employees of an organization. It is a cliché to say that all people are different but it is none the less true, and it is a truth that organizations sometimes fail to appreciate when they assume, for example, that all their employees will be motivated to the same degree by money.

Types of motivation

There are two types of motivation as originally described by Herzberg *et al* (2):

- *Intrinsic motivation* – this was defined by Herzberg as 'motivation through the work itself'. It takes place when people feel that the work they do is intrinsically interesting, challenging and important and involves the exercise of responsibility (having control over one's own resources), autonomy or freedom to act, scope to use and develop skills and abilities and opportunities for advancement and growth.
- *Extrinsic motivation* – what is done to or for people to motivate them. This includes rewards such as increased pay, recognition, praise or promotion, and punishments such as disciplinary action, withholding pay, or criticism.

Extrinsic motivators can have an immediate and powerful effect, but it will not necessarily last long. The intrinsic motivators, which are concerned with the notion of the 'quality of working life' (a phrase promoted by advocates of the notion of intrinsic motivation but little used today), are likely to have a deeper and longer-term effect because they are inherent in individuals and not imposed from outside. But it should not be assumed that intrinsic motivation is good and extrinsic motivation is bad. They both have a part to play.

The role of job design in motivation

Intrinsic motivation is provided when jobs are well designed. This is the case when the job has the following characteristics:

- autonomy, discretion, self-control and responsibility;
- variety;
- use of abilities;
- availability of constructive feedback;
- belief that the work is significant.

The role of rewards and incentives in motivation

Rewards provide recognition to people for their achievements and contribution. If rewards are worth having and attainable and people know how they can attain them, they can act as motivators. Rewards can be either financial or non-financial.

Incentives are designed to encourage people to achieve objectives. They are intended to provide direct motivation: 'do this and we will make it worth your while'. Incentives are generally financial but they can promise non-financial rewards such as recognition, promotion or a particularly interesting assignment.

MOTIVATION THEORIES

The process of motivation as described above is broadly based on a number of motivation theories that attempt to explain in more detail what it means. The main theories as described below are:

- instrumentality, behaviourist and reinforcement theories;
- needs or content theories;
- Herzberg's two-factor theory;
- process or cognitive theories (expectancy, goal and equity).

Instrumentality theory

'Instrumentality' is the belief that if we do one thing it will lead to another. In its crudest form, instrumentality theory states that people work only for money. The theory emerged in the second half of the 19th century, when the emphasis was on the need to rationalize work and to concentrate on economic outcomes. It assumes that people will be motivated to work if rewards and penalties are tied directly to their performance. Instrumentality theory has its roots in the scientific management methods of Taylor (3), who wrote: 'It is impossible, through any long period of time, to get workmen to work much harder than the average men around them unless they are assured a large and permanent increase in their pay.' This belief is often described as 'Taylorism'.

Instrumentality theory is based on the principle of reinforcement, which states that, with experience in taking action to satisfy needs, people perceive that certain actions help to achieve their goals while others are less successful. Success in achieving goals and rewards therefore acts as a positive incentive and reinforces the behaviour, which is repeated the next time a similar need emerges. Conversely, failure or punishment provides negative reinforcement, suggesting the need to seek alternative means of achieving goals. This process has been called the law of effect.

Motivation using this approach has been and still is widely adopted and can be successful in some circumstances. But it is based exclusively on a system of external controls and fails to recognize a number of other human needs. Nor does it take account of the fact that the formal control system can be seriously affected by the informal relations between workers.

Needs (content) theory

The basis of this theory is the belief that an unsatisfied need creates tension and disequilibrium. To restore the balance a goal is identified that will satisfy the need, and a behaviour pathway is selected that will lead to the achievement of the goal. All behaviour is therefore motivated by unsatisfied needs.

Not all needs are equally important to a person at any one time. Some may constitute a more powerful drive towards a goal than others, depending on the individual's background and situation. Complexity is increased because there is no simple relationship between needs and goals. The same need could be satisfied by a number of different goals. The stronger the need and the longer its duration, the broader the range of possible goals. At the same time, one goal may satisfy a number of needs. A new car provides transport as well as an opportunity to impress the neighbours.

The best-known contributor to needs theory is Maslow (1). He formulated the concept of a hierarchy of needs, which start from the fundamental physiological needs and lead through safety, social and esteem needs to the need for self-fulfilment, the highest need of all. He said that 'man is a wanting animal'; only an unsatisfied need can motivate behaviour, and the dominant need is the prime motivator of behaviour. This is the best-known theory of needs, but it has never been verified by empirical research.

Herzberg's two-factor model

Herzberg's two-factor model theory states that the factors giving rise to job satisfaction (and motivation) are distinct from the factors that lead to job dissatisfaction. It is sometimes called the motivation–hygiene theory.

There are two groups of factors. The first consists of the satisfiers or motivators, which are intrinsic to the job. These include achievement, recognition, the work itself, responsibility and growth. The second group comprises what Herzberg calls the 'dissatisfaction avoidance' or 'hygiene' factors, which are extrinsic to the job and include pay, company policy and administration, personal relations, status and security. These cannot create satisfaction but, unless preventive action is taken, they can cause dissatisfaction. He also noted that any feeling of satisfaction resulting from pay increases was likely to be short-lived compared with the long-lasting satisfaction from the work itself. One of the key conclusions derived from the research is therefore that pay is not a motivator, except in the short term, although unfair payment systems can lead to demotivation.

Herzberg's two-factor model draws attention to the distinction between intrinsic and extrinsic motivators, and his contention that the satisfaction resulting from pay increases does not persist has some face validity. But his research and the conclusions he reached have been attacked – first because, it is asserted, the original research is flawed and fails to support the contention that pay is not a motivator, and secondly because no attempt was made to measure the relationship between satisfaction and performance. As David Guest (4) has written: 'Many managers' knowledge of motivation has not advanced beyond Herzberg and his generation. This is unfortunate. Their theories are now over thirty years old. Extensive research has shown that as general theories of motivation the theories of Herzberg and Maslow are wrong. They have been replaced by more relevant approaches.'

Process or cognitive theory

The more relevant approaches to which Guest refers are the process or cognitive theories. They are known as process theories because they describe the psychological processes or forces that affect motivation, as well as basic needs. The term 'cognitive theories' is used because they refer to people's perception of their working environment and the ways in which they interpret and understand it. Process theory can be more useful to managers than needs theory because it provides more realistic guidance on motivation techniques. The processes covered by the most relevant theories are:

- expectations (expectancy theory);
- goal achievement (goal theory);
- feelings about equity (equity theory).

Expectancy theory

The core process theory is expectancy theory. As Guest (4) notes, most other approaches adapt or build on it. The concept of expectancy was originally contained in the valency–instrumentality–expectancy (VIE) theory formulated by Vroom (5). Valency stands for value, instrumentality is the belief that if we do one thing it will lead to another, and expectancy is the probability that action or effort will lead to an outcome.

The strength of expectations may be based on past experience (reinforcement), but individuals are frequently presented with new situations – a change of job, payment system or working conditions imposed by management – where past experience is an inadequate guide to the implications of the change. In these circumstances, motivation may be reduced.

Motivation is likely only when a clearly perceived and usable relationship exists between performance and outcome, and the outcome is seen as a means of satisfying needs. This explains why extrinsic financial motivation – for example, an incentive or bonus scheme – works only if the link between effort and reward is understood (there is a clear 'line of sight') and the value of the reward is worth the effort. It also explains why intrinsic motivation arising from the work itself can be more powerful than extrinsic motivation. Intrinsic motivation outcomes are more under the control of individuals, who can judge from past experience the extent to which advantageous results are likely to be obtained by their behaviour.

This theory was developed by Porter and Lawler (6) into a model that follows Vroom's ideas by suggesting that there are two factors determining the effort people put into their jobs: 1) the value of the reward to individuals in so far as they satisfy their need for security, social esteem, autonomy and self-actualization; and 2) the probability that reward depends on effort, as perceived by individuals – in other words, their expectations of the relationship between effort and reward. Thus, the greater the value of a set of rewards, and the higher the probability that receiving each of these rewards depends upon effort, the greater the effort that will be made in a given situation.

But, as Porter and Lawler emphasize, mere effort is not enough. It has to be effective effort if it is to produce the desired performance. The two variables additional to effort that affect task achievement are: 1) ability – individual characteristics such as intelligence, manual skills and know-how; and 2) role perceptions – what individuals want to do or think they are required to do. Role perceptions are good from the viewpoint of the organization if they correspond with what it thinks the individual ought to be doing. They are poor if the views of the individual and the organization do not coincide.

A model of expectancy theory as produced by Lawler and Porter is shown in Figure 8.2.

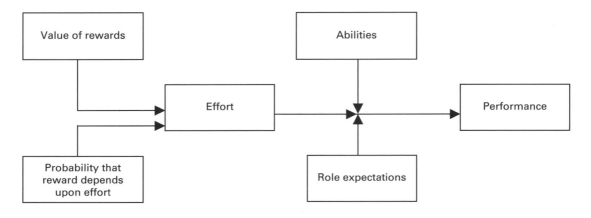

Figure 8.2   Motivation model (Porter and Lawler)

Goal theory

Goal theory as formulated by Latham and Locke (7) states that motivation and performance are higher when individuals are set specific goals, when the goals are difficult but accepted, and when there is feedback on performance. Participation in goal setting is important as a means of securing agreement to the setting of higher goals. Difficult goals must be agreed, and achieving them must be helped by guidance and advice. Finally, feedback is vital in maintaining motivation, particularly towards the achievement of even higher goals.

Goal theory provided the theoretical underpinning to processes such as management by objectives where the emphasis was on setting goals and measuring performance. Management by objectives, or MbO as it was known, is no longer a fashionable term, partly because MbO systems tended to be bureaucratic and overemphasize quantitative targets. But they still provide the basis for traditional performance-related pay schemes where the focus is on objectives and the measurement of achievements as a means of providing financial rewards in the shape of performance pay.

Equity theory

Equity theory as described by Adams (8) states that people will be better motivated if they are treated equitably and demotivated if they are treated inequitably. It is concerned with people's perceptions of how they are being treated in relation to others. To be dealt with equitably is to be treated fairly in comparison with another group of people (a reference group) or a relevant other person. Equity involves feelings and perceptions, and it is always a comparative process. It is not synonymous with equality, which means treating everyone alike. That would be inequitable if they deserved to be treated differently.

Equity theory is linked with the 'felt-fair' principle as defined by Jaques (9), which states in effect that pay systems will be fair if they are felt to be fair.

MOTIVATION AND FINANCIAL INCENTIVES AND REWARDS

Financial incentives and rewards can motivate. People need money and therefore want money. It can motivate but it is not the only motivator. It has been suggested by Wallace and Szilagyi (10) that money can serve the following reward functions:

- It can act as a goal that people generally strive for although to different degrees.
- It can act as an instrument that provides valued outcomes.
- It can be a symbol that indicates the recipient's value to the organization.
- It can act as a general reinforcer because it is associated with valued rewards so often that it takes on reward value itself.

Money motivates because it is linked directly or indirectly with the satisfaction of many needs. It satisfies the basic need for survival and security, if income is regular. It can also satisfy the need for self-esteem (it is a visible mark of appreciation) and status – money can set you in a grade apart from your fellows and can buy you things they cannot afford. Money satisfies the less desirable but nevertheless prevalent drives of acquisitiveness and cupidity. So money may in itself have no intrinsic meaning, but it acquires significant motivating power because it comes to symbolize so many intangible goals. It acts as a symbol in different ways for different people, and for the same person at different times. Pay is often a dominant factor in the choice of employer, and pay is an important consideration when people are deciding whether or not to stay with an organization.

But doubts have been cast on the effectiveness of money as a motivator by Herzberg *et al* (2). As noted above, he claimed that, while the lack of it may cause dissatisfaction, money does not result in lasting satisfaction. There is something in this, especially for people on fixed salaries or rates of pay who do not benefit directly from an incentive scheme. They may feel good when they get an increase, as, apart from the extra money, it is a highly effective way of making people believe they are valued. But the feeling of euphoria can rapidly die away. However, it must be re-emphasized that different people have different needs, and Herzberg's two-factor theory has not been validated.

Some will be much more motivated by money than others. What cannot be assumed is that money motivates everyone in the same way and to the same extent.

But do financial incentives motivate people? The answer, according to Kohn (11), is absolutely not. He challenges what he calls the behaviourist dogma about money and motivation. And he claims that 'no controlled scientific study has ever found a long-term enhancement of the quality of work as a result of any reward system'. When you look at how people are motivated, claims Kohn, 'It becomes disturbingly clear that the more you use rewards to "motivate" people, the more they tend to lose interest in whatever they had to do to get the rewards.' He quotes research that has 'repeatedly shown that the more salient or reinforcing the reward is, the more it erodes intrinsic interest' and points out that 'various devices can be used to get people to do something, but that is a far cry from making people *want* to do something'.

Pfeffer (12) also contends that: 'People do work for money – but they work even more for meaning in their lives. In fact, they work to have fun. Companies that ignore this fact are essentially bribing their employees and will pay the price in lack of loyalty and commitment.' He believes that pay cannot substitute for a working environment 'high on trust, fun and meaningful work'.

In contrast, Gupta and Shaw (13) emphasize the instrumental and symbolic meaning of money. The instrumental meaning of money concerns what we get for it – better houses, clothes, cars, etc. The symbolic meaning of money concerns how it is viewed by ourselves and others – money signals our status in and worth to society. They take the basic behaviourist line on money: 'When certain behaviours are followed by money, then they are more likely to be repeated. This means that employees will do the things for which they are rewarded; it also means that they ignore the things for which they are not rewarded.'

The views expressed by Kohn are convincing except that he seems to think that the only types of rewards to be considered in this debate are financial. He does not recognize that non-financial rewards *can* motivate if handled properly. Pfeffer, however, makes this point when he emphasizes the importance of trust and meaningful work. Gupta and Shaw weaken their argument by adopting a crude behaviourist viewpoint.

To assume that financial incentives will always motivate people to perform better is as simplistic as to assume, like Kohn, that they *never* motivate people to perform better. Some people will be more motivated by money that others and, if handled properly, an incentive scheme can encourage them to perform more effectively as long as they can link their effort to the reward and the reward is worth having. Sometimes cash sums (bonuses) can be more effective rewards because they can be immediately converted into things that people want. But others may be less interested in money and will respond more to intrinsic or non-financial rewards. It seems likely that the majority will react positively to a judicious mix of both financial and non-financial rewards, although how positively will depend on their own needs and aspirations.

What is clear is that simplistic assumptions about the power of money to motivate can lead organizations into developing simplistic performance-related pay schemes or other forms of incentives. And we can be reasonably certain that a multiplicity of interdependent factors are involved in motivating people. Money is only one of those factors, which may work for some people in some circumstances, but may not work for other people in other circumstances.

It should also be remembered that, while an increase in pay arising from a contingent pay scheme may motivate the people who get it, for a limited period perhaps it will almost certainly demotivate those who don't get it or feel that they are not getting enough compared with other people. The likelihood is that the number of people demotivated in this way will be larger than the number who have been motivated. Paradoxically, therefore, contingent pay schemes are in danger of increasing the amount of demotivation existing in the organization rather than enhancing motivation.

FACTORS AFFECTING SATISFACTION WITH PAY

As Lawler (14) points out, people's feelings about the adequacy of their pay are based upon comparisons they make between their own and others'. External market comparisons are the most critical because they are the ones that strongly influence whether individuals want to stay with the organization. Many people, however, are unlikely to leave for pay reasons alone unless the increase they expect from a move is substantial, say 10 per cent.

Lawler also suggests, 'Sometimes it seems that individuals are never satisfied with the pay.' One of the reasons put forward by Lawler for low pay satisfaction is that individuals tend to seek unfavourable comparisons. First they look externally. If comparisons there are favourable, they then focus on internal comparisons. Only if these are favourable as well are they likely to be satisfied. He comments that: 'A finding that employees are dissatisfied with pay is, in effect, a non-finding. It is to be expected. The key thing that the organization needs to focus on is whether its employees are more dissatisfied with their pay than are employees in other organizations.'

Reactions to reward policies and practices will depend largely on the values and needs of individuals and on their employment conditions. It is therefore dangerous to generalize about the causes of satisfaction or dissatisfaction. However, it seems reasonable to believe that, as mentioned above, feelings about external and internal equity (the 'felt-fair' principle) will strongly influence most people. Research by Porter and Lawler (6) and others has also shown that higher-paid employees are likely to be more satisfied with their rewards but the satisfaction resulting from a large pay increase may be short-lived. People tend to want more of the same. In this respect, at least, the views of Maslow and Herzberg have been supported by research.

Other factors that may affect satisfaction or dissatisfaction with pay include the degree to which:

- individuals feel their rate of pay or increase has been determined fairly;
- rewards are commensurate with the perceptions of individuals about their ability, contribution and value to the organization (but this perception is likely to be founded on information or beliefs about what other people, inside and outside the organization, are paid);
- individuals are satisfied with other aspects of their employment – for example, their status, promotion prospects, opportunity to use and develop skills, and relations with their managers.

MOTIVATION AND JOB SATISFACTION AND PERFORMANCE

There is no research evidence that there is always a strong and positive relationship between job satisfaction and performance. A satisfied worker is not necessarily a high performer and a high performer is not necessarily a satisfied worker. Satisfaction may lead to good performance but good performance may just as well be the cause of satisfaction. The relationship can be reciprocal.

The relationship between motivation and performance is even more complex. Vroom (5) formulated it as $P = M \times A$ where P is performance, M is motivation and A is ability. Note that the relationship is multiplicative – if the value of either M or A is zero, then there will be no performance. Performance depends on both motivation and ability.

A more recent formulation of the relationship has been produced by Boxall and Purcell (15). This is that $P = M + A + S$ where P is performance, M is motivation, A is ability and S is scope to use and develop abilities. Note that the relationship is not multiplicative as in Vroom and there is an additional factor (scope).

By including ability and scope as factors, the latter formulation underlines the importance of adopting an integrated approach to reward and other HR strategies. Motivation by pay or any other means is not enough. Reward strategies must be associated with human resource development and resourcing strategies to maximize their impact on performance.

THE KEY MESSAGES OF MOTIVATION THEORY

The key practical messages delivered by motivation theory are summarized below.

Extrinsic and intrinsic rewards

Extrinsic rewards provided by employers in the form of pay will help to attract and retain employees and, for limited periods, may increase effort and minimize dissatisfaction. Intrinsic non-financial rewards related to responsibility, achievement and the work itself may have a longer-term and deeper impact on motivation. Reward systems should therefore include a mix of extrinsic and intrinsic rewards.

The significance of needs

People will be better motivated if their work satisfies their social and psychological needs as well as their economic needs. Needs theory underpins the concept of total reward, which recognizes the importance of the non-financial rewards as motivators. For example, recognition as a non-financial motivator is important because it addresses one of the most significant needs. A total reward policy makes use both of intrinsic and extrinsic rewards and of financial and non-financial rewards in a reward framework as set out in Table 8.1.

Performance management processes as described in Chapter 24 provide a basis for redesigning jobs or roles and for agreeing and implementing development programmes.

Table 8.1 The reward framework

	Financial Rewards	Non-Financial Rewards
Intrinsic rewards		– Job design and role development (responsibility, autonomy, meaningful work, the scope to use and develop skills) – Opportunities to achieve and develop – Quality of working life – Work/life balance
Extrinsic rewards	– Pay and benefits	– Recognition – Praise – Feedback

Table 8.2 Summary of motivation theories and their practical implications

Theory	Theorist	Summary of Theory	Practical Implications
Instrumentality	Taylor	People will be motivated to work if rewards and penalties are tied directly to their performance.	Conceptual basis of incentive and pay-for-performance schemes.
Needs	Maslow	Unsatisfied needs create tension and disequilibrium. To restore the balance a goal is identified that will satisfy the need, and a behaviour pathway is selected that will lead to the achievement of the goal. Only unsatisfied needs motivate.	Identifies a number of key needs for consideration in developing total reward policies.
Two-factor	Herzberg	The factors giving rise to job satisfaction (and motivation) are distinct from the factors that lead to job dissatisfaction. Any feeling of satisfaction resulting from pay increases is likely to be short-lived compared with the long-lasting satisfaction from the work itself. Makes a distinction between intrinsic motivation arising from the work itself and extrinsic motivation provided by the employer, eg pay.	A useful distinction is made between intrinsic and extrinsic motivation that influences total reward decisions. The limited motivational effects of pay increases are worth remembering when considering the part contingent pay can play in motivating people.
Expectancy	Vroom	Motivation is likely only when: 1) a clearly perceived and usable relationship exists between performance and outcome; and 2) the outcome is seen as a means of satisfying needs.	Provides the foundation for good practice in the design and management of contingent pay. The basis for the concept is the 'line of sight', which emphasizes the importance of establishing a clear link between the reward and what has to be done to achieve it.

Table 8.2 *Continued*

Theory	Theorist	Summary of Theory	Practical Implications
Goal	Latham and Locke	Motivation and performance are higher when individuals are set specific goals, when the goals are difficult but accepted, and when there is feedback on performance.	Provides a theoretical underpinning for performance management processes to ensure that they contribute to motivation through goal setting and feedback.
Equity	Adams	People will be better motivated if they are treated equitably and demotivated if they are treated inequitably.	Emphasizes the need to develop an equitable reward system involving the use of job evaluation.

The importance of expectations

The degree to which people are motivated will depend not only upon the perceived value of the outcome of their actions – the goal or reward – but also upon their perceptions of the likelihood of obtaining a worthwhile reward, ie their expectations. They will be highly motivated if they can control the means of attaining their goals. This indicates that contingent pay schemes – that is, those where pay is related to performance, competence, contribution or skill – are effective as motivators only if: 1) people know what they are going to get in return for certain efforts or achievements – there is 'a line of sight' between effort and reward; 2) they feel that what they may get is worth having; and 3) they expect to get it.

The influence of goals

Individuals are motivated by having specific goals to work for, and they perform better when they are aiming at difficult goals that they have accepted, and when they receive feedback on performance. This emphasizes the importance of performance management processes as motivators when they are based on *agreed* goals (note the emphasis) that are demanding but attainable and feedback on attainments in relation to those goals.

REFERENCES

1 Maslow, A (1954) *Motivation and Personality*, Harper & Row, New York
2 Herzberg, F, Mausner, B and Snyderman, B (1957) *The Motivation to Work*, Wiley, New York
3 Taylor, FW (1911) *Principles of Scientific Management*, Harper, New York
4 Guest, D (1992) Motivation after Herzberg, Unpublished paper delivered at the Compensation Forum, London
5 Vroom, V (1964) *Work and Motivation*, Wiley, New York
6 Porter, L and Lawler, EE (1968) *Management Attitudes and Behaviour*, Irwin-Dorsey, Homewood, IL
7 Latham, G and Locke, EA (1979) Goal setting: a motivational technique that works, *Organizational Dynamics*, Autumn, pp 68–80
8 Adams, J (1965) Injustice in social exchange, in *Advances in Experimental Psychology*, ed L Berkowitz, Academic Press, New York
9 Jaques, E (1961) *Equitable Payment*, Heinemann, London
10 Wallace, MJ and Szilagyi, L (1982) *Managing Behaviour in Organizations*, Scott, Glenview, IL
11 Kohn, A (1993) Why incentive plans cannot work, *Harvard Business Review*, September/October, pp 54–63
12 Pfeffer, J (1998) Six dangerous myths about pay, *Harvard Business Review*, May/June, pp 42–51
13 Gupta, N and Shaw, JD (1998) Financial incentives *are* effective!, *Compensation and Benefits Review*, March/April, pp 26, 28–32
14 Lawler EE (1990) *Strategic Pay*, Jossey-Bass, San Francisco
15 Boxall, P and Purcell, J (2003) *Strategic Human Resource Management*, Palgrave Macmillan, Basingstoke

9

Engagement and organizational commitment

The notion of 'engagement' has become prominent in recent years. But it is not always clear what it is. The *Oxford English Dictionary* defines engagement as the act of pledging oneself to do something. In human resource and reward management circles it has a number of meanings. It is sometimes used as a 'catch-all' word that covers both motivation and commitment. It is often treated as being synonymous with commitment.

Engagement, commitment and motivation are indeed closely linked but when considering how they influence reward policy and practice it is useful to distinguish between them. That is the purpose of this chapter, which starts with definitions and continues with a more detailed analysis of the meaning of the concepts of job engagement and organizational commitment and their practical implications.

DEFINITIONS

As usually conceived, and as defined below, engagement, commitment and motivation are complementary processes; they interlink and they overlap. But they can be distinguished from one another.

Engagement

Engagement, sometimes known as job engagement, is concerned with people and their work. It happens when people are caught up in and interested in, even excited about, their jobs and are therefore prepared to exert discretionary effort in getting them done.

The Hay Group (Helen Murlis, 1) defines engaged performance as: 'A result that is achieved by stimulating employees' enthusiasm for their work and directing it towards organizational success. This result can only be achieved when employers offer an implied contract to their employees that elicits specific positive behaviours aligned with the organization's goals.'

Commitment

Commitment, sometimes referred to as organizational commitment, refers to identification with the goals and values of the organization, a desire to belong to the organization and a willingness to display effort on its behalf.

Motivation

Motivation takes place when people have well-defined goals and take action that they expect will achieve those goals.

Similarities and differences

All three concepts provide ways of defining how people behave at work and therefore indicate what actions can be taken to encourage positive discretionary behaviour. As described by Purcell *et al* (2), discretionary behaviour refers to the choices that people at work often have on the way they do the job and the amount of effort, care, innovation and productive behaviour they display. It can be positive when people 'go the extra mile' to achieve high levels of performance. It can be negative when they exercise their discretion to slack at their work.

Engagement and commitment are both states of being. So is motivation in a sense, but it is more dynamic. Motivation is about wanting to do something and then doing it. Engagement and commitment are broader terms describing a range of behaviours that are desirable from the organization's viewpoint.

Although highly engaged and committed people may be motivated, people who are motivated are not necessarily engaged or committed. They may be pursuing their own ends not that of their job or the organization.

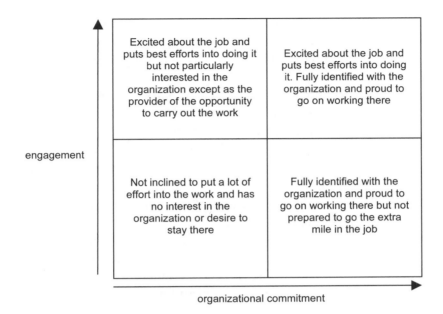

Figure 9.1 Combinations of the impact of engagement and organizational commitment

An engaged person can be committed to the organization. But people can be engaged with their work even when they are not committed to the organization except in so far as it gives them the opportunity to use and develop their skills. For example, researchers may be more interested in the facilities for research they are given and the opportunity to make a name for themselves. They therefore join and stay with an organization only if it gives them the opportunities they seek. Combinations of engagement and organizational commitment are illustrated in Figure 9.1.

ENGAGEMENT

The significance of the concept of engagement is that it is at the heart of the employment relationship. It is about what people do and how they behave in their roles and what makes them act in ways that further the achievement of the objectives of both the organization and themselves. The importance attached to the notion of engagement has intensified recently in association with the rise of total reward concepts. It is high on the reward agenda of a number of leading organizations. For example, Tim Fevyer, Senior Manager, Compensation and Benefits, Lloyds TSB, comments that: 'Pay is no longer the great differentiator. The only way we are going to keep people is by engaging them.'

Trevor Blackman, Head of Reward at the Royal Bank of Scotland, explains that the desire to enhance engagement underpins much of the work undertaken by Human Resources in the bank and is a key principle underlying the approach to the design of reward programmes. Quantifying the relationship between reward and engagement is one of the methods used to measure the impact of those programmes. He notes that: 'Reward done well can drive engagement throughout the organization.' Kevin Brady, HR Director, Reward and Employee Relations at BT, feels the most important thing for employers to do is 'engage, engage, engage'.

Standard Chartered Bank also attaches importance to engagement. The bank measures it through its 'Q12' staff attitude survey and conducts regular reviews. The surveys show that branches with higher levels of engagement achieve greater growth in their profit margins, higher customer ratings and increased productivity.

What is an engaged employee?

An answer to this question was provided by Bevan et al (3), who describe an engaged employee as someone 'who is aware of business context, and works closely with colleagues to improve performance within the job for the benefit of the organization'.

A more detailed answer was given by Dilys Robinson, Principal Research Fellow, Institute of Employment Studies (IES). She presented to the 2005 e-reward/CIPD reward symposium (4) a summary of discussions held by the IES with 46 organizations in the private and public sectors. These led to a picture of an engaged employee, who:

- is positive about the job;
- believes in, and identifies with, the organization;
- works actively to make things better;
- treats others with respect, and helps colleagues to perform more effectively;
- can be relied upon, and goes beyond the requirements of the job;
- sees the bigger picture, even sometimes at personal cost;
- keeps up to date with developments in his or her field;
- looks for, and is given, opportunities to improve organizational performance.

Dilys Robinson commented that the role of pay and benefits in fostering engagement is somewhat ambiguous. So far, the IES research suggests that pay is important to employees, but that improvements in pay are rarely at the top of their 'wish list'.

However, getting reward wrong – for example, withdrawing benefits, failing to promote or allocating bonuses unfairly – has a huge impact and is very 'disengaging', as these aspects of working life are held as proxies of the extent to which the organization values the individual. In this sense, pay remains a 'hygiene' factor. And their research also illustrates the manner in which the emphasis on the various HR and reward policies in generating engagement varies in each organizational setting.

What are the factors that influence engagement?

Levels of engagement are influenced by four factors as discussed below and modelled in Figure 9.2:

1. *Intrinsic motivation.* As identified by Frederick Herzberg (5) there are five key motivation factors that are intrinsic to the job: achievement, recognition for achievement, the work itself, responsibility (autonomy) and growth or advance-

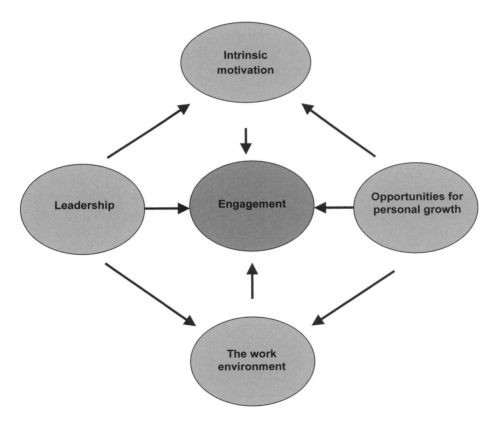

Figure 9.2 Model of the factors affecting engagement

ment. This is still a relevant list of the basic factors that influence engagement. It applies particularly to roles where there is scope for discretionary behaviour. But it can apply to more routine jobs. Lands' End, the mail-order clothing company, believes that, where jobs are repetitive or less challenging, it is particularly important to provide some challenge and fun. And at Lands' End, if it isn't possible to give people a choice as to the type of work they do, they can be given some choice as to how they do it.

2. *The work environment.* An enabling, supportive and inspirational work environment creates experiences that impact on engagement by influencing how people regard their roles and carry them out. An enabling environment will create the conditions that encourage high performance and effective discretionary behaviour. These include work processes, equipment and facilities, and the physical conditions in which people work. A supportive environment will be one in which proper attention is paid to achieving a satisfactory work/life balance, emotional demands are not excessive, attention is paid to providing healthy and safe working conditions, job security is a major consideration and personal growth needs are taken into consideration. An inspirational environment will be one where what John Purcell and his colleagues (2) refer to as 'the big idea' is present – the organization has a clear vision and a set of integrated values that are 'embedded, collective, measured and managed'.

3. *Leadership.* The degree to which jobs provide intrinsic motivation and therefore encourage engagement and positive discretionary behaviour depends more on the way in which job holders are led and managed than on any formal process of job design. Managers and team leaders often have considerable discretion on how they allocate work and how much they delegate and provide autonomy. They can spell out the significance of the work people do. They can give them the opportunity to achieve and develop, and provide feedback that recognizes their contribution.

4. *Opportunities for personal growth.* Most people want to get on. As Ed Lawler (6) put it: 'People enjoy learning – there's no doubt about it – and it touches on an important "treat people right" principle for both organizations and people: the value of continuous, ongoing training and development.' Learning is a satisfying and rewarding experience and makes a significant contribution to intrinsic motivation. Alderfer (7) emphasized the importance of the chance to grow as a means of rewarding people. He wrote: 'Satisfaction of growth needs depends on a person finding the opportunity to be what he or she is most fully and become what he or she can.' The opportunity to grow and develop is a motivating factor that directly impacts on engagement when it is an intrinsic element of the work.

Strategies for enhancing engagement

An overall approach to improving engagement was described by Helen Murlis at the e-reward/CIPD symposium (1). She warned that pay, and especially variable pay, is very hard to get right and requires care in both design and implementation. But our leaders in both the public and the private sector 'buy' and like the idea of 'pay at risk' and reward for performance, since it matches values and beliefs they have or aspire to. 'There are still people around who believe that pay systems can be used to manage people – from the shop floor to the boardroom.' If everyone was only interested in wealth creation, variable pay would make more sense, but people go to work for a wide range of reasons, which arise from their personalities, preferences and stage of life as well as their role in the organization. This means that they have 'diverse engagement factors'. If you do not take account of these, you are unlikely to get high performance with any reward mechanism that you introduce.

Total reward is therefore an important consideration. The experience of being at work is 'multifaceted'. Hay Group's Engaged Performance Model captures the most important of these, which are:

● tangible rewards;
● quality of work;
● work/life balance;
● inspiration and values;
● enabling environment;
● future growth opportunity.

All of these elements will be important to some staff, but they will not all be equally important. Hay's own research found that inspiration and values – especially quality of leadership – are most important to staff, followed by opportunities for career advancement and learning as well as development, with tangible rewards typically coming third on a list of important issues.

Specific engagement strategies

Specifically, engagement strategies can be developed under the headings of the four factors affecting engagement set out above.

Intrinsic motivation

Intrinsic motivation depends basically on the way in which work or jobs are designed. Three characteristics have been distinguished by Lawler (8) as being required in jobs if they are to be intrinsically motivating:

- *Feedback* – individuals must receive meaningful feedback about their performance, preferably by evaluating their own performance and defining the feedback. This implies that they should ideally work on a complete product/process/service, or a significant part of it that can be seen as a whole.
- *Use of abilities* – the job must be perceived by individuals as requiring them to use abilities they value in order to perform the job effectively.
- *Self-control (autonomy)* – individuals must feel that they have a high degree of self-control over setting their own goals and over defining the paths to these goals.

The work environment

A strategy for increasing engagement through the work environment will be generally concerned with developing a culture that encourages positive attitudes to work, promoting interest and excitement in the jobs people do and reducing stress. Lands' End believes that staff who are enjoying themselves, who are being supported and developed and who feel fulfilled and respected at work will provide the best service to customers. The thinking behind why the company wants to inspire staff is straightforward – employees' willingness to do that little bit extra arises from their sense of pride in what the organization stands for, ie quality, service and value. It makes the difference between a good experience for customers and a poor one.

The strategy also needs to consider particular aspects of the work environment, especially communications, involvement, work/life balance and working conditions. It can include the formulation and application of 'talent relationship management' policies, which are concerned with building effective relationships with people in their roles, treating individual employees fairly, recognizing their value, giving them a voice and providing opportunities for growth.

Leadership

The leadership strategy should concentrate on what line managers have to do if they are going to exercise leadership in order to play their vital and immediate part in increasing levels of engagement. This will include the implementation of learning programmes that help them to understand what they are expected to do and the skills they need to use. The programmes can include formal training (especially for potential managers or those in their first leadership role), but more impact will be made by 'blending' various learning methods such as e-learning, coaching and mentoring.

It should also be recognized that a performance management process can provide line managers with a useful framework in which they can deploy their skills in improving performance through increased engagement. This applies particularly to the performance management activities of role definition, performance improvement planning, joint involvement in monitoring performance and feedback. The strategy should therefore include the steps required to make performance management more effective by increasing the commitment of managers to it and developing the skills they require.

Opportunities for personal growth

A strategy for providing development and growth opportunities should be based on the creation of a learning culture. This is one that promotes learning because it is recognized by top management, line managers and employees generally as an essential organizational process to which they are committed and in which they engage continuously.

It is suggested by Reynolds (9) that to create a learning culture it is necessary to:

1. develop and share the vision – the belief in a desired and emerging future;
2. empower employees – provide 'supported autonomy': freedom for employees to manage their work within certain boundaries (policies and expected behaviours) but with support available as required;
3. adopt a facilitative style of management in which responsibility for decision making is ceded as far as possible to employees;
4. provide employees with a supportive learning environment where learning capabilities can be discovered and applied, eg peer networks, supportive policies and systems, protected time for learning;
5. use coaching techniques to draw out the talents of others by encouraging employees to identify options and seek their own solutions to problems;
6. guide employees through their work challenges and provide them with time, resources and, crucially, feedback;
7. recognize the importance of managers acting as role models;
8. encourage networks – communities of practice;
9. align systems to vision – get rid of bureaucratic systems that produce problems rather than facilitate work.

Measuring the impact of engagement

The effectiveness of engagement strategies needs to be evaluated by measuring their impact and therefore indicating any areas for improvement. An example of how this can be done was provided by Paul Bissell, Senior Rewards Manager, Nationwide Building

Society, who at the 2005 reward symposium described their project Genome as 'the process of identifying, characterizing and mapping the key drivers (or corporate DNA) of employee engagement in our business to establish their effect on and importance to member commitment and business performance'.

For example, the Genome business simulator predicts that, if Nationwide increases the average length of service of employees from 10.2 to 11.2 years, then this will increase customer commitment by almost 1 per cent, which will improve mortgage completions against target by almost 2 per cent, bringing in an additional £5.6 million in revenue. Similarly, a 1 per cent increase in employees' perceptions of coaching leads to almost a 1 per cent increase in personal loan sales against target. Nationwide says that it uses the information from the Genome project to 'improve the characteristics of our employee brand/proposition, to increase employee engagement and in so doing improve the value our members derive from doing business with us'.

ORGANIZATIONAL COMMITMENT

People are committed to their organization when they are proud of it and want to go on working there. As Purcell *et al* (2) explain, if people feel committed they are more likely to engage in discretionary behaviour to help the organization be successful. They suggest that successful organizations are able to meet people's needs both for a good job and to work 'in a great place'. In this way they become an 'employer of choice'. People will want to work there because their individual needs are met – for a worthwhile job with prospects.

Factors affecting organizational commitment

The factors affecting the level of organizational commitment have been defined by Kochan and Dyer (10) as follows:

1. *strategic level* – supportive business strategies, top management value commitment and effective voice for HR in strategy making and governance;
2. *functional (human resource policy) level* – staffing based on employment stabilization, investment in training and development and contingent compensation that reinforces cooperation, participation and contribution;
3. *workplace level* – selection based on high standards, broad task design and teamwork, employee involvement, and a climate of cooperation and trust.

Developing an organizational commitment strategy

An organizational commitment strategy will cover what needs to be done to:

- communicate the values and aims of management and the achievements of the organization, so that employees are more likely to identify with it as one they are proud to work for;
- demonstrate to employees that management is committed to them by recognizing their contribution as stakeholders and by striving to maximize job security;
- develop a climate of trust by ensuring that management is honest with people, treats them fairly, justly and consistently, keeps its word and shows willingness to listen to the comments and suggestions made by employees during processes of consultation and participation;
- create a positive psychological contract by treating people as stakeholders, relying on consensus and cooperation rather than control and coercion and focusing on the provision of opportunities for learning, development and career progression;
- establish performance management processes that provide for the alignment of organizational and individual objectives;
- help to increase employee identification with the organization through rewards related to organizational performance (profit sharing or gain sharing) or employee share ownership schemes;
- overall, establish and maintain a working environment that makes the organization an 'employer of choice' because it is 'a great place to work'.

Developing the employment brand at B&Q

B&Q recognized that it faced a daunting challenge if it was to present itself as an employer of choice. The findings of internal and external research on B&Q as an employer had told senior managers something very important about what employees and potential employees actually thought of the employment relationship at B&Q. They realized that its 'employment brand' had to change. Work was carried out with consultants TMP on developing a clearly defined employment brand proposition. The stated aims of the exercise were to:

- create high awareness of the B&Q brand;
- change the negative misconceptions of B&Q as an employer;
- raise awareness of the company's positive employment attributes both internally and externally;
- attract and select the right kind of people to deliver great service.

The 'employment value proposition' is the name given to B&Q's approach to a distinct employer brand. According to the company, the employment value proposition 'sits behind the entire relationship that B&Q has with our employees throughout the entire life cycle of their employment'. In essence, it is a way of determining what drives people to join B&Q, stay in the company and be motivated to higher levels of performance.

But as Will Astill, B&Q's Reward Manager, explains, it was not just about trying to sell B&Q as an employer to potential recruits. 'B&Q wanted to be the type of employer with the systems and practices actually in place. We needed to formulate strategy and plans, so the reality is similar to perception before we sell the vision externally.' By assembling and marketing a compelling employment offer that will attract, engage and retain the people needed for organizational success, B&Q was confident that a good brand would create a competitive advantage. Says Astill: 'Engaged employees will go beyond the strict boundaries of the job and offer better service. This means customers become more loyal and increase their overall spend thereby boosting profits.'

REFERENCES

1   Murlis, H (2005) Diverse engagement factors, Unpublished, e-reward/CIPD Reward Symposium

2   Purcell, J *et al* (2003) *People and Performance: How people management impacts on organisational performance*, Chartered Institute of Personnel and Development, London

3   Bevan, S, Barber, I and Robinson, D (1997) *Keeping the Best: A practical guide to retaining key employees*, Institute for Employment Studies, Brighton

4   Robinson, D (2005) Employee engagement, Unpublished, e-reward/CIPD Reward Symposium

5   Herzberg, F (2003) One more time: how do you motivate employees?, *Harvard Business Review*, **81** (1), pp 87–96

6   Lawler, EE (2003) *Treat People Right! How organisations and individuals can propel each other into a virtuous spiral of success*, Jossey-Bass, San Francisco

7   Alderfer, C (1972) *Existence, Relatedness and Growth*, Free Press, New York

8   Lawler, EE (1969) Job design and employee motivation, *Personnel Psychology*, **22**, pp 426–35

9   Reynolds, J (2004) *Helping People Learn*, Chartered Institute of Personnel and Development, London

10 Kochan, TA and Dyer, L (1993) Managing transformational change: the role of human resource professionals, *International Journal of Human Resource management*, **4** (3), pp 569–90

10

The psychological contract

The employment relationship contains a combination of beliefs held by individuals and their employers about what they expect of one another. This is the psychological contract, and it is necessary to understand what the psychological contract is and its significance as a key aspect of relationships with employees when formulating and implementing reward policy.

THE PSYCHOLOGICAL CONTRACT DEFINED

A psychological contract is a system of beliefs that encompasses the actions employees believe are expected of them and what response they expect in return from their employer. It has been defined by Stiles, Gratton and Truss (1) as: 'The set of reciprocal expectations between an individual employee and the organization'. As described by Guest *et al* (2): 'It is concerned with assumptions, expectations, promises and mutual obligations.' It creates attitudes and emotions that form and govern behaviour. A psychological contract is implicit. It is also dynamic – it develops over time as experience accumulates, employment conditions change and employees re-evaluate their expectations.

The psychological contract may provide some indication of the answers to the two fundamental employment relationship questions that individuals pose: 'What can I reasonably expect from the organization?' and 'What should I reasonably be expected to contribute in return?' But it is difficult, often impossible, to ensure that the psychological contract and therefore the employment relationship will be fully understood by either party.

Employees may expect to be treated fairly as human beings, to be provided with work that uses their abilities, to be rewarded equitably in accordance with their contribution, to be able to develop and display competency, to have opportunities for further growth, to know what is expected of them and to be given feedback (preferably positive) on how they are doing. Employers may expect employees to do their best on behalf of the organization ('to put themselves out for the company'), to be fully committed to its values, to be compliant and loyal, and to enhance the image of the organization with its customers and suppliers. Sometimes these assumptions are justified – often they are not. Mutual misunderstandings can cause friction and stress and lead to recriminations and poor performance, or to a termination of the employment relationship.

To summarize, in the words of Guest and Conway (3), the psychological contract lacks many of the characteristics of the formal contract: 'It is not generally written down, it is somewhat blurred at the edges, and it cannot be enforced in a court or tribunal.' They believe that: 'The psychological contract is best seen as a metaphor; a word or phrase borrowed from another context which helps us make sense of our experience. The psychological contract is a way of interpreting the state of the employment relationship and helping to plot significant changes.'

THE SIGNIFICANCE OF THE PSYCHOLOGICAL CONTRACT

As suggested by Spindler (4), 'A psychological contract creates emotions and attitudes which form and control behaviour.' The significance of the psychological contract was further explained by Sims (5) as follows: 'A balanced psychological contract is necessary for a continuing, harmonious relationship between the employee and the organization. However, the violation of the psychological contract can signal to the participants that the parties no longer share (or never shared) a common set of values or goals.' The concept highlights the fact that employee/employer expectations take the form of unarticulated assumptions. Disappointments on the part of management as well as employees may therefore be inevitable. These disappointments can, however, be alleviated if managements appreciate that one of their key roles is to manage expectations, which means clarifying what they believe employees should achieve, the competencies they should possess and the values they should uphold. And this is a matter not just of articulating and stipulating these requirements but of discussing and agreeing them with people.

Guest *et al* (2) comment that:

> While employees may want what they have always wanted – security, a career, fair rewards, interesting work and so on – employers no longer feel able or obliged to provide these. Instead, they have been demanding more of their employees in terms of greater input and tolerance of uncertainty and change, while providing less in return, in particular less security and more limited career prospects.

DEVELOPING AND MAINTAINING A POSITIVE PSYCHOLOGICAL CONTRACT

As Guest *et al* (2) remark, 'A positive psychological contract is worth taking seriously because it is strongly linked to higher commitment to the organization, higher employee satisfaction and better employment relations. Again this reinforces the benefits of pursuing a set of progressive HRM practices.' They also emphasize the importance of a high-involvement climate and suggest in particular that HRM practices such as the provision of opportunities for learning, training and development, focus on job security, promotion and careers, minimizing status differentials, fair reward systems and comprehensive communication and involvement processes will all contribute to a positive psychological contract.

The part played by reward management in developing a positive psychological contract

Reward and, especially, performance management processes can help to clarify the psychological contract and make it more positive by:

- providing a basis for the joint agreement and definition of roles;
- communicating expectations in the form of targets, standards of performance, behavioural requirements (competencies) and upholding core values;
- obtaining agreement on the contribution both parties (the manager and the individual) have to make to getting the results expected;
- defining the level of support to be exercised by managers;
- providing financial rewards through schemes that deliver messages about what the organization believes to be important;
- providing non-financial rewards that reinforce the messages about expectations;
- giving employees opportunities at performance review discussions to clarify points about their work.

REFERENCES

1 Stiles, P, Gratton, L and Truss, C (2001) Performance management and the psychological contract, *Human Resource Management Journal*, **7** (1), pp 57–66

2 Guest, DE *et al* (1996) *The State of the Psychological Contract in Employment*, Chartered Institute of Personnel and Development, London

3 Guest, DE and Conway, N (1998) *Fairness at Work and the Psychological Contract*, IPD, London

4 Spindler, GS (1994) Psychological contracts in the workplace: a lawyer's view, *Human Resource Management*, **33** (3), pp 325–33

5 Sims, RR (1994) Human resource management's role in clarifying the new psychological contract, *Human Resource Management*, **33** (3), pp 373–82

Part 3

Establishing job values and relativities

11

Job evaluation schemes

Job evaluation is of fundamental importance in reward management. It provides the basis for achieving equitable pay and is an essential means of dealing with equal-pay-for-work-of-equal-value issues. In the 1980s and 1990s job evaluation fell into disrepute because it was alleged to be bureaucratic, time-consuming and irrelevant in a market economy where market rates dictate internal rates of pay and relativities. However, as the e-reward 2002 survey of job evaluation (1) showed, job evaluation is still practised quite widely (44 per cent of respondents had a scheme) and, indeed, its use is increasing in the UK, not least because of the pressures to achieve equal pay.

This chapter starts with a definition of job evaluation and an assessment of its aims and the cases for and against it. The different categories and types of job evaluation schemes are then described and the use of computers discussed. The chapter concludes with an assessment of the criteria for choice and suggestions on how to use job evaluation effectively.

DEFINITION OF JOB EVALUATION

Job evaluation is a systematic process for defining the relative worth or size of jobs within an organization in order to establish internal relativities. It provides the basis for designing an equitable grade and pay structure, grading jobs in the structure, managing job and pay relativities and guiding the achievement of equal pay for work of equal value.

AIMS

Job evaluation aims to:

- establish the relative value or size of jobs, ie internal relativities based on fair, sound and consistent judgements;
- produce the information required to design and maintain equitable and defensible grade and pay structures;
- provide as objective as possible a basis for grading jobs within a grade structure, thus enabling consistent decisions to be made about job grading;
- enable sound market comparisons with jobs or roles of equivalent complexity and size;
- be transparent – the basis upon which grades are defined and jobs graded should be clear;
- ensure that the organization meets equal-pay-for-work-of-equal-value obligations.

The last aim is important. In its *Good Practice Guide: Job evaluation schemes free of sex bias*, the Equal Opportunities Commission (EOC) (2) states that: 'Non-discriminatory job evaluation should lead to a payment system which is transparent and within which work of equal value receives equal pay regardless of sex.'

FEATURES

The main features of job evaluation are described below.

Based on factual evidence

The relative value or 'size' of jobs is determined on the basis of information on the characteristics of the jobs. In analytical schemes this information is assessed within a structured framework of criteria or factors.

Judgemental

Human judgement has to be exercised at a number of points in the job evaluation process. Although job evaluations are based on factual evidence, this has to be interpreted. The information provided about jobs through job analysis can sometimes fail to provide a clear indication of the levels at which demands are present in a job.

The definitions in a factor plan used in an analytical scheme (see below) or grade definitions in a non-analytical scheme will not precisely indicate the level of demand that should be recorded. Judgement is required in making decisions on the level and therefore, in a point-factor or factor comparison scheme, the score.

The aim is to be objective, but it is difficult to eliminate a degree of subjectivity. As the EOC states (2), 'it is recognised that to a certain extent any assessment of a job's total demands relative to another will always be subjective'.

A fundamental aim of any process of job evaluation is to ensure, as far as possible, that consistent judgements are made based on objectively assessed information. To refer to an evaluation as 'judgemental' does not necessarily mean that it is inaccurate or invalid. Correct judgements are achieved when they are made within a defined framework and are based on clear evidence and sound reasoning. This is what job evaluation can do if the scheme is properly designed and properly applied.

Concerned with the job not the person

This is the iron law of job evaluation. It means that when evaluating a job the only concern is the content of that job in terms of the demands made on the job holder. The performance of the individual in the job must not be taken into account. But it should be noted that while *performance* is excluded, in today's more flexible organizations the tendency is for some people, especially knowledge workers, to have flexible roles. Individuals may have the scope to enlarge or enrich their roles and this needs to be taken into account when evaluating what they do. Roles cannot necessarily be separated from the people who carry them out. It is people who create value not jobs.

Concerned with internal relativities

When used within an organization, job evaluation in the true sense as defined above (ie not market pricing as described later) can only assess the relative size of jobs in that organization. It is not concerned with external relativities, that is, the relationship between the rates of pay of jobs in the organization and the rates of pay of comparable jobs elsewhere (market rates).

THE CASE FOR AND AGAINST JOB EVALUATION

The case for

The case for properly devised and applied job evaluation, especially analytical job evaluation, is that:

- it can make the criteria against which jobs are valued explicit and provide a basis for guiding the judgement process;
- an equitable and defensible pay structure cannot be achieved unless a structured and systematic process is used to assess job values and relativities;
- a logical framework is required within which consistent decisions can be made on job grades and rates of pay;
- the factor plan and the process of job evaluation can be aligned to the organization's value system and competency framework and therefore reinforce them as part of an integrated approach to people management;
- analytical schemes provide the best basis for achieving equal pay for work of equal value and are the only acceptable defence in an equal pay case;
- a formal process of job evaluation is more likely to be accepted as fair and equitable than informal or ad hoc approaches – and the degree of acceptability will be considerably enhanced if the whole process is transparent.

The case against

The case against job evaluation has been presented vociferously. It has been called a 'bogus science'. Critics emphasize that it can be bureaucratic, inflexible, time-consuming and inappropriate in today's organizations. Graef Crystal (3) stated that 'all systems of job evaluation essentially boil down to organized rationalization'. Ed Lawler (4) claims that job evaluation can create unnecessary and undesirable pecking orders and power relationships in organizations. He also believes that people realize that creatively written job descriptions can lead to pay increases (he calls this 'point grabbing' in point-factor schemes). Maeve Quaid (5) suggested that job evaluation functions as a rationalized, institutional myth and believes that it 'provides organizations with a set of language, rituals and rhetoric that has transported an otherwise impossible and indeterminate process to the realm of the possible and determinable. In this way, what job evaluation seems to do is to code and re-code existing biases and value systems to re-present them as objective data.' Niels Nielsen (6) takes exception to the fact that job evaluation is not concerned with external relativities, which he considers are what really matter.

Schemes can decay over time through use or misuse. People learn how to manipulate them to achieve a higher grade, and this leads to the phenomenon known as grade drift – upgradings that are not justified by a sufficiently significant increase in responsibility.

Job evaluators can fall into the trap of making a priori judgements. They may instinctively prejudge the level of a job on the basis of their own conception of its value. The information presented to them about a job may be filtered through these preconceptions and the scheme is used to justify them. The so-called 'felt-fair' test is often used to assess the acceptability of job evaluations, but a rank order is felt to be fair if it simply reproduces the evaluator's notion of what the rank order ought to be, not what it is.

Response to criticisms

Job evaluation schemes do decay, they are misused, and evaluators do make a priori judgements. It has to be accepted that job evaluation is not a scientific process. It can never achieve complete objectivity as long as it is conducted by human beings. Computer-assisted systems do not eliminate this as they ultimately depend on the inputs of potentially fallible people.

The criticisms about schemes used to assess internal relativities focus on the way in which job evaluation is operated rather than the concept of job evaluation itself. Like any other management technique, job evaluation schemes can be misconceived and misused. All that can be done is to provide those involved in job evaluation with as much help as possible in guiding their judgements and the training necessary to minimize subjectivity even though realistically it will never be eliminated.

Those who criticize job evaluation because it is only concerned with internal relativities fail to understand that job evaluation exists to grade jobs not to price them. Of course, when developing the pay structures superimposed on grade structures it is necessary to take account of external relativities, and this will mean reconciling the different messages provided by job evaluation and market rate surveys. If the latter indicate that attracting and retaining good-quality staff are only feasible through rates of pay higher than those indicated by the grading of the job, then it may be necessary to pay market supplements, but to avoid claims that equal pay is not being provided these must be objectively justified on the basis of evidence on competitive rates.

CATEGORIES OF JOB EVALUATION

The three main categories of job evaluation are analytical schemes, non-analytical schemes and market pricing. The first two rely on internal comparisons and do not directly 'price' the jobs, ie attach rates of pay to them. Market pricing is not a job evaluation scheme as usually defined because it relies totally on external comparisons, but it is included in this chapter because it is a method of determining the relative value of jobs, albeit in financial terms.

Analytical job evaluation

Analytical job evaluation is the process of making decisions about the value or size of jobs, which are based on an analysis of the level at which various defined factors or elements are present in a job in order to establish relative job value. The set of factors used in a scheme is called the 'factor plan', which defines each of the factors used (which should be present in all the jobs to be evaluated) and the levels within each factor. Analytical job evaluation is the most common approach to job evaluation The two main types of analytical job evaluation schemes are point-factor schemes and analytical factor comparison schemes, as described later. Another variety of analytical scheme is factor comparison but it is little used except by independent experts in equal pay cases and as a basis for the Hay Guide Chart method of job evaluation.

Non-analytical job evaluation

Non-analytical job evaluation compares whole jobs to place them in a grade or a rank order – they are not analysed by reference to their elements or factors. Non-analytical schemes do not meet the requirements of equal value law. They operate either on a job-to-job basis in which a job is compared with another job to decide whether it should be valued more, or less, or the same (ranking and 'internal benchmarking' or job-matching processes) or a job-to-scale basis in which judgements are made by comparing a whole job with a defined hierarchy of job grades (job classification) – this involves matching a job description to a grade description.

Market pricing

Market pricing is the process of assessing rates of pay by reference to the market rates for comparable jobs. It can be described as external benchmarking.

Comparison of approaches

The approaches described above are compared in Table 11.1.

TYPES OF ANALYTICAL SCHEMES

The main types of analytical schemes are described below.

Point-factor evaluation

Point-factor schemes are the most commonly used type of analytical method of job evaluation. The basic methodology is to break down jobs into factors or key

Table 11.1 Comparison of approaches to job evaluation

Approach	Features	Types*	Advantages	Disadvantages
Analytical	Decisions are made about the relative value or size of jobs by reference to an analysis of the level at which various defined factors or elements are present in a job. The set of factors used in a scheme is called the factor plan, which defines each of the factors used (these should be present in all the jobs to be evaluated), the levels within each factor and, in point-factor schemes, the scores available at each level.	– Point-factor – Analytical matching – Factor comparison	– Systematic – Provide evaluators with defined yardsticks that help to increase the objectivity and consistency of judgements – Provide a defence against an equal pay claim	– Expensive and time-consuming to design or implement – Can be over-complex – Do not ensure either complete objectivity or consistency
Non-analytical	Whole jobs are compared to place them in a grade or a rank order – they are not analysed by reference to their elements or factors.	– Job classification – Job ranking – Non-analytical matching	– Can be developed quite easily – Provide a simple and quick method of grading jobs or establishing relativities (rank orders)	– Rely on overall and potentially subjective judgements that may be insufficiently guided by a factor plan and do not take account of the complexity of jobs – No defined standards for judging relative worth are provided – Do not provide a defence in an equal pay case
Market pricing	Jobs valued by reference to market rates		– Realistic – it's the marketplace that determines the value of jobs – Relatively easy as long as appropriate market data are readily available – Market relativities can be used as a guide to internal relativities	– Accurate market data may not be available readily – Ignores internal equity considerations – May create unequal pay if the market rate comparisons simply reproduce existing inequities

* A detailed comparison of the main schemes is given in Table 12.1.

elements representing the demands made by the job on job holders, for example skill requirements, responsibility for resources, decision making. It is assumed that each of the factors will contribute to job size (ie the value of the job) and is an aspect of all the jobs to be evaluated but to different degrees. Using numerical scales, points are allocated to a job under each factor heading according to the extent to which it is present in the job. The separate factor scores are then added together to give a total score, which represents job size.

Analytical matching

Like point-factor job evaluation, analytical matching is based on the analysis of a number of defined factors. There are two forms of analytical matching. One is role profile to grade/level profile matching; the other is role profile to benchmark role profile.

In *role-to-grade matching*, profiles of roles to be evaluated are matched to grade, band or level profiles. Reference is made to a grade structure incorporating the jobs covered by the evaluation scheme. This consists of a sequence or hierarchy of grades, bands or levels into which groups of benchmark jobs that are broadly comparable in size are placed following a point-factor job evaluation exercise or on an ad hoc basis (see Chapters 17 and 18). Definitions of each of the grades in the structure (grade or level profiles) are produced, which set out the characteristics of the jobs in each grade. The definitions may be based on the job evaluation factors in a point-factor scheme or a selection of them. They may also or alternatively refer to levels of competency and accountability especially in job and career family structures. Role profiles are produced for the jobs to be evaluated under the same headings as the grade profiles. The role profiles are then 'matched' with the range of grade or level profiles to establish the best fit and thus grade the job.

In *role-to-role matching*, role profiles for jobs to be evaluated are matched analytically with benchmark role profiles for jobs that have already been graded as a result of an initial job evaluation exercise. Roles are analysed against a common set of factors or elements. Generic role profiles will be used for any class or cluster of roles that are essentially similar although there may be minor differences, eg team leader, administrative assistant (see Chapter 16). Role-to-role matching may be used to supplement role-to-grade matching.

Analytical matching may be used to grade jobs following the initial evaluation of a sufficiently large and representative sample of 'benchmark' jobs, ie jobs that can be used as a basis for comparison with other jobs. This can happen in big organizations when it is believed that it is not necessary to go through the whole process of point-factor evaluation for every job, especially where 'generic' roles are concerned. When this follows a large job evaluation exercise, as in the NHS Agenda for Change Programme, the factors used in the grade and role profiles will be the same as those used in the point-factor job evaluation scheme.

Factor comparison

The original but obsolete factor comparison method compared jobs factor by factor using a scale of money values to provide a direct indication of the rate for the job. The main form of factor comparison now in use is graduated factor comparison, which involves comparing jobs factor by factor with a graduated scale. The scale may have only three value levels – for example lower, equal, higher – and factor scores are not necessarily used.

It is a method often used by the independent experts engaged by employment tribunals to advise on an equal pay claim. Their job is simply to compare one job with one or two others, not to review internal relativities over the whole spectrum of jobs in order to produce a rank order. Independent experts may score their judgements of comparative levels, in which case graduated factor comparison resembles the point-factor method except that the number of levels and range of scores are limited, and the factors may not be weighted.

Analytical schemes available from consultants (proprietary brands)

There are a number of analytical job evaluation schemes offered by management consultants. By far the most popular is the Hay Guide Chart Profile Method, which is a factor comparison scheme. It uses three broad factors (know-how, problem solving and accountability), each of which is further divided into sub-factors. Definitions of each level have been produced for each sub-factor to guide evaluators and ensure consistency of application.

TYPES OF NON-ANALYTICAL SCHEMES

There are four main types of non-analytical schemes: job classification, job ranking, paired comparison (a statistical version of ranking) and non-analytical matching or internal benchmarking.

Job classification

This is the most common non-analytical approach. Roles or jobs as defined in role profiles or job descriptions are 'slotted' into grades in a hierarchy by comparing the whole job with a grade definition and selecting the grade that provides the best fit (slotting). It is based on an initial definition of the number and characteristics of the grades into which jobs will be placed. The grade definitions may therefore refer to such job characteristics as skill, decision making and responsibility but these are not treated analytically, ie the role profiles are not compared factor by factor, as in a point-factor scheme or analytical matching (this is what is meant by 'whole job comparison').

Job ranking

Whole job ranking is the most primitive form of job evaluation. The process involves comparing whole jobs with one another and arranging them in order of their perceived size or value to the organization. In a sense, all evaluation schemes are ranking exercises because they place jobs in a hierarchy. The difference between simple ranking and analytical methods such as point-factor rating is that job ranking does not attempt to quantify judgements. Instead, whole jobs are compared – they are not broken down into factors or elements although, explicitly or implicitly, the comparison may be based on some generalized concept such as the level of responsibility.

Paired comparison ranking

Paired comparison ranking is a statistical technique that is used to provide a more sophisticated method of whole job ranking. It is based on the assumption that it is always easier to compare one job with another than to consider a number of jobs and attempt to build up a rank order by multiple comparisons.

The technique requires the comparison of each job as a whole separately with every other job. If a job is considered to be of a higher value than the one with which it is being compared it receives two points; if it is thought to be equally important, it receives one point; if it is regarded as less important, no points are awarded. The scores are added for each job and a rank order is obtained.

The advantage of paired comparison ranking over normal ranking is that it is easier to compare one job with another rather than having to make multi-comparisons. But it cannot overcome the fundamental objections to any form of whole job ranking – that no defined standards for judging relative worth are provided and it is not an acceptable method of assessing equal value. There is also a limit to the number of jobs that can be compared using this method – to evaluate 50 jobs requires 1,225 comparisons. Paired comparisons can also be used analytically to compare jobs on a factor-by-factor basis.

A simplified example of a paired comparison ranking is shown in Figure 11.1.

Job reference	a	b	c	d	e	f	Total score	Ranking
A	–	0	1	0	1	0	2	5=
B	2	–	2	2	2	0	8	2
C	1	0	–	1	1	0	3	4
D	2	0	1	–	2	0	5	3
E	1	0	1	0	–	0	2	5=
F	2	2	2	2	2	–	10	1

Figure 11.1   A paired comparison

Non-analytical matching or internal benchmarking

Non-analytical matching or internal benchmarking is what people often do intuitively when they are deciding on the value of jobs, although it is not usually dignified in job evaluation circles as a formal method of job evaluation. It simply means comparing the job under review with any internal job that is believed to be properly graded and paid and placing the job under consideration into the same grade as that job. The comparison is made on a whole job basis without analysing the jobs factor by factor.

MARKET PRICING

As mentioned earlier, strictly speaking market pricing is not a process of job evaluation in the sense that those described above are.

However, the term market pricing in its extreme form is used to denote a process of directly pricing jobs on the basis of external relativities with no regard to internal relativities. This approach has been widely adopted in the United States. It is associated with a belief that 'the market rules, OK', disillusionment with what was regarded as bureaucratic job evaluation, and the enthusiasm for broad-banded pay structures (ie structures as described in Chapter 17 with a limited number of grades or bands). It is a method that often has appeal at board level because of the focus on competitiveness in relation to the marketplace for talent.

The acceptability of market pricing is dependent on the availability of robust market data and, when looking at external rates, the quality of the job-to-job matching process, ie comparing like with like. It can therefore vary from analysis of data by job titles to detailed matched analysis collected through bespoke surveys focused on real market equivalence (see Chapter 15). Market pricing can produce an indication of internal relativities even if these are market-driven. But it can lead to pay discrimination against women where the market has traditionally been discriminatory. It does not satisfy UK equal pay legislation.

Market pricing can be done formally by the analysis of published pay surveys, participating in 'pay clubs', conducting special surveys, obtaining the advice of recruitment consultants and agencies and, more doubtfully, studying advertisements. In its crudest form, market pricing simply means fixing the rate for a job at the level necessary to recruit or retain someone. To avoid a successful equal pay claim, any difference in pay between men and women carrying out work of equal value based on market rate considerations has to be 'objectively justified'.

COMPUTER-ASSISTED JOB EVALUATION

Computer-assisted evaluation systems are often used to help directly with the job evaluation process in national schemes such as those developed for local government, higher education establishments and further education colleges. But they do not occur extensively elsewhere (only 27 per cent of the respondents to the e-reward survey had them). Perhaps this was because in many cases it was thought that they were an expensive and unnecessary addition to a process that could be carried out successfully using a purely paper scheme or a simple spreadsheet.

Types of schemes

The two types of computer-assisted systems are:

1. *Job analysis-based schemes* such as that offered by Link Consultants in which the job analysis data are either entered direct into the computer or transferred to it from a paper questionnaire. The computer software applies predetermined rules based on an algorithm that reflects the organization's evaluation standards to convert the data into scores for each factor and produce a total score. The algorithm replicates panel judgements both on job factor levels and on overall job score.
2. *Interactive schemes* using software such as that supplied by Pilat UK (Gauge) in which the job holder and his or her manager sit in front of a PC and are presented

with a series of logically interrelated questions forming a question tree; the answers to these questions lead to a score for each of the built-in factors in turn and a total score.

Advantages of computer-assisted job evaluation

Computer-assisted job evaluation systems can:

- provide for greater consistency – the same input information will always give the same output result because the judgemental framework on which the scheme is based (the algorithm) can be applied consistently to the input data;
- offer extensive database capabilities for sorting, analysing and reporting on the input information and system outputs;
- speed up the job evaluation process once the initial design is complete.

Disadvantages of computer-assisted job evaluation

Computer-assisted job evaluation systems can:

- lack transparency – the evaluation in a job analysis-based scheme is made in a 'black box' and it can be difficult to trace the connection between the analysis and the evaluation and therefore to justify the score; this is not such a problem with interactive schemes in which job holders participate in evaluations and the link between the answer to a question and the score can be traced in the 'question trees';
- appear to bypass the evaluation process through joint management/employee panels, which is typical in conventional schemes; however, this problem can be reduced if panels are used to validate the computer-generated scores.

EXAMPLES OF THE USE OF JOB EVALUATION

Most of the organizations surveyed by e-reward in 2002 adopted a fairly conventional approach to job evaluation, using either a proprietary brand (most commonly Hay) or a scheme developed in-house, often with help of consultants. GlaxoSmithKline is an example of the latter. However, there were examples of companies that settled for a non-analytical approach on the grounds that a points scheme would be too time-consuming and unwieldy. Aegon and Tesco are in this category.

GlaxoSmithKline

With the introduction of the new grading process, individuals were, and continue to be, allocated to their grades using a home-grown factor-based scheme, which is based around a combination of a number of different job evaluation schemes found in the market. This was a demanding exercise, keeping many of the company's compensation team busy for around nine months.

Aegon

Job evaluation now relies on whole job comparisons consisting of internal bench-marking or matching along with external benchmarking against survey data, using generic role definitions. The relative emphasis on job evaluation and detailed, common standards of internal job measurement and grading has been reduced.

Tesco

The retailer found that its 22-grade pay structure and job evaluation processes were inflexible and did not provide a sufficient link between pay and performance. They also inhibited the career development and horizontal movement the organization needed to manage in a period of expansion and change. The company's response has been to introduce a six-level broad-banded structure that gives line managers more discretion over how they develop and pay their staff.

CONCLUSION

Organizations have to use some method of valuing jobs that ensures that their pay system is externally competitive or internally equitable. Every time a decision is made on what a job should be paid it requires the use of either job evaluation or market pricing. Job evaluation proper is all about creating an internally equitable grade structure to which pay levels or ranges are attached that take account of market rates although they are not allowed to drive the structure. But it can be resource-intensive. Market pricing is, in a sense, realistic and is not so bureaucratic or time-consuming as the conventional forms of job evaluation, although it ignores the claims of internal equity.

Considerations affecting the choice of schemes are discussed in Chapter 12.

REFERENCES

1 e-reward (2002) *Survey of Job Evaluation*, e-reward.co.uk, Stockport
2 Equal Opportunities Commission (2003) *Good Practice Guide: Job evaluation schemes free of sex bias*, EOC, Manchester
3 Crystal, G (1970) *Financial Motivation for Executives*, AMA, New York
4 Lawler, EE (1986) What's wrong with point-factor job evaluation?, *Compensation and Benefits Review*, March/April, pp 20–28
5 Quaid, M (1993) *Job Evaluation: The myth of equitable settlement*, University of Toronto Press, Toronto
6 Nielsen, NH (2002) Job content evaluation techniques based on Marxian economics, *WorldatWork Journal*, **11** (2), pp 52–62

Developing and maintaining job evaluation schemes

This chapter covers how to develop and manage a job evaluation scheme. It starts by examining the initial stages and continues with descriptions of the programmes required to develop the three main types of job evaluation scheme: point-factor rating, job classification and analytical matching. Consideration is then given to market pricing. The chapter ends with a review of methods of managing, maintaining and introducing job evaluation.

DEVELOPING A JOB EVALUATION SCHEME: INITIAL STAGES

The initial stages in developing a job evaluation scheme are shown in Figure 12.1. This leads into the detailed design programmes as described later in this chapter.

Stage 1: decide to introduce or modify a job evaluation scheme

The case for introducing job evaluation

There is a good case for introducing job evaluation if any of the following conditions apply:

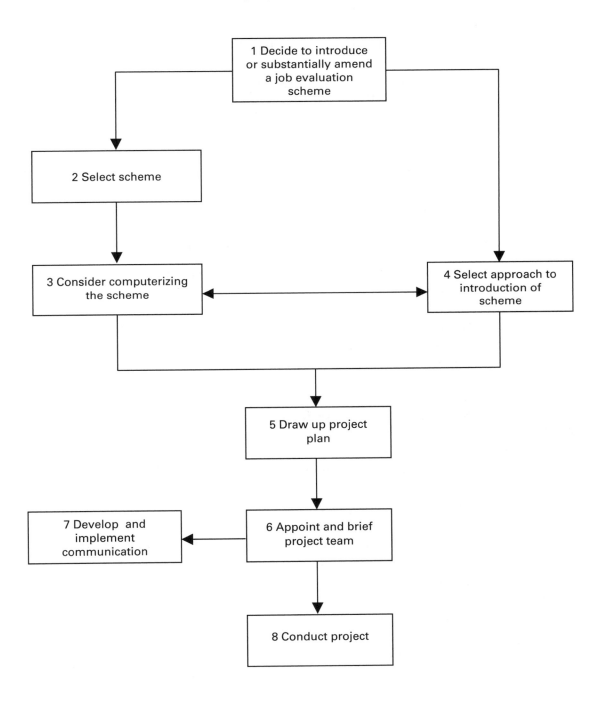

Figure 12.1 Developing a job evaluation scheme: initial stages

- There are a considerable number of grading anomalies – people clearly over- or under-graded without good reason.
- There is pronounced grade drift, ie a large number of jobs have been or are being upgraded without justification in terms of an increase in responsibilities.
- There is general dissatisfaction at the way in which the grade and pay system is being managed.
- The existing grade structure is wholly inappropriate.
- An equal pay review has revealed considerable pay gaps between similar jobs held by men and women.
- There has been a successful equal pay claim.

The case for modifying an existing job evaluation scheme

There is a good case for modifying an existing job evaluation scheme in any of the following circumstances:

- There is evidence that the job evaluation scheme has decayed to the extent that it no longer provides a fair and reliable method of determining the relative size of jobs and their grading.
- Management and/or employees have lost confidence in the scheme.
- The scheme is being manipulated to facilitate unjustified upgradings.
- The scheme has failed to provide an adequate defence in an equal pay case.
- The scheme is unable to support an equal pay review or produce the information needed to ensure that equal pay is provided for work of equal value.
- The scheme is over-bureaucratic, time-consuming or too complicated.

The decision to introduce a new job evaluation scheme or replace an existing one should not be taken lightly. It will involve considerable work, expense and trouble. Job evaluation exercises may aim to remove the causes of dissatisfaction with the pay or grading system but they can result in higher levels of dissatisfaction than before if expectations are not met.

If it is decided to go ahead, the next two decisions to be made concern the type of scheme and who is involved in its implementation.

Stage 2: select the scheme

The first choice to be made is whether an analytical or non-analytical scheme is to be developed or whether market pricing is to be the primary method. The features of each of these approaches, the types of scheme under each heading and their advantages and disadvantages were set out in Table 11.1.

Making a choice between an analytical approach, non-analytical approach and market pricing often boils down to providing answers to the following three questions:

1. Do we want an analytical scheme, which, although it may be troublesome and expensive to develop, will produce a reasonably consistent and fair method of judging relativities and will provide a defence in an equal pay claim? Or:
2. Do we want a non-analytical scheme, which, although it will not provide a framework for making consistent judgements and will not be usable in defence of an equal pay case, will be easier to develop and operate and will provide us with a sufficient basis for grading jobs? Or:
3. Do we want to depend on market pricing, which is realistic – it's the marketplace that determines the value of jobs – and relatively easy as long as appropriate market data are readily available and good matching is possible, bearing in mind potential internal equity problems?

Most organizations in the UK considering the introduction or redesign of job evaluation are likely to answer 'yes' to the first question. In the United States they are more likely to say 'yes' to market pricing.

The advantages and disadvantages of the main schemes are set out in Table 12.1.

The first critical decision is whether to rely entirely on market pricing or whether to adopt one of the other conventional forms of job evaluation. The choice is affected by the amount of importance attached to internal equity as against the need to be competitive. Zingheim and Schuster (1) have no doubt which is to be preferred. They point out that 'the history of job evaluation involves entitlement disguised as a nearly singular emphasis on internal equity'. The future as they see it 'depends on our ability to develop and implement a base salary system… that is anchored in the marketplace'.

The other point of view, as argued by Heneman and LeBlanc (2), is that 'it is premature to abandon traditional job evaluation for market pricing'. Internal equity considerations and powerful equal pay legislation support the use of job evaluation.

And the implication by those who advocate market pricing that organizations that use 'conventional' job evaluation schemes ignore market rate considerations is nonsense. When it comes to deciding on pay levels every organization must consider how much they should pay to attract and retain the people they need, and this means that they must take account of market rates. The difference is that they are not driven by the marketplace, although there is often tension between the pursuit of both internal equity and external competitiveness

If market pricing is not adopted, the choice of a conventional job evaluation scheme should be made by reference to the features and pros and cons of different schemes

Table 12.1 Comparison of job evaluation schemes

Scheme	Characteristics	Advantages	Disadvantages
Point-factor rating	An analytical approach in which separate factors are scored and added together to produce a total score for the job, which can be used for comparison and grading purposes.	As long as it is based on proper job analysis, point-factor schemes provide evaluators with defined yardsticks that help to increase the objectivity and consistency of judgements and reduce the oversimplified judgement made in non-analytical job evaluation. They provide a defence against equal value claims as long as they are not in themselves discriminatory.	Can be complex and give a spurious impression of scientific accuracy – judgement is still needed in scoring jobs. Not easy to amend the scheme as circumstances, priorities or values change.
Analytical matching	Grade profiles are produced that define the characteristics of jobs in each grade in a grade structure in terms of a selection of defined factors. Role profiles are produced for the jobs to be evaluated set out on the basis of analysis under the same factor headings as the grade profiles. Role profiles are 'matched' with the range of grade profiles to establish the best fit and thus grade the job.	If the matching process is truly analytical and carried out with great care, this approach saves time by enabling the evaluation of a large number of jobs, especially generic ones, to be conducted quickly and in a way that should satisfy equal value requirements.	The matching process could be more superficial and therefore suspect than evaluation through a point-factor scheme. In the latter approach there are factor-level definitions to guide judgements, and the resulting scores provide a basis for ranking and grade design that is not the case with analytical matching. Although matching on this basis may be claimed to be analytical, it might be difficult to prove this in an equal value case.

Table 12.1 *Continued*

Scheme	Characteristics	Advantages	Disadvantages
Job classification	Non-analytical – grades are defined in a structure in terms of the level of responsibilities involved in a hierarchy. Jobs are allocated to grades by matching the job description with the grade description (job slotting).	Simple to operate; standards of judgement when making comparisons are provided in the shape of the grade definitions.	Can be difficult to fit complex jobs into a grade without using over-elaborate grade definitions; the definitions tend to be so generalized that they are not much help in evaluating borderline cases or making comparisons between individual jobs; does not provide a defence in an equal value case.
Ranking	Non-analytical – whole job comparisons are made to place them in rank order.	Easy to apply and understand.	No defined standards of judgement; differences between jobs not measured; does not provide a defence in an equal value case.
Internal benchmarking	Jobs or roles are compared with benchmark jobs that have been allocated into grades on the basis of ranking or job classification and placed in whatever grade provides the closest match of jobs. The job descriptions may be analytical in the sense that they cover a number of standard and defined elements.	Simple to operate; facilitates direct comparisons, especially when the jobs have been analysed in terms of a set of common criteria.	Relies on a considerable amount of judgement and may simply perpetuate existing relativities; dependent on accurate job/role analysis; may not provide a defence in an equal value case.

Table 12.1 Comparison of job evaluation schemes (*continued*)

Scheme	Characteristics	Advantages	Disadvantages
Market pricing	Rates of pay are aligned to market rates – internal relativities are therefore determined by relativities in the marketplace. Not strictly a job evaluation scheme.	In line with the belief that 'a job is worth what the market says it is worth'. Ensures that pay is competitive.	Relies on accurate market rate information, which is not always available; relativities in the market may not properly reflect internal relativities; pay discrimination may be perpetuated.

listed in Table 12.1. The criteria for choice are that the selected job evaluation scheme should be:

- *Thorough in analysis and capable of impartial application* – the scheme should have been carefully constructed to ensure that its methodology is sound and appropriate in terms of all the jobs it has to cater for. It should also have been tested and trialled to check that it can be applied impartially to those jobs.
- *Appropriate* – it should cater for the particular demands made on all the jobs to be covered by the scheme.
- *Comprehensive* – the scheme should be applicable to all the jobs in the organization covering all categories of staff, and the factors, if used, should be common to all those jobs. There should therefore be a single scheme that can be used to assess relativities across different occupations or job families and to enable benchmarking to take place as required.
- *Transparent* – the processes used in the scheme from the initial role analysis through to the grading decision should be clear to all concerned.
- *Capable of contributing to the achievement of equal pay* – the scheme should enable discrimination to be identified, provide a defence in an equal pay claim, assist in an equal pay review and not be discriminatory in itself. If this is the key criterion, then the use of market pricing or a non-analytical scheme is ruled out.

Making the choice

The choice has to be made by reference to the advantages and disadvantages of the alternative schemes and the criteria set out above. But the advantages of using a recognized analytical approach that satisfies equal value requirements are considerable.

The e-reward 2002 survey of job evaluation (3) revealed that in those organizations with job evaluation there was an overwhelming preference (79 per cent) for analytical schemes. The most popular type of analytical scheme was point-factor rating, used in 70 per cent (89 per cent of all analytical schemes). The advantages of using a recognized analytical approach that satisfies equal value requirements appear to be overwhelming.

However, organizations such as the NHS are increasingly adopting point-factor methodology as the basic scheme but using analytical factor comparison in a supporting role to deal with large numbers of generic roles not covered in the original benchmarking exercise. Matching through analytical factor comparison can be used to allocate generic roles to grades as part of the normal job evaluation operating procedure to avoid having to resort to job evaluation in every case. This avoids the considerable time and energy required to use a points scheme for all jobs. Once the benchmark jobs have been evaluated with the point-factor scheme it is held in reserve to deal with new and unusual jobs, equal pay issues and equal pay reviews and appeals against gradings.

Stage 3: consider computerization

A final decision may be made at this stage either to computerize or not to computerize. Alternatively, the decision may be delayed until a paper-based job evaluation scheme has been designed and tested.

Computer-supported job evaluation uses computers to help directly with the job evaluation process. As described in Chapter 11 there are two types of systems: job analysis-based schemes and interactive schemes. Computer-assisted schemes save time and administrative effort and can result in more consistent evaluations. But they do not obviate the need for judgement in preparing the job data that are entered into the system, can be complex and difficult to introduce and operate and lack transparency. These difficulties may explain why only 28 per cent of respondents to the e-reward survey had them.

Stage 4: select an approach to the introduction of the scheme

There are three approaches to introducing a scheme:

1. Purchase a ready-made analytical scheme from a consultant (a 'proprietary brand'), which applies predetermined factors and a standard scoring model that

have been tried and tested across a range of organizations or designed specifically for a sector.

2. Develop a tailor-made scheme entirely in-house or with the aid of an external adviser.
3. Develop a hybrid scheme by adapting an existing scheme, usually one provided by consultants, to the particular needs of the organization.

Based on the views expressed by the respondents to the e-reward survey, the advantages and disadvantages of each approach are summarized in Table 12.2.

Stage 5: draw up a project plan

When drawing up a project plan it is first necessary to determine the time required. Clearly, this depends on the type of scheme, the resources available, including internal staff and outside help, and the size and complexity of the organization. An analytical estimating approach can be used. For example, the estimate of time for designing and applying a point-factor scheme and conducting an analytical job-matching exercise might be made in the following steps:

1. Develop and test scheme. This would include identifying and analysing test jobs, testing the scheme on those jobs and iterations as necessary.
2. Determine the number of benchmark jobs to be analysed and evaluated.
3. Establish the resources available to carry out analyses and evaluations. These will include job analysts and members of the job evaluation panel.
4. Calculate the time taken for analysis of the benchmark jobs. This would include getting questionnaires completed, conducting interviews and preparing the job analyses for the job evaluation panel.
5. Calculate the time for evaluating the benchmark jobs. An experienced job evaluation panel cannot be expected to evaluate more than six jobs a day properly. Initially, they may only evaluate two or three – they speed up when they become familiar with the scheme and can use previous evaluations to guide their decisions.
6. Estimate the time taken to design a grade structure, define grade or level profiles and obtain the approval of management to the proposal.
7. Allow time to prepare for an analytical matching exercise to grade all the jobs, including the benchmark jobs. This involves developing protocols for the matching process and briefing those involved.
8. Estimate the time taken to conduct the analytical matching exercise with line managers. It might be possible to match 20 or so jobs in a day but managers cannot usually be asked to spare more than half a day at a time once a week

Table 12.2 Pros and cons of different approaches to introduction

Approach	Advantages	Disadvantages
Ready-made (proprietary)	– Tried and tested, with an established reputation. – The consultants can draw on extensive experience of implementing similar schemes. – Does not require intensive design effort. – May link to pay database. – Computer support may be available as part of the package. – Consultancy may have international network for implementation.	– Factors may not suit the requirements, characteristics and culture of the organization. – May not lead to high level of internal ownership. – May be difficult to explain rationale for scoring and weighting. – Can lead to ongoing reliance on external provider. – May include elements or supporting processes that do not meet organizational requirements, eg lengthy job descriptions.
Tailor-made	– Reflects the values and language of the organization – focuses on what is important. – Fits the particular needs at the time. – Participative design process likely to lead to greater buy-in. – No ongoing reliance on external provider. – Can be aligned to competency framework.	– Needs investment of considerable time and resources to develop scheme. – Unless expertise is available in-house, needs external support through development process.
Hybrid	– Enables the standard scheme to be customized to a degree. – Draws on external experience, so saves on design time. – Gives a starting point to the design process, but gives opportunities to engage employees.	– Needs careful design input and implementation to avoid same risks as for proprietary scheme. – Need to avoid 'cherry-picking' factors or scheme design elements that do not logically hang together.

on job evaluation. The elapsed time taken depends on the number of managers involved and the number of job evaluation specialists available to facilitate the matching process.

9. Calculate the time to price the jobs and develop pay or zone ranges. A survey of market rates lasting, say, three months could take place during the earlier stages of the project. Time would need to be allowed to design the pay structure and gain approval for it.

10. Validate the gradings, review pay levels and deal with any inconsistencies.

Time would also be taken during the project in communicating to employees and formulating and agreeing assimilation and protection policies.

Assuming 50 benchmark jobs out of a total of 500, two analysts, one job evaluation panel, 10 managers and the use of a questionnaire-plus-interview method of job analysis, Table 12.3 is an example of how the time taken might be estimated.

The basic principles to follow in drawing up a project plan are:

- Allow plenty of time – it always takes longer than you think.
- Set up a structure for the project: a steering group to oversee it and make the key decisions; a project team with representatives from management, trade unions and other employees besides HR specialists and, where relevant, the outside consultants; and a project manager to carry out the detailed management of the project. Define the terms of reference and responsibilities of each of these bodies.
- Identify the key stages in the project – the events that have to take place and the activities required to make those events happen.
- Clarify any interdependencies between stages.
- Define the criteria to be used to assess whether satisfactory progress has been made.
- Identify the key decisions to be made.
- Identify the responsibilities for managing the project, conducting each stage, monitoring and reporting on progress, reviewing progress and making decisions.
- Remember when planning the project that a frequent major cause for delay is getting decisions agreed by steering groups or other authorities.
- Allocate a timescale for each stage.
- Set out when 'milestone' meetings will need to take place at which progress will be reviewed and decisions made.
- Draw up a bar chart as illustrated in Figure 12.2, supplemented where there are a number of interdependencies by a network as illustrated in Figure 12.3.

Table 12.3 Estimate of time taken for a job evaluation exercise

Activity	Minimum Days Taken	Maximum Days Taken	Minimum Elapsed Time in Weeks*	Maximum Elapsed Time in Weeks*
Formulate strategy	3	5	2	4
Develop and test scheme	40	60	15	30
Analyse and evaluate benchmark jobs	10	15	10	15
Develop and agree grade structure	3	5	4	8
Prepare for analytical matching	5	10	1	2
Conduct analytical matching	25	40	10	20
Price jobs and design pay structure	5	10	4	8
Validate gradings and deal with anomalies	10	20	4	8
Total	101	165	50	95

* The elapsed time allows for the fact that the work will be discontinuous and delays will occur for communications and consultation and obtaining approval.

Stage 6: appoint and brief the project team

The role of the project team is to be involved in the detailed conduct of the project: planning and reviewing progress and collectively developing and testing the scheme and evaluating jobs. Individual members may also act as job analysts, obtaining details of jobs as a basis for evaluation. The project team can evolve into a job evaluation panel that is concerned with the implementation and maintenance of job evaluation once the scheme has been designed.

Careful consideration should be given to the selection of the project team. It could consist of managers, the trade unions and other employees. In addition the project manager, HR staff associated with the project and outside consultants, if any, would be members. The team should be chaired by someone who is acceptable to all parties

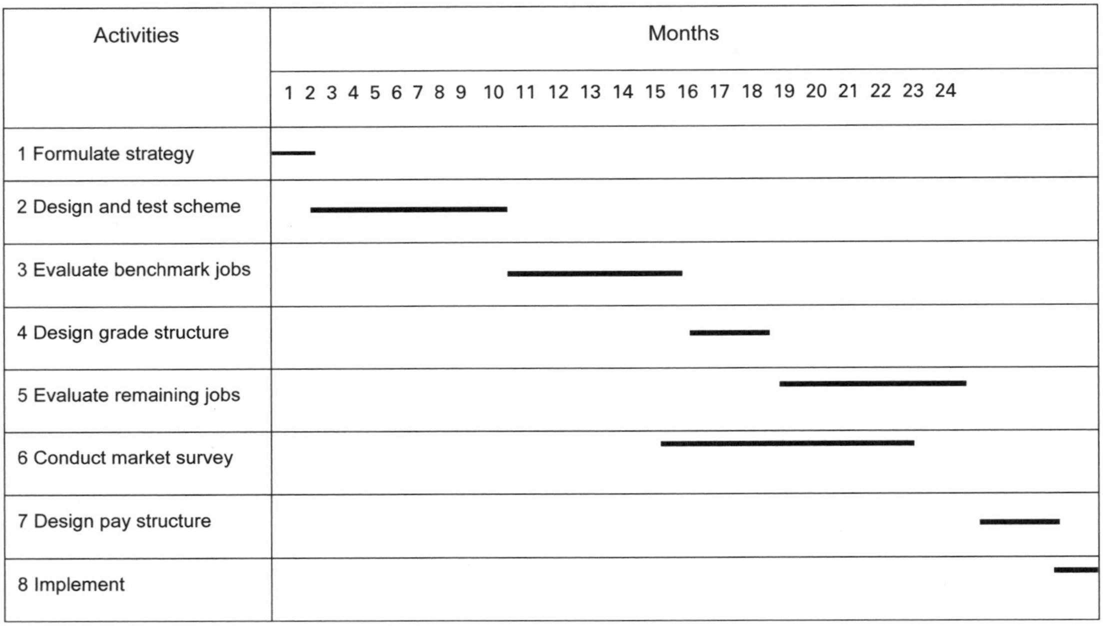

Activities	Months
	1 2 3 4 5 6 7 8 9 10 11 12 13 14 15 16 17 18 19 20 21 22 23 24
1 Formulate strategy	▬
2 Design and test scheme	▬▬▬▬▬
3 Evaluate benchmark jobs	▬▬▬▬▬
4 Design grade structure	▬▬
5 Evaluate remaining jobs	▬▬▬▬
6 Conduct market survey	▬▬▬▬▬
7 Design pay structure	▬▬
8 Implement	▬

Figure 12.2   Project plan bar chart

as being objective and capable. Terms of reference need to be drawn up and the team briefed on its duties.

Stage 7: develop and implement a communications strategy

A job evaluation exercise will create interest and concern amongst all those who will be affected by it. There will be expectations and fears that may or may not be reasonable. It is the job of the project team to manage these expectations and allay the fears by developing and implementing a communications programme.

DESIGNING A POINT-FACTOR JOB EVALUATION SCHEME

The steps required are set out in Figure 12.4.

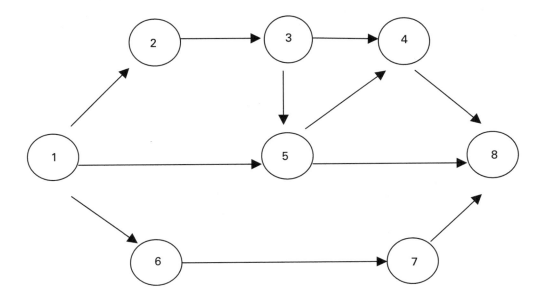

1 Formulate strategy
2 Design and test job evaluation scheme
3 Evaluate benchmark jobs
4 Evaluate remaining jobs
5 Design grade structure
6 Conduct market rate survey
7 Attach pay ranges to grade structure
8 Implement

Figure 12.3   A job evaluation project network

Step 1: identify and define the factors

Job evaluation factors are the characteristics or key elements of jobs that are used to analyse and evaluate them in an analytical job evaluation scheme. Although many of the job evaluation factors used in different organizations capture similar job elements (this is an area where there are some enduring truths), the task of identifying and agreeing factors can be challenging.

The following guidelines should be used when choosing factors:

1. The factors must be capable of identifying relevant and important differences between jobs that will support the creation of a rank order of the jobs to be covered by the scheme.

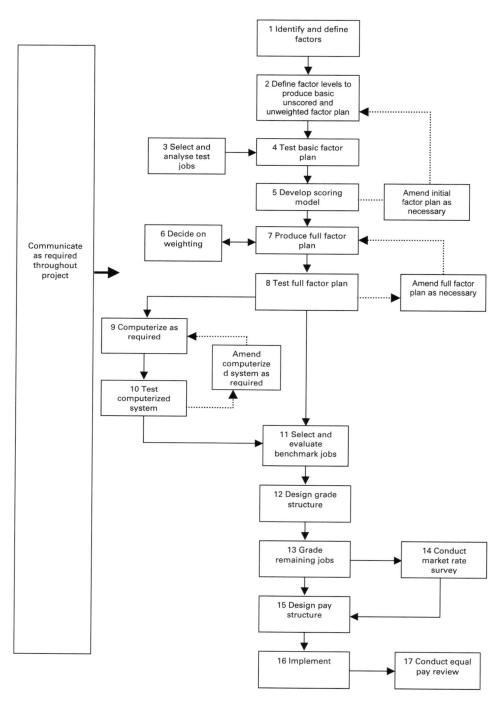

Figure 12.4 Point-factor scheme design sequence

2. The factors should between them measure all significant job features and should be of broadly comparable scope.
3. They should apply equally well to different types of work including specialists and generalists, lower-level and higher-level jobs, and not be biased in favour of one gender or group.
4. The whole range of jobs to be evaluated at all levels should be covered without favouring men or women, people belonging to a particular racial group, or any particular job or occupation.
5. Job features frequently found in jobs carried out by women should not be omitted, for example manual dexterity, interpersonal skills and 'caring' responsibilities.
6. Double-counting should be avoided, ie each factor must be independent of every other factor – the more factors (or sub-factors) in the plan, the higher the probability that double-counting will take place.
7. Elision or compression of more than one significant job feature under a single factor heading should be avoided. If important factors are compressed with others it means that they will probably be undervalued.
8. The factor definitions should be clear, relevant and understandable and written in a way that is meaningful to those who will use the scheme.
9. The factors should be acceptable to those who will be covered by the scheme.
10. The choice should not lead to discrimination on the grounds of gender, race or disability or for any other reason. The scheme should fairly measure features of female-dominated jobs as well as male-dominated jobs. Experience should not be included as a factor because it may prejudice the evaluation of jobs held mainly be females, who may not have had the same opportunity to obtain experience as men. The same principle applies to education or qualifications as stand-alone factors.

The e-reward survey established that the most frequently used factors by the respondents with analytical schemes were:

1. knowledge and skill;
2. communications and contacts;
3. judgement and decision making;
4. impact;
5. people management;
6. freedom to act;
7. working environment;
8. responsibility for financial resources.

The following sources of information and approaches to support the development of factors are available.

Reviewing internal strategy/business documents

Looking through existing written materials such as organization or human resources strategy documents can give an insight into the current values and language.

Reviewing people-related frameworks or processes

In the past, job evaluation criteria were not necessarily linked to other human resources processes or frameworks. However, many organizations have now accepted the need to adopt a more coherent approach by applying the organization's values and language across related processes. Reviewing existing job descriptions may be a place to start. The most obvious potential link is with an organization's competency framework, as many of the concepts reflected in competencies are similar to job evaluation criteria, albeit expressed in behavioural or skills-based language. The extent to which a link can be made with an existing competency framework will depend on how the competency framework has been defined. The desirability of achieving a degree of linkage was a finding from the e-reward survey, and was one of the main reasons for companies favouring a tailor-made scheme.

Interviews with line managers and other stakeholders

Discussions with key managers can help to get an early perspective on the senior management priorities for the scheme. This group is most likely to have a view about the future demands on the organization and what work will be valued. Early senior manager involvement can also help to dispel myths and misconceptions about job evaluation, and will support the overall communications process – particularly if the managers concerned are those who will later be responsible for approving the scheme.

Focus groups

Structured meetings with employees can be a good way of understanding what aspects of jobs are currently valued and what people think are the most important. Such meetings can also contribute to achieving better involvement and communications. Because employees may be unfamiliar with job evaluation concepts, the agenda will normally need to cover an overview of what job evaluation is, the rationale for introducing job evaluation, what factors are, and what makes a 'good' factor. Views can be explored on possible factors. Focus groups can also be used to obtain the views of employees about how the scheme should be communicated.

Focus groups can be particularly useful for organizations with geographically or functionally diverse constituencies or for developing sector-wide schemes. In developing the further education scheme, focus groups were run in about a dozen colleges around the country. They were selected to represent different types of institution as well as geographic diversity. The focus groups generated a long list of possible factor headings, which showed a high degree of consistency across the institutions. This input was clustered into 11 main groups, which became the factors.

Consideration should also be given to whether input from other stakeholders is necessary. Trade unions or other employee representatives should be involved at an early stage. A voluntary organization may want to include volunteers in focus groups or to obtain the views of key trustees.

Project team input

The project team can explore possible factors in a number of ways, for example:

- Open discussion – drawing on the inputs that are available to the team from other sources.
- Selecting a number of jobs/roles and exploring the differences between them – what makes one 'bigger' or 'smaller' than another. This can be done informally or through a process such as whole job ranking or paired comparison.
- Using an existing database or list of common factor headings, posting these up on a flipchart and drawing out and clustering the job dimensions that seem most relevant to the organization. If a consultant is being used, this exercise is likely to use headings from his or her factor database.

Step 2: define factor levels to produce the basic factor plan

The factor plan is the key job evaluation document. It guides evaluators on making decisions about the levels of demand and responsibility present in a job. The basic factor plan defines the levels within each of the selected factors. The full factor plan attaches points scores to the levels.

A decision has to be made on the number of levels (often four, five, six or seven), which has to reflect the range of responsibilities and demands in the jobs covered by the scheme. The starting point can be an analysis of what would characterize the highest or lowest level for each factor and how these should be described. For example, the highest level in a judgement and decision-making factor could be defined as: 'Deals with widely differing problems calling for extreme clarity of thought in assessing conflicting information and balancing the risks associated with possible solutions. Additionally, one of the main requirements of the role may be to develop fundamentally new strategies and approaches.' The lowest level could be defined as: 'The work is well defined and relatively few new situations are encountered. The causes of problems are readily identifiable and can be dealt with easily.'

It might then be decided that there should be three levels between the highest and lowest level on the basis that this truly reflects the graduation in responsibilities or demands. The outcome would then be the definition of the factor and each of the five levels illustrated in Table 12.4. This process is repeated for each factor.

The following guidelines should be used in defining levels:

1. Each level should be defined as clearly as possible to help evaluators make 'best fit' decisions.
2. The levels should cover the whole range of demands in this factor that are likely to arise in the jobs with which the evaluation scheme is concerned.
3. The link between the content of level definitions should be related specifically to the definition of the factor concerned and should not overlap with other factors.
4. There should be uniform progression in the definitions level by level from the lowest to the highest level. There should be no gaps or undefined intermediate levels that might lead to evaluators finding it difficult to be confident about the allocation of a level of demand.
5. The factor levels should represent clear and recognizable steps in demand.
6. The levels should be defined in absolute, not relative, terms. So far as possible any dimensions should be defined. They should not rely upon a succession of undefined comparatives, eg small, medium, large.
7. Each level definition should stand on its own. Level definitions should not be defined by reference to a lower or higher level, ie it is insufficient to define a level in words to the effect that it is a higher (or lower) version of an adjacent level.

Step 3: select and analyse test jobs

A small representative sample of jobs should be identified to test the basic factor plan. The proportion depends on the size and complexity of the organization but typically it is about 10–15 per cent of the jobs to be covered. These are then analysed in terms of the factors. This generally means using a questionnaire followed up by an interview that will obtain information about the overall purpose of the job, the main activities carried out, the demands made by the job and the responsibilities involved with regard to each factor.

Table 12.4 Definition of a factor and the five levels

Judgement and decision making: The requirement to exercise judgement in making decisions and solving problems, including the degree to which the work involves choice of action or creativity.

1 The work is well defined and relatively few new situations are encountered. The causes of problems are readily identifiable and can be dealt with easily.

2 Evaluation of information is required to deal with occasional new problems and situations and to decide on a course of action from known alternatives. Occasionally required to participate in the modification of existing procedures and practices.

3 Exercises discriminating judgement in dealing with relatively new or unusual problems where a wide range of information has to be considered and the courses of action are not obvious. May fairly often be involved in devising new solutions.

4 Frequently exercises independent judgement when faced with unusual problems and situations where no policy guidelines or precedents are available. May also frequently be responsible for devising new strategies and approaches that require the use of imagination and ingenuity.

5 Deals with widely differing problems calling for extreme clarity of thought in assessing conflicting information and balancing the risks associated with possible solutions. Additionally, one of the main requirements of the role may be to develop fundamentally new strategies and approaches.

Step 4: test the basic factor plan

No one ever gets the definitions of factors and their levels right first time. The draft definitions must be tested on actual jobs.

The aim of this initial test is to check on the extent to which:

- the factors are appropriate;
- the factors cover all aspects of the jobs to be evaluated;
- the factors are non-discriminatory;
- the factors avoid double-counting and are not compressed unduly;
- level definitions are worded clearly, graduated properly and cover the whole range of demands applicable to the jobs to be evaluated so that they provide good

guidance on the allocation of factor levels to evaluators and thus enable consistent evaluations to be made.

A more comprehensive test should be carried out later when the full factor plan with scoring systems and weightings has been devised.

Step 5: develop a scoring model

The aim is to design a point-factor scheme that will operate fairly and consistently to produce a rank order of jobs, based on the total points score for each job. Each level in the factor plan has to be allocated a points value so that there is a scoring progression from the lowest to the highest level.

A decision needs to be made on how to set the scoring progression within each factor. There are two methods: 1) the 'arithmetic' or linear approach assumes that there are consistent step differences between factor levels, eg a four-level factor might be scored 1,2,3,4; 2) alternatively, geometric scoring assumes that there are progressively larger score differences at each successive level in the hierarchy to reflect progressive increases in responsibility. Thus the levels might be scored 1,2,4,8 rather than 1,2,3,4. This increases the scoring differentiation between higher-level jobs. The rank order produced by either of these methods is unlikely to differ much, but senior managers sometimes like to think that there should be larger gaps between levels at their end of the scale. It can also indicate clearer breaks between grades when it comes to designing the structure as described below.

It is best to allocate a single finite score for each level because giving a choice from a range of scores can complicate evaluations. If it is decided that there should be some choice, this should be as simple as possible, for example low, standard and high.

Step 6: decide on the factor weighting

Weighting is the process of attaching more importance to some factors than others. There are two approaches: 1) *explicit weighting*, by increasing the maximum points available for what are regarded as more important factors; and 2) *implicit weighting*, which takes place when some factors have more levels than others but the same scoring progression per level exists as in the other factors. The factors with more levels have more points available to them and have therefore been implicitly weighted.

The number and choice of factors may also implicitly weight a scheme. If two factors that would normally be treated as being of equal importance are compressed into one and the scoring has not been increased proportionately, then implicit weighting of that combined factor has taken place, ie it is undervalued in terms of its significance.

Most job evaluation factor plans use explicit weighting because it accords with the belief that some factors are more important than others. Implicit weighting is more likely to take place when there is a large number of factors – 10 or more – and the impact of explicitly weighting any factors is less (unless the weighting is so disproportionate that the non-weighted factors become immaterial).

There should be a rationale for the scoring and weighting system, eg relative value of factors to the organization, agreed relative values – it should not just give the answers people want.

Step 7: produce the full factor plan

The outcome of Steps 5 and 6 is a draft fully scored and weighted factor plan, which is tested in Step 8.

Step 8: test the full factor plan

The full factor plan is tested on the same jobs used in the initial test of the draft factors. Further jobs may be added to extend the range of the test. Each test job is evaluated and scored by the project team and ranked according to the total score. The project team then considers the extent to which it is believed the rank order is valid in the sense that the evaluations correctly indicate relative job size. There is no single, simple test that will establish the validity of a factor plan. The methods available are as follows:

1. *Reference ranking* – the team compares the ranking produced by the job evaluation with the rank order produced by a ranking exercise. The technique of paired comparison (see Chapter 11) may be used to guide the ranking process.
2. *Hierarchy comparisons* – the rank order produced by the test is compared with the existing organizational hierarchy and any obvious discrepancies are investigated.
3. *External market test* – the internal rank order is compared with that existing in comparable jobs elsewhere. But this may replicate existing inequities between male and female jobs.
4. *The 'felt-fair test'* – the rank order produced by the test is compared with what the job evaluation panel 'feels' is the fair and therefore appropriate ranking, and discrepancies are identified. This is dangerous because it is liable simply to reproduce existing prejudices. Inevitably, however, a 'felt-fair' approach will be adopted by some of those reviewing the test. It is therefore necessary to be particularly alert to the possibility of prejudgements affecting opinions and to challenge any apparent move in that direction. The first three tests can be used for this purpose.

Step 9: computerize

The steps set out above will produce a paper-based scheme, which is the most common approach. But full computerization as described earlier can offer many advantages including greater consistency, speed and the elimination of much of the paperwork.

Computer-assisted schemes use software provided by suppliers but the system itself is derived from the paper-based scheme devised by the methods set out above. If they are adopted, the job evaluation project team or panel will not be required to spend time carrying out detailed paper evaluations but it is necessary to set up a review panel that can validate and agree the outcomes of the computerized process. No one likes to feel that a decision about their grade has been made by a computer on its own, and hard lessons have been learnt by organizations that have ended up with fully automated but unacceptable systems.

Step 10: test the computerized scheme

If the computerized scheme has been derived from a paper-based scheme, it is necessary to test it on the same jobs used to test the paper scheme to establish that similar results will be produced.

Step 11: select and evaluate benchmark jobs

Benchmark jobs are a sample of typical jobs representing the different occupations and levels in the organization and also representing jobs held mainly by women or members of particular racial groups. When evaluated, the benchmark jobs provide the basis for designing the grade structure. The jobs used for tests can become benchmark jobs but it is often advisable to extend the number to provide a satisfactory basis for grading. The proportion of distinct jobs varies according to the complexity and size of the organization. Even in a simple structure it will be 10 per cent or more and it could be much higher in some organizations (30 per cent or more).

Step 12: design the grade structure

There is a choice amongst the grade structures described in Chapter 17. The advantages and disadvantages of the various options and methods of structure design are set out in Chapter 18.

Step 13: grade the remaining jobs

If a reasonable sample of benchmark posts has been used, the remaining jobs can be graded by a process of analytical matching rather than evaluating each job in full.

Step 14: conduct a market rate survey

Information on market rates for all or a selection of the benchmark jobs is required as the basis for the design of a pay structure (see Chapter 15).

Step 15: design the pay structure

Pay ranges are attached to the grade structure by reference to current actual salaries. Account is taken of the outcome of a market survey to ensure that rates of pay are competitive. The cost of implementation may be calculated at this stage. Costs arise because, while it is the usual policy not immediately to reduce anyone's pay if they are over-graded, those who are under-graded will have their pay brought up to the minimum of their new grade. The scale of cost depends on the number of anomalies (ie under-gradings) in existence before the job evaluation exercise, but it can be 4–5 per cent of payroll. The fewer the grades, the fewer the anomalies and therefore the lower the cost, although limiting the number of grades (eg broad-banding) can create equal pay problems.

Step 16: implement

Implementation involves communicating the outcome and implications of the exercise. It will also involve the implementation of assimilation policies that provide guidance on where jobs should be allocated in the structure and how to deal with those who have been 'green-circled', ie are now paid below the minimum for their new grade. The basis upon which the pay of those who have been 'red-circled' because they are paid more than the upper limit of their new grade (protection policy) will also have to be determined. It is advisable to agree assimilation and protection policies well before implementation.

Step 17: conduct an equal pay review

An equal pay review as described in Chapter 14 can be related to the outcome of a job evaluation and grade and pay structure design programme as described above. Its aims would be to:

● establish whether there are pay inequities arising because of gender, race or disability;
● analyse in more detail the nature of any inequities;
● analyse the factors creating inequities and diagnose the cause or causes;
● determine what action is required to deal with any inequities revealed by the analysis and diagnosis.

DESIGNING A JOB CLASSIFICATION SCHEME

The steps required to design a job classification scheme are:

1. *Decide on the number of grades required.* This is sometimes an a priori decision that is made empirically by reference to the existing hierarchy or a belief that the present number of grades should be reduced to a more manageable number, say from 14 to 8. A less judgemental approach is to base the decision on a ranking of benchmark posts, possibly using paired comparisons and an analysis of the clustering of jobs based on the identification of common characteristics. The ranked jobs are then divided into grades according to views on the number of the distinct levels of responsibility that need to be differentiated in terms of pay and, possibly, benefits provision. In either case, the number may be amended at a later stage if it is shown to be inappropriate.

2. *Define the grades.* The hierarchy of grade definitions could consist of overall statements such as the following: '*Grade 1* – the work involves standard routines such as maintaining straightforward record systems or operating simple office equipment. Close supervision is exercised or the work is easily controlled by self-checking. Tasks are clearly defined and the choice of action is within narrow limits. Contacts are limited to routine exchanges of information with colleagues.'

   This example does in fact describe the job under a number of headings covering skill requirements, responsibility and contacts with others. These could be expanded and form an analytical grade definition or profile that would facilitate the use of analytical matching if jobs were described under the same headings and compared, factor by factor. Thus job classification becomes more analytical.

   It is also possible to define the grade by reference to the jobs placed within it and evaluation is carried out by comparing the role profile of those jobs with a role profile of the job to be evaluated, again under analytical headings.

3. *Grade the jobs.* Allocate jobs to grades by overall 'whole job' comparisons between a job description and the grade definition or through analytical matching.

4. *Create a pay structure.* Attach pay brackets to the grade structure by reference to market rate data.

5. *Implement.* Anomalies will have to be dealt with but this approach can often reduce the problems of assimilation and protection.

DEVELOPING AN ANALYTICAL MATCHING SCHEME

Analytical matching takes place in the form of role to grade/level matching, role to benchmark role matching or a combination of the two.

The steps required to develop role to a grade/level profile matching scheme are:

1. *Identify and define the analytical factors.* These can be the factors used in a point-factor scheme or, if analytical matching is to be used as a stand-alone approach, the decisions on the factors can be made as described earlier in this chapter. If competencies are going to be a major criterion in defining levels in the grade structure then reference should be made to any existing competency frameworks.

2. *Decide on the grade structure.* This may have already been designed following the initial benchmarking exercise when developing a point-factor scheme. If not, decisions on the grade structure should be made along the lines suggested in Chapter 18. These will initially cover whether the structure should be a single one covering all jobs or whether it should be a career or job grade and pay structure (see Chapter 17). A decision will also have to be made on the provisional number of bands or grades (this number may be amended when the grade definition process takes place).

3. *Define grade, band or level profiles.* The definitions may be based on the job evaluation factors in a point-factor scheme or a selection of them. In job and career family structures, they may refer to levels of competency and accountability. The least desirable but easiest way of producing definitions is simply to draw up the grade profiles on the basis of assumptions about the characteristics of any jobs that would be placed in the various levels. An alternative but still questionable approach is to select benchmark jobs covering all levels, analyse and rank them, allocate them to grades on a judgemental (felt-fair) basis and then prepare grade profiles by reference to the analyses of the benchmark jobs. The preferable method is to refer to the analyses of benchmark jobs that have already been graded following a point-factor evaluation and distil these to produce a generic definition. Further information on the definition of grade or level profiles is given in Chapter 18.

   The career band profiles used by Friends Provident Insurance are shown in Figure 12.5.

4. *Develop a matching protocol.* A protocol or guidelines on matching will be necessary. These should cover the formation and role of a matching panel, the documentation to be made available to it and the procedure it should follow. The rules should specify:
   - what constitutes a perfect profile match, ie all the factors in the role profile match all the factors in the grade profile;

Career band A *Job example: clerical and administrative staff*	
Technical knowledge/business experience and qualifications	Developing a knowledge of one or more key areas within the function or business unit, together with an understanding of the systems utilized. Ensures that technical information is appropriately presented and correct.
Problem solving	Solves problems by following well-defined procedures and precedents. Will consult with more experienced colleagues on more difficult or novel situations.
Leadership	Takes responsibility for management of own workload, delivering against performance standards and individual/team objectives.
Communication/influence	Communicates information clearly and concisely, applying standards of common courtesy to all contacts.

Career band B *Job example: customer services consultant*	
Technical knowledge/business experience and qualifications	Demonstrates a good understanding of a range of non-standard processes, procedures and systems to be utilized in carrying out responsibilities. Is likely to have two or more years' relevant experience working within the function or business unit or have gained relevant experience elsewhere. May be starting to study for specific technical exams, eg FPC or ACII.
Problem solving	Works within procedures and precedents determining solutions from a number of appropriate alternatives.
Leadership	Offers guidance and technical support to less experienced members of the team.
Communication/influence	Applies developed communication skills in effectively handling more challenging contacts.

Career band C *Job example: customer services team leader*	
Technical knowledge/business experience and qualifications	Fully conversant with the procedures, policies and systems applied within the function or business unit, having gained relevant experience over a period of five or more years. Demonstrates a comprehensive understanding of one or more well-defined areas for which they will provide technical leadership. Is developing an understanding of the relationship between different subject areas/business units. Is likely to have gained a qualification in a technical subject in a relevant discipline.
Problem solving	Applies specialist knowledge of own area in making judgements based on the analysis of factual information in straightforward situations.
Leadership	Plans and coordinates the work of the team and/or provides technical leadership, eg through delivery of on-the-job training, quality audits or application of developed specialist skills and knowledge.
Communication/influence	Explains technical information clearly and effectively, adopting a style of communication to fit differing levels of audience understanding. Is able to persuade colleagues and gain commitment to new ideas or approaches by expressing own views confidently and logically.

Figure 12.5 Friends Provident career band profiles

Career Band D *Job examples: customer services team manager, analyst, programmer*	
Technical knowledge/business experience and qualifications	Is able to apply and consolidate specialist skills and knowledge gained over a period of eight or more years' relevant experience to ensure essential procedures are followed and standards maintained. Demonstrates an understanding of the relationship between different subject areas and applies this knowledge in delivering cross-functional support, projects or advice. As a professional entrant to the business, will be developing professional skills through exam success and be increasing their contribution to the business.
Problem solving	Uses analytical skills and evaluative judgement, based on the analysis of factual and qualitative information to solve problems of a non-routine or more complex nature. Will be guided by precedents.
Leadership	In a team management role will be handling staff management issues including recruitment, resource management, training, coaching and performance management, and playing a leading role in determining salary recommendations for team members. Alternatively, will be a technical specialist with well-developed technical skills and specialist knowledge.
Communication/influence	Demonstrates strong verbal and written communication skills in influencing the outcome of decisions. Involves appropriate contacts in developing the final solution.

Figure 12.5 *Continued*

- the number of matches required of individual factors to indicate that a profile match is justified, for example 6 out of 10; but it is usual to restrict the mismatches allowed to fairly small variations – if there are any large ones, the match would be invalidated (this is easier when profiles include job evaluation ratings as in the NHS);
- any factors that *must* match for there to be a profile match, for example it may be decided that there must be a match for a factor covering knowledge and skills.

The NHS protocol requires matching panels to record the profile level in the profile level column of the matching form and the proposed level for the job in the job level column, referring to the job evaluation scheme factor levels only when the job evaluation levels do not appear to match the profile level(s), in order to determine the appropriate level. Where the job level is the same as the profile level or within the profile range, evaluators are required to mark M (for match) in the match column. Where it is one level higher or lower than the profile level or range, they mark V (for variation) in the match column. Where the job level is more than one level higher or lower than the profile level or range, they mark NM (no match). The possible outcomes are: 1) if all factor levels are within the range specified on the profile, this is a perfect profile match; and 2) if most factor levels match, but there are a small number of variations, there may still be a band match if *all* the following conditions apply:

 - the variations are of *not more* than one level above or below the profile level or range; *and*
 - the variations do *not* relate to the knowledge or freedom to act factors (variations in these factors are indicative of a different profile and/or band); *and*
 - the variations do not apply to more than *five* factors (multiple variations are indicative of a different profile or the need for a local evaluation); *and*
 - the score variations do not take the job over a grade boundary.

If there are any NM variations in the match column, there is no match.

5. *Test the matching procedure.* It is essential to test the grade profiles and the matching protocol by preparing a representative set of individual role profiles using the same format of factors and then matching the latter to the former. Any difficulties in doing this and achieving a sensible result, or any problems with the matching rules, will indicate what changes need to be made to the grade profiles.

6. *Prepare role profiles for matching.* These will take account of any lessons learnt from the test.

7. *Train the matching panel.* The panel should be trained in the matching process and the use of the protocols using real examples.

DEVELOPING MANAGEMENT PROCEDURES

The management procedures should cover setting up a job evaluation or job-matching panel, conducting reviews of evaluations and maintenance.

Job evaluation panel

A job evaluation panel should be set up to manage and maintain job evaluation, either by conducting 'paper' evaluations or by reviewing the outcomes of computerized job evaluations. The panel can also operate as a 'matching' panel as described above. The design team may be converted into a panel but it will also be necessary to ensure that additional job evaluators are trained so that substitutes are available. The training should include sitting in on design team meetings. It is important to include training in what needs to be done to avoid biased evaluations.

Evaluation appeals and reviews

Employees should be given the right to appeal against evaluations by requesting a review of the decisions made by the design team or job evaluation panel. Managers can also ask for an evaluation to be reviewed. A formal evaluation appeal and review procedure should be prepared, agreed and issued before any evaluation results are made known. An appeal takes place when the job is first allocated to a grade and that grade is made known to the parties concerned. A review takes place when the content of a job changes (or is about to change) sufficiently to place doubt on the existing grading of that job.

Appeals against reviews of the initial evaluations carried out by the design team should be conducted by a specially convened appeals review group. This might be composed of two members of the original design team plus two additional trained evaluators who were not associated with the original decision and an independent chair. A request for the re-evaluation of a job should be dealt with by the job evaluation panel.

When dealing with an appeal against the original evaluations of the design team the stages are typically as follows:

1. The employee discusses his or her concern with the line manager, who will decide whether or not to support the review.
2. The employee, supported if appropriate by the line manager, submits his or her case for a grading review.
3. The manager responsible for job evaluation should examine the request, add notes as necessary and submit it to the review group together with all available details of the original evaluation. If the request is based on a comparison with another job, details of that evaluation should also be provided.
4. The review group should examine the documents and decide whether a re-evaluation is justified. If the request is based on the way job information has been interpreted rather than on matters of fact the review group should try to establish why this was not identified during the original evaluation or review.
5. The review group should re-evaluate the job. If the review group believes that a request based on a comparison with another job is potentially valid but that it is the comparator job that was wrongly evaluated, it should re-evaluate both jobs. The re-evaluation process should be the same as for the original evaluation. There should be no right of appeal to the review group but employees could be allowed to take up the case as a grievance through the normal grievance procedure.

A request for the re-evaluation of a job should be dealt with by the job evaluation panel. This should be supported by evidence of changes in the role that indicate for consideration by the panel why either the manager, the employee or both believe that regrading is appropriate.

INTRODUCING JOB EVALUATION

The following advice on introducing job evaluation was given by respondents to the e-reward survey:

- 'Overkill communication.'
- 'Better and more open communications of how the process works and why we are using it.'
- 'Need greater involvement of management to ensure commitment – job evaluation as "business-owned" system rather than "HR-owned".'
- 'Involvement and collaboration at an early stage of all trade unions, senior managers and a cross-section of staff.'
- 'Managers need to understand more about the principles of job evaluation. Pay and grading issues are often confused.'
- 'The business leaders should have been involved more from the outset to ensure their buy-in.'
- 'Widen pool of trained evaluators.'
- 'Set more realistic timescales to manage employee expectations.'
- 'It should be run like a project with specific success criteria and regular reviews and not be afraid to amend it as appropriate rather than letting the job evaluation system run the organization.'
- 'Prepare the technical work within HR. Present to senior managers with a good description of the advantages to them (some real-life examples they can relate to). Then communicate the project to the whole organization (a specific project team needs to be working on the plan). Give information on different media to the employees.'
- 'The scheme was introduced through a rigorous process of pilot testing and cascaded throughout the firm by a range of means. This worked well.'

MAINTAINING A JOB EVALUATION SCHEME

The following advice on maintaining job evaluation was provided by respondents to the e-reward survey:

- 'All systems should be constantly monitored and reviewed to ensure that they continue to meet the scheme requirements. Full review should be introduced in three/five years.'

- 'Regular meetings between human resources, unions and managers on outcomes so that the bigger picture can be reviewed. Yearly reviews of the scheme to ensure that it is fit for the purpose and amend accordingly.'
- 'Adequate training for those operating the scheme.'
- 'Ensure trained facilitators do not get rusty through lack of opportunity to evaluate jobs.'
- 'Computerize so that managers can enter their own information, and receive a job evaluation, job description, competency listing and costing without any need to refer to HR.'
- 'Find a less time-consuming way of managing it; see how computers can help.'
- 'Need to communicate with employees more.'
- 'More line accountability and involvement.'
- 'Make managers accountable for the roles that they manage. If a role that reports to them is not reflected in the classification programme, make sure that it is truly unique and that suitable benchmark jobs exist in the marketplace.'
- 'Need to ensure that we are not supporting managers abdicating their responsibility for making decisions about gradings etc.'
- 'Make it clear what the purpose is – "equal pay for work of equal value" rather than an upgrading scheme. To have specific times of the year when job evaluation is done and verified, rather than whenever someone feels like it.'
- 'Tighter policing and clearer rationale for a new job evaluation to take place.'
- 'More clarity on job families and job titles in grade groups. More attention by managers to keeping job profiles updated.'
- 'Ensure jobs are re-evaluated more frequently.'
- 'Have better systems for maintaining scheme – central system linked to job profiles etc.'

REFERENCES

1   Zingheim, PK and Schuster, JR (2002) Pay changes going forward, *Compensation and Benefits Review*, **34** (4), pp 48–53

2   Heneman, RL and LeBlanc, PV (2002) Developing a more relevant and competitive approach for valuing knowledge work, *Compensation and Benefits Review*, **34** (4), pp 43–47

3   e-reward (2002) *Survey of Job Evaluation*, e-reward.co.uk, Stockport

13

Equal pay for work of equal value

This chapter deals with: 1) why discrimination takes place; 2) the legislation concerning equal pay for work of equal value; 3) what organizations can do to avoid discrimination in their job evaluation practices to avoid gender bias; and 4) how pay structures can discriminate. The chapter focuses on equal pay for women, but pay discrimination can take place because of race, disability or age, and equal pay reviews as described in Chapter 14 need to consider these potential areas of inequality.

WHY DISCRIMINATION TAKES PLACE

As Robert Elliott (1) has stated: 'Discrimination arises when equals are treated unequally.' Historically, it has been generally accepted by men in a man's world that women's place was in the home, unless they were needed to carry out menial and therefore underpaid jobs. Women's work has been undervalued because of the low rates of pay. It has been a vicious circle. Prior to the Equal Pay Act in 1970, collective agreements tended to have only one rate of pay for women workers, with no differentiation between grades of work or levels of skill.

The entry of women into the professions in the 19th century and pressures for women's rights in the 20th heralded a very gradual change in this climate of discrimination. But it needed the Treaty of Rome (1957), Article 119 of which enshrined the principle of equal pay for equal work, to stimulate anti-discriminatory law in the United Kingdom. The first British legislation was the Equal Pay Act of 1970, amended by the Equal Pay Amendment Regulations in 1983.

The incidence of discrimination

Discrimination in the determination of the relative rates of pay for men and women may not be so blatant now as it was before 1975, when the 1970 Equal Pay Act came into force, but there is still a significant gap nationally between the earnings of men and women. The Government's Annual Survey of Hours and Earnings revealed that in 2006 the gap between the mean earnings of men and women (the gender pay gap) was 17.2 per cent, the same as the 2005 figure.

Causes of the gender pay gap

The 2001 research conducted by the National Institute of Economic and Social Research (NIESR) (2) into the causes of the gender pay gap identified the following five key factors:

1. *Human capital differences*, ie differences in educational levels and work experience. Historical differences in the levels of qualifications held by men and women have contributed to the pay gap. Women are still more likely than men to have breaks from paid work to care for children and other dependants. These breaks impact on women's level of work experience, which in turn impacts on their pay rates.
2. *Part-time working* – the pay gap between women's part-time hourly earnings and men's full-time hourly earnings is particularly large and, because so many women work part time, this is a major contributor to the gender pay gap. Some of this gap is due to part-time workers having lower levels of qualifications and less work experience. However, it is also due to part-time work being concentrated in less well-paid occupations.
3. *Travel patterns* – on average women spend less time commuting than men. This may be because of time constraints due to balancing work and caring responsibilities. This can impact on women's work in two ways: a smaller selection of jobs to choose from and/or lots of women wanting work in the same location (ie near to or where they live), which leads to lower wages for these jobs.
4. *Occupational segregation* – women's work is highly concentrated in certain occupations (60 per cent of working women work in just 10 occupations). And these occupations that are female-dominated are often the lowest-paid. In addition,

women are still under-represented in the higher-paid jobs within occupations – the 'glass ceiling' effect.

5. *Workplace segregation* – at the level of individual workplaces, high concentrations of female employees are associated with relatively low rates of pay. And higher levels of part-time working are associated with lower rates of pay, even after other factors have been taken into account.

Other factors that affect the gender pay gap include: job grading practices, appraisal systems, reward systems, retention measures and pay determination practices. In the latter case, pay levels set entirely on the basis of external comparisons (market rates) can lead to unequal pay for women within the organization because external rates may simply reflect the pay inequities already existing in the labour market.

The design and operation of pay structures can contribute to maintaining or even enlarging the pay gap. For example, experienced men with skills that, because of unequal opportunities, women do not have to the same extent may be started at higher rates of pay within a pay range for the job. Extended pay ranges, especially where progression is based on length of service, will favour men, who are much less likely than women to have career breaks and may therefore progress further and faster. The assimilation of men on their present higher rates of pay in the upper reaches of new pay ranges may leave women behind, and women may take a long time to catch up if they ever do. Broad-banded pay structures as described in Chapter 17 can also lead to discrimination

It is noteworthy that none of the key factors identified by the NIESR research refers specifically to pay inequities as a cause of the gender pay gap. Indeed, Diana Kingsmill, author of the 2001 *Review of Women's Employment and Pay* (3), commented that: 'Unlawful wage inequality – the occurrence of unequal pay… does not appear to be so commonplace as the 18% headline gap would suggest.' This opinion seems to be backed up in part by the report of the 2001 Equal Pay Task Force (4) to the Equal Opportunities Commission (EOC). The Task Force stated that, in their view, pay discrimination contributed to 25 per cent to 50 per cent of the pay gap – a wide range that seems to be a matter of opinion rather than evidence.

However, the Kingsmill Review focused mainly on the other factors creating the pay gap, and Diana Kingsmill commented that: 'Time and time again I have been confronted with data demonstrating that women are clustered towards the bottom of organizational hierarchies while men are clustered towards the top. This distribution clearly has a profound impact on the pay gap.'

The better use of human capital and the provision of equal opportunities for women are therefore important ways of reducing the pay gap. But this does not detract from the necessity of dealing with pay inequities. The rest of this chapter therefore concentrates on the equal pay legislation affecting pay policy and practice and how information on the incidence of unequal pay can be identified by equal pay audits as a basis for initiating corrective action.

THE LEGAL FRAMEWORK

The equal-pay-for-work-of-equal-value legal framework is based on the provisions of European legislation, the 1970 Equal Pay Act as amended by the Equal Pay (Amendment) Regulations 1983, plus the case law. The legislation essentially provides that pay differences are allowable only if the reason for them is not related to the sex of the job holder. The Act and its amendment are implemented through employment tribunals. The Employment Act 2002 provided for the use of equal pay questionnaires.

The same principles of fairness and equity of course apply to other potential areas of discrimination because of race, religion, disability or age that results in pay inequities.

European legislation

Article 119 of the EC founding Treaty of Rome of 1957 (now subsumed and expanded as Article 142 of the Treaty of Maastricht) stated that men and women should receive equal pay for equal work – in order to achieve what is often described as a 'level playing field' in terms of wages. Article 119 was extended by the Equal Pay Directive of 1975, which stated that:

● men and women should receive equal pay for work of equal value;
● job classification systems (which is Euro-English for any formal grading system and thus encompasses job evaluation schemes) should be fair and non-discriminatory;
● EC member states should take steps to implement the equal pay principle.

The Equal Pay Act 1970

The 1970 Equal Pay Act effectively outlawed separate women's rates of pay by introducing an implied equality clause into all contracts of employment. Under the Act, which came into force in 1975, an employee in the United Kingdom is entitled to claim pay equal to that of an employee of the opposite sex in the same employing organization in only two situations: 1) where they are doing the same, or broadly similar, work – 'like work'; and 2) where the work they do is rated equivalent under a job evaluation scheme.

The basis of the Act is that every contract of employment is deemed to contain an equality clause, which is triggered in either situation. The equality clause modifies any terms in a woman's contract that are less favourable than those of the male comparator. Thus, if a woman is paid less than a man doing the same work, she is entitled to the same rate of pay. Although the Act refers to pay it extends to all aspects of the employee benefits package.

The three important points to note about the original Act are that:

1. Because it was confined to like work and work rated as equivalent the scope of comparison was fairly narrow.
2. It did not make job evaluation compulsory, but did establish the important point (or made the important assumption) that where job evaluation did exist and valued two jobs equally there was a prima facie entitlement to equal pay.
3. It recognized that a job evaluation scheme could be discriminatory if it set 'different values for men and women on the same demand under any heading'. It gave effort, skill and decision as examples of headings.

However, the European Commission's Equal Pay Directive of 1975 stated that the principle of equal pay should be applied to work of equal value. The Commission successfully argued before the European Court of Justice in 1982 that the United Kingdom had failed to implement the directive, because the Equal Pay Act enabled individuals to obtain equal pay for work of equal value only where their employer had implemented job evaluation. As a result the United Kingdom government had to introduce the 1983 Equal Pay (Amendment) Regulations of the Act, which came into force in 1984. These are often referred to as the equal value regulations.

The Equal Pay (Amendment) Regulations 1983

Under this equal value amendment, women are entitled to the same pay as men (and vice versa) where the work is of equal value 'in terms of the demands made on a worker under various headings, for instance, effort, skill, decision'.

This removed the barrier built into the Act that had prevented women claiming equal pay where they were employed in women's jobs and no men were employed in the same work. Now any woman could claim equal pay with any man and vice versa, subject to the rules about being in the same employment. Equal value claims can now be brought even if there are no job evaluation arrangements, although the existence of a non-discriminatory job evaluation scheme that has been applied properly to indicate that the jobs in question are not of equal value can be a defence in an equal value case.

The amendment also provided for the assignment of 'independent experts' by employment tribunals to assess equality of value between claimant and comparator under such headings as effort, skill and decision without regard to the cost or the industrial relations consequences of a successful claim.

The Employment Act 2002

One of the biggest barriers to bringing equal pay claims has been a lack of access to information regarding other people's pay. The Equal Pay (Questions and Replies) Order 2003 of the Employment Act 2002 provided for an equal pay questionnaire, which can be used by an employee to request information from his or her employer about whether the employee's remuneration is equal to that of named colleagues. Unions may also lodge these forms on behalf of their members.

The questionnaire includes:

- A statement of why the individual (the complainant) thinks he or she is not receiving equal pay, followed by a statement of who the individual believes the comparators are. A comparator is the person the complainant is comparing him- or herself with. A complainant can compare him- or herself with a predecessor or successor in the job. The comparator must be in the same employment as the complainant.
- Factual questions to ascertain whether the complainant is receiving less pay than the comparator and, if so, the reason why.
- A question asking whether the employer (the respondent) agrees or disagrees (with reasons) that the complainant is being paid less than the comparator.
- A question asking whether the employer agrees or disagrees (with reasons) that the complainant and the comparator are doing equal work.
- Space for the complainant's own questions.

The employer is asked to respond within eight weeks but is not required to reply to the complainant's questions. But if, without reasonable excuse, the employer fails to reply within eight weeks or replies in 'an evasive or ambiguous way', the employment tribunal may conclude that a respondent did not provide a proper explanation for a difference in pay because there was no genuine reason for the difference.

Case law

The following are some of the leading cases that provide guidance in a number of areas as indicated on how the equal pay legislation should be applied in a number of areas.

The basis of comparison

In the case of *Hayward* v *Cammell Laird* (1988) the House of Lords ruled that the Act required a comparison of each term of the contract considered in isolation. The applicant was therefore entitled to the same rates of basic and overtime pay as the comparator even though the other terms of her contract were more favourable.

The definition of pay

In *Barber* v *Guardian Royal Exchange Assurance Group* (1990) the European Court of Justice held that occupational pensions under a contracted-out pensions scheme constitute 'pay' under Article 119 and so must be offered to men and women on equal terms.

Extended pay scales

In *Crossley* v *ACAS* (1999) the applicant claimed that she was doing work of equal value to the comparator but earned significantly less because of the fact that the ACAS pay scales required many years' experience to reach the top of the pay band, which, it was argued, discriminated against women, who are more likely to have shorter periods of service. Although the tribunal accepted that there was a period during which the job was being learnt, it agreed the period in this case was too long.

Market forces

In *Enderby* v *Frenchay Health Authority* (1993) the European Court of Justice ruled that 'the state of the employment market, which may lead an employer to increase the pay of a particular job in order to attract candidates, may constitute an objectively justified ground for a difference in pay'. But tribunals will want clear evidence that a market forces material factor defence is based on such grounds, bearing in mind that the labour market generally discriminates against women. They may view with suspicion evidence gleaned only from published surveys, which they may hold to be inherently discriminatory because they simply represent the status quo.

Red-circling

In *Snoxell* v *Vauxhall Motors Ltd* (1977) it was held that if an employee's pay is not reduced, ie is 'protected', following a regrading exercise when his or her pay falls above the maximum for the new grade (red-circling) the protection should not last indefinitely.

Transparency

In what is usually referred to in abbreviated form as the Danfoss case, the European Court of Justice in 1989 ruled that:

> The Equal Pay Directive must be interpreted as meaning that when an undertaking applies a pay system which is characterised by a total lack of transparency, the burden of proof is on the employer to show that his pay practice is not discriminating where a female worker has established, by comparison with a relatively large number of employees, that the average pay of female workers is lower than that of male workers.

Use of job evaluation as a defence in an equal pay claim

In *Bromley* v *Quick* (1988) the Court of Appeal ruled that a job evaluation system can provide a defence only if it is analytical in nature. The employer must demonstrate the absence of sex bias in the job evaluation scheme, and jobs will be held to be covered by a job evaluation scheme only if they have been fully evaluated using the scheme's factors.

Pay related to experience

In *Cadman* v *The Health and Safety Executive* (2006) the European Court ruled that pay could be related to service but might have to be objectively justified.

THE EOC CODE OF PRACTICE ON EQUAL PAY

The Code of Practice on Equal Pay as reissued by the Equal Opportunities Commission in December 2003 (5) describes:

- the equal pay legislation;
- the scope of the Equal Pay Act;
- how individuals can raise equal pay matters with their employers, request information and bring an equal pay claim;
- how to conduct equal pay reviews.

It also provides an example of an equal pay policy.

EQUAL PAY CLAIMS

Claims for equal pay, which may be supported by a completed equal pay questionnaire, can be made to an employment tribunal on any of the following three grounds:

1. where the work is *like work*, meaning the same or very similar work;
2. where the work is *work rated as equivalent* under a job evaluation 'study';
3. where the work is of *equal value* 'in terms of the demands made on a worker under various headings, for instance, effort, skill, decision'.

If a tribunal finds that the work is like, equivalent or of equal value it can invoke the equality clause in the legislation and rule that the man and the woman should be paid the same.

Defending an equal pay claim

The two most common grounds for defending a claim are: 1) that the work is not equal; and 2) that, even if they are equal, there is a genuine material factor that justifies the difference in pay. As the EOC Code of Practice states, justification has to be objective, which means demonstrating that: the purpose of the provision or practice is to meet a real business need; and the provision or practice is appropriate and necessary as a means of meeting that need.

Employers cannot defend equal value cases on the grounds of the cost of implementation or the effect a decision could have on industrial relations, and part-time working per se cannot provide a defence to a claim. A tribunal can ask an independent expert to analyse the jobs and report on whether or not they are of equal value.

Proving that the work is not equal

The onus is on the employer to prove that the complainant is not carrying out like work, work rated as equivalent or work of equal value when compared with the comparator. If the employer invokes job evaluation to provide support to a claim that the jobs are not equal, the scheme must be analytical, unbiased and applied in a non-discriminatory way.

Analytical means that the scheme must analyse and compare jobs by reference to factors such as, in the words of the Equal Pay Regulations, 'effort, skill, decision'. Slotting jobs on a whole job comparison basis is not acceptable as a defence. The legislation and case law do not specify that a point-factor or a scored factor comparison scheme should be used, and even if an 'analytical matching' process is followed (see

Chapter 11) a tribunal may need to be convinced that this is analytical within the meaning of the Act and has not led to biased decisions.

Genuine material factor

The legislation provides for a case to be made by the employer that there is a 'genuine material factor' creating and justifying the difference between the pay of the applicant and the comparator. A genuine material factor could be the level of performance or length of service of the comparator, which means that he or she is paid at a higher level than the applicant in the pay range for a job. But this only applies if the basis for deciding on additions to pay and the process of doing so are not discriminatory. The Crossley case referred to above is an example of where a tribunal found that length-of-service criteria could be discriminatory if they meant that women are paid less than men and find it hard to catch up.

Pay differences because of market supplements can be treated as genuine material factors as long as they are 'objectively justified'. In the case of a claim that market pressures justify unequal pay the tribunal will need to be convinced that this was not simply a matter of opinion and that adequate evidence from a number of sources was available. In such cases, the tribunal will also require proof that the recruitment and retention of the people required by the organization were difficult because pay levels were uncompetitive.

Independent experts

If there is any doubt as to whether or not work is of equal value employment tribunals will require an independent expert to prepare a report. The expert must:

- evaluate the jobs concerned analytically;
- take account of all information supplied and representations that have a bearing on the question;
- before reporting, send the parties a written summary of the information and invite representations;
- include the representations in the report, together with the conclusion reached on the case and the reason for that conclusion;
- take no account of the difference in sex, and at all times act fairly.

The independent expert's task differs in a number of ways from that of someone carrying out a conventional job evaluation within an organization. This is because the aim in the latter case is to establish relative value by ranking a number of jobs, while an independent expert will be concerned with comparative value – comparing the value of a fairly narrow range of jobs.

Avoiding equal pay claims

To avoid successful equal pay claims, which can be very expensive and time-consuming, there are five things an organization must do:

1. Use a non-discriminatory analytical job evaluation scheme designed and operated to avoid discrimination as explained later in this chapter.
2. Conduct regular equal pay reviews or audits as described in the next chapter and take action if they reveal pay discrimination.
3. Ensure that there is objective and non-discriminatory justification for any differences in pay between men and women.
4. Adopt a non-discriminatory grade and pay structure as described in Chapter 18.
5. Ensure that everyone is aware that one of the most important core values of the organization is the provision of equal opportunities to enable women to have the same chance as men to progress their careers and therefore their pay and to be given equal pay for work of equal value. Steps must be taken to ensure that this core value is acted upon.

AVOIDING DISCRIMINATION IN JOB EVALUATION

The main points on avoiding discrimination made by the Equal Opportunities Commission in its *Good Practice Guide: Job evaluation schemes free of sex bias* (6) and in case law are:

- The scheme should be analytical.
- The scheme should be appropriate for the jobs it is intended to cover – it should incorporate all the important and relevant differentiating characteristics of those jobs.
- The scheme should be designed and operated to measure fairly all significant features of jobs typically carried out by women as well as of those generally carried out by men.
- The factors should operate fairly.
- The factor and level definitions should be exact, and detailed descriptions should be provided for each factor.

- The factors should cover all important job demands. A scheme will be discriminatory if it fails to include or properly take into account a demand such as caring that is an important element in the jobs carried out by women – the exclusion of an important factor will result in it being undervalued compared with other jobs.
- Knowledge and skills factors should measure what is actually required for the job (not recruitment level or what the current job holder has), measure all forms of knowledge and skills, not just occupational knowledge, measure actual knowledge (qualifications as indicators, not determinants) and avoid measuring years of experience.
- The factor levels should represent clear and recognizable steps in demand and be defined in absolute, not relative, terms, ie they should define the differences in terms of what is done at each level not in terms such as small, bigger or big.
- There should be no double-counting of factors.
- Factors that are characteristic of jobs largely held by one sex should not unjustifiably have a greater number of levels than the number of levels in factors mainly held by the other sex.
- Factors that are characteristic of male-dominated jobs should not have a wider dispersion of scores than factors that are characteristic of female-dominated jobs.
- There should be a rationale for the scoring and weighting system, eg relative value of factors to the organization, agreed relative values – it should not just give the answer people want.
- The method of scoring for each factor should be reasonably similar.
- Variation between points should reflect real differences in demand.
- The weighting system should not favour men or women.
- The selection of benchmark jobs should not favour men or women.
- Job evaluation on the basis of a traditional organizational job description is likely to be unsatisfactory because it leaves evaluators to use their own experience or make assumptions when assessing jobs against factors for which no information is provided.
- Job analysts, facilitators and evaluators should be trained on how to avoid bias.
- The selection of grade boundaries should be objectively based on the evidence provided by job evaluation, irrespective of the sex of the job holders.
- The outcome of a new job evaluation scheme should be monitored to check for sex bias; other things being equal, it is to be expected that a new job evaluation scheme will result in some upward movement of female-dominated jobs as historical pay discrimination is eliminated, particularly those that show typical features of work carried out by women, relative to other jobs.
- Existing schemes should be kept up to date and reviewed to ensure that sex discrimination has not crept in.

- Evaluation outcomes should be properly recorded with reasons, consistency should be checked by factor and by whole job and the outcome should be revised if there is good reason, eg faulty job information or a bad evaluation day.

Use of slotting

The use of traditional 'slotting' techniques is a further potential cause of discrimination. In even a medium-size organization, it is time-consuming to evaluate the job of every individual employee separately. In a large organization, it is impossible. Historically, therefore, it was common practice in larger organizations to evaluate only a benchmark sample of jobs and to 'slot' other jobs against the benchmark through some form of whole job comparison.

However, in its decision in the case of *Bromley* v *Quick*, the Court of Appeal said that the applicant and comparator jobs that had been 'slotted' in this way had not been analysed and evaluated under the scheme in question, so were not covered by the 'job evaluation study' defence. There was not such a study 'where the jobs of the women and their comparators were slotted into the structure on a "whole job" basis and no comparison was made by reference to the selected factors between the demands made on the individual workers under the selected headings'. This decision has significant implications for job evaluation in large organizations, as it implies that all employees should be attached to a job description, which has either been analysed and evaluated or, at minimum, has been matched to an evaluated benchmark job, using an analytical process.

The process of analytical matching as described in Chapters 11 and 12 aims to avoid the problems of slotting by ensuring that the comparisons are made by reference to an analytical framework.

DISCRIMINATORY PAY STRUCTURES

Pay structures can be discriminatory in the following ways:

- The grade boundary lines in a multi-graded structure are based purely on judgements, which may simply reinforce existing inequalities.
- Generic job descriptions take insufficient account of significant differences between male and female roles.
- Whole jobs are slotted into a graded, broad-banded or job family structure by a process of internal benchmarking that is not analytical in itself and is not underpinned by an analytical job evaluation scheme, with the result that the outcome could simply be the perpetuation of existing discrimination.

- Benchmark jobs do not fairly represent the distribution of male and female jobs.
- Market-related pay levels and differentials reproduce marketplace gender discrimination and do not take account of internal relativities.

Approaches to designing non-discriminatory pay structures are described in Chapter 18.

REFERENCES

1   Elliott, RF (1991) *Labor Economics*, McGraw-Hill, Maidenhead
2   National Institute of Economic and Social Research (2001) *The Gender Pay Gap*, Women and Equality Unit, Department of Trade and Industry, London
3   Kingsmill, D (2001) *Review of Women's Employment and Pay*, Department of Trade and Industry, London
4   Equal Pay Task Force (2001) *Just Pay*, Report of the Equal Pay Task Force to the Equal Opportunities Commission, EOC, Manchester
5   Equal Opportunities Commission (2003) *Code of Practice on Equal Pay*, EOC, Manchester
6   Equal Opportunities Commission (2003) *Good Practice Guide: Job evaluation schemes free of sex bias*, EOC, Manchester

14

Equal pay reviews

As described in Chapter 13, UK organizations have a legal obligation to provide equal pay for equal work that is free from sex bias. They therefore need to understand whether their practices and policies are achieving this outcome. The Equal Opportunity Commission (EOC)'s *Code of Practice on Equal Pay* (1) says that an internal review is 'the most appropriate method of ensuring that a pay system delivers equal pay free from sex bias'.

This section of the chapter describes the equal pay review process (sometimes termed equal pay audits). However, it does not intend to replicate the comprehensive guidance that is available though other sources such as the EOC *Equal Pay Review Kit* (2) or the CIPD *Equal Pay Guide* (3). It focuses instead on how organizations can respond to the analysis challenges presented by equal pay reviews in the context of their existing approach to valuing jobs.

PURPOSE OF EQUAL PAY REVIEWS

The purpose of equal pay reviews is to:

- establish whether any gender-related pay inequities have arisen;
- analyse the nature of any inequities and diagnose the cause or causes;
- determine what action is required to deal with any inequities that are revealed.

In doing so they should give organizations confidence about whether they are meeting their legal obligations with respect to equal pay for equal work. There is also the broader benefit from being seen to apply a fair and equitable reward system, and the positive impact this has on employee perceptions and satisfaction.

Equal pay reviews will also support an organization's ability to respond to employee requests for information about its pay practices in accordance with the 2002 Employment Act. This provides for a statutory equal pay questionnaire to help individuals who believe that they may not have received equal pay to obtain information from their employer on whether this is the case, and why, before deciding whether to submit an equal pay claim.

PLANNING A REVIEW

Before embarking on the data collection and analysis that are essential parts of an equal pay review it is necessary to decide on the scope of the review: whether it should focus on gender only, or include other possible areas of pay inequity such as racial groups and those with disabilities. It is certainly advisable to consider the conduct and outcomes of an equal pay review in the context of all the other equality policies, procedures and processes in the organization.

The review should cover employees on different employment terms, specifically part-time and hourly paid staff if there are any and those on short-term contracts or contracts of unspecified duration as well as full-time staff.

Part of the planning process will inevitably involve consideration of how to source and access the data that will be needed to feed the analysis. The initial data required may well sit across payroll and the HR database. The data for follow-up analyses may rest in individual files or reside in the memory of longer-serving staff – if such data exist at all. Issues that have come up in equal pay reviews include data that are not retrievable without HR support, data not collected in standardized form and the need to convert data from multiple sources on to a common database in order to generate reports.

Some software tools are available to support analyses. These range from database tools that enable data to be imported from a range of sources to generate pay gap analyses, such as the e-reward equal pay toolkit, to more sophisticated tools that allow for a broader range of analysis possibilities using different data cuts, including the tool developed by Link Consultants. What is clear is that analysis needs will vary from one organization to the next and it is not always possible to specify in advance what analyses will be needed. Therefore advice to organizations planning to replace their

HR database is that one criterion should be the flexibility of customized reporting to support future equal pay review analyses.

There are other process decisions to be made, for example about how intensive the review should be and at what point staff or unions should be involved. These process decisions are all well covered in the EOC *Equal Pay Review Kit* and other sources.

THE EQUAL PAY REVIEW PROCESS

Although the EOC *Equal Pay Review Kit* describes a five-stage process, there are essentially three main stages to an equal pay review:

1. *analysis* – the collection and analysis of relevant data to identify any gender gaps;
2. *diagnosis* – the process of reviewing gender gaps, understanding why they have occurred and determining what remedial action might be required if the differences cannot be objectively justified;
3. *action* – agreeing and enacting an action plan that eliminates any inequalities.

These stages are described below, and the chapter continues with a review of analysis options, based around an organization's existing approach to valuing jobs.

Stage one: analysis

This stage involves collecting and analysing pay and benefits practices and policies in order to test the extent of any differences in policy or application that might lead to unequal pay between men and women. There are three elements to this analysis stage:

1. *Review the organization's equal pay policy.* This is the most straightforward part of the initial analysis. It involves establishing whether or not an equal pay policy exists. If there is one, the organization should:
   - compare the policy with the model policy set out in the EOC *Code of Practice on Equal Pay* (see the box);
   - examine the extent to which it has been communicated internally;
   - identify who is responsible for implementing the policy and what steps have been taken to ensure that it has been implemented.

   Where there is no existing equal pay policy the EOC model as set out in the box can be used as a basis for establishing one.

Model equal pay policy: the Equal Opportunities Commission

We are committed to the principle of equal pay for all our employees. We aim to eliminate any bias in our pay systems.

We understand that equal pay between men and women is a legal right under both domestic and European law.

It is in the interest of the organization to ensure that we have a fair and just pay system. It is important that employees have confidence in the process of eliminating sex bias and we are therefore committed to working in partnership with the recognized trade unions. As good business practice we are committed to working with trade union/employee representatives to take action to ensure that we provide equal pay.

We believe that in eliminating sex bias in our pay system we are sending a positive message to our staff and customers. It makes good business sense to have a fair, transparent reward system and it helps us to control costs. We recognize that avoiding discrimination will improve morale and enhance efficiency.

Our objectives are to:

● Eliminate any unfair, unjust or unlawful practices that impact on pay
● Take appropriate remedial action.

We will:

● Implement an equal pay review in line with EOC guidance for all current staff and starting pay for new staff (including those on maternity leave, career breaks, or non-standard contracts)
● Plan and implement actions in partnership with trade union/employee representatives
● Provide training and guidance for those involved in determining pay
● Inform employees of how these practices work and how their own pay is determined
● Respond to grievances on equal pay as a priority
● In conjunction with trade union/employee representatives, monitor pay statistics annually.

2. *Pay analysis.* This is about generating the first set of statistics that will help to indicate whether or not an organization may have an equal pay issue, and the extent to which further analysis will be needed. The analysis requirements are discussed later in this chapter (pages 222–25).

3 *Benefits comparison.* This involves establishing the extent to which men and women have access to, and on average receive, equal benefits for equal work, such as pensions, sick pay, medical insurance, company cars and holidays. Benefits design, eligibility criteria and actual practice will need to be examined.

   Benefits comparison is an essential part of the analysis phase because, although the publicity surrounding equal pay reviews focuses mainly on cash reward, equal pay legislation allows comparison to be made in respect of any remuneration item. There is no 'total remuneration' concept in equal pay law. This means that an equal pay claim can be submitted in respect of any remuneration item, where an individual feels that he or she is not being fairly treated in comparison with a colleague of the opposite sex doing equal work – even if the total remuneration package is worth the same.

Stage two: diagnosis

The aim of stage two is to establish the nature of any inequities and their causes with the intent of establishing whether the difference in pay is genuinely due to a material difference between the man's and the woman's job rather than due to gender. The review should first seek explanations of why the gap exists and then establish the extent to which the gap can be objectively justified. This stage involves delving into the data, using intuition and judgement about where to focus effort, in order not to be overwhelmed by the mass of options for further analysis.

If this diagnostic phase suggests that any pay differences are gender based the remedial action needed to rectify the situation should feed into stage three. Table 14.1 gives examples of the types of analyses and issues that could arise from this diagnostic phase, together with the remedial actions that may be required.

Stage three: action

Any issues that have been identified in stage two must be remedied. The course of action that will remove pay gaps must be defined, planned and implemented. The action plan should incorporate proposals on:

● introducing or amending an equal pay policy if necessary;
● the steps required to remove pay gaps;

Table 14.1 Factors creating pay gaps and remedial actions

Possible Factors	Data Required to Identify Factors	Possible Remedial Actions
Men and women on like work, work rated equivalent or work of equal value are paid differently.	1 An analysis of the average and individual rates of pay of all those on like work, work rated equivalent or work of equal value. 2 An assessment of possible reasons for differences, eg traditional differentials, higher entry pay levels for certain categories of staff, market rate supplements, red- or green-circling.	Investigate each case to establish whether or not there is a material factor such as differences in the performance of those concerned, market forces or red-circling that might justify the inequality. But a claim by an employer that a difference arose from different levels of performance or market forces would have to be objectively justified, and red-circling that favours any category could be regarded as discriminatory. If there is no material factor that demonstrably justifies the difference, the jobs in question should be compared by means of an analytical job evaluation scheme. If this indicates that the jobs are of equal value, steps will have to be taken to equalize pay.
Other measures of equal value, eg qualification levels, show pay inequalities between jobs in different occupational groups.	The use of a job evaluation scheme to establish whether the inequalities are caused by the systematic under-evaluation of one occupational group as against another.	As set out above.
Disproportionate distribution of men or women at the upper or lower part of a pay range or an incremental scale. This might result from the unequal impact of women's family responsibilities such as the effect of career interruptions because of maternity.	Distribution of men or women in the range or scale.	Review: 1) the length of the range or scale. If this is longer than is necessary to reflect the additional value that experience can bring to a role, this will discriminate against women and others who have less opportunity to obtain continuous experience; 2) the policy on fixing recruitment salaries (see below).

Table 14.1 *Continued*

Possible Factors	Data Required to Identify Factors	Possible Remedial Actions
Men or women placed at higher points in the scale on appointment or promotion.	The most common point on the pay scale for the grade at which men or women are placed on appointment or promotion.	Ensure that policies and procedures are implemented that will prevent such discrimination. For example, produce guidelines that specify when staff can be recruited or promoted to higher points in the range or scale and emphasize the importance of adopting a non-discriminatory approach. Monitor such decisions to ensure that they are objectively justified and do not discriminate.
Men or women receive higher merit or performance pay awards or benefit more from accelerated increments.	The comparative level of merit or performance pay awards or the comparative incidence of the award of accelerated increments. The comparative distribution of performance ratings. The extent to which differences can be objectively justified.	Ensure that: – men and women are equally entitled to participate in merit or performance pay schemes or to obtain accelerated increments; – the criteria and processes used to determine merit or performance pay increases are not biased; – managers are aware of the possibility of gender or race bias and are trained in how to avoid it; – proposals for merit or performance pay or for accelerated increments are monitored to ensure that they are objectively justified and to detect and correct any bias.
Discriminatory use of a threshold merit bar resulting in more men or women achieving a level of pay above the merit bar.	The proportion of men and women whose pay is above the threshold merit bar.	– Review criteria for crossing the threshold or merit bar to ensure that they are not discriminatory. – Monitor threshold or merit bar decisions to ensure that they have been objectively justified and are free of bias.

Table 14.1 *Continued*

Possible Factors	Data Required to Identify Factors	Possible Remedial Actions
Market supplements applied differentially to men or women.	The comparative number of men and women receiving market supplements and their relative value.	Ensure that no supplements are awarded unless they have been objectively justified. Such justification should include evidence that the recruitment and retention of the staff concerned would be seriously prejudiced unless market rates were paid. It should use a number of information sources and should not rely solely on published survey material, which could simply reproduce existing marketplace inequalities.
Red- or green-circling applied in a way that results in pay discrimination between men and women doing work of equal value or like work.	The incidence and duration and impact in terms of pay differentials of red- or green-circling for the different categories being compared.	Ensure that red- or green-circling does not unjustifiably favour either women or men.
Men or women in work of equal value or like work receive higher allowances.	The distribution and amount of allowances for the different categories being compared.	Equalize the distribution and amount of allowances.
A discriminating job evaluation scheme in terms of factors or weightings or the job evaluation scheme applied in a discriminatory way.	Details of the factor plan and an analysis of the process of job evaluation followed by an assessment.	Revise the plan or the process to take account of any bias revealed by its assessment.

- how future bias can be eliminated by changing the processes, rules or practices that gave rise to unequal pay;
- a programme for implementing change;
- accountabilities for drawing up and implementing the plan;
- how employee representatives or recognized trade unions should be involved in preparing and implementing the plan;
- the arrangements for monitoring the implementation of the plan and for evaluating outcomes.

With regard to how long an organization should take to address any inequities, the answer depends on the scale of change that is needed; the causes and costs involved in rectifying inequities are wide and varied. However, the timetable should be realistic in the light of change required, whilst demonstrating an immediate intention to implement change. In the interim the organization remains at risk of an equal pay claim – the intent to redress the difference is not sufficient to avoid a claim.

It is, of course, important to address both the cause and the effect of the inequity. For example, if the cause of pay differences within grades rests in an organization's recruitment processes, the short-term remedy may be to rectify existing pay differentials – but to avoid the situation arising again more fundamental issues will need to be addressed relating to recruitment, perhaps including actions such as manager training and generating new guidelines on how to set recruitment salaries.

ANALYSING PAY

The rest of this chapter focuses on the types of pay analyses that may be involved in an equal pay review. In particular it focuses on the initial analyses that are needed to check whether there appears to be a gender-related pay gap. The nature of analyses that are possible will be affected by the existing pay and grading structure. Some preparatory analysis of the employee population is needed before the statistical analyses can start.

Determining initial analysis options

In the experience of organizations that have undertaken equal pay reviews, this step can be the most difficult part of the process. This is determining what kind of analyses an organization is able to do in relation to the three definitions of equal work. These are:

- *Like work* – this means identifying jobs anywhere in the organization where the work is the same or broadly similar. Where there is no job evaluation this is the only type of equal work comparison that can readily be made. Although this should be a straightforward comparison there are potential pitfalls, such as over-reliance on unrepresentative job titles. If existing job titles are not a good guide, it might be necessary to re-categorize jobs in order to arrive at who is doing 'like work'.
- *Work rated as equivalent* – this means work that has been rated as equivalent using the organization's own analytical job evaluation scheme. Clearly analyses can only be readily applied where the organization has a job evaluation scheme that covers the whole organization.

- *Work of equal value* – this is the 'catch-all' in equal pay legislation. It means that an equal pay claim can be brought by any employee where he or she believes that his or her job is of equal worth to any other role in the organization that is occupied by someone of the opposite sex. As with the 'work rated as equivalent' test the only organizations that can readily conduct analyses under this heading are those with an organization-wide job evaluation scheme that enables different types of jobs to be compared using criteria that apply equally across the organization.

These last two definitions of equal pay rely on job evaluation, and fully to satisfy an equal pay test in law the scheme should be analytical. But it is unrealistic to expect that every organization will introduce an analytical job evaluation scheme in order to provide a legal defence to equal pay claims, even those organizations that aim to be fair and equitable employers. Decisions about how to value and reward jobs are based on a wide range of organizational and business factors, and organizations must balance the relative benefits and risks of alternative approaches, of which the ability to meet all the tests laid down in equal pay legislation is just one – albeit an important one.

However, it is reasonable to expect organizations to apply a range of tests in good faith that will enable them to be satisfied that their pay practices and outcomes are non-discriminatory.

Undertaking the initial pay analyses

As a minimum organizations need to be able to undertake straightforward statistical checks to investigate the percentage pay difference between men and women doing the same or similar ('like') work and thus define any 'pay gap' that exists.

To do this women's base pay and total pay should be calculated as a percentage of men's pay for all incumbents doing like work. It is helpful to separate the calculation into the different elements of total earnings in order to see where any pay differences lie. As mentioned earlier, in order to compare like with like this analysis needs to be based on a standard norm, eg annual or hourly pay.

The aim is to establish the degree to which inequality exists in the form of a significant pay gap. The EOC recommends that a pay gap in favour of one gender of more than 5 per cent for one job is significant enough to warrant further investigation, as is a pattern of differences in favour of one group of 3 per cent or more (eg a pay gap in favour of men at all or most levels of the organization).

However, the guideline percentages are, at best, a rule of thumb. It is more important to get an understanding of the pattern of differences and to investigate suspected problem areas, even if the results do not lie within these guideline percentages. It is also important to remember that an individual can make a claim whatever the aggregate statistics say.

The discovery of a gender pay gap does not automatically mean that there is a problem. However, differences must be objectively justifiable – so further investigation will be needed to check whether this is so. If the reason for the pay difference is gender related the law requires that the inequity is remedied.

If job evaluation is used on an organization-wide basis it is possible to conduct pay gap analyses that meet all three equal work categories. This can be done by conducting both a like work and an organization-wide comparison between the pay for men and the pay for women in the same grade irrespective of their occupational groups. This is because, where organizations use analytical job evaluation, different types of jobs on the same grade defined in terms of a range of job evaluation scores will generally be regarded as being of 'equal worth', thus enabling a pay gap analysis that covers all employees in the same grade.

However, this is unlikely to be a satisfactory assessment of equal worth where bands or grades are so broad that they include jobs with a wide range of responsibilities and skills. Where this is the case, it may be necessary to split the grades/bands into narrower groups. This can be done fairly easily using a point-factor scheme's total job scores, but will not be so straightforward where other job evaluation techniques have been used (eg classification) without some adaptation to the scheme or alternative approach to deriving additional levels. Of course, the type of job evaluation approach used also impacts on the perceived robustness of the equal worth comparison in the first place.

Where there is no organization-wide job evaluation scheme, further steps need to be taken by an organization if it wants to satisfy itself that there is no potential pay gender gap. The extent to which an organization may need to extend analysis beyond the initial 'like' work check will depend on a number of factors:

● the outcome of the 'like work' analysis;
● the extent to which it wants to explore the potential risk of an equal pay claim;
● the extent to which it wants to be seen as adhering to 'best practice' in conducting an equal pay review.

The options for extending the analysis depend both on the level of rigour that the organization wants to apply and on the nature of existing remuneration arrangements. In particular the options for further analysis will depend on whether:

● analytical job evaluation is used in one or more parts of the organization – and can be extended across the organization;

- analytical job evaluation is not normally used, but the organization may be prepared to apply it purely for equal pay review purposes;
- the organization is not prepared formally to apply analytical job evaluation.

CONCLUSION

As those organizations that have conducted equal pay reviews have found out, the causes of pay inequity are many and varied – there is the risk of getting overwhelmed by the data requirements needed to carry out a comprehensive review. It is therefore important to prioritize effort, and to undertake those analyses that are most likely to throw light on whether any potential inequities exist.

It should be noted that where an organization satisfies itself through an equal pay review and continuing monitoring that there is no systematic pay discrimination it is still possible to be subject to an equal pay claim. However, the likelihood of claims occurring should be reduced, and any claims that do occur are more likely to be one-offs rather than reflecting a wider problem.

Ultimately the test of an equal pay review is whether the organization has reached evidence-based conclusions that it is systematically applying non-discriminatory criteria for determining pay and for achieving outcomes that are defensible and justifiable or, if not, it knows what is needed to address any inequities. Looking for such evidence should be an ongoing responsibility of any organization to enable it to demonstrate that employees are being treated fairly. For this reason the demand for robust, analytical approaches to valuing jobs will remain a constant organizational requirement.

It is also necessary to remember that simply installing a job evaluation scheme, designing a new grade and pay structure and allocating jobs to the structure do not, as some organizations believe, obviate the need for an equal pay review. As mentioned in Chapter 13, there can be all sorts of reasons for unequal pay that are not caused by discriminatory basic rates of pay, eg the practices used to progress pay in graded structures, decisions on where people should be placed in a pay range on recruitment or promotion, and 'career gaps' that restrict the progress of women through pay ranges. And even if a new structure has been introduced, it will still include inequalities arising from green- and red-circling. The existence of these needs to be checked and controlled.

REFERENCES

1   Equal Opportunities Commission (2003) *Code of Practice on Equal Pay*, EOC, Manchester

2   Equal Opportunities Commission (2002) *Equal Pay Review Kit*, EOC, Manchester

3   Chartered Institute of Personnel and Development (2001) *Equal Pay Guide*, CIPD, London

15

Market rate analysis

One of the vital ingredients of an effective reward management strategy is the development and maintenance of a competitive pay and benefits position that enables organizations to attract and retain high-quality people. This can only be done if data on the levels of pay in the external market are systematically monitored by a process of market rate analysis.

This chapter starts with definitions of market rate analysis and its aims. Attention is then given to the concept of a market rate, which is by no means as straightforward as it seems. The next sections of the chapter cover sources of data and methods of collecting it. The chapter ends with a review of methods of presenting and interpreting data.

MARKET RATE ANALYSIS DEFINED

Market rate analysis is the process of collecting and comparing data on the rates and benefits provided for similar jobs in other organizations and the rates at which pay is increasing elsewhere. It is conducted by means of surveys that review published data and/or collect data from various sources.

AIMS OF MARKET RATE ANALYSIS

The aims of market analysis are to:

- obtain relevant, accurate, representative and up-to-date data on levels of pay and benefits for specified jobs within the organization;
- deduce from this information the market (going) rate or market range for a position, taking into account the type and size of the job and such variables as company size, sector and location;
- maintain a competitive pay and benefit position in relation to the marketplace, thus enabling the organization to attract and retain people of the quality it needs;
- inform decisions on levels of pay for individual jobs, and pay brackets or scales for pay structure grades;
- provide guidance on pay review decisions concerning any adjustments required to general or individual pay levels;
- support a market pricing approach to valuing jobs – this will be particularly important when the organization decides that its pay levels should be 'market-driven';
- offer guidance on internal differentials by reference to the differentials in the external labour market.

THE PROBLEM OF DEFINING THE MARKET RATE

The process of market analysis focuses on obtaining information about 'market rates', ie the rates of pay or 'going rates' paid by employers in national or local labour markets for particular categories of jobs. But the concept of a market rate is elusive. It is not so simple as it sounds and establishing what the market rate for a job is can be a matter of judgement rather than certainty.

All too many managers and senior executives – and, indeed, many employees – commonly believe that it is not only possible, but relatively easy, to establish a 'correct' rate for any given job, in any industry, in any location, for any age or experience level, preferably to the nearest pound. But as a report by online pay database CubikSurvey. com (1) explained, accurate market rate information may be difficult to obtain:

> The expectation is that reward specialists, and the surveys they provide, can wave a magic wand and come up with the only right answer. This rather overlooks the complexity of remuneration issues. It is rare that two companies, even within the same industry and location, are managed in identical ways. Different corporate values,

perceptions of the contribution of each job to the effectiveness of the organization, and the experience and performance of the individuals holding the jobs all impact on the remuneration paid to people in apparently similar positions.

Ultimately those differences are reflected in the market. There is always a choice of rates. No survey is able, despite the claims of some surveyors, to provide a single 'right' rate of pay for any position or range of positions. This is because different organizations have different policies as to what they need to pay. Employees in effect have their own market rate, depending on their expertise and ability and the degree to which their talents are unique. This individual 'market worth' varies widely and is often as much a matter of perception as of fact. When making comparisons between internal and external rates for jobs the aim is to compare like with like. But it may be difficult or even impossible to obtain precise matches between jobs in the organization and jobs elsewhere. 'Like' jobs may not exist. The comparisons may be approximate with the result that the range between the highest and lowest levels of pay for a job as established by an individual survey can be as much as 50 per cent or more. Different surveys will produce different results depending on the sample of organizations covered, the quality of matching and the timing of the survey.

The translation of salary market data into competitive pay levels for individuals, or into an acceptable company pay structure, is a process based on intuition, judgement and compromise. It means striking a balance between the competing merits of the different sources of data and extracting what may be called a 'derived market rate'. But the judgements will be more accurate if they are based on the systematic analysis of valid and reliable data gained from reputable published surveys or well-conceived surveys conducted by the organization.

The validity and reliability of market rate data

This is based on three factors:

1. *Job matching* – the extent to which good job matching has taken place.
2. *Sample frame* – the extent to which the sample of organizations from which the data have been collected is fully representative of the organizations with which comparisons need to be made in such terms as sector, technology or type of business, size and location.
3. *Timing* – the degree to which the information is up to date or can be updated reliably. By its very nature, the information in published surveys, upon which many people rely, can soon become out of date. Indeed, the moment surveys are produced they are out of date – pay levels may have changed and people may

have moved in or out since the date of the survey. Whilst it is not possible to overcome this completely, as data must be gathered and analysed, surveys that aim to have as short a time as possible between data collection and the publication of results are likely to be of more use than those with longer lead times. Estimates can be made of likely movements since the survey took place, but they are mainly guesswork.

Job matching

Inadequate job matching is a major cause of inaccuracies in the data collected by market analysis. So far as possible the aim is to match the jobs within the organization and those outside (the comparators) so that like is being compared with like. It is essential to avoid crude and misleading comparisons based on job titles alone or vague descriptions of job content. It is first necessary to ensure that a broad match is achieved between the organization and the types of organizations used as comparators in terms of sector, industry classification, size and location.

The next step is to match jobs within the organizations concerned. The various methods in ascending order of accuracy are:

- *Job title* – this can be misleading. Job titles by themselves give no indication of the range of duties or the level of responsibility and are sometimes used to convey additional status to employees or their customers unrelated to the real level of work done.
- *Brief description of duties and level or zone of responsibility* – national surveys frequently restrict their job-matching definitions to a two- or three-line description of duties and an indication of levels of responsibility in rank order. The latter is often limited to a one-line definition for each level or zone in a hierarchy. This approach provides some guidance on job matching, which reduces major discrepancies, but it still leaves considerable scope for discretion and can therefore provide only generalized comparisons.
- *Capsule job descriptions* – club or specialist 'bespoke' surveys frequently use capsule job descriptions that define main responsibilities and duties in about 100 to 200 words. To increase the refinement of comparisons, modifying statements may be made indicating where responsibilities are higher or lower than the norm. Capsule job descriptions considerably increase the accuracy of comparisons as long as they are based on a careful analysis of actual jobs and include modifying statements. But they are not always capable of dealing with specialist jobs, and the accuracy of comparisons in relation to levels of responsibility may be limited, even when modifiers are used.

- *Full role profiles*, including a factor analysis of the levels of responsibility involved, may be used in special surveys when direct comparisons are made between jobs in different organizations. They can be more accurate on a one-for-one basis but their use is limited because of the time and labour involved in preparing them. A further limitation is that comparator organizations may not have available, or be prepared to make available, their own full role profiles for comparison.
- *Job evaluation* – can be used in support of a capsule job description or a role profile to provide a more accurate measure of relative job size. A common method of evaluation is necessary. In the UK, market information sources are created on this basis by consultants such as Hay and Watson Wyatt. This approach will further increase the accuracy of comparisons but the degree of accuracy will depend on the quality of the job evaluation process.

THE PROCESS OF MARKET RATE ANALYSIS

The process of market rate analysis consists of the following steps as described in the rest of this chapter:

1. Decide that it is necessary to collect market rate data by means of surveys for a defined purpose or purposes such as those listed above.
2. Decide on the jobs for which market rate data will be collected.
3. Identify potential sources of market rate data and select the most appropriate ones.
4. Prepare information on the jobs to be surveyed.
5. Analyse and interpret the data from the various sources.
6. Present the outcome of the analysis with proposals for action.

INITIAL DECISION TO CONDUCT MARKET RATE ANALYSIS

The initial decision is made following an assessment of the need for a market survey and a definition of its purpose, eg to ensure pay is competitive, to provide guidance on market pricing, to inform the design of a pay structure or to deal with specific attraction and retention problems. Responsibility for conducting the survey has to be allocated and consideration given to the use of consultants.

DECIDE ON BENCHMARK JOBS

The survey should aim to collect data on a representative sample of benchmark jobs, which will be used to provide guidance on the design of a pay structure (see Chapter 18) or as a basis for market pricing. The jobs selected should be ones for which it is likely that market data will be available. There are usually some jobs that are unique to the organization and for which comparisons cannot be made. When conducting a market pricing exercise it is necessary to make a judgement on the positioning of these jobs in the structure on the basis of comparisons with the benchmark jobs. A point-factor evaluation scheme, if available, would help to make these comparisons more accurate.

SOURCES OF MARKET DATA

Once it has been decided that market data are needed, the potential sources need to be identified. There is a wide variety of sources of varying quality and it is advisable to select more than one to ensure that a spread of information is obtained. The main sources are:

- online pay data;
- general published national surveys;
- general local surveys;
- sector and industry surveys;
- occupational surveys;
- management consultants' databases including online services;
- bespoke surveys conducted by the organization;
- pay clubs;
- published data in journals;
- official sources;
- recruitment consultants and agencies;
- analysis of recruitment data;
- job advertisements.

Each of these sources is described and assessed below.

Online pay data

There has been a considerable increase in recent years of pay data obtainable online. This is quicker, cheaper and often more up to date than paper publications, and search facilities are usually available. Instead of ordering pre-designed, standard analyses delivered in a static survey format, survey results can be individually tailored to suit the organization's needs. Users have the ability to extrapolate salary figures for different job positions and adjust them for company size (turnover), sector and location. They can decide how the market should be segmented and drill down and analyse the raw source data and create reports. Data submission is easier. It is simply a matter of entering the organization's data online, which is still there for the next survey. Alternatively, data can be downloaded from the HR system and submitted offline on Excel spreadsheets. Online data are available from the following suppliers:

- Croner Reward, www.salarysearch.co.uk;
- Cubiks, www.cubiksurvey.com;
- Hay Group, www.haypaynet.com.

Pay databases are also available from:

- IDS Pay Benchmark, www.incomesdata.co.uk;
- Labour Research Department, www.lrd.org.uk;
- PayWizard, www.paywizard.co.uk – this is a free service, offered by the Trades Union Congress and pay analysts Incomes Data Services (IDS), enabling people to compare their earnings against what others receive for doing similar jobs.

General published surveys

General published surveys can be purchased from providers such as Monks, Remuneration Economics (PricewaterhouseCoopers) and Croner Reward. Hay Group also provides clients who use its job evaluation system with market rate data where survey contributors achieve job matching through use of the common evaluation process.

The surveys contain data on a variety of occupations (sometimes restricted to managerial and professional jobs), usually for the whole of the United Kingdom, and often analysed by regions. They may be produced as paper-based documents but, as mentioned above, this is increasingly being replaced by electronic formats such as standard computer spreadsheet presentations or PDF documents that can be delivered directly via e-mail or published on and downloaded from websites.

The data include details of base salary and total earnings levels at a given date, with some information on the provision of employee benefits. Pay movements may also be included. The data are presented by job title and function. There is usually some indication of the level of the job and sometimes a brief description of typical responsibilities. The data will probably be analysed in terms of organization size (sales turnover or number of employees), location and industry sector.

General surveys are produced by expert providers and offer wide coverage of pay levels in the national and regional labour markets. However, their value is diminished by the problems of job matching, except in the case of the Hay survey. This difficulty and differences in sampling explain why data on seemingly similar jobs may vary widely between surveys. Variations are also caused because the surveys may have been conducted on different dates.

General local published surveys

Some organizations such as locally based management consultants and recruitment agencies conduct and publish surveys of the local labour market, covering office and manual occupations as well as managerial and professional jobs.

Such surveys can usefully provide relevant information for the market in which an organization is doing most of its recruiting. It is necessary, however, to ensure that the survey includes data from a reasonable number of organizations (no fewer than 20 or so), and that it has been conducted professionally, with some care to ensure an acceptable level of job matching.

Sector and industrial surveys

Sector surveys can produce helpful information on a sector where pay levels and occupations may be distinct from those in other sectors, for example the electronics industry, the insurance industry and the voluntary sector. These are conducted by a range of organizations, including specialist salary survey firms, management consultants, employers and trade associations. Many of the main providers of general surveys publish specialist surveys. Their advantage is that they provide information about relevant labour markets but they have the same disadvantages as any published survey.

Occupational surveys

Occupational surveys conducted by consultants or professional institutions provide information on the pay of people in occupations such as accountants, HR specialists, IT staff, sales staff and office staff. They can give useful information on general levels of pay for professional people but they may be confined to pay in relation to age, qualifications and membership status rather than to jobs.

Management consultants' databases

The larger management consultancy firms, especially those specializing in pay, maintain their own database of salary levels. They can provide useful information on general salary levels for managers and professional staff but matching may be difficult.

Bespoke surveys

An organization can conduct its own special survey or arrange for a firm of management consultants to conduct one on its behalf. This may be a national, regional or sector survey, or it may be confined to the local labour market. It could cover a range of occupations or focus on particular jobs.

Such surveys can be as sophisticated as those conducted by the organizations that publish general surveys, or they can be relatively simple. They have the advantage of being able to concentrate on the jobs in which the organizations are particularly interested. They can also seek information from organizations competing in the same national or local labour market, which may be quite willing to cooperate as long as they think the benefit of the extra information with which they are provided on a reciprocal basis justifies the time and effort in replying to a survey questionnaire. But they do entail a considerable amount of work and it may be frustrating to get people to cooperate and provide the information on time. The steps required are described below:

1. *Draw up a list of participating organizations.* The first step in conducting a special pay survey is to draw up list of participating organizations. Those invited to take part should be chosen on the basis of their compatibility with regard to sector, size and the sort of jobs they have. Selection will also be governed by estimates of the likelihood of the organizations agreeing to participate. It is obviously best to start with organizations and individuals known to the originator of the survey. Preferably the organizations selected should be ones where there are HR or pay specialists who will be able to obtain and present the information required. It is generally easier to conduct a local market survey because good networks are more likely to exist.

    The number of organizations invited will depend on the time available and on whether the survey is to be by post or by personal visit. Personal visits are ideal, but they are time-consuming and the participating organizations may prefer to deal quickly with a return rather than having to entertain a visitor. Clearly, the more sources of information the better. The aim should be to attract at least 20 participants, although in a specialized area it may be necessary to be content with a smaller number. Experience has shown that, unless the originating company is fortunate, at least a third of the companies invited to take part will decline on the grounds that they do not reveal pay data, or that they will get nothing out of it, or that they have contributed to enough surveys already. The proportion of refusals can be minimized by adopting an impressively professional approach, but some refusals are inevitable and should be allowed for when drawing up the list of organizations.

2. *Decide on the data required, the format in which they should be made available and the information that should accompany the invitation to participate.* The data requested will include levels of pay for specified jobs (base rates and earnings) and details of benefits provision as required. The format usually includes a request for information on the median rate for particular jobs and an indication of dispersion, eg the upper and lower quartile rate. The format for the survey should be as simple as possible to encourage comparators to participate. An example of a survey form restricted to pay data is given in Figure 15.1. Further columns could be added as required to obtain information on such benefits, allowances and terms and conditions as pension schemes, life insurance, company cars, location allowances, holidays and hours of work. The terms used, eg base rates, total earnings and median and quartiles, need to be defined. Capsule job descriptions should be supplied.

3. *Approach comparators.* When approaching potential comparator organizations it is best to deal with known contacts, but a direct approach often has to be made out of the blue. There is much to be said for making the approach by e-mail, possibly followed up by a telephone call. The e-mail can lead to the use of electronic means to collect and analyse data, which is infinitely preferable to the traditional paper exercise from the point of view of both the participant and the originator of the survey. When inviting someone you do not know to participate, the three messages to be got across are that: 1) a responsible individual is conducting the survey, which will be carried out competently; 2) the respondent organization will obtain relevant and useful information in return in the form of a summary of the survey results; and 3) they will not be put to too much trouble. The date by which it is hoped responses will be made available should also be stated. People tend to complete such forms at the last minute and it is best to restrict the time to three or four weeks.

4. *Collect, analyse and distribute data.* Respondents may have to be reminded to supply the data. If the worst comes to the worst, an attempt can be made to collect the data over the telephone. When sufficient data are received, a summary should be provided to participants on an anonymous basis.

Job title	No. in job	Base rates £			Total earnings £		
		Lower quartile	Median	Upper quartile	Lower quartile	Median	Upper quartile

Figure 15.1 Example of a pay and benefits survey form

Pay clubs

Pay clubs consist of members who regularly exchange information amongst themselves on the pay and benefits provided for a selected range of jobs. The methods used to produce and analyse the data and the format of the capsule descriptions are similar to those used for special surveys as described above. A considerable number of such clubs have been set up by employers in a particular sector or part of a sector and in industries or localities. Their advantage is that more accurate job matching can be achieved and the information is obtained in a standardized form on a regular basis.

Pay clubs should consist of a sufficient number of members, 10 or more, to ensure that a good spread of information is obtained. They can be set up by an existing network, the members of which already exchange information informally and who want to obtain comparative data more systematically. If such a network does not exist, a company may decide to form a club.

It is useful to invite interested parties to a meeting at which agreement can be reached on the jobs to be covered, the data to be collected for those jobs, the preparation of capsule job descriptions, the method of analysis and presentation and how the club may be run. The originating company may undertake to administer the drawing up of capsule job descriptions and the initial survey. However, the aim is to get club members interested enough to take turns in administering the survey. They may agree to contribute to retaining a management consultant to conduct it.

Many existing pay clubs are oversubscribed and will not accept new members.

Published data in journals

Up-to-date company and national pay data can be obtained from:

- Incomes Data Services and IRS Employment Review (Pay and Benefits Section), which monitor pay settlements and publish details of agreements. Details of pay structures and trends in individual companies are also supplied but there is little or no information on the rate of pay of individual jobs.
- The government's Labour Force Survey and Annual Survey of Hours and Earnings, which provide information on earnings levels by industry, occupation, region, age group and hours worked (contact www.statistics.gov.uk). This is readily available but statistics are based on broad occupational categories and are not usually specific enough for accurate benchmarking.
- The business news sections of the *Financial Times* and other quality newspapers, which give general information on pay trends.

Recruitment consultants and agencies

Recruitment consultants and agencies should have a good 'feel' for levels of pay in the posts that they are helping to fill. They obtain data from employers and from applications. Executive search consultants are particularly knowledgeable about rates of pay in the senior management job market. They will sometimes conduct their own surveys, which can provide useful information.

Analysis of recruitment data

It is sometimes possible to get ancillary data about levels of pay by analysing information obtained from recruitment campaigns. Data provided in CVs may be suspect, but some indication of what is the going rate can be obtained by establishing how much money is required to attract a particular type and level of applicant.

Job advertisements

A lot of people, especially line managers, rely on job advertisements in the national and local press or in specialist journals. Advertisements provide some indication of levels of pay but they should be treated with great caution, especially in the case of managerial and professional jobs advertised nationally. Differences in the levels of responsibility and scope of jobs with the same job title can be considerable and levels of pay vary accordingly. The brief descriptions of the jobs are often full of hyperbole and may be misleading. The quoted pay levels may be misleading. This problem is not so acute for the clerical, sales and manual workers who are advertised for in local papers.

Nevertheless, even for managerial and professional jobs, advertisements provide an additional source of information that cannot be ignored. Employees will also be looking at them and will be drawing their own conclusions about what they are worth in the marketplace.

Other market intelligence

Data on market rates can be obtained from informal contacts or networks. Information can usefully be exchanged on rates of pay for specific jobs, increases in pay levels, performance or merit pay increases, and data obtained from separate market rate surveys. Building up and maintaining an informal or semi-formal network can be very helpful, especially if it consists of employers or personnel managers who are interested in the local labour market.

Selecting data sources

Because it is unlikely that precise job matching, a perfect sample and coincidence of timing will be achieved, it is advisable to obtain data from more than one source. Ultimately, a judgement has to be made about market levels of pay and this will be helped if a range of information is available, which enables a view to be taken on what should be regarded as 'the market rate' for internal use. This is more convincing if it has been derived from a number of sources. It will also provide the objective justification for any market premiums, which might create unequal pay.

Published surveys, which are readily accessible and are based on a large sample, can be used to back up individual or club surveys. If the information can be obtained online, so much the better. But it has to be relevant to the needs of the organization and particular attention should always be paid to the range of data and the quality of job matching. General market data can be supplemented by specialist surveys covering particular jobs. Should the quality of job matching be important, an individual survey can be conducted or a salary club can be joined if there is room.

Market intelligence and published data from journals and associated sources should always be used as back-up material and for information on going rates and trends. They can provide invaluable help with updating.

Although the analysis of job advertisements has its dangers, it can be used as further back-up or to give an instant snapshot of current rates, but it is risky to rely on this source alone.

Published surveys are of widely varying content, presentation and quality and are sometimes expensive. When selecting a published survey use the following guide-lines:

- Does it cover relevant jobs in similar organizations?
- Does it provide the information on the pay and benefits required?
- Are there enough participants to provide acceptable comparisons?
- So far as can be judged, is the survey conducted properly in terms of its sampling techniques and the quality of job matching?
- Is the survey reasonably up to date?
- Are the results well presented?
- Does it provide value for money?

As a starting point to identifying a relevant survey, look at the regular reviews included in publications from Incomes Data Services and IRS. Pay analysts Incomes Data Services also publish a directory that brings together information on virtually every available survey of salaries and benefits produced in the UK, providing an unmatched guide to data sources. It currently lists some 290 surveys of salaries and benefits from 76 UK survey producers, covering national surveys, local surveys, benefit surveys and international surveys, and gives details of employee groups and jobs covered by each survey, sample size, date of the survey data and the length and price of the report. Subscribers to the directory can also access it online and search for data by job title, type of benefit, sector, UK region or overseas region. Contact www.salarysurveys. info.

The main sources and their advantages and disadvantages are analysed in Table 15.1.

ANALYSE DATA

Market analysis requires the understanding of a number of statistical terms as described below.

Measures of central tendency, ie the point about which the several values cluster, consist of:

- The arithmetic mean or *average* (A), which is the total of the values of the items in the set divided by the number of individual items in the set. The average can, however, be distorted by extreme values on either side of the centre.

Table 15.1 Analysis of data sources

Source	Brief Description	Advantages	Disadvantages
Online data	Access data from general surveys.	Quick; easy; can be tailored.	May not provide all the information required.
General national published surveys	Available for purchase – provide an overall picture of pay levels for different occupations in national and regional labour markets.	Wide coverage; readily available; continuity allows trend analyses over time; expert providers.	Risk of imprecise job matching; insufficiently specific; quickly out of date.
Local published surveys	Available for purchase – provide an overall picture of pay levels for different occupations in the local labour market.	Focus on local labour market especially for administrative staff and manual workers.	Risk of imprecise job matching; insufficiently specific; quickly out of date; providers may not have expertise in pay surveys.
Sector surveys	Available for purchase – provide data on a sector such as charities.	Focus on a sector where pay levels may differ from national rates; deal with particular categories in depth.	Risk of imprecise job matching; insufficiently specific; quickly out of date.
Industrial/ occupational surveys	Surveys often conducted by employer and trade associations on jobs in an industry or specific jobs.	Focus on an industry; deal with particular categories in depth; quality of job matching may be better than general or sector surveys.	Job matching may still not be entirely precise; quickly out of date.
Management consultants' databases	Pay data obtained from the databases maintained by management consultants.	Based on well-researched and matched data.	Only obtainable from specific consultants.

Table 15.1 Continued

Source	Brief Description	Advantages	Disadvantages
Special surveys	Surveys specially conducted by an organization.	Focused; reasonably good job matching; control of participants; control of analysis methodology.	Take time and trouble; may be difficult to get participation; sample size may therefore be inadequate.
Pay clubs	Groups of employers who regularly exchange data on pay levels.	Focused; precise job matching; control of participants; control of analysis methodology; regular data; trends data; more information may be available on benefits and pay policies.	Sample size may be too small; involve a considerable amount of administration; may be difficult to maintain enthusiasm of participants.
Published data in journals	Data on settlements and pay levels available from IDS or IRS, and on national trends in earnings from the New Earnings Survey.	Readily accessible.	Mainly about settlements and trends; little specific well-matched information on pay levels for individual jobs.
Analysis of recruitment data	Pay data derived from analysis of pay levels required to recruit staff.	Immediate data.	Data random and can be misleading because of small sample.
Job advertisements	Pay data obtained from job advertisements.	Readily accessible; highly visible (to employees as well as employers); up to date.	Job matching very imprecise; pay information may be misleading.
Other market intelligence	Pay data obtained from informal contacts or networks.	Provide good background.	Imprecise; not regularly available.

- The *median* (M), which is the middle item in the distribution of individual items – 50 per cent of the sample falls above the median, 50 per cent below. This is unaffected by extremes and is generally preferred to the arithmetical mean, as long as there are a sufficient number of individual items (the median of a sample much less than 10 is suspect). Medians are often lower than arithmetic means because of the tendency in the latter case for there to be a number of high values at the top of the range.

Measures of dispersion, ie the range of values in the set, which provides guidance on the variations in the distribution of values of items around the median, consist of:

- *The upper quartile* (UQ) – the value above which one-quarter of the individual values fall (this term is sometimes used incorrectly to indicate the range of values above the upper quartile).
- *The lower quartile* (LQ) – the value below which one-quarter of the individual values fall (also sometimes used incorrectly as in the case of the upper quartile).
- *The inter-quartile range* – the 50 per cent difference between the upper and lower quartile values; this is a good measure of dispersion.
- *Upper and lower deciles* – the values above and below which 10 per cent of the individual values fall. This is less frequently used but does provide for greater refinement in the analysis of distribution.
- *Total range* – the difference between the highest and lowest values. This can be misleading if there are extreme values at either end, and is less often used than the inter-quartile range, except where the sample is very small.

PREPARE INFORMATION ON THE JOBS TO BE SURVEYED

The information may be prepared by role analysis leading to the production of capsule job descriptions, as illustrated in Figure 15.2.

Information will also be required on current rates of pay and earnings and benefits.

INTERPRET AND PRESENT MARKET DATA

Data need to be interpreted by reference to the details provided from each source and by assessments of data reliability, accuracy and relevance. If data have been obtained

---

CAPSULE JOB DESCRIPTION

Retail marketing analyst

1 Provide annual and monthly forecasts of retail sales on the basis of given assumptions to assist in generating retail one- and three-year plans.
2 Maintain database of information on sales, retail prices and customer discounts.
3 Provide information on products to the trade and other interested parties.
4 Deal with queries on products and prices from customers.
5 Provide general support to marketing and sales managers in analysing retail sales data.
6 Undertake special investigations and ad hoc exercises as required to support marketing and sales planning activities.

Figure 15.2   Example of a capsule job description

from a number of sources these will also have to be interpreted to produce a derived market rate, which will be used as the basis of comparison. This can be entirely judgemental, but a quantified method of analysing and interpreting multi-source data can be used, as shown in a simplified form in Figure 15.3. This approach commits the statistical sin of averaging averages but at least it provides some rationale for the judgement.

The significance of information can sometimes be revealed more clearly if the tables are supplemented by graphs, which can highlight significant data and comparisons, as in the example in Figure 15.4.

Figure 15.5 shows how a graphical presentation can be made of the outcome of a pay survey based on job evaluation scores compared with the organization's practice line of actual salaries and the policy line defining where the organization would like its pay levels to be. This example shows that pay practice is falling behind pay policy and is ahead of median market rates in the lower part of the scale but market rates are higher in the upper part of the scale.

Source	Assessment of source: reliability, relevance, sample size, quality of job matching: 3 = excellent 2 = good 1 = acceptable	Lower quartile £	Median £	Upper quartile £
A	3	19,000	20,000	21,000
B	2	20,000	21,000	22,000
C	2	21,000	22,000	23,000
D	2	19,000	20,000	21,000
Derived market rate – average weighted by assessment		19,600	20,600	21,600

Figure 15.3 Presentation of market data from different sources and a derived market rate

USING MARKET DATA

The available data have to be collected and presented in the most accessible manner possible (ie job by job for all the areas the structure is to cover). In a graded or career/job family structure (see Chapter 17), a 'reference point' can be established for each

Marketing Director	Survey data						
			LQ		M		UQ
	Actual pay				X		
UK Sales Director	Survey data						
			LQ		M		UQ
	Actual pay				X		
Marketing Executive	Survey data						
		LQ	M	UQ			
	Actual pay		X X X				
Annual pay		35K	40K	50K	55K	60K	65K

Figure 15.4 Comparison of survey data and actual salaries

grade level based on the place in the market the company wishes to occupy, ie its 'market stance'. The establishment of this reference point will be based not only on assessment of current and updated pay data, but also on indications of movements in earnings and the cost of living that are likely to affect the life of the whole structure. The reference point is commonly placed at the mid-point of the grade. For organizations needing to stay ahead of the market, this point will often be between the median and the upper quartile (of a significant population). For others, closer alignment with the median may be sufficient. Once the series of reference points in relation to the market has been established and assessed, the principles of grade and pay structure design construction set out in Chapter 18 can be applied. Market rate data can contribute to the development of market groups in a job family structure.

The market rate data can also be used to determine spot rates (ie rates of pay for specific jobs not incorporated into a conventional grade and pay structure) and the

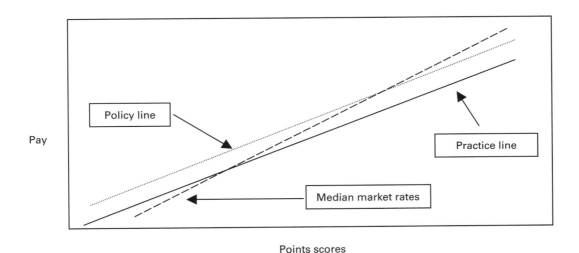

Figure 15.5 A graphical presentation of comparative survey data

positioning of jobs in a broad-banded structure when the design of such a structure is largely market-driven.

Guidance from market rate data will be available to determine where market rate supplements may be necessary to maintain competitive pay rates for any category of staff for which special measures need to be taken to ensure that they join and stay with the organization. Market rate supplements (sometimes called recruitment premiums when they are primarily designed to attract staff) are special payments made in addition to the standard rate for the job. They are reviewed regularly and can be abolished if the market conditions no longer justify them. But if this happens, the pay of existing staff will need to be protected. A record needs to be kept of the rationale for supplements to enable any market differentials to be objectively justified in an equal pay case.

A database should be set up of the information, which can be updated regularly.

A FINAL WORD

Market analysis is all about judgement and compromise. Judgement has to be exercised when selecting sources of data and analysing data. Compromise is required because it is not possible for any survey to show the single correct rate for a job and it is necessary to produce derived market rates from a range of data.

REFERENCE

1   CubikSurvey.com (2005) *Market Rate Survey Report*, Cubik, London

16

Role analysis

The reliability and validity of many reward management processes, including job evaluation, job matching when conducting market rate surveys, and pay structure design, depend largely on the quality of the analysis of roles. Role analysis is a fundamental HR process. It provides the information needed to produce role profiles for use in recruitment, learning and development, performance management and job evaluation. This chapter covers: 1) the terms used in role analysis; 2) the contribution made by role analysis to reward management; 3) the methods used in role analysis; 4) role profile definition; and 5) the use of generic role profiles with examples.

DEFINITIONS

Roles and jobs

The terms 'role' and 'job' are often used interchangeably but they can be distinguished from one another.

A *role* is the part played by people in carrying out their work. It refers to the competencies they require to do the work, as well as the outcomes produced by using those competencies. It is set out in a role profile.

A *job* consists of a group of finite tasks to be performed, responsibilities to be exercised and duties to be carried out as set out in a job description.

The term 'job evaluation' rather than 'role evaluation' has been retained in this book because the former is still common parlance. But this chapter focuses on *role analysis* as the means of providing the information required for job evaluation because the concept of a role draws attention to the significance of competencies while the concept of a job is more limited. This reflects the emphasis on competencies both in factor plans and in grade or level profiles.

Individual and generic roles

Individual roles are those carried out by one person. Generic roles are those in which essentially similar activities are carried out by a number of people. They may cover a whole occupation.

Role profile

A role profile defines the outcomes role holders are expected to deliver in terms of key result areas or accountabilities. It also lists the competencies required to perform effectively in the role – what role holders need to know and be able to do. Role profiles can be individual or generic.

Role analysis

Role analysis is the process of obtaining the information required to produce a role profile.

ROLE ANALYSIS AND REWARD MANAGEMENT

The contribution made by role analysis to job evaluation, market rate analysis, the design of graded pay structures and performance management is described below.

Job evaluation

For job evaluation purposes, role analysis generates the information required to generate a role profile, which enables evaluators to form a judgement on the levels of demand and responsibility in a role and how a role should be graded. In point-factor evaluation this judgement determines the level in the factor plan into which the role fits. In analytical matching the information obtained by role analysis is used by evaluators to match the role with a grade profile or a benchmark role.

In point-factor evaluations, the role analysis is built round the factor plan so that information about the demands made by the role or the levels of responsibility for each factor is available to the evaluator. In analytical matching, the role profile may use the same headings as a factor plan or a special set of factors may be used for this purpose.

Market rate analysis

Role analysis provides the essential data needed to produce the capsule descriptions used for job matching.

Graded pay structure design

The design of grade structures may involve the production of grade definitions or profiles that will enable matching to take place. Guidance on producing these will be provided by role analysis (further information on the definition of grade profiles is given in Chapter 18).

Performance management

As described in Chapter 24, an essential part of performance management is an agreement on role expectations. This agreement may start by referring to an existing role profile but it is necessary to update and revise that as necessary, and this means further role analysis.

METHODOLOGY

Role analysis uses systematic methods to collect the information required. It starts with a definition of the information required. This information is then collected by interviews or questionnaires or a combination of the two.

Information requirements

The information should consist of:

- A brief definition of the purpose of the role.
- A list of the outcomes expected from the role holder. These should be limited to seven or eight key result areas or accountabilities.
- Details of the demands made on the role holder and the responsibilities involved. Where appropriate, these are set out under the headings of the point-factor scheme factor plan where the factor and level definitions will indicate what is needed. If role-to-grade analytical matching is to take place, the information on role demands

relates to the factors used in defining grade or level profiles. These may refer to technical competencies that describe what people are expected to know and be able to do to perform their work, or they can also refer to behavioural competencies that define how people are expected to behave in order to perform their work well.

Interviews

To obtain the full flavour of a role, it is best to interview role holders and check the findings with their managers or team leaders. The aim of the interview is to obtain all the relevant facts about the role to provide the information required for a role profile. It is helpful to use a checklist when conducting the interview. Elaborate checklists are not necessary. They only confuse people. The basic questions to be answered are:

1. What is the title of your role?
2. To whom are you responsible?
3. Who is responsible to you? (An organization chart is helpful.)
4. What is the main purpose of your role? Ie in overall terms, what are you expected to do?
5. What are the key activities you have to carry out in your role? Try to group them under no more than 10 headings.
6. What are the results you are expected to achieve in each of those key activities?
7. What are you expected to know to be able to carry out your role?
8. What skills should you have to carry out your role?

The answers to these questions may need to be sorted out – they can often result in a mass of jumbled information that has to be analysed so that the various activities can be distinguished and refined to seven or eight key areas.

The advantages of the interviewing method are that it is flexible, can provide in-depth information and is easy to organize and prepare. It is therefore the most common approach. But interviewing can be time-consuming, which is why, in large role analysis exercises, questionnaires as described below may be used to provide advance information about the job. This speeds up the interviewing process. It may even replace the interview altogether, although this means that much of the 'flavour' of the job – ie what it is really like – may be lost.

Questionnaires

Questionnaires about their roles can be completed by role holders and approved by their manager or team leader. They are helpful when a large number of roles have to be covered. They can also save interviewing time by recording purely factual information and by enabling the analyst to structure questions in advance to cover areas that need to be explored in greater depth. The simpler the questionnaire the better. It need only cover the eight questions listed above.

The advantage of questionnaires is that they can produce information quickly and cheaply for a large number of jobs. But a substantial sample is needed, and the construction of a questionnaire is a skilled job that should only be carried out on the basis of some preliminary fieldwork. It is highly advisable to pilot-test questionnaires before launching into a full-scale exercise. The accuracy of the results also depends on the willingness and ability of job holders to complete questionnaires. Many people find it difficult to express themselves in writing about their work.

Generic roles

The same methods can be used to prepare generic role profiles. However, it is advisable to obtain information from a number of role holders – three or four at least – which can then be distilled into a generic format.

ROLE PROFILE DEFINITION

Both individual and generic role profiles can be set out under the following headings:

- *Role title.*
- *Department.*
- *Responsible to.*
- *Responsible to role holder.*
- *Purpose of the role* – defined in one reasonably succinct sentence that defines why the role exists in terms of the overall contribution the role holder makes.
- *Key result areas* – if at all possible these should be limited to seven or eight, and certainly not more than 10. Each key result area should be defined in a single sentence beginning with an active verb (eg 'identify', 'develop', 'support') that provides a positive indication of what has to be done and eliminates unnecessary wording. Describe the object of the verb (what is done) as succinctly as possible, for example 'Test new systems', 'Post cash to the nominal and sales ledgers', 'Schedule production', 'Ensure that management accounts are produced', 'Prepare marketing plans'. State briefly the purpose of the activity in terms of outputs or standards to be achieved, for example 'Test new systems to ensure they meet agreed systems specifications', 'Post cash to the nominal and sales ledgers in order to provide up-to-date and accurate financial information', 'Schedule production in order to meet

Role title: Database administrator

Department: Information systems

Purpose of role: Responsible for the development and support of databases and their underlying environment.

Key result areas

- Identify database requirements for all projects that require data management in order to meet the needs of internal customers.
- Develop project plans collaboratively with colleagues to deliver against their database needs.
- Support underlying database infrastructure.
- Liaise with system and software providers to obtain product information and support.
- Manage project resources (people and equipment) within predefined budget and criteria, as agreed with line manager and originating department.
- Allocate work to and supervise contractors on day-to-day basis.
- Ensure security of the underlying database infrastructure through adherence to established protocols and develop additional security protocols where needed.

Need to know

- Oracle database administration.
- Operation of Designer 2000 and Oracle forms SQL/PLSQL, Unix administration, shell programming.

Able to:

- Analyse and choose between options where the solution is not always obvious.
- Develop project plans and organize own workload on a timescale of 1–2 months.
- Adapt to rapidly changing needs and priorities without losing sight of overall plans and priorities.
- Interpret budgets in order to manage resources effectively within them.
- Negotiate with suppliers.
- Keep abreast of technical developments and trends, bring these into day-to-day work when feasible and build them into new project developments.

Behavioural competencies

- Aim to get things done well and set and meet challenging goals, create own measures of excellence and constantly seek ways of improving performance.
- Analyse information from range of sources and develop effective solutions/recommendations.
- Communicate clearly and persuasively, orally or in writing, dealing with technical issues in a non-technical manner.
- Work participatively on projects with technical and non-technical colleagues.
- Develop positive relationships with colleagues as the supplier of an internal service.

Figure 16.1   Example of an individual role profile

output and delivery targets', 'Ensure that management accounts are produced that provide the required level of information to management and individual managers on financial performance against budget and on any variances', 'Prepare marketing plans that support the achievement of the marketing strategies of the enterprise, are realistic, and provide clear guidance on the actions to be taken by the development, production, marketing and sales departments'.

- *Need to know* – the knowledge required overall or in specific key result areas of the business and its competitors and customers, techniques, processes, procedures or products.
- *Need to be able to do* – the skills required in each area of activity.
- *Expected behaviour* – the behaviours particularly expected of the role holder (behavioural competencies), which may be extracted from the organization's competency framework.

EXAMPLES OF ROLE PROFILES

An example of an individual role profile is given in Figure 16.1. Examples of generic role profiles are given in Figures 16.2, 16.3 and 16.4.

Elements	Role analysis
1 Teaching and learning support	• Plan, design and deliver a number of modules within subject area. • Deliver at undergraduate and/or postgraduate levels across a range of modules. • Use appropriate teaching, learning support and assessment methods. • Supervise projects, field trips and, where appropriate, placements. • Supervise postgraduate students. • Identify areas where current course provision is in need of revision or improvement. • Contribute to the planning, design and development of course objectives and material. • Ensure in conjunction with colleagues that modules complement other courses taken by students. • Set, mark and assess coursework and examinations and provide feedback to students.
2 Research and scholarship	• Develop research objectives and proposals, obtain funding and design research projects. • Conduct individual and collaborative research projects, lead small research teams or play a major part in research teams. • Identify sources of funding and contribute to the process of securing funds. • Extend, transform and apply knowledge acquired through scholarly activities. • Write and referee journal articles, or write or contribute to textbooks and make presentations at national and international conferences.
3 Communication	• Communicate straightforward through to complex information to a variety of audiences, including students, peers and external contacts. • Use high-level presentation skills and a range of media.
4 Liaison and networking	• Liaise with colleagues in other departments and/or institutions on professional matters. • Participate in departmental and other committee meetings. • Join external networks to foster collaboration and share information and ideas. • May represent the department at external meetings.
5 Managing people	• Lead the delivery of teaching in a module or programme: plan the timetable, allocate teaching responsibilities, and monitor the delivery of programmes to ensure that they achieve learning objectives and are meeting quality standards. • Lead small research teams. • Act as mentor to more junior lecturers. • Appraise staff and advise them on their personal development.
6 Teamwork	• Attend and actively participate in regular team meetings at which course development and delivery issues are discussed. • Collaborate with colleagues to identify and respond to students' needs.
7 Pastoral care	• Use listening, interpersonal and pastoral care skills to deal with sensitive issues concerning students and provide support. • Refer students as appropriate to services providing further help. • Act as personal tutor.
8 Initiative, problem solving and decision making	• Identify the need for developing the content or structure of a course and put proposals together in conjunction with colleagues on how this should be achieved. • Develop creative ideas as a result of research and scholarship. • Deal with admission queries and problems concerning student performance. • Sole responsibility to decide how to deliver own modules and assess students.

Figure 16.2   Example of a generic role profile for a higher education lecturer

9 Planning and managing resources	• As module leader or tutor, liaise with colleagues on content and method of delivery. • May plan and implement consultancy projects to generate income for the institution.
10 Emotional demands	• Work under pressure to deliver results.
11 Work environment	• Work in a stable environment or a laboratory or workshop.
12 Expertise	• Possess in-depth knowledge of the subject. • Possess the required levels of expertise in teaching and research. • Update skills and knowledge continuously. • Understand equal opportunity issues as they impact upon the delivery of teaching and collegiate working.

Figure 16.2 *Continued*

Overall purpose of role:

To lead teams in order to attain team goals and further the achievement of the organization's objectives.

Key result areas

1   Agree targets and standards with team members that support the attainment of the organization's objectives.
2   Plan with team members work schedules and resource requirements that will ensure that team targets will be reached or, indeed, exceeded.
3   Agree performance measures and quality assurance processes with team members that will clarify output and quality expectations.
4   Agree with team members the allocation of tasks, rotating responsibilities as appropriate to achieve flexibility and the best use of the skills and capabilities of team members.
5   Coordinate the work of the team to ensure that team goals are achieved.
6   Ensure that the team members collectively monitor the team's performance in terms of achieving output, speed of response and quality targets and standards and agree with team members any corrective action required to ensure that team goals are achieved.
7   Conduct team reviews of performance to agree improvement.

Competencies

- Builds effective team relationships, ensuring that team members are committed to the common purpose.
- Encourages self-direction amongst team members but provides guidance and clear direction as required.
- Shares information with team members.
- Trusts team members to get on with things – not continually checking.
- Treats team members fairly and consistently.
- Supports and guides team members to make the best use of their capabilities.
- Encourages self-development by example.
- Actively offers constructive feedback to team members and positively seeks and is open to constructive feedback from them.
- Contributes to the development of team members, encouraging the acquisition of additional skills and providing opportunities for them to be used effectively.

Figure 16.3   Example of a generic role profile for a team leader

Overall purpose of role:
To act in partnership with line management and contribute to the effective management of the division by delivering the HR services required.

Key result areas:
- Work alongside line managers and provide help and advice on HR issues.
- Deal with people issues in the division.
- Ensure the division has the skilled people it requires.
- Promote a learning culture in the division and set up and deliver learning and development programmes to meet divisional needs.
- Ensure that performance management processes work effectively in the division, providing advice and guidance to line managers as necessary.
- Provide help and guidance to line managers in conducting pay reviews.
- Contribute to the development of corporate HR strategy and policy.

Knowledge required of:
- HRM techniques at the level of Member, CIPD with at least four years' experience;
- business imperatives in the division;
- employment law;
- corporate policies and procedures – employment, performance and reward management, employee relations;
- labour markets for people required by the division;
- techniques of performance and reward management.

Skills required in:
- analysing business requirements and the needs of people within the division and their implications for people management;
- anticipating the requirements of line managers and employees in the division;
- promoting the empowerment of line managers to make HR decisions but providing advice and guidance as required;
- change management;
- providing efficient and cost-effective services in each HR area;
- oral and written communication.

Competencies required:
- personal credibility;
- strategic capability;
- selects courses of action that will produce added-value outcomes for the division;
- high levels of interpersonal skills;
- coaches clients to deal with their own problems, transfers skills;
- diagnoses problems, builds relationships with clients;
- deploys intuitive/creative thinking to generate innovative solutions and proactively seize opportunities;
- customer focus.

Figure 16.4   Example of a generic role profile for an HR business partner

Part 4

Grade and pay structures

17

Types of grade and pay structures

Grade and pay structures provide a logically designed framework within which an organization's pay policies can be implemented. They enable the organization to determine where jobs should be placed in a hierarchy, define pay levels and the scope for pay progression and provide the basis upon which relativities can be managed, equal pay achieved and the processes of monitoring and controlling the implementation of pay practices take place. A grade and pay structure can also serve as a medium through which the organization communicates the career and pay opportunities available to employees.

This chapter starts with definitions of grade and pay structures and then describes the following types: narrow-graded, broad-graded, broad-banded, career family, combined, job family and pay spine. Spot rate and individual job grades are also described as methods of establishing and defining pay levels and pay ranges.

GRADE STRUCTURES

A grade structure consists of a sequence or hierarchy of grades, bands or levels into which groups of jobs that are broadly comparable in size are placed. There may be a single structure, which is defined by the number of grades or bands it contains.

Alternatively the structure may be divided into a number of career or job families consisting of groups of jobs where the essential nature and purpose of the work are similar but the work is carried out at different levels.

The main types of graded structures as described in this chapter are:

- *Narrow-graded structures*, which consist of a sequence of narrow grades (generally 10 or more). They are sometimes called multi-graded structures.
- *Broad-graded structures*, which have fewer grades (generally six to nine).
- *Broad-banded structures*, which consist of a limited number of grades or bands (often four to five). Structures with six or seven grades are often described as broad-banded even when their characteristics are typical of broad grades.
- *Career family structures*, which consist of a number of families (groups of jobs with similar characteristics) each divided typically into six to eight levels. The levels are described in terms of key responsibilities and knowledge, skill and competence requirements and therefore define career progression routes within and between career families. There is a common grade and pay structure across all the career families.
- *Job family structures*, which are similar to career families except that pay levels in each family may differ to reflect market rate considerations (this is sometimes referred to as market grouping). The structure is therefore more concerned with market rate relativities than mapping careers. The number of levels in families may also vary.
- *Combined structures*, in which broad bands are superimposed on career/job families or broad bands are divided into families.
- *Pay spines*, consisting of a series of incremental 'pay points' extending from the lowest- to the highest-paid jobs covered by the structure.

In addition, some organizations have spot rates or individual job grades as described at the end of this chapter. Strictly speaking, these are simply methods of describing a rate or pay range, not a structure in the sense defined above.

PAY STRUCTURES

A grade structure becomes a pay structure when pay ranges, brackets or scales are attached to each grade, band or level. In some broad-banded structures as described later in this chapter, reference points and pay zones may be placed within the bands and these define the range of pay for jobs allocated to each band.

Pay structures are defined by the number of grades they contain and, especially in narrow- or broad-graded structures, the span or width of the pay ranges attached to each grade. Span is the scope the grade provides for pay progression and is usually measured as the difference between the lowest point in the range and the highest point in the range as a percentage of the lowest point. Thus a range of £20,000 to £30,000 would have a span of 50 per cent.

Pay structures define the different levels of pay for jobs or groups of jobs by reference to their relative internal value as determined by job evaluation, to external relativities as established by market rate surveys and, sometimes, to negotiated rates for jobs. They provide scope for pay progression in accordance with performance, competence, contribution or service.

There may be a single pay structure covering the whole organization or there may be one structure for staff and another for manual workers, but this is becoming less common. There has in recent years been a trend towards 'harmonizing' terms and conditions between different groups of staff as part of a move towards single status. This has been particularly evident in many public sector organizations in the UK, supported by national agreements on 'single status'. Executive directors are sometimes treated separately.

The main types of grade and pay structures described in this chapter are narrow-graded structures, broad-graded structures, broad-banded structures, career and job family structures, pay spines, spot rates and individual job grades. Their features are summarized in Table 18.2 (page 300).

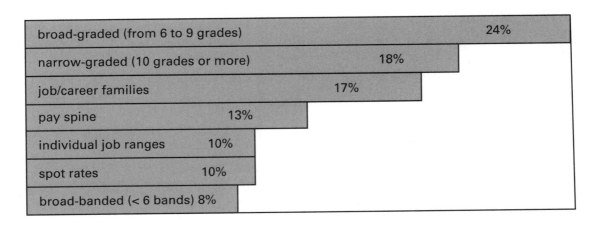

Figure 17.1 Incidence of grade and pay structures

Source: e-reward, 2004

INCIDENCE OF GRADE AND PAY STRUCTURES

The incidence of different types of grade and pay structure in the UK as established by e-reward (1) in 2004 is shown in Figure 17.1.

NARROW-GRADED STRUCTURES

Until fairly recently the typical type of structure was the narrow, multi-graded pay structure illustrated in Figure 17.2.

However, this type of structure is being replaced in many organizations by structures that have fewer grades (broad-graded structures) or with broad-banded, career family or job family structures.

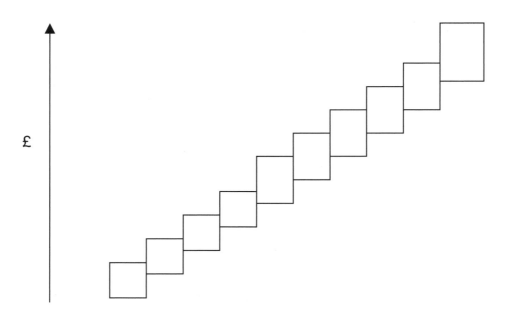

Figure 17.2 A narrow, multi-graded structure

Grades in a narrow-graded structure

A narrow-graded structure consists of a sequence of job grades into which jobs of broadly equivalent value are placed. There may be 10 or more grades, and long-established structures, especially in the public sector, may have as many as 18 grades. Grades may be defined by a bracket of job evaluation points so that any job for which the job evaluation score falls within the points bracket for a grade would be allocated to that grade. Alternatively, grades may be defined by grade definitions or profiles, which, if analytical factor comparison is used as described in Chapter 11, provide the information required to match jobs set out under job demand factor headings. This information can be supplemented by reference to benchmark jobs that have been already graded as part of the structure design exercise.

Pay ranges

A pay range is attached to each grade. This allows scope for pay progression, which is related to performance, competence or contribution. In a narrow-graded pay spine, progression is through fixed increments based on length of service in the job. The four characteristics of pay ranges as described below are span, reference points or target rates, differentials and overlap.

Span

Pay ranges may be described in terms of their span (the percentage by which the highest point exceeds the lowest point). This is usually between 20 per cent and 50 per cent (30 to 40 per cent is typical). The centre of the range is called the mid-point.

Alternatively, ranges are described as a percentage of the mid-point, for example 80 per cent to 120 per cent. In this case, the mid-point of 100 per cent could be £25,000 and the minimum and maximum would be £20,000 (80 per cent) and £30,000 (120 per cent) respectively. The span in this case is on the high side at 50 per cent.

Mid-point management techniques as described in Chapter 33 can be used to control the structure. They use compa-ratios, which express the actual rate of pay as a percentage of the mid-point when the latter is regarded as the policy rate of pay or the reference point.

Reference point

A reference point or target rate is often defined in each grade, which is the rate for a fully competent individual who is completely qualified to carry out the job. This is sometimes called the policy rate because it is usually aligned to market rates in accordance with company policies on the relationship between its pay levels and market rates for similar jobs (its 'market stance'). The reference point is commonly the mid-point of the pay range for a grade. It may be called a target rate when it is regarded as the consolidated rate to which individuals should aspire when they are fully competent and experienced in their roles. In some schemes people who reach this rate are only entitled to non-consolidated cash bonuses for exceptional achievement although this may be consolidated (ie incorporated in the base rate) if the level of achievement is sustained over two or three years.

Differentials

Differentials between pay ranges – the percentage by which the mid-point of a range is higher than the mid-point of the range below – are typically between 15 per cent and 20 per cent but they can be as high as 25 per cent. Too low a differential means that the scope for pay progression on upgrading is limited. Too high a differential means that a decision to upgrade may mean that the increase in pay is disproportionate to the increase in responsibility.

Overlap

There is usually an overlap between ranges. This is measured by the proportion of a grade which is covered by an adjacent grade. Thus if the range below is £20,000–£24,000 and the range above is £22,000–£26,000 the overlap is:

$$\frac{24,000 - 22,000}{24,000 - 20,000} \times 100 = 50\%$$

In this example the differential between the mid-points of the adjacent grades is fairly low at 9 per cent. Increasing the differential to about 15 per cent and adjusting the higher range to £23,000–£28,000 would decrease the overlap to 25 per cent. The degree of overlap can be manipulated at the design stage by varying differentials and ranges. An overlap provides more flexibility. It enables recognition to be given to the fact that a highly experienced individual at the top of a range may be contributing more than someone who is still in the learning curve portion of the next higher grade.

Advantages and disadvantages of narrow-graded structures

Narrow-graded structures provide a framework for managing relativities and for ensuring that jobs of equal value are paid equally. In theory they are easy to manage because the large number of grades enables fine distinctions to be made between different levels of responsibility. They define career ladders and staff may favour them because they appear to offer plenty of opportunities for increasing pay by upgrading.

The main problem with narrow, multi-graded structures is that, if there are too many grades, there will be constant pressure for upgrading, leading to grade drift (unjustified upgradings). They can be aligned to a traditional extended hierarchy that may no longer exist, and can function rigidly, which is at odds with the requirement of flexibility in new team- and process-based organizations. They also reinforce the importance of promotion as a means of progression, which may run counter to the need for organizations to be more flexible and grow capability by moving people within grades to broaden their experience and competencies.

BROAD-GRADED STRUCTURES

Broad-graded structures generally have six to nine grades rather than the 10 or more grades contained in narrow-graded structures. More and more organizations are adopting them because they represent the realities of hierarchies in today's 'flatter' structures, are easier to manage, can be used more flexibly and can reduce grade drift.

The grades and pay ranges are defined and managed in the same way as narrow-graded structures except that the wider pay range spans mean that organizations sometimes introduce mechanisms to control progression in the grade so that staff do not inevitably reach its upper pay limit. The mechanisms available consist of:

- *Reference point control* – scope is provided for progression according to competence by increments to the reference point. Thereafter, individuals may earn cash bonuses for high achievement, which may be consolidated up to the maximum pay for the grade if high achievement levels are sustained.
- *Threshold control* – a point is defined in the pay range beyond which pay cannot increase unless individuals achieve a defined level of competence and achievement.
- *Segment or zone control* – an extension of threshold control that involves dividing the grade into, typically, three segments or zones.

All these mechanisms require the use of some form of contingent pay as described in Chapter 19.

Broad-graded structures are used to overcome or at least alleviate the grade drift problem endemic in multi-graded structures. If the grades are defined, it is easier to differentiate them, and matching (comparing role profiles with grade definitions or profiles to find the best fit) becomes more accurate. But it may be difficult to control progression and this would increase the costs of operating them, although these costs could be offset by better control of grade drift.

Examples of broad-graded structures

Broad-grading at Bristol-Myers Squibb

Pay is determined in relation to the market, and is pitched at the median, though the total reward package is upper quartile. There are eight overlapping bands, each with a span of between 80 per cent and 100 per cent, covering everyone, apart from the UK's dozen or so senior executives. The bands are:

D 1   Basic clerical, factory semi-skilled
D 2   Clerical and factory semi-skilled
D 3   Clerical and factory supervisor
D 4   Senior supervisor, entry level for professionals (eg scientists), customer-facing sales staff
D 5   Customer-facing sales staff
D 6   First-level manager, head of department
D 7   Function heads
D 8   Business heads, eg oncology, finance

These eight bands are used in all the countries in which Bristol-Myers Squibb operates, though the salaries attached to them are locally determined. But the bands are seen as more of a safety net than anything else and something that the US parent is keen to retain, although the market is more important in the UK. The company says the bands are helpful if there is an intention to recruit someone at a salary way over or under the band, which signals that the job may need to be regraded.

Camelot

The broad-graded structure at Camelot is market-driven – its focus is on paying the market rate for each job. Every salary is benchmarked against the market to ensure that job holders are being 'paid fairly for the job that they do', with base pay set at the median market rate. The following six-level banding structure, covering everyone except the chief executive, is used:

- *Bands A and B* cover administrative support and IT roles.
- *Band C* includes supervisors, professionals and specialists.
- *Band D* is for middle management.
- *Band E* is for heads of department.
- *Band F* covers functional directors.

Bands have some overlap, and each job has its own pay range within a band. The range is 85 per cent to 115 per cent, with 100 per cent being the rate for the job. The ranges are benchmarked against the market twice a year.

Broad-grading at COLT Telecom

Nine job levels or grades were introduced at COLT Telecom as a way of:

- providing transparency in the organizational structure;
- providing an equitable reward framework for base pay, variable pay and long-term incentives;
- ensuring consistency and fairness across functions and countries;
- allowing cross-function and country comparison;
- beginning to clarify career development and progression;
- supporting the One COLT culture and values of open and honest communication;
- aiding internal and external benchmarking of remuneration.

Vivian Leinster, Director of Compensation and Benefits, says that:

> COLT levels seek to aid succession planning and promotion; an advantage of having a formal job-level structure is that managers will be able to communicate how and when their teams can progress within COLT. As the levels are fairly broad, not all promotions or role changes will result in a level change. However, if your role changes or you move within the organization to a different department, the job level will be reviewed and adjusted as appropriate.

Broad-grading at Friends Provident

At Friends Provident there are eight broad career bands, five for non-management staff, to replace the nine previous grades, and three additional bands to cover everyone below executive director level. Generic skills and competency levels have been established to describe the broad requirements for each band. Each of the career bands is broad and although there is a mid-point the company tells staff that they should not believe that the rate for the job is the mid-point or control point. As Peter Harris, Reward and Benefits Manager, explains:

> Generally speaking, staff who are developing their role should be in the lower quartile of the range, staff who are fully performing are at the median while those who are regularly exceeding all requirements should be being paid at the upper quartile. A normal distribution would be 25 per cent developing, 50 per cent fully performing and 25 per cent exceeding requirements.

Broad-grading at Lloyds TSB

Every role in Lloyds TSB has a market reference point, which indicates the normal rate of pay for a fully effective performer. The company has introduced new pay zones within grades two to eight to help indicate normal progression and to give more structure and openness to the way in which pay is managed. An internal briefing paper sent to all staff explains: 'The zones mean that you'll be able to see more clearly how your pay is managed in line with your contribution, and how your salary should increase as you develop in your role.'

There is a published salary range for each grade (in other words, a minimum and maximum salary) based on pay rates within the market and these are reviewed every year to keep them in line with market movements. Each grade has three zones:

1. *Primary zone* – for people new to the role and still developing in that role. Typically – but not normally in every case – Lloyds TSB expects an employee to be performing to a 'fully effective' level after two or three years in the role and to move to the next zone. If an employee's salary is currently below the bottom zone and his or her work is judged satisfactory, pay will automatically be adjusted upwards.
2. *Market zone* – if an employee is fully effective in a role, his or her pay should be managed towards or in the 'market' zone (if an employee moves to a new role, pay will start in the market zone as long as he or she has the necessary knowledge, competencies and skills to be fully effective from the outset). Broadly speaking, the market zone reflects the rate that other employers would pay for a particular job. These rates are set with data provided by independent pay consultants.

3. *High-performance zone* – if an employee consistently makes a superior contribution to the business, his or her pay is managed towards or in the high-performance zone.

Work levels at Unilever

Unilever rejected the notion of broad-banding and introduced its 'work level' structure in the mid-1990s. This is a variation of broad-grading using different nomenclature and a special approach to defining levels. There are six work levels, each subdivided into a number of pay grades. The levels were determined according to the idea of the time-span of discretion developed by Eliot Jaques (2) and also measure the strategic importance of particular jobs. The three principles underlying levels are:

1. The major tasks of any job fall into a single work level. This is the case despite the fact that a job may include a mixture of tasks, with an executive making strategic decisions also undertaking less demanding administrative tasks.
2. At each successive higher work level, decisions of a broader nature are taken in an increasingly complex environment. Discretion and the authority required to do the job also increase, and more time is required to assess the impact of these decisions. Assigning jobs to work levels involves identifying the decisions that are unique to a job. This helps to highlight differences in management decision making and accountability, which in turn allows the management structure to be more clearly delineated.
3. Each work level above the first requires one and only one layer of management. A layer of management is necessary only where a manager makes decisions that could not be taken by subordinates, who may be more than one level below their boss. The company's work levels approach ensures that job holders take decisions that cannot be taken at a lower level.

BROAD-BANDED STRUCTURES

Broad-banded structures have four or five 'bands' as distinct from the 10 or more grades in a narrow-graded structure and the six to nine grades in a broad-graded structure, as illustrated in Figure 17.3. The process of developing broad-banded structures is called 'broad-banding'.

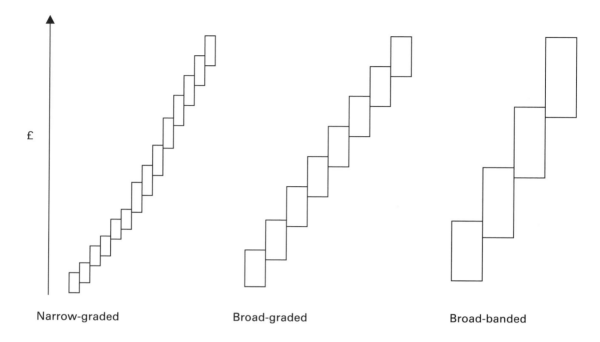

Figure 17.3 Narrow-graded, broad-graded and broad-banded structures

Genesis of the concept

The notion of broad-banding crossed the Atlantic in the early 1990s, although it was referred to, briefly, by Michael Armstrong and Helen Murlis (3) in 1988. An article by LeBlanc (4) in 1992 produced one of the earliest definitions of broad-banding – 'Fewer pay grades for all types of jobs and more horizontal (lateral) movement'. Broad-banding really came to the fore in the mid-1990s when Gilbert and Abosch (5) wrote about how it had been developed in General Electric in support of the Jack Welch philosophy of boundary-less (and de-layered) organizations. Since then it has burgeoned.

The difference between a broad-graded structure and a broad-banded structure is important. It was originally made by Gilbert and Abosch in 1996. They referred to broad-grade structures with seven or eight grades in which a fairly conventional approach to pay management is often adopted using mid-point management, compa-ratio analysis and pay matrix techniques. They contrasted these with what they called 'career band' structures with four to five bands where the emphasis is on individual career development, flexible roles and competence growth.

The original concept of broad-banding

In its original version, a broad-banded structure contained no more than five bands, each with, typically, a span of 70 per cent to 100 per cent. Bands were unstructured and pay was managed much more flexibly than in a conventional graded structure (no limits may be defined for progression) and much more attention was paid to market rates, which governed what were in effect the spot rates for jobs within bands. Progression in bands depended on competency and the assumption of wider role responsibilities. Bands were described verbally, not by reference to the results of analytical job evaluation. More authority was devolved to line managers to make pay decisions within a looser framework.

Armstrong and Brown (6) established that, in organizations with broad bands, 62 per cent had bands with widths between 50 per cent and 75 per cent, while the rest had bands with widths between 75 per cent and 100 per cent. Typically, there were between four and six bands in such structures. The band boundaries were often, but not always, defined by job evaluation. Jobs were placed in the bands purely by reference to market rates or by a combination of job evaluation and market rate analysis. Bands were described by an overall description of the jobs allocated to them (senior management etc) or by reference to the generic roles they contained, eg technical support.

This concept was, and still is, beguiling. Broad-banded structures are simpler and therefore easier to design. They satisfy the desire for more flexibility, and the research conducted by Armstrong and Brown (6) in 2001 established that this was by far the most important reason for introducing broad bands. Flexibility is achieved by catering for broader roles rather than tightly defined jobs, by adopting less rigid approaches to the allocation of roles to bands and how people progress within them, and by being able to respond more quickly to market rate pressures. In the United States the advantages of doing without formal job evaluation and using market pricing were originally the most powerful arguments in favour of broad-banding. This remains the case there, but in the UK the use of job evaluation rather than market pricing is still common, and the original concept of broad-banded structures has never been taken up as enthusiastically as in the United States. An aspect of flexibility that is seldom discussed in public is that when introducing broad bands the wider span of pay means that fewer anomalies are created and the cost of implementation is reduced.

Moreover, broad-banding was in accord with the drive for de-layering. The reduction in the number of grades meant that the pressure for upgrading was reduced, there was less likelihood of grade drift and it was thought that they would be easier to manage.

Further developments in the concept

The original notion of unstructured broad bands is now no longer general practice in the UK. It created expectations of the scope for progression that could not be met. Progression had to stop somewhere if costs were going to be controlled, and no rationale was available for deciding when and why to stop. Line managers felt adrift without adequate guidance and staff missed the structure they were used to. Questions were asked on the point of having broad bands at all when in effect all they consisted of was spot rates determined mainly by market relativities. Why, people asked, should organizations not be honest with themselves and their staff and revert to the complete freedom and therefore flexibility that spot rates provide?

Inevitably, therefore, structure crept in. It started with reference points aligned to market rates around which similar roles could be clustered. These were then extended into zones for individual jobs or groups of jobs as illustrated in Figure 17.4 (based on a structure in a financial services company). Reference points are frequently placed in zones so that they increasingly resemble conventional structure grades. The research conducted by Armstrong and Brown (6) established that 80 per cent of organizations had introduced some controls in the form of zones (43 per cent) and zones with reference points (37 per cent). Job evaluation was used not only to define the boundaries of the band but to size jobs as a basis for deciding where reference points should be placed in conjunction with market pricing. Progressively, therefore, the original concept of broad-banding was eroded as more structure was introduced and job evaluation became more prominent to define the structure and meet equal pay requirements. Zones within broad bands began to look very like conventional grades. An example of a broad-banded structure linked to job evaluation in a housing association is given in Figure 17.5.

Reservations about broad-banding

The two reservations that emerged from the experience of developing broad bands in the 1990s and early 2000s were: 1) What's the point of unstructured broad bands if they simply consist of spot rates? and 2) What's the difference between, say, a four-banded structure with three zones in each band and a 12-graded structure? The answer given by broad-band devotees to the first question was that at least there was some overall structure within which spot rates could be managed. In reply to the second question, the usual answer was that, as roles develop, movements between zones within bands could be dealt with more flexibly. Neither of these responses is particularly convincing.

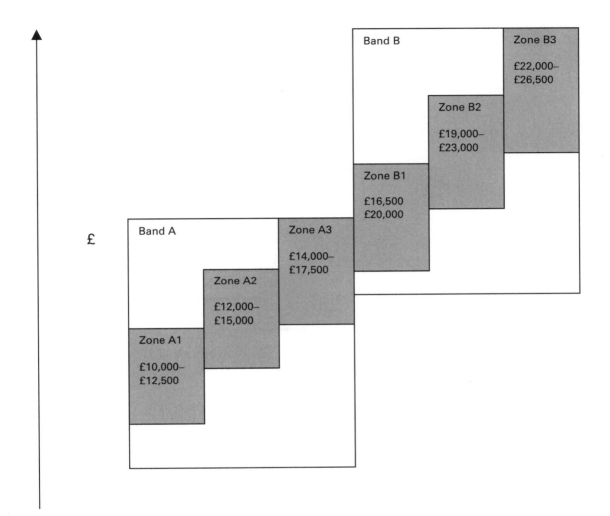

Figure 17.4   Zones in a broad-banded structure

Objections to broad-banding

Apart from these fundamental reservations, there are a number of other objections to broad-banding. In general, it has been found that broad-banded structures are harder to manage than narrower-graded structures in spite of the original claim that they would be easier – they make considerable demands on line managers as well as HR. Broad-banding can build employee expectations of significant pay opportunities, which are doomed in many cases if proper control of the system is maintained. It

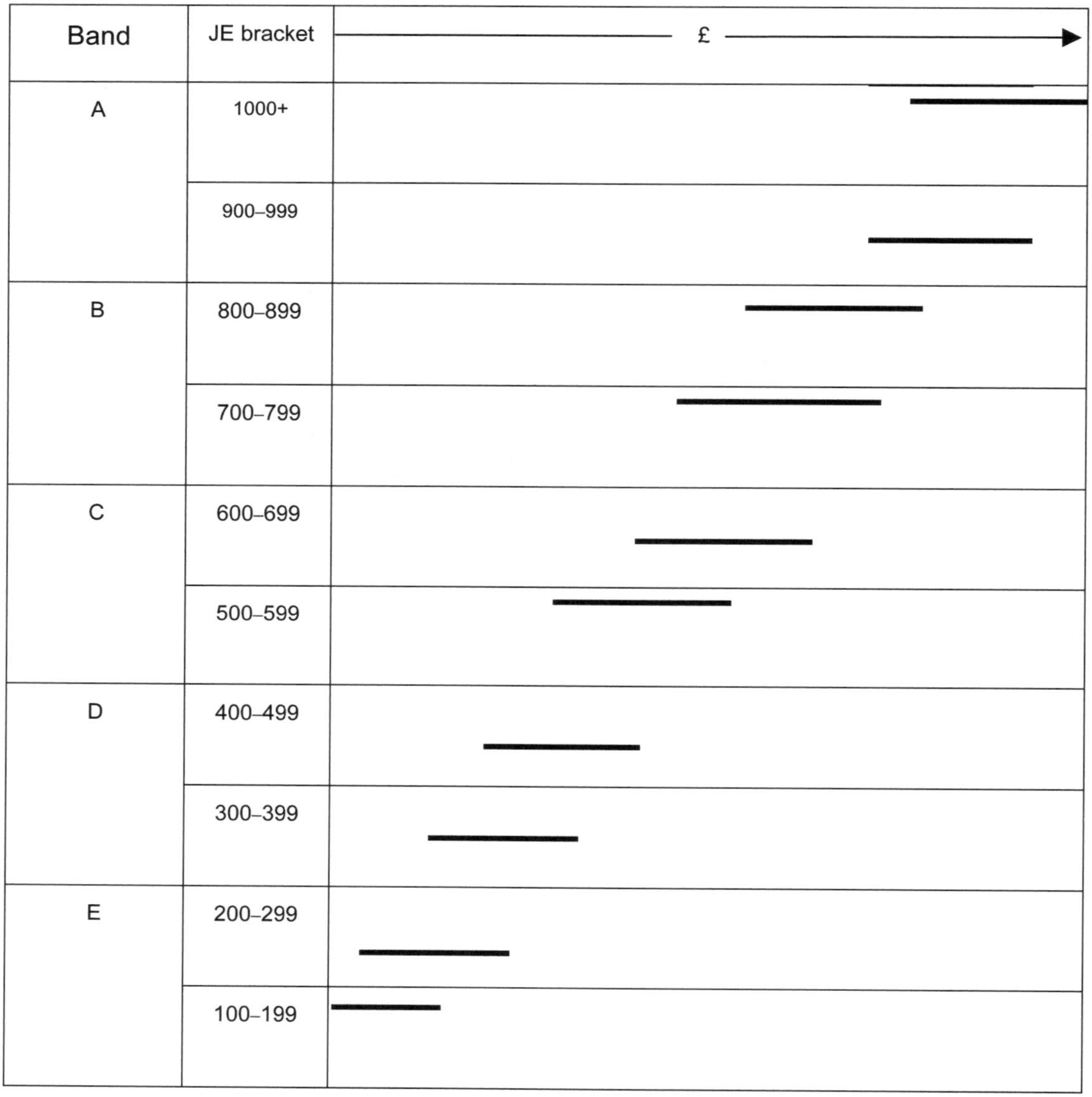

Band	JE bracket	£
A	1000+	
	900–999	
B	800–899	
	700–799	
C	600–699	
	500–599	
D	400–499	
	300–399	
E	200–299	
	100–199	

Figure 17.5 A broad-banded structure with zones defined by job evaluation score brackets

can be difficult to explain to people how broad-banding works and how they will be affected and they may be concerned by the apparent lack of structure and precision. Decisions on movements within bands can be harder to justify objectively than in other types of grade and pay structures.

Broad-banded structures may be more costly than more conventional structures because there is less control over pay progression. Research conducted by Charles Fay and others (7) in the United States in 2000–01 found that both wages and total cash compensation were significantly higher in the companies with broad-banded structures than in those with more conventional structures. They estimated that broad-banding increased payroll costs by 7 per cent plus.

Another major objection to broad-banding is that it can create the following equal pay problems:

- Reliance on external relativities (market rates) to place jobs in bands can reproduce existing inequalities in the labour market.
- The broader pay ranges within bands mean that they include jobs of widely different values or sizes, which may result in gender discrimination.
- Women may be assimilated at their present rates in the lower regions of bands and find it impossible, or at least very difficult, to catch up with their male colleagues who, because of their existing higher rates of pay, are assimilated in the upper reaches of bands.

Broad-banding in its original sense is therefore not the panacea it was once thought to be. More organizations are settling for a broad-graded structure with six to nine grades with the possibility of restricting the number to five but recognizing that they have to contain control mechanisms, which might take the form of a series of zones.

Examples

Examples of broad-banded structures at Britannia Building Society, GlaxoSmithKline and Tesco are given below.

Britannia Building Society

As reported by IRS (8) the Britannia Building Society introduced a six-band structure although within these there are 38 separate role profiles. The pay ranges for the bands are based on external market comparisons. Mapping individual staff to the role profiles involved a process of job evaluation and validation by management teams.

GlaxoSmithKline

GlaxoSmithKline has five bands: A and B are for top executives, band C is for directors and managers, band D covers professional and technical staff and band E is for

administrative staff. These bands determine benefit entitlements. Pay for manufacturing staff is negotiated with the trade unions; these job grades are subject to local
agreement and are not included in the grading structure.

Each band is divided into a number of zones for pay purposes. For example, band D
is divided into six zones, and band E has five zones. The combination of band and zone
produces the grade, and there are 29 grades in total. These grades are also important
for determining bonus entitlement. The pay for each grade ranges approximately 25
per cent either side of the range mid-point.

This kind of job-evaluated multi-graded structure can sometimes cause problems
with grade drift, as there may not be the flexibility to reward lateral development
within pay bands. Where this happens, individuals who take on extra responsibilities
expect to be promoted. This is not a problem at GSK. First, there is a fair degree of
flexibility as to how managers can use the ranges. Staff can be recruited high or low
within a grade, if this is necessary to keep pace with the market. Managers can be paid
one grade above or below the grade at which their job has been evaluated, again to
keep their pay relative to their capabilities and hence in line with the market. Secondly,
there are a number of career ladders (such as the HR and R&D scientific career ladders),
which provide an established means of moving up the structure. Finally, while staff
are not automatically promoted or given a salary increase when they move laterally as
part of their development plan, this is likely to lead to promotion in the long run.

With the introduction of the new grading process, individuals were, and continue to
be, allocated to their grades using a home-grown factor-based scheme, which is based
around a combination of a number of different job evaluation schemes found in the
market. This was a demanding exercise, keeping many of the company's compensation
team busy for around nine months.

Pay ranges are benchmarked against the market. The company's policy is to base
pay rates on the median, but for total cash to range from median to the 65th percentile
for good performers.

Tesco

When the new structure was introduced at Tesco it converted the previous 22 grades,
which covered all staff from the shop floor to the main board, into six 'work levels':

- *Work level 1* covers all clerical and some administrative (non-executive) jobs.
- *Work levels 5 and 6* are for main board and senior directors, whose pay is determined
  on an individual basis.
- All other jobs are covered by *work levels 2, 3 and 4*, and it is the occupants of these
  posts who are covered by the new broad-banded pay structure. The maximum of
  each of the bands is at least 100 per cent above the minimum.

CAREER FAMILY STRUCTURES

Career families consist of jobs in a function or occupation such as marketing, operations, finance, IT, HR, administration or support services that are related through the activities carried out and the basic knowledge and skills required, but in which the levels of responsibility, knowledge, skill or competency needed differ. In a career family structure as illustrated in Figure 17.6, the different career families are identified and the successive levels in each family are defined by reference to the key activities carried out and the knowledge and skills or competencies required to perform them effectively. They therefore define career paths – what people have to know and be able to do to advance their career within a family and to develop career opportunities in other families. Typically, career families have between six and eight levels as in broadgraded structures. Some families may have more levels than others.

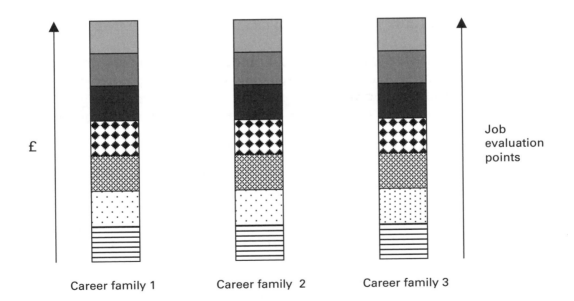

Figure 17.6   A career family structure

In effect, a career structure is a single graded structure in which each grade has been divided into families. The difference between a conventional graded structure and a career family structure is that in the former the grade definitions are all the same. In a career family structure, although the levels may be defined generally for all families, separate definitions expressed as competency requirements exist for levels in each of the career families. These define career paths and are the distinguishing characteristic of career family structures, which are as much about defining career progression routes as they are about defining a pay structure.

Advantages and disadvantages

Career family structures provide the foundation for personal development planning by defining the knowledge, skills and competencies required at higher levels or in different functions, and describing what needs to be learnt through experience, education or training. Level definitions in a family can be more accurate than in a conventional structure because they concentrate on roles within the family with common characteristics and do not attempt to cover wide and in some ways unconnected sets of skills across the whole organization. Furthermore, the existence of a common grading system when it is supported by job evaluation facilitates the achievement of equal pay for work of equal value. Finally, linking pay and grade management with career development is in accordance with good-practice human resource management in the shape of 'bundling' – the belief, supported by extensive research, that HR practices will be more effective if they are interrelated and therefore complement and reinforce one another.

But career structures can be more difficult to develop, explain and manage than single grade structures. A considerable amount of work is required to produce clear analytical level definitions that are properly graded and provide good career guidelines. A broad-graded structure, for example, is a simple and straightforward concept and splitting it into families may increase the complexity without providing commensurate benefits. Maintaining the accuracy of the level definitions also demands much care and attention. It is these problems that are perhaps the main reason why career structures have not yet caught on.

Furthermore, whatever emphasis is placed on career development between as well as within families, they could be perceived as being divisive and in conflict with the principle of identical treatment for all enshrined in a single grade structure. It may be inferred that progression can only take place in an occupational 'silo'. This has meant that career family approaches have been abandoned where the silos have been narrowly drawn and managed rigidly – the simpler they are the better.

Examples of career families

Career family structure at Norwich Union Insurance

At Norwich Union Insurance a career framework helps staff to understand how their jobs fit within their business unit and the organization as a whole. The career families support movement across the organization, since individuals can identify jobs at a similar level in other families that they might like to join. The skills, knowledge and behaviours profile for each role is published to facilitate this.

This career framework had been used for some time before a pay structure was attached to it. Each family contains between four and seven levels, each with a pay range with an 80 per cent minimum, a market salary guide for competent performance and no maximum.

A career family structure in a university

In this university's career family structure, illustrated in Figure 17.7, the range of pay for all staff in a level is the same. Each of the generic roles has a role profile, which is used for job-matching purposes. There are only three families, and the structure is presented to demonstrate that, while teaching, learning and research are the reason the university exists, managerial and learning support is essential for this purpose to be achieved. This arrangement also facilitates the definition of career paths between families, especially from learning support roles to teaching and research roles.

Career family structure at XANSA

There are about 150 generic job titles at XANSA, the IT programming and systems company, covering everyone from receptionists to the board directors. All new recruits must be appointed to one of these jobs, which are positioned on a 'job map' in seven broad bands and 14 career (job) families. The bands reflect the accountability, complexity and influence in the nature of the work undertaken, while career families are groups of jobs with similar skills. For each job there is a generic job description, which outlines the main purpose of the job, its key responsibilities and a skills profile that identifies the generic requirements of the job. There is also a competency framework, which defines the attributes that contribute to high performance.

The career families fall into four groups:

- *delivery* – design; build/integrate; run and support; management; business services; and training;

Levels	Career Families		
	Managerial, professional, administrative and support	Teaching, learning and research	Learning and research support
1	Support worker		Learning support assistant
2	Administrator Senior support worker		Learning support worker
3	Senior administrator Section head Craft worker		Senior learning support worker
4	Specialist or professional Activity leader	Associate lecturer Research associate	Advanced learning support worker
5	Senior specialist or professional Head of small or medium-sized department	Lecturer Researcher	Learning support expert Team leader
6	Leading specialist or professional Head of large operational department	Senior lecturer Research fellow Reader	Leading learning support expert Departmental manager
7	Head of major department	Professor Head of department	Head of major department
8	Head of major function		

Figure 17.7   Career family structure in a university

- *consultancy*;
- *business development* – general management; sales and strategic development; and client development;
- *professional support* – business support; finance; human resources; and marketing/ communications.

JOB FAMILY STRUCTURES

Job family structures as illustrated in Figure 17.8 resemble career structures in that separate families are identified and levels of knowledge, skills and competency requirements defined for each level, thus indicating career paths and providing the basis for grading jobs by matching role profiles to level definitions. Like career families, job families may have different numbers of levels depending on the range of responsibility they cover.

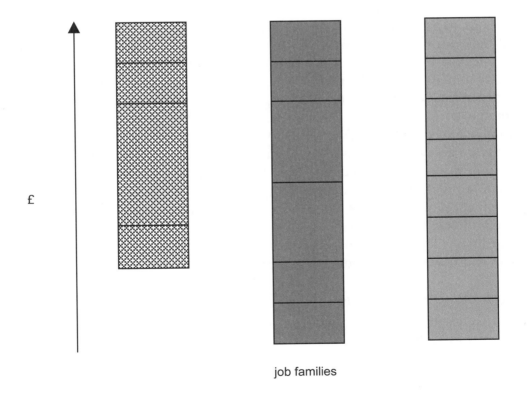

job families

Figure 17.8 A job family structure

The difference between a career family structure and a job family structure is that in the former there is a common grade and pay structure. Jobs in the same level in each career family are deemed to be the same size as assessed by job evaluation and the pay ranges in corresponding levels across the career families are the same. In contrast, the families in a job family structure have in effect their own pay structures, which take account of different levels of market rates between families (this is sometimes called 'market grouping'). The size of jobs and rates of pay can vary between the same levels in different job families, which means that there may be no read-across between them unless they are underpinned by job evaluation. Because they may cover a number of market groups, there are often more families in a job family structure than in a career family structure.

Advantages and disadvantages

Job family structures can help organizations to flex rates of pay for different occupations to reflect variations in market rates and therefore provide for competitive pay to attract and retain people with essential skills. They can also indicate career paths within and, to a certain extent, between families.

But they can result in unequal pay for work of equal value between job families. This can arise if jobs of the same size are paid differently when pay levels vary between families to cater for market rate pressures. Such variations may be difficult to justify objectively because the market pay differentials in job family structures are common to a whole family. In other structures, including career family structures, the alternative and preferable approach is to use market supplements, which are easier to justify on an individual basis. Pay inequities in job family structures can also arise because of read-across difficulties when trying to assess the relative size of jobs in different families. In theory this problem can be solved by the use of job evaluation but in practice this is difficult when there are considerable differences in the structure and definition of family levels.

In addition, like career family structures, job families can be more difficult to develop, explain and manage than single grade structures.

Examples of job family structures

Job family structure in BT

The overall objective of setting up the new grade and pay structure in BT was to be simple and complete, avoiding over-complicated structures. More specifically, the company decided to opt for a system of job families in order to:

- achieve internal consistency of reward in alignment with external market rates;
- ensure that status, rank and relative position within hierarchies would become less important than what an individual achieves;
- help to clarify the roles and potential career paths available to individuals, particularly within a job family and, to a certain extent, between families;
- offer visibility of roles and salary ranges across other job families;
- achieve more flexibility in managing reward for different occupations to reflect differences in market rates and therefore provide for competitive pay to attract and retain people with essential skills.

The job family structure was developed to replace a traditional graded structure containing eight core grades together with a separate sales structure. Ranges were 'quite broad' with significant overlap. According to the Connect trade union, there were 'deep-rooted problems' with the system. In what was once a typical multi-graded pay structure the emphasis was very much on hierarchy: the only way ahead was upward, through promotion or regrading. The focus is now on flexible roles and the individual's contribution in the role, and more priority is given to external competitiveness. A salary range provides BT line managers with flexibility in managing reward within their teams. Gone are the days when pay progression and career development at BT were simply a matter of getting promotion to a higher grade.

Job family structure in the Financial Services Authority (FSA)

The FSA has 12 job families, which vary in size from 38 people in economics and research to 900 in regulatory. Within each job family there are a number of broad levels, ranging from four to six, according to the family. The levels reflect the different contributions that individuals make according to their skills, knowledge and experience, and the roles they perform.

Each level has an associated indicative pay range, which has been determined by comparing levels in the markets in which the FSA competes for staff. Pay ranges are used rather than a specific rate for the job, to reflect that there is no single market rate of pay for a given job. Instead, there is a range of pay in the market related to the specific backgrounds, experience and delivery of individuals performing the roles. The broad overlapping ranges are designed to give management the flexibility to reflect the differences in contribution that individuals are making.

Job family structure at Nationwide

Nationwide decided to opt for a system of job families because they:

- offer the flexibility to respond to occupational and labour market pressures, in contrast to more rigid systems where market rates may fall outside the grading structure;
- encourage flexible working practices and multiskilling;
- encourage people to move jobs and build up a broad base of skills in different areas while still remaining in the same job family, although there must be flexibility in the pay ranges to reward people for this;
- clarify routes to career progression; and
- flatten the organizational structure, driving accountability down to the lowest possible level so that the person dealing with customers is empowered to solve their problems.

The job family structure was developed following a detailed analysis of work. Jobs across the whole organization were found to fall into three broad areas – customer service, support services and specialist advice – providing the basis on which to group roles into job families. The project considered whether to construct families on the basis of function or on the basis of similarities in the nature of people's work. They chose the latter because they believed that this would help to keep the number of families to a minimum. It was subsequently decided to base the new structure on 11 job families.

Other examples

As reported by IDS (9) the following are some other examples of the number of families in job family structures:

- Cannon – 23;
- Norwich Union Central Services – 22;
- University of Southampton – 4;
- Zarlink Semiconductor – 16.

COMBINED CAREER/JOB FAMILY AND BROAD-BANDED STRUCTURES

It is possible to combine career or job family structures with broad-banded structures. This can be done by superimposing a broad-banded structure on career/job families as illustrated in Figure 17.9. In effect this means that in each job or career family the levels are restricted to four or five rather than the more typical seven or eight.

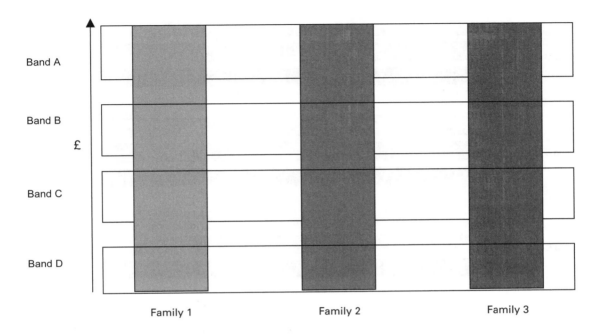

Figure 17.9 Broad-banded structure superimposed on a career/job family structure

Another approach to the combination of family and broad-banded structures is to divide each band in a broad-banded structure into job families as illustrated in Figure 17.10. This enables internal and external relativities to be dealt with individually for each family and also identifies career paths within families.

PAY SPINES

Pay spines are found in the public sector or in agencies and charities that have adopted a public sector approach to reward management. They consist of a series of incremental 'pay points' extending from the lowest- to the highest-paid jobs covered by the structure. Typically, pay spine increments are between 2.5 per cent and 3 per cent. They may be standardized from the top to the bottom of the spine, or the increments may vary at different levels, sometimes widening towards the top. Job grades are aligned to the pay spine, and the pay ranges for the grades are defined by the relevant scale of pay points. The width of grades can vary and job families may

Figure 17.10 Broad bands divided into career families

have different pay spines. Progression through a grade is based on service although an increasing number of organizations provide scope for accelerating increments or providing additional increments above the top of the scale for the grade to reward contribution or merit. The age discrimination regulations only permit-service related pay for a maximum of five years. Further points in a pay spine can only be used if there is an objectively justifiable reason.

Advantages and disadvantages

The first advantage of pay spines is that they just about manage themselves. Either no decisions on pay progression have to be made by management and line managers, or decisions on additional increments, if they are provided for, are made within an explicit framework. Additionally, because the need for managers to make possibly biased or inconsistent judgements on pay increases does not exist or is severely limited, they give the impression of being fairer than structures where progression is governed by managerial decisions on performance or contribution. For this reason they are favoured by trade unions and many managements in the public sector.

The disadvantages are that: 1) relating pay almost entirely to service means that people are rewarded for 'being there' and not for the value of their contribution; 2) pay spines can be costly in organizations with low staff turnover where everyone drifts to the top of the scale; and 3) where there are a large number of incremental points in the scale, equal value complications can arise as men progress to the top while the progress of women is delayed because of career breaks. For this reason the Local Government Pay Commission recommended a move away from service-related increments on to pay for contribution, restricting increments to the first few years in a job.

SPOT RATES

Some organizations do not have a graded structure at all for any jobs or for certain jobs such as directors. Instead they use 'spot rates'. Such a rate may also be called the 'rate for the job', more typically for manual jobs where there is a defined skilled or semi-skilled market rate that may be negotiated with a trade union. Spot rates are quite often used in retail firms such as B&Q for customer service staff (see Chapter 27).

Spot rates are sometimes attached to a person rather than a job. Unless they are negotiated, rates of pay and therefore relativities are governed by market rates and managerial judgement. Spot rates are not located within grades and there is no defined scope for progression while on the spot rate. There may, however, be scope for moving on to higher spot rates as skill, competence or contribution increases. Job holders may be eligible for incentive bonuses on top of the spot rate.

Spot rates can be used where there is a very simple hierarchy of jobs as in some manufacturing and retailing companies. They may be adopted by organizations that want the maximum amount of scope to pay what they like. They often exist in small or start-up organizations that do not want to be constrained by a formal grade structure and prefer to retain the maximum amount of flexibility. But they can result in serious inequities that may be difficult to justify.

INDIVIDUAL JOB GRADES

Individual job grades are, in effect, spot rates to which a defined pay range of, say, 20 per cent on either side of the rate has been attached to provide scope for pay progression based on performance, competence or contribution. Again, the mid-point of the range is fixed by reference to job evaluation and market rate comparisons.

Individual grades are attached to jobs not persons but there may be more flexibility for movement between grades than in a conventional grade structure. This can arise when people have expanded their role and it is considered that this growth in the level of responsibility needs to be recognized without having to upgrade the job. Individual job grades may be restricted to certain jobs, for example more senior managers where flexibility in fixing and increasing rates of pay is felt to be desirable. They provide for greater flexibility than more conventional structures but can be difficult to manage and justify and can result in pay inequities. As described earlier in this chapter, the 'zones' that are often established in broad-banded structures have some of the characteristics of individual job grades.

REFERENCES

1   e-reward (2004) *Survey of Grade and Pay Structures*, e-reward.co.uk, Stockport
2   Jaques, E (1961) *Equitable Payment*, Heinemann, London
3   Armstrong, M and Murlis, H (1988) *Reward Management*, 1st edn, Kogan Page, London
4   LeBlanc, PV (1992) Banding: the new pay structure for the transformed organization, *Journal of Compensation and Benefits*, January/February, pp 34–38
5   Gilbert, D and Abosch, KS (1996) *Improving Organizational Effectiveness through Broad-Banding*, American Compensation Association, Scottsdale, IL
6   Armstrong, M and Brown, D (2001) *New Dimensions in Pay Management*, Chartered Institute of Personnel and Development, London
7   Fay, CH *et al* (2004) Broadbanding, pay ranges and labour costs: an empirical test, *WorldatWork Journal*, **13** (2), Second quarter, pp 26–34
8   IRS (2005) Rejecting pay hierarchy: broadbanding at Britannia, *IRS Employment Review*, 828, pp 33–36
9   Incomes Data Services (2006) *IDS HR Studies: Job families*, IDS, London

18

Developing grade and pay structures

This chapter is concerned with approaches, options and guidelines for the development of grade and pay structures. It starts with a statement of guiding principles and, as an introduction to the process, quotes the views of some practitioners on managing design projects. The chapter continues with a description of the design process covering the analysis of present arrangements and the selection of a structure, including the criteria for choice, design options and the use of job evaluation. The focus is then on the design of the most typical structures, ie graded, broad-banded and career/job family structures. Because the approach to developing narrow and broad-graded structures is the same, even if the result in terms of the number of grades is different, these two types of structure are considered together. The chapter ends with a discussion of the process of implementing new or radically changed structures with particular reference to assimilation and protection issues.

GUIDING PRINCIPLES FOR GRADE AND PAY STRUCTURES

Grade and pay structures should:

- be appropriate to the culture, characteristics and needs of the organization and its employees;
- facilitate the management of relativities and the achievement of equity, fairness, consistency and transparency in managing gradings and pay;
- be capable of adapting to pressures arising from market rate changes and skill shortages;
- facilitate operational flexibility and continuous development;
- provide scope as required for rewarding performance, contribution and increases in skill and competence;
- clarify reward, lateral development and career opportunities;
- be constructed logically and clearly so that the basis upon which they operate can readily be communicated to employees;
- enable the organization to exercise control over the implementation of pay policies and budgets.

THE DESIGN PROGRAMME

The design or redesign of a grade and pay structure is often a massive project. On the basis of his experience of a major reward system development programme, Will Astill, Reward Manager at B&Q, recommends the following guiding principles:

1. *Without cooperation change strategies are likely to fail.* A key challenge is getting the people in all of the different departments involved in the project – recruitment, employment policy, internal communications, human resources and reward – to work together. If change strategies do not carry everyone in the organization willingly forward, the process can be painful and even damaging. So it's vital that the reward manager builds relationships with the right people. 'You need to get key individuals to work together without them feeling that they are losing control of their initiatives', says Will Astill.

2. *Secure directors' 'buy-in' right away.* You will need to build a compelling case for the recommended approach and it should be accepted and supported by directors at an early stage. As Will Astill puts it: 'Don't go to the board meeting without having talked the directors through it beforehand.' Additionally, time spent thinking about each and every individual decision maker is time well spent. Says Will Astill: 'You must sell it to every individual. For example, with the new store team bonus we had to anticipate how it would impact on the finance director and the property director. You must build that into the project management process.'

Will Astill is keen to extol the virtues of a more strategic use of reward: 'Reward is so strategic. If it is not being discussed in the boardroom, you are doing something wrong. It has so much impact on changes management, performance, and business strategy. You cannot hope to design a reward strategy if you are not close to the board.'

3. *Never underestimate the value of in-depth employee consultation.* As Will Astill explains: 'It is necessary to spend money on professional research – market research, HR consultants to design and facilitate focus groups – as though you are conducting a market research exercise. Employees are consumers. You need to sell the initiative to them and help them understand why it is taking place.'

4. *Remember that strategy formulation is an evolutionary process.* 'Our business is changing rapidly and there are significant differences in our business needs compared with, say, the early 1990s, so we need policies, procedures and people to follow them', says Will Astill. 'We work on the basis of an emerging strategy and there is always a three-year rolling plan. New challenges emerge through the business changing. There are whole new profit areas of B&Q that simply didn't exist a few years ago, for example the financial services and installation part of the business. Clearly, this has an impact on the type of people we recruit and the way we reward them. Customer advisers now need to be educated to sell financial services.'

5. *Look at how much you spend on communicating your reward package.* Does every employee have an effective induction? Do they know what the total package is worth? Do they know how their bonus has been tracking?

6. *No initiative should be implemented without examining the return on investment.* This means that processes and schemes will not be introduced or updated at B&Q without assessing the effect they are expected to have on the business. 'Make a business case for everything', says Will Astill. 'The return on investment analysis also justifies what priority you assign to implementation.'

7. *Evaluate the effectiveness of programmes and take action as required.* B&Q carries out a post-implementation review one year after implementation to ensure the scheme is meeting its key objectives and it examines what will need to change in the next year.

Dos and don'ts

The 'dos and don'ts' of developing and implementing new or amended grade and pay structures, as expressed by respondents to the 2004 e-reward survey (1), are set out in Table 18.1.

Table 18.1 Grade and pay structure design – dos and don'ts

Do	Don't
– make the structure congruent to the values and methods of work in your business;	– be rushed into launching before you are ready (all employees will want to know what it means for their pay and progression on day one, so have the answers before you launch);
– ensure it fits with how the organization wants to operate;	– lose sight of the detail when discussing the strategy!
– ensure that the company is ready and supports the approach and that flexibility over structure is valued;	– expect people to understand first time round;
– work out why you are doing it and if anyone else will understand it;	– try to put in a structure that other companies have and then adapt it as yours;
– keep the structure as simple as possible (if people don't understand the structure, it is too complicated);	– try to do it without a process for job evaluation;
– resource your project full time, not in someone's spare time;	– spend a fortune implementing an unwieldy system;
– ensure you have accurate data relating to each job and person within it;	– rely on one survey, but make sure you have other sources to verify data you are gathering;
– get good market data but be honest about data limitations;	– be secretive about the process;
– monitor internal consistency;	– underestimate levels of internal resistance to change;
– ensure you have the buy-in of senior managers;	– assume that launch communication will be sufficient to enable the structure to be fully understood (reinforcement of the message is required over a longer period of time);
– talk to the line managers (at least 20 times!);	– underestimate the resources such a project will use up;
– get line managers involved at an early stage;	– underestimate the level of perseverance required;
– allow managers flexibility;	– be pressurized into a system that does not fit your organization culture, eg by a US parent;
– allow time for managers to adapt to the new approach and support them appropriately;	– think of a structure and force-fit the jobs into it;
– ensure you have a structure that can be managed without becoming cumbersome;	– neglect the 'status symbol' that grades have for certain people (they can be a very emotive subject!);
– ensure you have the correct processes in place to deal with movements and changes of job;	– expect to please everyone;
– ensure that performance management disciplines are embedded;	– assume anything or try to hide the unpalatable, but be honest about any aspects that aren't ideal;
– make sure that the structure is available to all staff with no hidden agenda (people like to know there is something to work towards and that the system is fair);	– misunderstand the amount of work involved in changing, either partially or totally, elements of the current pay framework/system;
– communicate very widely and very often what is being done and why;	– try for perfection (fit for purpose will do);
– involve key operational sponsors throughout;	– regrade people in response to market pressures on pay;
– be determined to achieve!	– introduce it without training managers (ensuring they understand the system) and the rest of the employees.
– keep the faith!	

THE DESIGN PROCESS

A flow chart of the design process is set out in Figure 18.1. The emphasis is on communication and involvement throughout the programme, specifically through a steering group and task force or project team and generally with line managers and other employees. The approaches to defining guiding principles and objectives, analysing present arrangements, selecting the structure and considering its main features, selecting and developing the approach to job evaluation, designing the three main types of structures and implementation are covered in the remaining sections of this chapter.

DEFINE GUIDING PRINCIPLES AND OBJECTIVES

Guiding principles for the design of the grade and pay structure along the lines set out at the beginning of this chapter should be discussed and agreed with stakeholders and communicated to employees.

Specific objectives should be defined for the project, for example:

1. To develop a new grade and pay structure by...
2. To ensure that the grade and pay structure provides for internal equity and external competitiveness as far as possible.
3. To implement the new structure by...
4. To ensure that no employees suffer a reduction of pay when the structure is implemented.

ANALYSE PRESENT ARRANGEMENTS

The analysis of present arrangements should aim to establish the extent to which these fit the changing requirements of the organization, to check on how far the guiding principles are satisfied and to identify any specific problems that need to be dealt with. The 10 most common problems are:

1. too many grades, causing grade drift;
2. lack of precision in grade definitions;
3. inconsistent and poorly justified decisions on grading;
4. too many anomalies (over-graded or under-graded jobs);
5. equal pay for work of equal value is not provided for adequately;

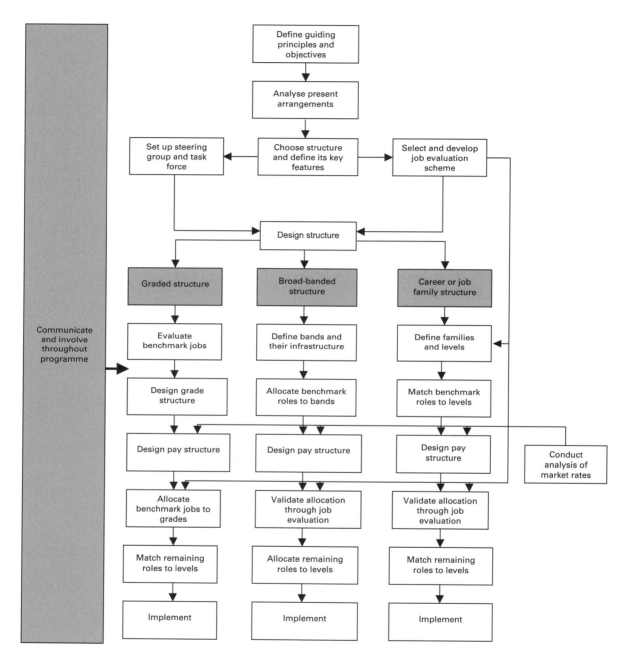

Figure 18.1 Flow chart: design of a new grade and pay structure

6. the structure no longer fits the way in which work is organized;
7. a satisfactory basis is not provided for rewarding contribution;
8. the structure does not help with the management of relativities;
9. pay levels are not sufficiently aligned to market rates;
10. career paths are not clarified by the structure.

If it is decided that the changing requirements of the organization or the problems of the existing arrangements mean that a new or substantially changed structure is required, then decisions should be made on communications and involvement policies. These decisions will be concerned with how employees will participate in the design process and the communications strategy required to inform them of what is happening and why. The importance of involvement and communications cannot be overestimated.

SELECTING THE STRUCTURE

The next step is to consider the options concerning the type of structure and its design. The e-reward 2004 *Survey of Grade and Pay Structures* (1) established that the most popular type of structure was a broad-graded one. There was quite a lot of support for career and job family structures but few respondents had broad bands. Pay spines persist in the public sector.

The different types of structures and their advantages and disadvantages are summarized in Table 18.2, and this is followed by an assessment of the criteria for choice of structure and a description of the design options.

CRITERIA FOR CHOICE

The chosen structure should be the one that most closely fits the requirements of the organization. The considerations affecting the choice between structures are described below.

Narrow-graded structure

A narrow-graded structure may be considered more appropriate when:

● the organization is large and bureaucratic with well-defined and extended hierarchies;
● pay progression is expected to occur in small but relatively frequent steps;

Table 18.2 Summary description of different grade and pay structures

Type of Structure	Features	Advantages	Disadvantages
Narrow-graded	– A sequence of job grades: 10 or more – Narrow pay ranges, eg 20%–40% – Progression usually linked to performance	– Clearly indicate pay relativities – Facilitate control – Easy to understand	– Create hierarchical rigidity – Prone to grade drift – Inappropriate in a de-layered organization
Broad-graded	– A sequence of between six and nine grades – Fairly broad pay ranges, eg 40%–50% – Progression linked to contribution and may be controlled by thresholds or zones	As for narrow graded structures but in addition: – the broader grades can be defined more clearly – better control can be exercised over grade drift	– Too much scope for pay progression – Control mechanisms can be provided but they can be difficult to manage – May be costly
Broad-banded	– A series of, often, five or six 'broad' bands – Wide pay bands: typically between 50% and 80% – Progression linked to contribution and competence	– More flexible – Reward lateral development and growth in competence – Fit new-style organizations	– Create unrealistic expectations of scope for pay rises – Seem to restrict scope for promotion – Difficult to understand – Equal pay problems
Career family	– Career families identified and defined – Career paths defined for each family in terms of key activities and competence requirements – Same grade and pay structure for each family	– Clarify career paths within and between families – Facilitate the achievement of equity between families and therefore equal pay – Facilitate level definitions	– Could be difficult to manage – May *appear* to be divisive if 'silos' emerge
Job family	– Separate grade and pay structures for job families containing similar jobs – Progression linked to competence and/or contribution	– Can appear to be divisive – May inhibit lateral career development – May be difficult to maintain internal equity between job families unless underpinned by job evaluation	– Facilitate pay differentiation between market groups – Define career paths against clear criteria
Pay spine	– A series of incremental pay points covering all jobs – Grades may be superimposed – Progression linked to service	– Easy to manage – Pay progression not based on managerial judgement	– No scope for differentiating rewards according to performance – May be costly as staff drift up the spine

- the culture is one in which much significance is attached to status as indicated by gradings;
- some but not too much scope for pay progression is wanted.

Broad-graded structure

A broad-graded structure may be considered more appropriate when:

- it is believed that if there is a relatively limited number of grades it will be possible to define and therefore differentiate them more accurately as an aid to better precision when grading jobs;
- an existing narrow-graded structure is the main cause of grade drift;
- it is considered that pay progression through grades can be related to contribution and that it is possible to introduce effective control mechanisms.

Broad-banded structure

A broad-banded structure may be considered more appropriate when:

- greater flexibility in pay determination and management is required;
- it is believed that job evaluation should no longer drive grading decisions;
- the focus is on rewarding people for lateral development;
- the organization has been de-layered.

Career family structure

A career family structure may be considered more appropriate when:

- there are distinct families, and different career paths within and between families can be identified and defined;
- there is a strong emphasis on career development in the organization;
- robust methods of defining competencies exist;
- it is believed to be inappropriate to vary pay structures between families.

Job family structure

A job family structure may be considered more appropriate when:

- there are distinct market groups that need to be rewarded differently;
- the range of responsibility and the basis upon which levels exist vary between families.

Pay spine

A pay spine may be considered more appropriate when:

- this is the traditional approach in a public or voluntary sector organization and it fits the culture;
- it is believed to be impossible to measure different levels of contribution fairly and consistently;
- ease of administration is an important consideration.

DESIGN OPTIONS

Whichever structure is selected, there will be a number of design options. These consist of the number of grades, bands or levels, the width of the grades (the span of pay ranges), the differentials between grades, the degree to which there should be overlap between grades, if any, and the method of pay progression within grades. In broad-banded structures there is also choice on the infrastructure (the use of reference points or zones). In career or job family structures there are options concerning the number of families, the composition of families and the basis upon which levels should be defined.

Number of grades, levels or bands

The considerations to be taken into account when deciding on the number of grades, levels or bands are:

- the range and types of roles to be covered by the structure;
- the range of pay and job evaluation points scores to be accommodated;
- the number of levels in the organizational hierarchy (this will be an important factor in a broad-banded structure);
- decisions on where grade boundaries should be placed following a job evaluation exercise that has produced a ranked order of jobs – this might identify the existence of clearly defined clusters of jobs at the various levels in the hierarchy between which there are significant differences in job size;
- the problem of 'grade drift' (unjustified upgradings in response to pressure or lack of promotion opportunities or because job evaluation has been applied laxly), which can be increased if there are too many narrow grades.

Pay range spans

The factors affecting decisions on the span of pay ranges attached to grades are:

- views on the scope that should be allowed for performance, contribution or career progression within grades;
- equal pay considerations – wide spans, especially extended incremental scales, are a major cause of pay gaps between men and women simply because women, who are more likely to have career breaks than men, may not have the same opportunity as men to progress to the upper regions of the range; male jobs may therefore cluster towards the top of the range while women's may cluster towards the bottom;
- decisions on the number of increments in a pay spine – to meet the requirements of the Employment Equality (Age) Regulations (2006) no more than five service-related increments are allowable. Additional increments can be provided for as long as they are 'objectively justified' on the basis of additional contribution or competence. Alternatively, the pay span may have to be reduced or the size of the increments increased;
- in a broad-banded structure, the range of market rates and job evaluation scores covering the jobs allocated to the band.

Differentials between pay ranges

Differentials between pay ranges should provide scope to recognize increases in job size between successive grades. If differentials are too close – less than 10 per cent – many jobs become borderline cases, which can result in a proliferation of appeals and arguments about grading. Large differentials below senior management level of more than 25 per cent can create problems for marginal or borderline cases because of the amount at stake. Experience has shown that in most organizations with conventional grade structures a differential of between 15 and 20 per cent is appropriate except, perhaps, at the highest levels.

Pay range overlap

There is a choice on whether or not pay ranges should overlap and, if so, by how much. Overlap between ranges is measured as the difference between the highest point of the range below and the lowest point of the range above expressed as a percentage of the difference between the lowest and highest points in the range below. Large overlaps of more than 10 per cent can create equal pay problems where, as is quite common, men are clustered at the top of their grades and women are more likely to be found at the lower end.

Pay progression

There is a choice of methods of pay progression between the various forms of contingent pay, namely performance-, competence- or contribution-related, as described in Chapter 17 and the fixed service-related increments common in the public sector.

USE OF JOB EVALUATION

A point-factor analytical job evaluation scheme is often applied when designing a graded structure although it may be limited to the initial design of the structure with analytical matching being used to grade jobs.

This approach is used less often in the design of broad-banded or career/job family structures where the most common method is to make a provisional advance decision on the number of bands or career/job family levels and then position roles in bands (often by reference to market rates) or allocate roles into defined levels by analytical matching. Job evaluation may only be deployed at a later stage to validate the positioning of roles in bands or the allocation of jobs to family levels, check on relativities and, sometimes, define the bands or levels in job evaluation score terms. The initial decision on the number of bands or levels and their definition may, however, be changed in the light of the outcome of the allocation, matching and evaluation processes.

More rarely, the grade and pay structure design is conducted by means of a non-analytical job classification exercise that defines a number of single grades. Jobs are then slotted into the grades by reference to the grade definitions.

GRADED PAY STRUCTURE DESIGN

Graded pay structure involves first designing the grade structure and then deciding on the pay ranges that should be attached to it. Decisions have to be made on assimilation and protection policies and the cost of implementing the structure. This costing process may mean some iteration in design to select the most affordable structure. The process described below applies to both the narrow- and broad-graded structures.

The two approaches to design are: 1) the *derived method* in which decisions on the grade structure are led by point-factor job evaluation; and 2) the *pre-emptive method* in which the number of grades is determined first and each grade is then defined as a basis for analytical matching (role profile to grade profile or role profile to benchmark role profile as described in Chapter 11) or market pricing.

The derived method (use of point-factor job evaluation)

This approach starts with a point-factor job evaluation exercise. This produces a rank order of jobs according to their job evaluation scores. A decision then has to be made on where the boundaries that will define grades should be placed in the rank order. A preliminary view may be taken on the preferred number of grades or the rank order may be analysed to discern by inspection where jobs might be grouped into grades and how many grades emerge from this procedure.

So far as possible, the grade boundaries in the rank order should divide groups or clusters of jobs that are significantly different in size so that all the jobs placed in a grade are clearly smaller than the jobs in the next higher grade and larger than the jobs placed in the next lower grade.

Fixing grade boundaries is one of the most critical aspects of grade structure design following an analytical job evaluation exercise. It requires judgement – the process is not scientific and it is rare to find a situation when there is one right and obvious answer. In theory, grade boundaries could be determined by deciding on the number of grades in advance and then dividing the rank order into equal parts. But this would mean drawing grade boundary lines arbitrarily and the result could be the separation of groups of jobs that should properly be placed in the same grade.

The best approach is to analyse the rank order to identify any significant gaps in the points scores between adjacent jobs. These natural breaks in points scores will then constitute the boundaries between clusters of jobs that can be allocated to adjacent grades. A distinct gap between the highest-rated job in one grade and the lowest-rated job in the grade above will help to justify the allocation of jobs between grades. It will therefore reduce boundary problems leading to dissatisfaction with gradings when the distinction is less well defined. Clear grade breaks appear more naturally when job evaluation scores are based on geometric progression than when progression is arithmetic. This is because a 'step difference' principle is implicit in the former.

However, the existence of a number of natural breaks cannot be guaranteed, which means that judgement has to be exercised as to where boundaries should be drawn when the scores between adjacent jobs are close. In cases where there are no obvious natural breaks the guidelines that should be considered when deciding on boundaries are as follows:

● Jobs with common features as indicated by the job evaluation factors are grouped together so that a distinction can be made between the characteristics of the jobs in different grades – it should be possible to demonstrate that the jobs grouped into one grade resemble each other more than they resemble jobs placed in adjacent grades.

- The grade hierarchy should take account of the organizational hierarchy, ie jobs in which the job holder reports to a higher-level job holder should be placed in a lower grade although this principle should not be followed slavishly when an organization is over-hierarchical with, perhaps, a series of one-over-one reporting relationships.
- The boundaries should not be placed between jobs mainly carried out by men and jobs mainly carried out by women.
- The boundaries should ideally not be placed immediately above jobs in which large numbers of people are employed because this will result in a large number of appeals against the grading.
- The grade width in terms of job evaluation points should represent a significant step in demands on job holders as indicated by the job evaluation scheme.

The grades in the structure established in this manner can be defined in the form of grade profiles using the job evaluation factors as the headings for the profile. These form the basis for analytical matching as described in Chapter 11 and below.

The pre-emptive method

The pre-emptive method takes place in the following steps:

1. *Decide number of grades.* The decision on how many grades are required is based on an analysis of the existing hierarchy of roles and a judgement on how many levels are needed to produce a logical grouping of those roles, level by level. A logical grouping is one in which each grade contains roles whose levels are broadly comparable and there is a step difference in the degree of responsibility between each level. Judgements on the number of grades required may start with the belief that the excessive number of grades in an existing multi-graded structure should be reduced. This may lead to the opinion that, say, eight levels would be better. This is sometimes sheer guesswork based on feelings about what is likely to be right. Preliminary decisions often have to be amended if it is established at a later stage that the structure does not result in a logical hierarchy of grades that enables clear distinctions to be made between grades and jobs to be grouped together appropriately. Alternative grade structures may also have to be considered if estimates of the cost of implementation indicate that a more affordable structure is required.
2. *Define grades.* There is a choice between a simple non-analytical or semi-analytical job classification approach and a full analytical approach.

The job classification approach involves preparing an overall definition of the grade to enable 'job slotting' to take place. This means allocating 'whole jobs', ie ones that have not been analysed under job evaluation factor headings, to grades by comparing the whole job description with grade definitions, which may be 'semi-analytical', ie define the grades under a number of headings. A set of semi-analytical grade definitions for a housing association is illustrated in Figure 18.2.

A full analytical approach involves the preparation of grade profiles. These use job evaluation factors as the headings for the profile of each grade, which can be compared with role profiles set out under the same headings so that analytical matching can take place. The factors may be the same as those used in the organization's point-factor scheme or a special set of factors may be identified and defined. The process of definition may reveal that the number of grades assumed to be required initially was either too many (the distinctions between them could not be made with sufficient clarity) or too few (it becomes apparent that the range of roles to be fitted into the structure was too great to be accommodated into the number of grades available). If this is the case, the number of grades will have to be adjusted iteratively until a satisfactory result is obtained.

An example of grade profiles set out under job evaluation headings for the first three levels of an eight-level structure in a large not-for-profit organization is given in Table 18.3.

3. *Define role profiles.* To enable analytical matching to take place, generic or individual role profiles have to be set out under the same set of headings used in the grade profiles. Benchmark roles are selected and analysed under these headings. An example of a generic role profile is given in Figure 18.3 (other examples are given in Chapter 16).

4. *Match benchmark roles.* The benchmark roles are matched to grades in accordance with a predetermined analytical matching protocol as described in Chapter 12. When matched, the information on the benchmark roles may suggest changes to the grade profiles, which would thus become even more realistic.

5. *Match remaining roles.* The remaining roles can be matched to the grade profiles using the protocol. A confirmation of the match can be obtained by comparing them with the graded benchmark roles.

Grade	Description
1 Support worker/administrator (a)	• Provide basic support/administrative services in a defined area of activity • Meet service standards • Use and maintain basic equipment and facilities • Meet deadlines and fulfil work programme
2 Support worker/administrator (b)	• Deliver efficient and effective services in a key area of activity • Meet exacting deadlines • Achieve demanding service standards • Use and maintain a range of fairly complex equipment
3 Team leader/senior administrator	• Lead a small to medium-sized team and ensure that team goals and standards are achieved and/or • Advise client groups on administrative matters and procedures • Assist in the preparation of plans and budgets • Produce accurate and timely reports on administrative or operational matters • Use initiative to respond effectively to enquiries, queries and requests
4 Manager (a)	• Head up an operational or service unit or project or a small department • Formulate plans for the unit/department • Manage, monitor and review the work of the unit/department in order to achieve objectives • Provide leadership, support and learning opportunities to staff • Prepare budgets and control expenditure for the unit/department
5 Manager (b)	• Head up a large department or function • Formulate strategic plans for the department/function • Manage, monitor and review the work of the department/function in order to achieve objectives • Provide leadership, support and learning opportunities to staff • Prepare budgets and control expenditure for the department/function
6 Senior manager	• Head up a division or principal function • Contribute to formulation of corporate strategies relating to division/function • Achieve agreed objectives by making strategic decisions that have a major impact on the organization's results • Respond effectively to new organization-wide opportunities and threats • Provide visionary and inspirational leadership • Monitor the total performance of the division/function and take effective action as required

Figure 18.2 Grade definitions in a housing association

Table 18.3 Level profiles

Factor	Level 1	Level 2	Level 3
Supervisory responsibility	Little or no supervisory responsibility other than helping/ inducting less experienced staff in the work of the group.	Minor supervisory responsibility, eg in the absence of section head the allocation of work and checking for quality and quantity.	Occasional supervision of staff temporarily assigned or shared supervision of permanent staff.
Creativity	Work with very limited opportunity for creative work or innovatory thinking.	Work largely regulated by laid-down procedures, but needing occasional creative skills.	Creativity is a feature of the job but exercised within the general framework of recognized procedures.
Contacts	Contacts and exchanges information within the organization beyond the immediate associates, but usually within the post's own department. Exchange usually on non-contentious and well-established matters.	Contacts with employees of other departments or occasionally receives enquiries from outside the authority as first contact. Contacts beyond the organization's employees are within limited terms of reference and generally restricted to situations where information is readily available.	Contacts that are generally not contentious but where the need or potential outcome may not be straightforward, or where the circumstances call for an element of tact or sensitivity. Contacts at this level include interviewing to establish details or service needs, the supply of straightforward advice and initiating action to provide assistance. Contacts within the organization will require the provision of advice or guidance on matters that are less well established.

Table 18.3 *Continued*

Factor	Level 1	Level 2	Level 3
Decisions	Post requires little freedom to act, work is carried out within clearly defined rules or procedures and advice is available if required. Decisions have limited and short-term effect on employees beyond immediate colleagues or on the public. Effects of decisions will be quickly known and readily amended if necessary.	Work is carried out within clearly defined rules and procedures involving decisions chosen from a range of established alternatives. Decisions have an effect on the internal operations of the post's own or other departments or on the individual or on the provision of service to the public.	Work is carried out within policies and objectives where there is a wide range of choices and where advice is not normally available and/or involves decisions where policy, procedures and working standards provide only general guidelines. Decisions have significant implications for the organization or significant effects on employees or other individuals or other organizations.
Knowledge and skills	Ability to undertake work, consistent with a basic knowledge and skills requirement, which involves a limited range of tasks that can be carried out after initial induction.	Ability to undertake work, consistent with a comparatively basic knowledge and skills requirement, which encompasses a range of tasks involving application of readily understood rules.	Ability to undertake work concerning more involved tasks confined to one function or area of activity, which requires a good standard of practical knowledge and skills in that area of activity.
Work context	Work where the programme of tasks is not normally interrupted.	Work subject to interruption to programme of tasks but not involving any significant change to the programme.	Work subject to changing problems or circumstances or demand.

Administrative Assistant	
Overall purpose of role	To provide administrative support to a team or within a department or unit.
Key result areas	• Maintain database accurately. • Obtain and distribute data as required. • Word-process standard documents and reports efficiently. • Deal with routine queries promptly.
Supervisory responsibility	Occasionally supervise a temporary administrative assistant.
Creativity	Work fairly routine but sometimes has to deal with unfamiliar requirements.
Contacts	Contacts with members of the public to deal with routine enquiries.
Decisions	Work under fairly close supervision. Will sometimes have to take responsibility for dealing with a query or obtaining information from an unfamiliar source.
Knowledge and skills	Administrative or operational knowledge or skills applied within an area or section. Basic word-processing skills.
Work context	Work often subject to interruption with calls for support from a number of different people. Plan day-to-day activities.

Figure 18.3   Role profile: administrative assistant

Pay range design

The steps required to determine pay ranges are:

1. List the jobs placed within each grade on the basis of job evaluation (these might be limited to benchmark jobs that have been evaluated but there must be an adequate number of them if a proper basis for the design is to be provided).
2. Establish the actual rates of pay of the job holders.
3. For each grade, set out the range of pay for job holders and calculate their average or median rate of pay (the pay practice point). It is helpful to plot the pay practice data as illustrated in Figure 18.4, which shows pay in each grade against job evaluation scores and includes a pay practice trend line.

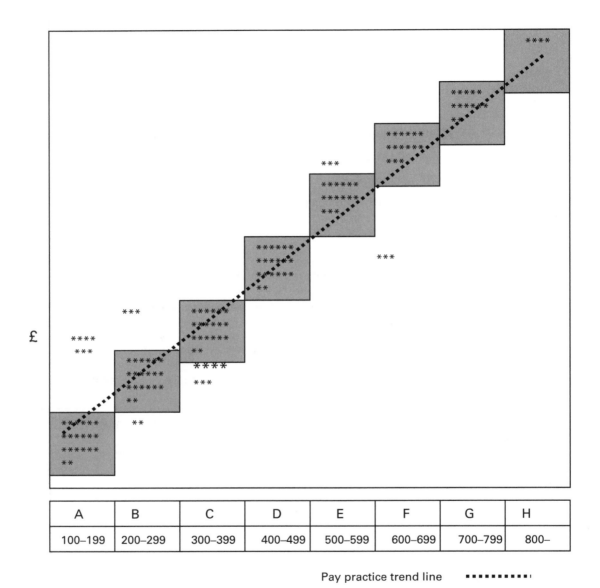

A	B	C	D	E	F	G	H
100–199	200–299	300–399	400–499	500–599	600–699	700–799	800–

Pay practice trend line ▪▪▪▪▪▪▪▪▪▪▪ˈ

Figure 18.4 Scattergram of evaluations and pay

4. Obtain information on the market rates for benchmark jobs where available. If possible this should indicate the median rate and the upper and lower quartiles. Remember that there may be some key jobs for which market rate data are not available. If market pricing is used, these will have to be slotted into the structure

later on the basis of comparisons with the benchmark jobs, possibly with the help of point-factor job evaluation, if available.

5. Agree policy on how the organization's pay levels should relate to market rates – its 'market stance'. This could be at the median, or above the median if it is believed that pay levels should be more competitive.

6. Calculate the average market rates for the benchmark jobs in each grade according to pay stance policy, eg the median rates. This produces the range market reference point.

7. Compare the practice and market reference points in each range and decide on the range reference point. This usually becomes the mid-point of the pay range for the grade and is regarded as the competitive rate for a fully competent job holder in that grade. This is a judgemental process, which takes into account the difference between the practice and policy points, the perceived need to be more competitive if policy rates are higher, and the likely costs of increasing rates.

8. Examine the pay differentials between reference points in adjacent grades. These should provide scope to recognize increases in job size and, so far as possible, variations between differentials should be kept to a minimum. If differentials are too close – less than 10 per cent – many jobs become borderline cases, which can result in a proliferation of appeals and arguments about grading. Large differentials below senior management level of more than 25 per cent can create problems for marginal or borderline cases because of the amount at stake. Experience has shown that in most organizations with conventional grade structures a differential of between 15 and 20 per cent is appropriate except, perhaps, at the highest levels.

9. Decide on the range of pay around the reference point. This might be 20 per cent on either side of the reference point; thus if that point is 100 per cent, the range is from 80 per cent to 120 per cent. The range can, however, vary in accordance with policy on the scope for progression and, if a given range of pay has to be covered by the structure, the fewer the grades the wider the ranges.

10. Decide on the extent, if any, to which pay ranges should overlap. Overlap recognizes that an experienced job holder at the top of a range may be making a greater contribution than an inexperienced job holder at the lower end of the range above. Large overlaps of more than 10 per cent can create equal pay problems where men are at the top of their grades and women are found at the lower end.

11. Review the impact of the above pay range decisions on the pay of existing staff in order to calculate implementation costs. Establish the number of staff whose present rate of pay is above or below the pay range for the grade into which their jobs have been placed and the extent of the difference between the rate of pay of

those below the minimum and the lowest point of that pay range. Calculate the costs of bringing them up to the minimum. Software such as the pay modellers produced by Link and Pilat or locally tailored Excel spreadsheets can be used for this purpose.

12. When the above steps have been completed it may be necessary to review the decisions made on the grade structure and pay reference points and ranges. Iteration is almost always necessary to obtain a satisfactory result that conforms to the criteria for grade and pay structures mentioned earlier and minimizes the cost of implementation. Alternatives can be modelled using the software mentioned above.

Implementation costs

If a new grade and pay structure is adopted, existing employees have to be assimilated into it. This may mean that some will be 'winners' – they will be placed in a grade with a higher pay range than their present one – and some will be 'losers' – their existing pay will be above the upper limit for their new range. In practice the pay of the 'losers' is always protected (they are 'red-circled'). This means that pay is not reduced on implementation and will be maintained at its present level (marking time) for a limited period of time (often three or four years). Because the pay of some people will go up and no pay will be decreased immediately, the implementation of a new structure always generates costs. These are frequently between 3 and 4 per cent of payroll but they can be more or less depending on the number of anomalies that are created by assimilation. This number will be affected by the design. Generally, the fewer and broader the grades the fewer the exceptions and therefore the lower the cost. This creates an affordability issue, and the choice of structure or the design features in a structure, such as the number of grades, may be affected by cost considerations. These cost considerations also apply to broad-banded and career/job family structures. However, in the case of broad-banded structures they are not so acute because the design can ensure that all the jobs or at least a very high proportion of them are placed in bands at rates of pay that do not need to be either red-circled or green-circled. Assimilation and protection policies are considered at the end of this chapter.

The graded structure design process

There are no absolutes about structure design. The process can start with views about the major characteristics of the structure (number and width of grades, differentials and overlaps) but in practice these have to be modified – trying out different configurations and altering them as required to produce a more desirable design. This is complicated by the fact that the design variables interact – the size of differentials and ranges affect the size of overlaps and the number of grades. Design therefore involves judgement, iteration and optimization. There is always a choice and there is no such thing as an ideal or inevitable structure.

The following is a somewhat simplified illustration of what is involved in a structure covering jobs in which existing rates of pay range from £11,000 to £68,000. The starting point may be a view on what the structure should ideally look like, for example:

- eight grades/pay ranges;
- 80–100–120 span for each pay range (50 per cent);
- differentials between grades that ensure that the whole range of pay to be covered by the structure can be accommodated in eight grades;
- a reasonable overlap between grades;
- the pay ranges at different levels generally encompass the market rates for the benchmark posts allocated to the grades;
- the cost of implementing the structure will not exceed 3 per cent of payroll.

A preliminary structure produced by applying the eight-grade and 80–100–120 span criteria is set out below. To accommodate the whole range of pay a differential of 25 per cent had to be used. On this basis the overlap between grades is 50 per cent.

Grade	Minimum	Midpoint	Maximum	Overlap %
1	9,600	12,000	14,400	
2	12,000	15,000	18,000	50
3	15,000	18,750	22,500	50
4	18,750	23,437	28,124	50
5	23,437	29,296	35,155	50
6	29,296	36,621	43,945	50
7	36,621	45,776	54,931	50
8	45,776	57,220	68,664	

A review of this initial draft may suggest that the differentials and overlap are too large. The differentials can be reduced by increasing the number of grades. To reduce them to 20 per cent would result in 10 grades, and to reduce them to 15 percent would result in 12 grades. These are multi-graded structures – broad-graded structures with from six to nine grades will have larger differentials than those with narrow-graded structures with 10 or more grades. It may be decided that, say, a 10-grade structure is acceptable but this decision is affected by cost considerations – the fewer the grades the less the cost of implementation because not so many pay anomalies are created when there is a smaller number.

Overlaps can be reduced by increasing the differential or reducing the span or a combination of the two. If in this example the span were reduced to 85–100–115, the overlap would go down to 29 per cent. The optimum size of an overlap is a matter of judgement: 10 per cent might be felt to be too low, while 50 per cent could be considered too high. Somewhere between the two might be preferred, which means that further experiments with the range spans would be necessary.

The design also has to take into account the need to attach pay ranges to jobs that are in line with policy on the relationship between internal rates of pay and market rates so that the rates of pay are competitive. This may mean further iteration – adjusting the width of grades, even the number of grades, to provide a reasonably good fit (a few exceptions, which can be dealt with by market supplements, are allowable).

Finally, implementation costs have to be taken into account. These arise when, after assimilation, the rate of pay of individuals is less than the minimum of their new grade and their pay has to be brought up to that minimum, ie they are green-circled. The costs of implementation (usually expressed as a percentage of payroll) can be estimated at the design stage with the help of software available from Link Consultants or Pilat that enables different grade configurations to be tested and their relative costs calculated. Alternatively, costs can be estimated manually, although this is a tedious and time-consuming exercise. A manual calculation involves identifying every benchmark job that will need to be green-circled, working out the difference between the present rate of pay and the new minimum and adding the results to produce a total cost. This calculation may have to be repeated with different grade configurations to produce a more acceptable cost. The fewer the grades the fewer the number of anomalies. This is because the pay spans when there are a small number of grades are wider than those in a structure with more grades and, therefore, the pay of a higher proportion of jobs is likely to be within the range of their new grade. One of the most powerful arguments in favour of broad-grading and, better still, broad-banding is that they reduce assimilation costs. In fact, with new broad-banded structures it is easy to eliminate such costs completely.

BROAD-BANDED STRUCTURE DESIGN

Broad-banded structures are much easier to design than graded structures and they cost less to implement. But they still require a lot of thought in the design stage, as the guiding principles adopted by Tesco set out below indicate.

Guiding principles

The following guiding principles recommended by Richard Sullivan, Group Reward Manager at Tesco, should be borne in mind when introducing broad bands:

1. Don't underestimate the old culture – it will take time to change it.
2. Deal with the move to broad-banding as a conversion rather than a new initiative, to minimize change issues.
3. Be prepared to challenge any return to the old ways.
4. Management capability is key to communicating issues.
5. Deal with cost issues before changing to broad bands.
6. If broad bands are not used for all staff, explain why carefully.
7. Consider equal pay issues.
8. Use market data, but ensure that the data are credible before making them public.
9. Allow at least nine months to move to broad-banding.
10. Employee communication is key to having the new system understood.
11. Don't have less than five layers across the business in a broad-band system.
12. Obtain managers' input when designing the new process; this will help them explain it to others and will increase their commitment to it.

Design steps

The steps required to design a broad-banded structure are set out below:

1. *Decide on objectives.* The objectives of the structure should be set out in terms of what it is expected to achieve, for example increase flexibility in the provision of rewards, especially in responding to market rate pressures, reflect organization structure, provide a better base for rewarding lateral development and growth in competency, eliminate or at least reduce the need for job evaluation, replace an over-complex and inappropriate grade and pay structure. The objectives may include providing for individual treatment to be given to job families in the structure (a combined structure as described in Chapter 17).
2. *Decide on the number of bands.* The decision on the number of bands will be based on an analysis of the existing organization structure and hierarchy of jobs. The aim is to identify the value-adding tiers that exist in the business. An initial assessment can be made, for example, that there are five tiers, consisting of: 1) senior managers; 2) middle managers; 3) first-line managers and specialists; 4) senior administrators and support staff; and 5) administrators and support staff. This structure should be regarded as provisional at this stage – it could be changed after the more detailed work in the next two stages.
3. *Decide on the band infrastructure.* A decision has to be made at this stage on the use of reference points and zones. If reference points are to be used, which is most often the case, the method of determining where they should be placed in bands (by market pricing, job evaluation or both) should be decided. If zones are to be

used, decisions need to be made on the width of the zones and the basis upon which people should progress within and between zones. The scope for flexibility in creating special reference points and zones for individuals should also be considered.

4. *Define the bands.* Broad initial definitions are now made of each of the bands. Figure 18.5 shows an example of the definition of a band for senior administrators and support staff.

5. *Incorporate job families.* It may be decided to divide each band into job families so that the relativities within the band and the relationship to external rates can be treated separately and the career path within a band can be identified for the separate families.

6. *Prepare role profiles for benchmark jobs.* Identify benchmark jobs that are representative of different functions at the levels covered by the structure and for which market price data can be obtained. They should include as many of the key generic roles as possible. Role profiles for each of them are then prepared. The profiles should provide sufficient information to enable them to be matched with the band definitions and for use in market comparisons.

7. *Match the benchmark roles to the bands.* The matching process should provisionally allocate each benchmark role to a band. It is best carried out by a team consisting of line managers and employee representatives facilitated by HR or an outside consultant. This initial matching may indicate that the bands need to be redefined.

8. *Obtain market prices.* Conduct surveys and/or access pay information databases to establish the market rates of the benchmark roles.

9. *Decide on reference points.* Assuming a decision has been made to have reference points and zones, decide on the reference points for the benchmark roles. These may entirely be based on market rates but internal relativities as determined by job evaluation may be taken into account. If both criteria are used it is a matter of judgement to strike a balance between them. The weight given to either criterion will be a policy matter depending on the extent to which pay is market-driven and the extent to which it is believed that internal equity is important. Typically, however, more weight is attached to market rates in spite of the danger of equal pay problems.

10. *Decide on zones.* Assuming a decision has been made to use zones, these should now be attached to the reference points for the benchmark roles in accordance with the policy determined at stage 3.

11. *Define the pay ranges of the bands.* This is usually done empirically by reference to the earlier decisions on reference points and zones – the range of pay for a band will be the range of pay from the bottom of the lowest zone in the band to the top of the highest zone.

Key activities

- Provide a range of fairly complex administrative or higher-level support services.

- May have responsibility for a small section or subsection of work.

- May prepare non-standard documentation.

- May deal with non-routine queries.

- Take action to deliver improved performance.

Performance requirements

- Plan and prioritize own day-to-day activities in order to achieve performance objectives.

- Work under general supervision.

Relationships

- Maintain helpful and supportive relationships with colleagues in own and other areas and with internal and external customers.

- Take a leadership role within team when appropriate.

Communications

- Communicate orally or in writing internally and externally on non-routine matters.

People management

- May act as instructor or mentor to more junior staff.

- May allocate work to members of section or subsection.

Figure 18.5 Example of band definition

12. *Define bands in terms of job evaluation scores.* If the benchmark roles have been evaluated this will indicate the bracket of job evaluation scores that can be used to define each band, which might provide a guide to allocating non-benchmark or new roles to bands.

13. *Allocate non-benchmark roles to bands.* In theory, the remaining non-benchmark jobs could be allocated to bands on the basis of job evaluation, but in practice

most organizations match role profiles for such jobs (which are often generic) with the profiles of the benchmark jobs. This is more likely to work well if a reasonably representative range of benchmark jobs has been used and if there is well-developed management capability to work on this process and deal with its implications.

14. *Communicate outcomes.* Staff should have been involved and kept informed of the progress of the design process throughout the exercise but in this final stage the way in which broad-banding works and how it will affect them must be explained in detail.

CAREER FAMILY STRUCTURE DESIGN

The steps required to design a career family structure are described below:

1. *Select and define career families.* Decide on what career families are required. Typically, not more than four or five families are identified. The choice of families is between functions, eg marketing, finance, or activities, eg administration, support staff, or a combination of functions and activities. Examples of two career family structures are given in Figures 18.6 and 18.7.

2. *Decide on the number of levels in the career family structure and define them with level profiles.* Level profiles are required that apply to all the families in the structure bearing in mind that the defining characteristic of a career family structure is that the levels and the pay ranges attached to them are common to all the families in the structure (as distinct from job family structures in which levels and ranges differ between some or all of the families). Career family structures tend to have no more than seven or eight levels. Using more than eight levels can create difficulties in differentiating level definitions. A broad-banded career structure (a combined structure as described in Chapter 17) may have only four or five bands.

   Level profiles applying across the structure can be defined in the same way as the grade profiles in a graded structure using job evaluation factor levels as the analytical framework. However, the levels of each individual career family also need to be defined in terms of the activities and competencies specific to that family. This defines career paths, which are essential elements in a career structure. The individual career family profiles will describe the typical activities carried out at each level and the knowledge and skill requirements and competencies associated with them. They should facilitate analytical role matching. It is best to relate level profiles to the factor definitions used in the job evaluation scheme as long as the latter cover competency and skill requirements. If not, competencies will need to

- Operations – contains roles concerned with managerial and operational activities in marketing, buying, distribution, selling and providing customer services.
- Professional services – contains roles concerned with managing the provision of professional and specialist services and with delivering those services. These services will include the following functions: finance, IT, HR, property and facilities management.
- Administration – contains roles concerned with general management, managing and leading administrative teams, and providing administrative, secretarial and support services.

Figure 18.6 Retail organization career family structure

be covered specifically in the family level profiles. Level profiles can be derived from the analysis of benchmark roles as described in step 3. An example of a set of career family level profiles is illustrated in Figure 18.8.

3. *Identify, define and match benchmark roles.* A representative sample of benchmark roles are identified, defined as role profiles and matched with the level profiles as described above for a graded structure.

4. *Conduct analytical matching.* Analytical matching procedures are used to allocate the remaining roles to levels. It is advisable to test the process first in one family – this will not only test the procedure but will also enable model career family structures to be used when dealing with the other career families. An example of the testing procedure used in a large not-for-profit organization is set out below.

5. *Attach pay ranges to levels.* Pay ranges are established for each level as described above for graded structures.

6. *Validate relativities between career families.* The allocation of jobs to levels through matching across the career families is validated by reference to job evaluation scores to ensure that the relativities between them look reasonable. Some adjustment may need to be made as a result of this cross-check if it exposes inequities between families.

Example of analytical matching test procedure

Objectives

1. To test the whole process of analytical matching, ie matching role profiles to level profiles in the career family in order to grade jobs in the function.
2. To validate the provisional level definitions.

Career Family	Definition
Teaching, learning and research	Roles in this family are mainly concerned with teaching, learning, scholarship or research, but they may also have academic leadership or managerial, administrative or pastoral care responsibilities. However, the relative emphasis on these elements will vary. Some roles will be almost entirely concerned with teaching or research. In others, there will be different proportions of teaching and research work. The responsibility for administration may also vary, with some roles concerned only with administering the teaching they carry out personally while others may have additional responsibilities for such matters as curriculum development, quality control, mentoring, leading teams, pastoral care, student admissions or examinations.
Managerial, professional, administrative and support services	Roles concerned with managing functions, departments and professional, administrative or support services, supporting learning activities and students such as library and student services, administrative services concerned with such activities as departmental administration, student records or admissions, and support services such as maintenance, security, canteen and cleaning.
Technical learning and research support services	Roles concerned with providing technical support to learning and research activities. Role holders may be involved in technical work in laboratories, learning resource centres, research centres or workshops. Alternatively they may be concerned with distance or e-learning. Those primarily supporting learning may be involved in demonstrating and instructing students or helping them to make the best use of e-learning programmes. More senior role holders will instruct and assess students. Those concerned more with research may be involved in setting up experiments, analysing data and helping with reports on the results of research activities.

Figure 18.7   University career family structure

3. To produce specific level definitions in each of the provisional eight levels in the structure to act as a model for use in other functions.

Preparation for test

- Prepare model role profile set out under the following headings:
    - overall purpose of the role: a one-sentence description of what the role holder is there to do;
    - key result areas: no more than seven or eight areas each defining in one sentence beginning with an active verb the outcomes expected in that area (without attempting to describe how the outcome is to be achieved);
    - knowledge, skills and competencies required.
- Identify benchmark posts to be matched. These should be jobs that are likely to cover each of the eight levels.
- Prepare role profiles using the model for those benchmark posts (also make available existing job descriptions).
- Make available the provisional level definitions.

Level	Benchmark Role	Level Description	
		Key Accountabilities	Key Competencies
8	HR Director	• Contribute to development of business strategy. • Develop HR strategies aligned to business strategy. • Exercise overall direction of all HR activities required to support achievement of business goals. • Oversee human capital management projects.	Knowledge of: • the business, its strategy and its drivers; • HRM/HCM at a strategic level. Ability to: • articulate a vision and set a leadership agenda; • contribute to business strategic planning on equal terms with other directors; • develop and implement HR strategies that are aligned to the business strategy and integrated with one another.
7	Head of HR	• Prepare and implement plans to support achievement of HR strategic goals. • Act as Deputy to HR Director. • Coordinate the provision of HR services through departmental managers and HR business partners. • Direct human capital management projects.	Knowledge of: • the business, its strategy and its drivers; • HRM/HCM at the level of a Fellow of the CIPD. Ability to: • develop and implement strategic plans for the function; • manage a diverse range of activities; • plan and coordinate the work of senior HR managers.
6	Learning and Development Manager	• Contribute to the development of the learning and development strategy. • Identify learning needs and plan blended learning and development programmes to meet them. • Deliver major programmes. • Direct the activities of learning and development consultants.	Knowledge of: • current thinking and good practice in learning and development; • advanced concepts and techniques in the field (Fellow CIPD). Ability to: • analyse key factors affecting activities in the function; • coordinate and direct complex HRD programmes.
5	Assistant Head of Talent Management	• Contribute to the preparation of human capital plans. • Assist in preparing management succession plans. • Coordinate performance management activities. • Analyse human capital data and prepare reports.	Knowledge of: • techniques of human resource and management succession planning; • HRM at the level of Member CIPD with at least six years' experience. Ability to: • analyse business plans and draw conclusions on talent management requirements; • carry out the analysis and diagnosis of people issues and propose practical solutions.
4	HR Business Partner	• Contribute to the effective management of the division. • Ensure the division has the skilled people it requires. • Work alongside line managers and provide help and advice on HR issues. • Deliver HR services required by the division.	Knowledge of: • HRM techniques at the level of Member, CIPD with at least four years' experience; • business imperatives in the division; • corporate HR policies and practices. Ability to: • provide efficient and cost-effective services in each HR area; • promote the empowerment of line managers to make HR decisions but provide guidance as required; • anticipate requirements and set up and operate appropriate services.
3	Reward Analyst	• Maintain information systems on pay and benefits. • Assist in the conduct and analysis of market surveys. • Maintain data bank of information on market rates. • Prepare role profiles for job evaluation purposes.	Knowledge of: • the labour market and sources of market data; • reward management techniques at the level of the CIPD Certificate in Reward Management. Ability to: • carry out numerical and statistical analysis; • use IT systems, software and spreadsheets; • conduct role analyses.

Figure 18.8 Career family level profiles

| 2 | HR Assistant (recruitment) | • Place job advertisements.
• Arrange interviews.
• Deal with routine correspondence to applicants including standard offer letters.
• Ensure records created for new employees. | Knowledge of:
• HR techniques relevant to recruitment (studying for CIPD).
Ability to:
• select appropriate media;
• administer fairly complex procedures. |
| 1 | Administrative Assistant | • Provide word-processing services.
• Maintain records.
• Operate office machinery.
• Deal with routine queries. | Knowledge of:
• Microsoft Office – Word, Excel, PowerPoint.
Ability to:
• word-process all types of documents, including reports and complex tabulations;
• prepare PowerPoint presentations;
• administer standard procedures. |

Figure 18.8 *Continued*

Analytical matching process

● Refer to the role profile for jobs, which should ideally be set out according to the model under the six job evaluation factor headings (if role profiles in this format are not available, refer to the job descriptions).
● Refer to the provisional level definitions and identify the level that appears to provide the best match.
● Compare the role profile with each of the factors in the level definitions to establish the extent to which they match.
● The matching rules are as follows:
    – if there is a good match to a level under each of the six headings then an overall match has been achieved;
    – if no more than two headings do not match then an overall match has still been achieved, as long as: 1) the match in both those headings does not vary significantly; and 2) neither of the headings is the knowledge and skills factor;
    – if there are multiple or large variations, or there is no match for the knowledge and skills factor, matching should be attempted at another level using the knowledge and skills factor level as determined at the first attempt as the indicator for the likely level;
    – if there is still no positive match according to the above rules, then as a last resort the allocation of the level will have to be a matter of judgement, although it should always correspond with the knowledge and skills level.

Functional level definitions

The functional level definitions covering key result areas, knowledge and skills should be prepared after the benchmark jobs have been matched by reference to the knowledge and skills characteristics of the jobs allocated to each level.

JOB FAMILY STRUCTURE DESIGN

The process of designing job family structures is essentially the same as that used for career family structures. The difference is that, because some individual families will have their own pay and level structure, the analysis of market rates and the organization of work in families will have a stronger influence on the design.

DESIGNING NON-DISCRIMINATORY PAY STRUCTURES

To design a non-discriminatory pay structure it is necessary to ensure that:

- great care is taken over grade boundary decisions – the aim should be to avoid placing them between jobs that have been evaluated as virtually indistinguishable, bearing in mind that the problem will be most acute if grade boundaries are placed between traditionally male and female jobs (in any situation where such boundary problems exist it is good practice to re-evaluate the jobs, possibly using a direct 'comparable worth' or equal value approach that concentrates on the particular jobs);
- 'read-across' mechanisms exist between different job families and occupational groups if they are not all covered by the same plan;
- market rate comparisons are treated with caution to ensure that differentials arising from market forces can be objectively justified;
- care is taken over the implementation of the pay structure to ensure that female employees (indeed, any employees) are not disadvantaged by the methods used to adjust their pay following regrading;
- a non-discriminatory analytical job evaluation system is used to define grade boundaries and grade jobs;
- discriminatory job descriptions are not used as a basis for designing and managing the structure;
- men's jobs or women's jobs do not cluster respectively at the higher and lower levels in the grade of the hierarchy;
- pay scales where progression is related to service should not be extended to more than five years – beyond five years, any further progression should be related to performance, competency or contribution and decisions on such pay increases should not be discriminatory in the sense of producing unjustifiable gaps between the pay of men and the pay of women carrying out work of equal value;
- any variation between pay levels for men and women in similarly evaluated jobs (for example for market rate reasons) can be objectively justified;

- red-circling, ie maintaining pay above the maximum for a grade, is free of sex bias;
- there are objectively justifiable reasons for any inconsistency in the relation of the grading of jobs in the structure to job evaluation results.

IMPLEMENTING NEW GRADE AND PAY STRUCTURES

The implementation of new or revised grade and pay structures provides a change management challenge of considerable proportions. The scale of this challenge will be reduced if employees have a voice in its design. But it is essential to communicate the purpose and features of the new structure and how everyone will be affected. If, as is usual, the new structure follows a job evaluation programme it is necessary to manage the expectations of staff. They should be informed that, while no one will necessarily get extra pay, no one will lose pay when the structure is implemented. This means that assimilation and protection policies should be discussed and agreed prior to implementation. It is also necessary to ensure that training is provided for everyone concerned in administering reward.

Above all, it is important to think about how implementation is to take place and plan each aspect carefully. As Armstrong and Brown (2) comment:

> Perhaps the worst thing you can do if you are in a situation where you think your pay structures need to be redesigned is to start with the solution and to rapidly implement it. Yes, in these fast moving times, the HR function needs to be agile, responsive and results-oriented, as Ulrich [3] tells us. But in respect of such a sensitive and politically and emotionally charged issue as base pay management, this is not an area where you want to be acting first and then thinking, and perhaps regretting later.

A planned approach to managing implementation

A planned approach to change management and enlisting the understanding and support of stakeholders is necessary. It is essential to provide for both involvement and participation in the design and development programme. As suggested by Armstrong and Brown (2) the implementation steps are:

1. Decide at the planning stage the overall change/transition strategy and timing.
2. Model the transition into the new structure and develop policies to manage this transition.
3. Develop detailed operating responsibilities and guidelines for the new structure including the procedures for grading or regrading jobs and managing pay pro-

gression. The authority to make pay and grading decisions and methods of budgetary control should also be covered.

4. Negotiate the introduction of the new arrangements with staff representatives and trade unions. They should have been involved throughout the process, but the detailed 'nitty-gritty' of actual pay levels and assimilation policies and procedures need to be thrashed out now.

5. Produce and distribute communications about the new structure – how it works, who will be involved in managing it and how people will be affected. This is when the benefits of regularly involving and communicating with staff throughout the design and development programme will become apparent. Broad details of the proposed changes and the reasons for them should thereby be known already. The focus at the implementation stage can then be on the detailed designs and their individual impact. It is best to use line managers as the main communicators, helping them with relevant support (booklets, question-and-answer sheets, PowerPoint presentations, etc) to get the key messages over to their staff. Information technology (the intranet) can be used to identify and address specific staff concerns.

6. Design and run training workshops for managers, and possibly all staff. In the case of broad-banded structures and some career/job family structures, managers are likely to have more freedom and discretion in positioning staff in bands or family levels and adjusting their pay. But they may well need more than an operating manual and entries on the intranet to help them manage this in an appropriate and fair manner. HR should be prepared to provide coaching to managers as well as more formal courses. They must make themselves available to give guidance, especially to the less committed or experienced managers. A cadre of line managers can be trained to coach their colleagues on managing pay in the new structure.

7. Run a pilot or simulation exercise, operating the new approach in parts of the organization, to test its workability and robustness. In one organization recently, for example, the new system was initially introduced in the IT department, where the market pressures were greatest; this assisted in estimating the HR support required for full roll-out, and also indicated the emphasis required in the staff communication and 'branding' of the changes when full implementation occurred.

8. Full implementation and roll-out. This will include giving every person information on how the new structure affects them and on their right to ask for a review of their grading if they are dissatisfied.

Assimilation policy

The hard part of implementing arrives when the assimilation of staff to the new structure has to take place. It is necessary to have a policy on where staff will be assimilated to the new structure. This is usually at their existing salary or, in the case of a revised pay spine, on the nearest point in a new incremental scale above their existing salary. The following categories of staff should be covered by the assimilation policy:

- *Employees with current pay and pay potential both within the new pay range.* In some ways this group is the easiest to deal with and the majority of staff will normally be included in it. The wider the grades the more likely that is to be the case. One point at issue is whether or not any increase should be awarded on transition and the answer should be 'no' except when, as mentioned above, the policy is to move each person's pay to the nearest higher pay point.

  Good advance communications should have conveyed the fact that job evaluation and a new pay structure do not necessarily mean any increase in pay. But some people in this group may still feel disadvantaged at seeing others getting increases. This negative reaction can be decreased by introducing the new structure at the same time as any annual pay increase, so that everyone gets at least something.

  It is necessary to be aware of the possibility of creating equal pay problems when assimilating staff to their new scale. For example, if two people with broadly equivalent experience and skills are on different current salaries and are assimilated into the same new grade but at those rates, it would appear that there is no equal pay problem – they are both on the same grade with the same grade and salary potential. But an equal value issue is only avoided if a lower-paid woman or man has the opportunity to catch up with the higher-paid man or woman within a reasonable period (say three or four years).

- *Employees whose current pay is within the new pay range but pay potential higher than the new maximum.* No immediate increase is necessary in this circumstance but employees should be told what will happen. If progression to the old maximum was based on service only, ie automatic annual increases to the maximum, this guarantee will have to be retained and, contractually, it may be necessary to go on awarding increments to the maximum of the previous scale. However, once a person's pay passes the maximum for the grade as a result of service-related increases, this will then become a red-circle situation and should be treated as such (see below).

  If progression to the old maximum was not guaranteed, but was based on per-formance, competencies, etc, then the new range maximum should normally be applied. Care will be needed to ensure that this does not adversely affect any specific category of employees, particularly female staff.

- *Employees whose current pay is below the minimum for the new grade.* Both justice and equity demand that, if someone has now been identified as being underpaid, that situation should be rectified as quickly as possible. Correcting this situation, by raising the pay to the minimum of the new pay range, should normally be the first call on any money allocated to the assimilation process. Each case should, however, be taken on its merits. If someone has recently been appointed to a post and given a pay increase at that time, it may be appropriate to wait until that person has completed a probationary period before awarding another pay increase.

  If the total cost of rectifying underpayments is more than the organization can afford, it may be necessary, however unpalatable to 'green-circle' them and phase the necessary increases, say one portion in the current year and the rest in the next year – it is undesirable to phase increases over a longer period unless the circumstances are exceptional. The simplest approach is to place a maximum on the increase that any one person may receive. This can be in absolute terms (eg maximum of £2,000) or in percentage increase terms (eg maximum of 20 per cent of current pay). Another alternative is to use an annual 'gap reduction' approach (eg pay increase of 50 per cent of the difference between current pay and range minimum or £500, whichever is the greater).

  Again, if any delay in rectifying underpayment situations is necessary and some staff have therefore to be green-circled, it must not disadvantage one staff group more than another. Most organizations introducing job evaluation for the first time (or replacing an outdated scheme) and using the outcome to devise a new pay structure will find that more women than men have to be green-circled. Failure to correct these underpayments would be a perpetuation of gender bias.

- *Employees whose current pay is above the maximum for the new grade.* These situations, which lead to red-circling, are usually the most difficult to deal with. They normally include a high proportion of people (often male) who have been in their current job a long time and who have been able to benefit from a lax approach to pay management in the past. People can take very different attitudes about what should be done about these situations and, as a result, the most protracted of the implementation negotiations are often centred on 'how to handle the red circles' (protection policy).

  At one end of the scale is the argument that these people are now known to be receiving more pay than the job is worth and that this should be stopped as soon as possible, especially if the organization needs that money to pay more to those people who have been (or are still) receiving less than they should. The opposite stance is that these people have become accustomed to a standard of living based on the pay that the organization has been willing to provide up to now and they should not suffer just because new standards are being applied. This is the principle that is usually adopted but there are different ways of applying it.

Any assimilation policy must set out how the red-circle situations will be handled. The starting point is normally that no one should suffer a reduction in pay – it should be 'protected' or 'safeguarded'. Thereafter, it is a matter of how quickly pay can and should be brought in line. Approaches to protection are discussed below.

Protection policies

'Indefinite protection', that is maintaining the difference between current pay and the range maximum for as long as the employee remains in the job, is highly undesirable, first because it will create permanent anomalies and, second, because, where there are a lot of men in this situation (which is often the case), it will perpetuate unacceptable gender gaps. The Equal Opportunities Commission in its *Good Practice Guide: Job evaluation schemes free of sex bias* (4) states that red-circling 'should not be used on such a scale that it amounts to sex discrimination'. And, as stated by the Equal Pay Task Force (5): 'The use of red or green circling which maintains a difference in pay between men and women over more than a phase-in period of time will be difficult to justify.'

Because of these considerations, the most common approach is now to provide for red-circled employees to receive any across-the-board (cost of living) increase awarded to staff generally for a protection period, which is usually limited to three or four years. They will no longer be entitled to general increases after the time limit has been reached (ie they will 'mark time') until their rate of pay falls within the new scale for their job. They will then be entitled to the same increases as any other staff in their grade up to the grade maximum. If a red-circled individual concerned leaves the job, the scale of pay for the job reverts to the standard range as set up following job evaluation. Where there is an incremental pay structure it is usual to allow staff to continue to earn any increments to which they are entitled under existing arrangements up to the maximum of their present scale.

If there is no limit to the protection period, red-circled staff continue to be eligible for general increases for as long as they remain in their present job. They are then on what is sometimes called a 'personal to job holder' scale.

Throughout the protection period, and particularly at the start of it, every attempt should be made to resolve the red-circle cases by other means. If job holders are thought to be worth the current salary, then they may well be underused in their existing job. Attempts should be made to resolve this by either increasing the job responsibilities so that the job will justify regrading to a higher grade or moving the person concerned to a higher-graded job as soon as an appropriate vacancy arises.

REFERENCES

1 e-reward (2004) *Survey of Grade and Pay Structures*, e-reward.co.uk, Stockport
2 Armstrong, M and Brown, D (2001) *New Dimensions in Pay Management*, Chartered Institute of Personnel and Development, London
3 Ulrich, D (1998) A new mandate for human resources, *Harvard Business Review*, January/February, pp 124–34
4 Equal Opportunities Commission (2003) *Good Practice Guide: Job evaluation schemes free of sex bias*, EOC, Manchester
5 Equal Pay Task Force (2001) *Just Pay*, Report of the Equal Pay Task Force to the Equal Opportunities Commission, EOC, Manchester

Part 5

Rewarding and reviewing contribution and performance

19

Individual contingent pay

Individual contingent pay is the term used to describe schemes for providing financial rewards that are related to individual performance, competency, contribution or skill. This chapter focuses on such schemes. However, pay related to service is also in a sense contingent pay and is therefore considered separately towards the end of the chapter.

Contingent pay may be made available in the form of consolidated increases to base rates or by cash bonuses (variable pay or 'pay at risk') or a combination of the two. This chapter examines one form of combined scheme under the heading of contribution-related pay. Cash bonuses by themselves are dealt with in Chapter 20, as bonus schemes have a number of specific features that need to be considered separately. Contingent pay for teams is covered in Chapter 21. Rewarding people according to organizational performance is discussed in Chapter 22. Sales force and shop floor incentive schemes can be classified as contingent pay but, because of their special nature, they are examined specifically in Chapters 27 and 29 respectively.

This chapter deals with contingent pay under the following headings:

- individual contingent pay defined;
- the incidence of contingent pay;
- contingent pay as a motivator;
- arguments for and against contingent pay;
- alternatives to contingent pay;

- criteria for success;
- performance-related pay;
- competency-related pay;
- contribution-related pay;
- skill-based pay;
- service-related pay;
- choice of approach;
- readiness for contribution pay;
- developing and implementing contingent pay.

INDIVIDUAL CONTINGENT PAY DEFINED

Individual contingent pay schemes other than service-related systems are based on processes for relating pay to performance, competence, contribution or skill. They provide an answer to the two fundamental reward management questions: 1) what do we value? and 2) what are we prepared to pay for?

The measures used may be expressed as ratings, which are converted by means of a formula to a payment. Alternatively, there may be no formal ratings and pay decisions are based on broad assessments rather than a formula.

THE INCIDENCE OF CONTINGENT PAY

The e-reward 2004 *Survey of Contingent Pay* (1) established that 189 schemes were used by the 100 respondents in the following proportions:

- performance-related pay – 65 per cent;
- contribution-related pay – 33 per cent;
- service-related pay – 15 per cent;
- competence-related pay – 8 per cent.

CONTINGENT PAY AS A MOTIVATOR

Many people see contingent pay as the best way to motivate people. But it is simplistic to assume that it is only the extrinsic motivators in the form of pay that create long-term motivation. The total reward concept as explained in Chapter 3 emphasizes the importance of non-financial rewards as an integral part of a complete package. The intrinsic motivators that can arise from the work itself and the working environment may have a deeper and longer-lasting effect.

Research conducted by Ryan (2) investigated the relationship of financial, extrinsic forms of motivation and intrinsic rewards. The research found that, in an environment of tight managerial control and limited communication, the two were inversely related, that is the stronger the emphasis placed on financial rewards such as performance pay, the lower the intrinsic motivation to work. Yet in an open, high-communications culture, both intrinsic and extrinsic motivation increased together. Context is key.

Incentives and rewards

When considering contingent pay as a motivator a distinction should be made between financial incentives and financial rewards.

Financial incentives are designed to provide direct motivation. They tell people how much money they will get in the future if they perform well – 'Do this and you will get that.' A shop floor payment-by-result scheme and a sales representative's commission system are examples of financial incentives.

Financial rewards act as indirect motivators because they provide a tangible means of recognizing achievements, as long as people expect that what they do in the future will produce something worthwhile, as expectancy theory suggests. Rewards can be retrospective – 'You have achieved this, therefore we will pay you that.' But rewards can also be prospective – 'We will pay you more now because we believe you have reached a level of competence that will produce high levels of performance in the future.'

ARGUMENTS FOR AND AGAINST CONTINGENT PAY

The concept of contingent pay has aroused strong feelings amongst those who support and those who oppose it. The arguments for and against contingent pay are set out below.

Arguments for

The most powerful argument for contingent pay is that those who contribute more should be paid more. It is right and proper to recognize achievement with a financial and therefore tangible reward. This is preferable to paying people just for 'being there' as happens in a service-related system.

The e-reward 2004 *Survey of Contingent Pay* (1) found that, in order of importance, the following were the main reasons produced by the respondents for using contingent pay:

1. to recognize and reward better performance;
2. to attract and retain high-quality people;
3. to improve organizational performance;
4. to focus attention on key results and values;
5. to deliver a message about the importance of performance;
6. to motivate people;
7. to influence behaviour;
8. to support cultural change.

Arguments against

The main arguments against contingent pay are that:

- the extent to which contingent pay schemes motivate is questionable – the amounts available for distribution are usually so small that they cannot act as an incentive;
- the requirements for success are exacting and difficult to achieve;
- money by itself will not result in sustained motivation – as Kohn (3) points out, money rarely acts in a crude, behaviourist, Pavlov's dog manner;
- people react in widely different ways to any form of motivation – it cannot be assumed that money will motivate all people equally yet that is the premise on which contribution pay schemes are based;
- financial rewards may possibly motivate those who receive them but they can demotivate those who don't, and the numbers who are demotivated could be much higher than the numbers who are motivated;
- contingent pay schemes can create more dissatisfaction than satisfaction if they are perceived to be unfair, inadequate or badly managed;
- employees can be suspicious of schemes because they fear that performance bars will be continuously raised; a scheme may therefore only operate successfully for a limited period;
- schemes depend on the existence of accurate and reliable methods of measuring performance, competence, contribution or skill, which might not exist;
- contingent pay decisions depend on the judgement of managers, which in the absence of reliable criteria could be partial, prejudiced, inconsistent or ill informed;
- the concept of contingent pay is based on the assumption that performance is completely under the control of individuals when, in fact, it is affected by the system in which they work;
- contingent pay, especially performance-related pay schemes, can militate against quality and teamwork.

Another powerful argument against contingent pay is that it has proved difficult to manage. Organizations, including the Civil Service, rushed into performance-related pay (PRP) in the 1980s without really understanding how to make it work. Inevitably problems of implementation arose. Studies such as those conducted by Bowey (4), Kessler and Purcell (5), Marsden and Richardson (6) and Thompson (7) have all revealed these difficulties. Failures are usually rooted in implementation and operating processes, especially those concerned with performance management, the need for effective communication and involvement, and line management capability.

The last factor is crucial. The success of contingent pay rests largely in the hands of line managers. They have to believe in it as something that will help them as well as the organization. They must also be good at practising the crucial skills of agreeing targets, measuring performance fairly and consistently, and providing feedback to their staff on the outcome of performance management and its impact on pay. Line managers can make or break contingent pay schemes.

Vicky Wright (8) has summed it all up: 'Even the most ardent supporters of performance-related pay recognise that it is difficult to manage well', and Oliver (9) made the point that 'performance pay is beautiful in theory but difficult in practice'.

Conclusions

A comprehensive study by Brown and Armstrong (10) into the effectiveness of contingent pay as revealed by a number of research projects produced two overall conclusions: 1) contingent pay cannot be endorsed or rejected universally as a principle; and 2) no type of contingent pay is universally successful or unsuccessful. They concluded their analysis of the research findings by stating that 'the research does show that the effectiveness of pay-for-performance schemes is highly context and situation-specific; and it has highlighted the practical problems which many companies have experienced with these schemes'.

ALTERNATIVES TO CONTINGENT PAY

The arguments against contingent pay convince many people that it is unsatisfactory; but what is the alternative? One answer is to rely more on non-financial motivators. But it is still necessary to consider what should be done about pay. The reaction in the 1990s to the adverse criticisms of PRP was to develop the concept of competency-related pay, which fitted in well with the emphasis on competencies. This approach, as described later, in theory overcame some of the cruder features of PRP but still created a number of practical difficulties and has never really become popular. In the late 1990s the idea of contribution-related pay emerged as advocated by Brown and Armstrong (10). This combines the output-driven focus of PRP with the input-(competence-)orientated focus of competence-related pay and has proved to be much more appealing than either performance- or competence-related pay.

However, many people still have reservations about this approach from the viewpoint of achieving the fair and consistent measurement of contribution. So what are the alternatives for them? Team pay is often advocated because it removes the individualistic aspect of PRP and accords with the belief in the importance of teamwork, but, as explained in Chapter 21, although team pay is attractive it is often difficult to apply and it still relies on performance measurement.

The traditional alternative is service-related pay as described at the end of this chapter. This certainly treats everyone equally (and therefore appeals to trade unions) but pays people simply for being there and this could be regarded as inequitable in that rewards take no account of relative levels of contribution.

The other common alternative is a spot rate system as described in Chapter 17. Most people, however, want and expect a range of base pay progression, however that is determined, and spot rates are not much used in larger organizations except for shop floor and sales staff and senior managers.

CRITERIA FOR SUCCESS

The following are the five criteria for effective contingent pay:

1. Individuals should have a clear line of sight between what they do and what they will get for doing it. A line-of-sight model adapted from Lawler (11) is shown in Figure 19.1. The concept expresses the essence of expectancy theory: that motivation only takes place when people *expect* that their effort and contribution will be rewarded. The reward should be clearly and closely linked to accomplishment or effort – people know what they will get if they achieve defined and agreed targets or standards and can track their performance against them.
2. Rewards are worth having.
3. Fair and consistent means are available for measuring or assessing performance, competence, contribution or skill.
4. People must be able to influence their performance by changing their behaviour and developing their competences and skills.
5. The reward should follow as closely as possible the accomplishment that generated it.

Figure 19.1 Line-of-sight model

These are ideal requirements and few schemes meet them in full. That is why contingent pay arrangements can often promise more than they deliver.

The various forms of contingent pay are described in the following sections of this chapter.

PERFORMANCE-RELATED PAY

Methods of operating PRP vary considerably but its typical main features are summarized in Figure 19.2 and described below.

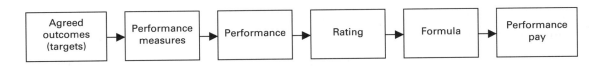

Figure 19.2 Performance-related pay

Basis of scheme

Pay increases are related to the achievement of agreed results defined as targets or outcomes.

Consolidated pay increases

Scope is provided for consolidated pay progression within pay brackets attached to grades or levels in a graded or career family structure or zones in a broad-banded structure. Such increases are permanent – they are seldom if ever withdrawn.

Cash bonuses (variable pay)

Alternatively or additionally, high levels of performance or special achievements may be rewarded by cash bonuses, which are not consolidated and have to be re-earned. Individuals may be eligible for such bonuses when they have reached the top of the pay bracket for their grade, or when they are assessed as being fully competent, having completely progressed along their learning curve. The rate of pay for someone who reaches the required level of competence can be aligned to market rates according to the organization's pay policy.

Pay progression

The rate and limits of progression through pay brackets in a grade and pay structure are typically but not inevitably determined by performance ratings, which are often made at the time of the performance management review but may be made separately in a special pay review. Some organizations do not base PRP increases on formal ratings and instead rely on a general assessment of how much the pay of individuals should increase by reference to performance, potential, the pay levels of their peers and their 'market worth' (the rate of pay it is believed they could earn elsewhere).

A formula in the shape of a pay matrix as illustrated in Figure 19.3 is often used to decide on the size of increases. This indicates the percentage increase payable for different performance ratings according to the position of the individual's pay in the pay range. This is sometimes referred to as an individual 'compa-ratio' (short for 'comparison ratio') and expresses pay as a percentage of the mid-point in a range. A compa-ratio of 100 per cent means that the salary would be at the mid-point.

Pay progression in a graded structure is typically planned to decelerate through the grade for two reasons. First, it is argued in line with learning curve theory that pay increases should be higher during the earlier period in a job when learning is at its highest rate. Second, it may be assumed that the central or reference point in a grade represents the market value of fully competent people. According to the pay policy of the organization this may be at or higher than the median. Especially in the latter case, it may be believed that employees should progress quite quickly to that level, but because beyond it they are already being paid well their pay need not increase so rapidly. This notion is reasonable but it can be difficult to explain to someone why they get smaller percentage increases when they are performing well at the upper end of their scale.

Amount of increases

The e-reward 2004 survey (1) found that the average increase was 3.9 per cent.

Conclusions on PRP

PRP has all the advantages and disadvantages listed for contingent pay. Many people feel the latter outweigh the former. It has attracted a lot of adverse comment, primarily

Rating	Percentage pay increase according to performance rating and position in pay range (compa-ratio)			
	Position in pay range			
	80%–90%	91%–100%	101%–110%	111%–120%
Excellent	12%	10%	8%	6%
Very effective	10%	8%	6%	4%
Effective	6%	4%	3%	0
Developing	4%	3%	0	0
Ineligible	0	0	0	0

Figure 19.3   PRP pay matrix

because of the difficulties organizations have met in managing it. Contribution-related pay schemes are becoming much more popular.

COMPETENCY-RELATED PAY

The main features of competency-related pay schemes are illustrated in Figure 19.4 and described below.

Basis of scheme

People receive financial rewards in the shape of increases to their base pay by reference to the level of competency they demonstrate in carrying out their roles. It is a method of paying people for the ability to perform now and in the future.

Consolidated pay increases

As in the case of PRP, scope is provided for consolidated pay progression within pay brackets attached to grades or levels in a narrow-graded or career family structure, or zones in a broad-banded structure (competence pay is often regarded as a feature of such structures).

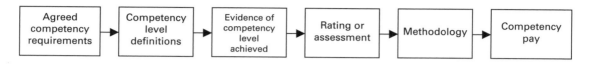

Figure 19.4 Competency-related pay

Pay progression

The rate and limits of progression through the pay brackets can be based on ratings of competence using a PRP-type matrix, but they may be governed by more general assessments of competence development.

Conclusions on competency-related pay

Competency-related pay is attractive in theory because it can be part of an integrated competency-based approach to HRM. It fits with the concept of human capital management, which emphasizes the skills and competencies people bring with them to the workplace. As Brown and Armstrong (10) comment: 'Increasingly, organizations are finding that success depends on a competent workforce. Paying for competence means that an organization is looking forward, not back.' Pay based on competence avoids the overemphasis in PRP schemes on quantitative, and often unrealistic, targets. It is appealing because it rewards people for what they are capable of doing, not for results over which they might have little control.

However, the idea of competency-related pay raises two questions. The fundamental question is 'What are we paying for?' Are we paying for behavioural competencies, ie how people behave, or technical competencies (competences), ie what people have to know and be able to do to perform well? If we are rewarding good behaviour (competencies) then a number of difficulties arise. It has been suggested by Sparrow (12) that these include the performance criteria on which competencies are based, the complex nature of what is being measured, the relevance of the results to the organization, and the problem of measurement. He concluded that 'we should avoid over-egging our ability to test, measure and reward competencies'.

Other fundamental objections to the behavioural approach have been raised by Ed Lawler (13). He expresses concern about schemes that pay for an individual's personality traits and emphasizes that such plans work best 'when they are tied to the ability of an individual to perform a particular task and when there are valid measures available of how well an individual can perform a task'. He also points out that 'generic competencies are not only hard to measure, they are not necessarily related to successful task performance in a particular work assignment or work role'.

This raises the second question: 'Are we paying for the possession of competency or the use of competency?' Clearly it must be the latter. But we can only assess the effective use of competence by reference to performance. The focus is therefore on results and, if that is the case, competency-related pay begins to look suspiciously like performance-related pay. It has been said that the difference between the two is all 'smoke and mirrors'. Competency-related pay could be regarded as no more than a more acceptable name for PRP.

There may be a case for rewarding the possession of competency but there is an even stronger one for linking the reward to outcomes (performance) as well as inputs (competence). This is the basis of the notion of contribution-related pay as described below and provides the explanation for the growing popularity of that approach compared with the more rarefied notion of competence-related pay.

CONTRIBUTION-RELATED PAY

Contribution-related pay as modelled in Figures 19.5 and 19.6 provides a basis for making pay decisions that are related to assessments of both the outcomes of the work carried out by individuals and the inputs in terms of the levels of competency that have influenced these outcomes. It focuses on what people in organizations are there to do, that is, to contribute by their skill and efforts to the achievement of the purpose of their organization or team.

Contribution-related pay is a holistic process, taking into account all aspects of a person's performance in accordance with the definition produced by Brumbach (14): 'Performance means both behaviours and results. Behaviours emanate from the performer and transform performance from abstraction to action. Not just the instruments for results, behaviours are also outcomes in their own right – the product of mental and physical effort applied to tasks – and can be judged apart from results.'

The case for contribution-related pay was made by Brown and Armstrong (10) as follows:

> Contribution captures the full scope of what people do, the level of skill and competence they apply and the results they achieve, which all contribute to the organization achieving its long-term goals. Contribution pay works by applying the mixed model of performance management: assessing inputs and outputs and coming to a conclusion on the level of pay for people in their roles and their work; both in the organization and in the market; taking into account both past performance and future potential.

Figure 19.5   Contribution pay model (1)

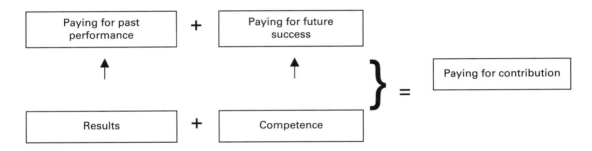

Figure 19.6   Contribution pay model (2)

Main features

The main features of contribution-related pay are illustrated in Figure 19.7.

An example of a pay-for-contribution scheme in a UK bank is shown in Figure 19.8. (The balanced scorecard is a set of performance measures that have to be taken equally into account when assessing overall performance.)

Methods of deciding contribution awards

There are six basic approaches as described below:

1. *Matrix formula.* Pay awards are governed by assessments of performance and competency and the amount is determined by a pay matrix such as the one illustrated in Figure 19.9.
    This approach is somewhat mechanistic.

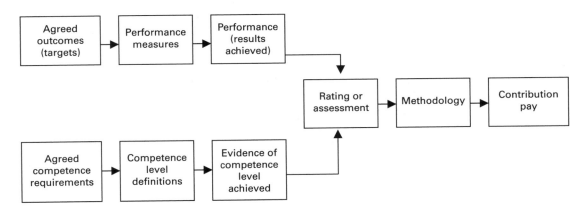

Figure 19.7 Contribution-related pay

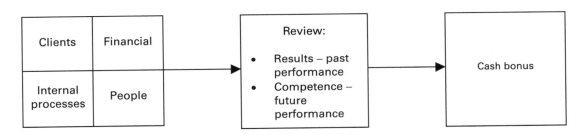

Figure 19.8 Paying for contribution in a UK bank

2. *Separate consolidated increases and bonuses.* Output is the only factor that governs cash bonuses but competency is the major component in determining base pay on the grounds that the latter is paid for what people are capable of doing while the former rewards them for what they achieve.

3. *Relate consolidated increases to competence up to a reference point and then pay cash bonuses for exceptional performance.* This is a version of the second approach. Its main features are:

   – a 'reference point' rate of pay is determined within each grade, band or level that includes jobs of broadly equal size;

   – the reference point is defined as the rate of pay for a person in a job who is highly competent, ie fully competent in all aspects of the job and therefore achieving high levels of performance;

   – the reference point takes account of both internal relativities and market rates;

   – the level of comparison for market rates is in accordance with the pay policy

Performance Rating	Percentage pay increase according to performance rating and competence assessment		
	Competence Assessment		
	Developing – does not yet meet all competence standards	Fully competent – meets all competence standards	Highly competent – exceeds most competence standards
Exceptional	–	8%	10%
Very effective	–	6%	7%
Effective	–	4%	5%
Developing	3%	–	–
Ineligible	0	–	–

Figure 19.9 Contribution pay matrix

of the organization – this might be set at above the median, eg at the upper quartile, to ensure that the high quality of staff required can be attracted and retained;

- the reference point is the maximum level of consolidated pay a high performer can expect to attain;
- a minimum level of pay for each grade is determined and progression to the reference point depends upon achieving defined levels of competence – there may be three or four levels;
- there is scope to reward those who perform exceptionally well with a re-earnable cash bonus, which could be consolidated if the level of exceptional performance is sustained over two to three years up to a maximum level defined for the grade.

A version of this contribution scheme developed for the Shaw Trust is modelled in Figure 19.10.

4. *Rewards as either consolidated increases or bonuses.* In this approach as illustrated in Figure 19.11 performers can earn a mix of base pay increase and bonus, which varies according to their position in the pay range. However, in the example in Figure 19.11 all outstanding performers receive a payment of 10 per cent of their base pay. Line managers would therefore not have to pass on the difficult message to outstanding individuals who are high in their pay range that they would be getting a smaller increase in spite of their contribution (this would be the case in a scheme using a typical PRP matrix as illustrated in Figure 19.3). Here, the higher up the range individuals are, the greater the proportion of their increase that is payable as a bonus. So those high in the range who are assessed as outstanding get 8 per cent as bonus and 2 per cent addition to their base pay, while outstanding individuals low in their range and below their market rates get an 8 per cent addition to their base pay and a 2 per cent bonus.

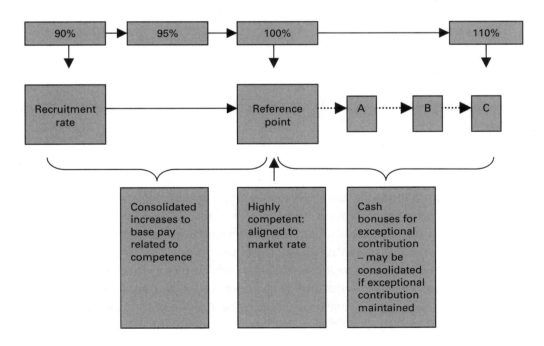

Figure 19.10 Contribution-related pay model: the Shaw Trust

Position in range	High – expert	Bonus	0%	2%	3%	6%	8%
		Base pay	0%	1%	2%	2%	2%
	Mid – competent market rate	Bonus	0%	1%	2%	4%	6%
		Base pay	0%	2%	3%	4%	4%
	Low – learning	Bonus	0%	0%	0%	1%	2%
		Base pay	0%	3%	6%	7%	8%
			U	S	G	E	O

Competency assessment*

* U = unsatisfactory   S = satisfactory   G = good   E = excellent   O = outstanding

Adapted from: Duncan Brown and Michael Armstrong (1999) *Paying for Contribution*, Kogan Page, London

Figure 19.11   Contribution matrix for base pay increases and bonuses

5. *Threshold payments.* A threshold is built into the pay range as illustrated in Figure 19.12 for an incremental payment scheme. To cross the threshold into a higher part of the range, individuals must meet contribution criteria that will define the level of competence required and indicate any performance (outcome) criteria that may be relevant.

   Threshold systems may be particularly relevant where there is a large pay span in a grade as in some incremental scales and it is felt that progression needs to be controlled. They could be regarded as a half-way house to a full contribution pay scheme and, because they do not rely on a suspect formula and contain defined and transparent criteria, they may be more acceptable to staff and their trade unions. However, their effectiveness depends on the definition of clear and assessable criteria and the willingness of all those concerned to assess contribution on the basis of evidence about the extent to which individuals meet the criteria. Judgements are still involved and this depends on the ability of managers to exercise them fairly and consistently and to be prepared to make hard decisions on the basis of objective evidence, which may mean that staff do not progress through the threshold. There is a real danger that, if managers do not have the courage of their convictions, staff will more or less automatically progress through

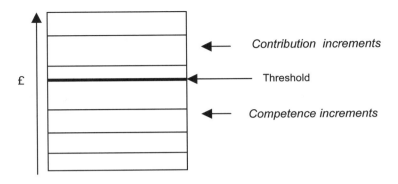

Figure 19.12   Contribution thresholds in a pay range

the thresholds as happened in the time of 'merit bars', although the criteria for crossing those bars were seldom defined explicitly.

6. *Holistic assessment.* A holistic approach can be adopted to assessing the level of contribution and therefore possible awards in the shape of base pay increases or bonuses. This approach leads to a decision on the level of pay appropriate for individuals in relation to the comparative levels of contribution of their peers and their own market worth, which will include consideration of their potential and the need to retain them.

Consideration is given both to what individuals have contributed to the success of their team and to the level of competence they have achieved and deployed. Team members who are contributing at the expected level will be paid at or around the reference point for the grade or zone and this reference point will be aligned to market rates in accordance with the organization's market pay policies. If, in the judgement of the line manager, individuals are achieving this level of contribution but are paid below their peers at the reference point, the pay of the individuals will be brought up to the level of their peers or towards that level if it is felt that the increase should be phased. Individuals may be paid above the reference point if they are making a particularly strong contribution or if their market worth is higher.

The policy guideline would be that the average pay of those in the grade should broadly be in line with the reference point (a compa-ratio of 100) unless there are special market rate considerations that justify a higher rate. Those at or above the reference point who are contributing well could be eligible for a cash bonus. A 'pay pot' would be made available for distribution, with guidelines on how it should be used.

This approach depends largely on the judgement of line managers although they would be guided and helped in the exercise of that judgement by HR. Its acceptability to staff as a fair process depends on precise communications generally on how it operates and equally precise communications individually on why decisions have been made. The assessment of contribution should be a joint one as part of performance management and the link between that assessment and the pay decision should be clear.

Other characteristics

The other characteristics of contribution pay are that:

- it is concerned with people as team members contributing to team performance, not acting as individuals;
- it can operate flexibly – approaches may be varied between different groups of people;
- it is tailored to suit the business and HR strategy of the organization;
- there is a clear business-related rationale that serves stated HR and reward purposes – individual and team contribution expectations are defined on the basis of the corporate and team business goals to be achieved and measured accordingly;
- it operates transparently – everyone understands how the scheme operates and how it affects them, and staff and their representatives will have contributed to the design of the system and will take part in regular reviews of its effectiveness, leading to modifications when required.

Conclusions

Contribution pay and performance pay are significantly different concepts as is shown in Table 19.1.

However, contribution-related pay decisions still ultimately depend on the decisions of line managers, and contribution pay will only work if line managers are capable of making sound judgements and are willing to spend time in doing so. Training and guidance are required and HR has an important role in providing them. The requirements for success are demanding and, as explained in the final two sections of this chapter, it is essential to ensure that the organization is ready for contribution pay and to plan its introduction with great care, including ample consultation and involvement. Organizations should never rush into contribution pay – more time than is usually thought necessary is needed to plan and implement it.

Table 19.1 Pay for performance compared with pay for contribution

	Pay for Performance	Pay for Contribution
Organizing philosophy	Formulae, systems	Processes
HR approach	Instrumentalist, people as costs	Commitment, people as assets
Measurement	Pay for results (the whats) – achieving individual objectives	Multidimensional, pay for results *and* how they are achieved
Measures	Financial goals	Broad variety of strategic goals: financial, service, operating, etc (balanced scorecard)
Focus of measurement	Individual	Multi-level: business, team
Design	Uniform merit pay and/or individual bonus approach throughout the organization	Diverse approaches using wide variety of reward methods to suit the needs of individual groups
Timescales	Immediate past performance	Past performance and contribution to future goals
Performance assessment	Performance appraisal – past review and ratings focus; top-down and quantitative	Performance management mixed model – past review and future development; partnership approach, quantitative and qualitative (possibly 360°)
Pay linkage	Fixed formula, matrix	Looser, more flexible linkages
Administration	Controlled by HR	Owned/operated by users
Communication and involvement	Top-down, non-transparent, imposed	Face to face, transparent, high involvement
Evaluation of effectiveness	Act of faith	Regular review and monitoring against clearly defined success criteria
Change over time	All or nothing	Regular incremental modification

Adapted from: Duncan Brown and Michael Armstrong (1999) *Paying for Contribution,* Kogan Page, London

SKILL-BASED PAY

Defined

Skill-based pay provides employees with a direct link between their pay progression and the skills they have acquired and can use effectively. It focuses on what skills the business wants to pay for and what employees must do to demonstrate them. It is therefore a people-based rather than a job-based approach to pay. Rewards are related to the employee's ability to apply a wider range or a higher level of skills to different jobs or tasks. It is not linked simply with the scope of a defined job or a prescribed set of tasks.

A skill may be defined broadly as a learned ability that improves with practice in time. For skill-based pay purposes the skills must be relevant to the work. Skill-based pay is also known as knowledge-based pay, but the terms are used interchangeably, knowledge being regarded loosely as the understanding of how to do a job or certain tasks.

Application

Skill-based pay was originally applied mainly to operatives in manufacturing firms. But it has been extended to technicians and workers in retailing, distribution, catering and other service industries. The broad equivalent of skill-based pay for managerial, professional and administrative staff and knowledge workers is competence-related pay, which refers to expected behaviour as well as, often, to knowledge and skill requirements. There is clearly a strong family resemblance between skill-based and competence-related pay – each is concerned with rewarding the person as well as the job. But they can be distinguished both by the way in which they are applied, as described below, and by the criteria used.

Main features

Skill-based pay works as follows:

- Skill blocks or modules are defined. These incorporate individual skills or clusters of skills that workers need to use and that will be rewarded by extra pay when they have been acquired and the employee has demonstrated the ability to use them effectively.
- The skill blocks are arranged in a hierarchy with natural break points between clearly definable different levels of skills.

- The successful completion of a skill module or skill block will result in an increment in pay. This will define how the pay of individuals can progress as they gain extra skills.
- Methods of verifying that employees have acquired and can use the skills at defined levels are established.
- Arrangements for 'cross-training' are made. These will include learning modules and training programmes for each skill block.

Conclusions

Skill-based pay systems are expensive to introduce and maintain. They require a considerable investment in skill analysis, training and testing. Although in theory a skill-based scheme will pay only for necessary skills, in practice individuals will not be using them all at the same time and some may be used infrequently, if at all. Inevitably, therefore, payroll costs will rise. If this increase is added to the cost of training and certification, the total of additional costs may be considerable. The advocates of skill-based pay claim that their schemes are self-financing because of the resulting increases in productivity and operational efficiency. But there is little evidence that such is the case. For this reason, skill-based schemes have never been very popular in the UK and some companies have discontinued them.

SERVICE-RELATED PAY

Defined

Service-related pay provides fixed increments that are usually paid annually to people on the basis of continued service either in a job or a grade in a pay spine structure. Increments may be withheld for unacceptable performance (although this is rare) and some structures have a 'merit bar' that limits increments unless a defined level of 'merit' has been achieved. The age discrimination regulations only permit service-related pay for a maximum of five years. Further points in a pay spine can only be used if there is an objectively justifiable reason, such as additional competencies.

Arguments for

Service-related pay is a simple concept based on the assumption that increased service in a job automatically enhances performance. It is supported by many unions because they perceive it as being fair – everyone is treated equally. It is felt that linking pay to time in the job rather than performance or competence avoids the partial and ill-informed judgements about people that managers are prone to make. Some people believe that the principle of rewarding people for loyalty through continued service is a good one.

Arguments against

The arguments against service-related pay are that:

- it is inequitable in the sense that an equal allocation of pay increases according to service does not recognize the fact that some people will be contributing more than others and should be rewarded accordingly;
- it does not encourage good performance and, indeed, it rewards poor performance equally;
- the assumption that performance improves automatically with service is difficult to justify – some people learn from experience over long periods of time (the eight years or more in a typical grade) and others do not; it has been said that a person with five years' experience may in practice only have had one year's experience repeated five times;
- it can be expensive – everyone may drift to the top of the scale, especially in times of low staff turnover, but the cost of their pay is not justified by the added value they provide.

The arguments against service-related pay have convinced most managements, in the private sector at least. Some managements, especially in the public and voluntary sectors, are concerned about managing any other form of contingent pay schemes (incremental pay scales do not need to be managed at all). They may also have to face strong resistance from their unions and can be unsure of what exit strategy they should adopt if they want to change. They may therefore stick with the status quo.

CHOICE OF APPROACH

The first choice is whether or not to have contingent pay related to performance, competence, contribution or skill. Public or voluntary sector organizations with fixed incremental systems (pay spines) where progression is solely based on service may want to retain them because they do not depend on possibly biased judgements by managers and they are perceived as being fair – everyone gets the same – and easily managed. However, the fairness of such systems can be questioned. Is it fair for a poor performer to be paid more than a good performer simply for being there?

The alternative to fixed increments is either spot rates or some form of contingent pay. Spot rate systems in their purest form are generally only used for senior managers or shop floor or retail workers and in smaller organizations and new businesses where the need for formal practices has not yet been recognized.

If it is decided that a more formal type of contingent pay for individuals should be adopted, the choice is between the various types of performance pay, competence-related or contribution-related pay and skill-based pay as summarized in Table 19.2.

Although contribution-related pay shares the disadvantages of other forms of contingent pay in that it relies on managerial judgement and is difficult to manage well it is probably the best choice in most circumstances. It is certainly the most popular. The last two sections of this chapter therefore concentrate on discussions of readiness for contribution pay and methods of developing and implementing it.

READINESS FOR CONTRIBUTION PAY

The 10 questions to be answered when assessing readiness for contribution pay are:

1. Is it believed that contribution pay will benefit the organization in the sense of enhancing its ability to achieve its strategic goals?
2. Are there valid and reliable means of measuring performance?
3. Is there a competency framework and are there methods of assessing levels of competence objectively (or could such a framework be readily developed)?
4. Are there effective performance management processes, which line managers believe in and carry out conscientiously?
5. Are line managers willing to assess contribution and capable of doing so?
6. Are line managers capable of making and communicating contribution pay decisions?
7. Is the HR function capable of providing advice and guidance to line managers on managing contribution pay?
8. Can procedures be developed to ensure fairness and consistency in assessments and pay decisions?
9. Are employees and trade unions willing to accept the scheme?
10. Do employees trust management to deliver the deal?

DEVELOPING AND IMPLEMENTING CONTRIBUTION PAY

The 10 steps required to develop and implement contribution pay are:

Table 19.2 Comparison of contingent pay schemes

Type of Scheme	Main Features	Advantages	Disadvantages	When Appropriate
Performance-related pay	Increases to basic pay or bonuses are related to assessment of performance.	– May motivate (but this is uncertain). – Links rewards to objectives. – Meets the need to be rewarded for achievement. – Delivers message that good performance is important and will be rewarded.	– May *not* motivate. – Relies on judgements of performance that may be subjective. – Prejudicial to teamwork. – Focuses on outputs, not quality. – Relies on good performance management processes. – Difficult to manage well.	– For people who are likely to be motivated by money. – In organizations with a performance-orientated culture. – When performance can be measured objectively.
Competence-related pay	Pay increases are related to the level of competence.	– Focuses attention on need to achieve higher levels of competence. – Encourages competence development. – Can be integrated with other applications of competency-based HR management.	– Assessment of competence levels may be difficult. – Ignores outputs: danger of paying for competences that will not be used. – Relies on well-trained and committed line managers.	– As part of an integrated approach to HRM where competencies are used across a number of activities. – Where competence is a key factor. – Where it may be inappropriate or hard to measure outputs. – Where well-established competency frameworks exist.

Table 19.2 *Continued*

Type of Scheme	Main Features	Advantages	Disadvantages	When Appropriate
Contribution-related pay	Increases in pay or bonuses are related both to inputs (competence) and outputs (performance).	Rewards people not only for what they do but how they do it.	As for both PRP and competence-related pay, it may be hard to measure contribution and it is difficult to manage well.	When it is believed that a well-rounded approach covering both inputs and outputs is appropriate.
Skill-based pay	Increments related to the acquisition of skills.	Encourages and rewards the acquisition of skills.	Can be expensive when people are paid for skills they don't use.	On the shop floor or in retail organizations.
Service-related pay	Increments related to service in grade.	– No scope for bias. – Easy to manage.	Fails to reward those who contribute more.	Where this is the traditional approach and trade unions oppose alternatives.

1. Analyse culture, strategy and existing processes including the grade and pay structure, performance management and methods of progressing pay or awarding cash bonuses.
2. Set out aims that demonstrate how contribution pay will help to achieve the organization's strategic goals.
3. Communicate aims to line managers and staff and involve them in the development of the scheme.
4. Determine how the scheme will operate covering:
   - the use of performance and competence measures;
   - the performance management processes required;
   - the scope for awarding cash bonuses as well as base pay increases;
   - the approach to making decisions on awards: one of the five approaches set out in this chapter or any other suitable method of deciding on pay progression and cash payments;

- the amount of money that will be available for contribution pay, and how that money should be distributed;
- the guidelines and procedures needed to govern contribution pay reviews and ensure that they are carried out fairly and consistently and within available budgets;
- the basis upon which the effectiveness of contribution pay will be evaluated.

5. Develop a competence framework and role profiles.
6. Develop or improve performance management processes covering the selection of performance measures, decisions on competence requirements, methods of agreeing objectives and the procedure for conducting joint reviews.
7. Communicate intentions to line managers and staff.
8. Pilot-test the scheme and amend as necessary.
9. Provide training to all concerned.
10. Launch the scheme and evaluate its effectiveness after the first review.

REFERENCES

1 e-reward (2004) *Survey of Contingent Pay*, e-reward.co.uk, Stockport

2 Ryan, R (1983) The relation of reward contingency and interpersonal context to intrinsic motivation, *Journal of Personality and Social Psychology*, **45** (4), pp 56–71

3 Kohn, A (1993) Why incentive plans cannot work, *Harvard Business Review*, September/October, pp 54–63

4 Bowey, A (1982) *The Effects of Incentive Pay Systems*, Department of Employment Research Paper No. 36, DOE, London

5 Kessler, J and Purcell, J (1992) Performance-related pay: objectives and application, *Human Resource Management Journal*, **2** (3), Spring, pp 16–32

6 Marsden, D and Richardson, R (1994) Performing for pay?, *British Journal of Industrial Relations*, June

7 Thompson, M (1992) *Pay and Performance: The employer experience*, Report No. 218, Institute of Manpower Studies, Brighton

8 Wright, V (1991) Performance related pay, in *The Performance Management Handbook*, ed E Neale, IPM, London

9 Oliver, J (1996) Cash on delivery, *Management Today*, August

10 Brown, D and Armstrong, M (1999) *Paying for Contribution: Real performance-related pay strategies*, Kogan Page, London

11 Lawler, EE (1988) Pay for performance: making it work, *Personnel*, October

12 Sparrow, PA (1996) Too good to be true, *People Management*, 5 December, pp 22–27

13   Lawler, EE (1993) Who uses skill-based pay, and why, *Compensation and Benefits Review*, March/April
14   Brumbach, GB (1988) Some ideas, issues and predictions about performance management, *Public Personnel Management*, Winter

20

Bonus schemes

Cash bonuses are an increasingly important part of the remuneration package. This chapter starts with a definition of bonus schemes and then covers:

- the aims of bonus schemes;
- the rationale for bonuses;
- the different types of schemes;
- the categories of staff taking part in bonus schemes;
- the design of bonus schemes;
- the introduction of a scheme.

BONUS SCHEMES DEFINED

Bonus schemes provide cash payments to employees that are related to the performance of their organization, their team or themselves, or a combination of two or more of these. Bonuses are often referred to as 'variable pay' or 'pay at risk'.

A defining characteristic of a bonus is that it has to be re-earned, unlike increases arising from individual contingent pay schemes such as performance- or contribution-related pay or pay related to service, which are consolidated into base pay. Such payments can be described as 'gifts that go on giving'.

Cash bonuses may be the sole method of providing people with rewards in addition to their base pay or they may be paid on top of individual contingent pay.

AIMS OF BONUS SCHEMES

The aims of bonus schemes may differ, but typically they include one or more of the following:

- Enable people to share in the success of the organization and therefore increase their commitment to it.
- Provide rewards related to business performance to increase motivation, commitment and engagement.
- Provide a reward that recognizes past performance or achievements and encourages individuals and teams to perform well in the future.
- Provide a direct incentive that increases motivation and engagement and generates higher future levels of individual and team performance.
- Ensure that pay levels are competitive and will attract and retain good-quality people.

RATIONALE FOR BONUS SCHEMES

The rationale for a bonus scheme will be based on the belief that it will fulfil one or more of the aims set out above, thus contributing to the creation of a high-performance culture and making a positive impact on bottom-line results.

When considering the rationale it is necessary to evaluate the case for having a bonus scheme either as an alternative to a more conventional individual contingent pay scheme (ie only provide cash bonuses) or as an addition to contingent pay (ie provide both cash bonuses and the opportunity to earn contingent pay that is consolidated in base pay). The advantages and disadvantages of these alternatives are summarized in Table 20.1.

TYPES OF SCHEME

Table 20.2 summarizes the features of the different types of bonus scheme and advantages and disadvantages.

Table 20.1 Advantages and disadvantages of alternative bonus arrangements

Approach	Advantages	Disadvantages
Bonus only	– Has to be re-earned. – Can be related to corporate or team performance as well as individual performance, thereby increasing commitment and enhancing teamwork. – Cash sums, as long as they are sizeable, can have a more immediate impact on motivation and engagement.	– May be perceived as arbitrary. – Many people may prefer the opportunity to increase their base pay rather than rely on potentially unpredictable bonus payments. – If unconsolidated, the payment will not be pensionable.
Bonus and contingent pay	– Get best of both worlds: consolidated increases and cash payments.	– Potentially complex. – The impact made by either bonuses or consolidated payments might be dissipated, especially when the sums available are divided into two parts.

CATEGORY OF STAFF COVERED

Bonus schemes based on organizational or individual performance are often only provided for directors and, possibly, senior managers on the grounds that they make the greatest impact on results and should be incentivized and rewarded for their contribution to those results. But this may frustrate other staff who, with justification, could argue that they also make a contribution that deserves a cash reward.

Bonuses based on organizational performance may be made available to all staff to provide a general reward and encourage identification with the business. Such bonuses can be in addition to contingent pay. They are sometimes provided in organizations that have team pay for certain categories of staff, eg branch staff in a financial services company, but are unable to extend team payments to other categories of staff who do not work in such well-defined teams. Combination plans may also be applied to all staff although they are sometimes restricted to senior managers. Bonuses based on individual performance may also be paid to all categories of staff or restricted to certain categories, eg directors or sales staff.

THE BUSINESS CASE FOR BONUS SCHEMES

The business cases made by a number of respondents to the 2006 e-reward *Survey of Bonus Schemes* (1) are illustrated below:

- The bonus structures are such that they are self-financing when people are over the 100 per cent target level. As the 100 per cent target level is set at the budget level, everything over this is of added benefit. The structure of the schemes also has a higher weighting of the products with more margin, which again helps to self-finance the schemes.
- The industry is driven by margins and total operating profit at branch and regional levels, so the bonus schemes reflect this requirement to deliver. The schemes are rigorously enforced and tested by finance.
- The organization has a pay-for-performance culture and in turn recognizes and awards high achievers. This is a key driver in motivating employees and organizational performance.
- The bonus scheme is a key to attaining scorecard performance at levels necessary to achieve the flexibility to manage costs finely in line with varying volumes of production and the lowest-margin products to ensure that the site can make a positive profit before tax contribution.

DESIGNING A BONUS SCHEME

The considerations affecting the design of a bonus scheme are set out below.

Criteria

The criteria for an effective bonus scheme are that it must:

- be designed to meet defined objectives;
- provide a clear line of sight between effort or contribution and the reward;
- result in meaningful rewards;
- be based on realistic, significant and measurable key performance indicators (KPIs) for organizational and team bonus schemes or combination plans;
- be based on a well-established and effective process of performance management for individual bonuses;
- operate fairly, equitably, consistently and transparently;
- be appropriate for the type of people to which it applies;

Table 20.2 Features and advantages and disadvantages of different bonus schemes

Type of Scheme	Main Features	Advantages	Disadvantages
Business performance schemes	Bonus payments related to the performance of the whole business or a major function such as a division, store or site. Performance is measured by key performance indicators (KPIs), eg profit, contribution, shareholder value, earnings per share or economic value added.	– Enable employees to share in the organization's success, thus increasing commitment. – Can focus on a range of key factors affecting organizational performance. – Can readily be added to other forms of contingent pay to recognize collective as distinct from individual effort.	– Do not provide an individual incentive.
Individual bonus or incentive plans	Bonus payments related to individual performance.	– Provide a direct reward related to individual performance. – Cash, if sufficiently high, can make an immediate impact on motivation and engagement.	– May not be pensionable. – Some people may prefer consolidated increases to their base pay rather than rely on possibly unpredictable bonus payments that may be perceived as arbitrary.
Team pay*	Payments to members of a formally established team are linked to the performance of that team. The rewards are shared among the members of the team in accordance with a published formula or on an ad hoc basis in the case of exceptional achievements.	– Encourage team working. – Enhance flexible working and multiskilling. – Clarify team goals. – Encourage less effective performance to improve by meeting team standards.	– May be difficult to identify well-defined teams with clear and measurable goals. – Individuals may resent the fact that their own performance is not recognized.

Table 20.2 *Continued*

Type of Scheme	Main Features	Advantages	Disadvantages
Combination plans	Bonuses are related to a combination of plans measuring performance across several levels, for example: corporate and individual performance; business, team and individual; team and individual.	– Combine the advantages of different types of bonus arrangements, eg business and individual (the most common form of combination scheme).	– May be over-complex. – Could disperse the impact of either the collective or the individual elements.
Cash-based profit sharing**	The payment of sums in cash related to the profits of the business. Such schemes operate on a corporate basis and usually make profit shares available to all employees except, possibly, directors or senior managers. They do not require Inland Revenue approval and are fully liable for income tax and national insurance.	– Increases identification with the firm. – Recognizes that everyone contributes to creating profit.	– Does not provide an individual incentive. – Amounts distributed are taken for granted.
Gain sharing**	A formula-based company- or factory-wide bonus plan that provides for employees to share in the financial gains made by a company as a result of its improved performance as measured, for example, by added value.	– Recognizes that everyone working in a plant contributes to creating added value and should benefit accordingly. – Provides a platform for the joint analysis of methods of improving productivity.	– Does not provide an individual incentive. – Can be complex. – Ineffective if too high a proportion of added value is retained by the company.

* See Chapter 21.
** See Chapter 22.

- be reasonably easy to understand and manage, ie not over-complex;
- only provide for payment if a demanding threshold of performance is achieved;
- contain arrangements to restrict (cap) the maximum payment to an acceptable sum;
- so far as possible be self-financing;
- provide for review at regular intervals to decide whether the scheme needs to be amended, replaced or cancelled;
- provide scope to moderate corporate bonuses by reference to personal performance.

Formula

Every bonus scheme is different. In an individual scheme a single criterion such as profit before tax may be used for directors with a threshold performance level to generate a bonus and a sliding scale up to a maximum that determines the size of the bonus. Alternatively, in a scheme applying to all staff, ratings may be used that determine the size of the bonus for individuals or teams by reference to the extent to which objectives have been achieved.

The formula for a combined scheme may be more complex:

- Individual or team payments may only be made if a threshold level of organizational performance is reached.
- The level of bonus related to organizational performance may be modified in accordance with the level of individual performance achieved.
- There are many variations on the split between corporate and individual bonuses although a 50/50 division is quite common.
- The split may vary at different levels, providing a greater proportion of bonus for corporate performance at higher levels.

Examples of the formulae used by the e-reward survey respondents are given in Table 20.3.

Table 20.3 Examples of bonus formulae

Business performance	Earnings per share, revenue growth and R&D reinvestment. Budgeted profit. Target set for financial performance: earnings before interest, tax, depreciation and amortization. If the first target is not met, no pool is generated. Three further targets are set, each generating a higher level of bonus. Key performance indicators and profit. Customer satisfaction levels, unique customer interactions and low cost interventions.
Individual performance	Determined by performance rating indicator – the top three performance ratings receive a bonus. Individual performance is based against pre-agreed objectives. Balanced scorecard – typically sales, customer service, call handling time and a development objective for call handling. Individual criteria linked to the area of responsibility, eg to achieve the budget target, a particular level of growth, etc. Demonstrable achievement over and above normal performance in one of the organization's six core competencies.
Combined	50% business performance, 50% individual performance. 20% company-wide performance, 30% business performance, 50% individual performance. 30% business performance, 70% individual performance. Group-wide business performance. Individual element 'flexes' the maximum business performance downward for bad performance, eg rating '1' to '3' get the full bonus; for rating '4' the business performance bonus is reduced by 25%; for a '5' rating the business performance bonus is reduced by 50%; a '6' rating gets zero award. Business performance creates a bonus opportunity for an individual, which is then flexed according to a personal performance factor.

INTRODUCING A BONUS SCHEME

The actions required when introducing a scheme are:

- Consult with those concerned on the purpose and features of the scheme.
- Define responsibilities for introducing, maintaining and evaluating the scheme.
- Pilot-test it if at all possible in a department or division or on a representative sample of employees to obtain information on how well the formula works, the appropriateness of the measures, the cost of the scheme, its impact, the effectiveness of the process of making decisions on bonuses (eg the application of performance management) and the reactions of staff.
- Make amendments as necessary in the light of the test.
- Prepare a description for communication to staff of the purpose of the scheme, how it works and how staff will be affected.
- Ensure that the scheme is bedded down in the organization's day-to-day operating processes, including management reports and performance reviews.
- Draw up a budget for the costs of the scheme.
- Define operating and control processes including responsibilities, the achievement of fairness and consistency and cost control.
- Prepare a plan for introducing the scheme covering the agreement of performance indicators and targets, methods of reviewing performance, the process of deciding on bonus payments and communications.

REFERENCE

1   e-reward (2006) *Survey of Bonus Schemes*, e-reward.co.uk, Stockport

21

Team pay

Two factors have combined to create interest in rewarding teams rather than individuals. The first is the significance attached to good teamwork and the belief that team pay would enhance it, and the second is dissatisfaction with the individual nature of performance-related pay, which is believed to be prejudicial to teamwork. The notion of team pay appeals to many people but the number of organizations that use it is small. The e-reward 2004 *Survey of Contingent Pay* (1) found that only 11 per cent of respondents had team pay and in the organizations covered by the CIPD 2006 reward survey (2) only one category of employee (middle and first-line management) had team pay on its own and that was for only 1 per cent of respondents. More people had team pay combined with other forms of contingent pay, eg individual performance pay: senior management – 10 per cent; middle and first-line management – 9 per cent; technical and professional – 6 per cent; and clerical and manual – 5 per cent. But these proportions are minute compared with, for example, the proportions with individual performance pay combined with competency pay (contribution-related pay), which were: senior management – 58 per cent; middle and first-line management – 53 per cent; technical and professional – 52 per cent; and clerical and manual – 43 per cent.

Team pay is an attractive idea but one difficult to put into practice. The limited number of schemes may arise because organizations find it difficult to meet the quite exacting conditions for team pay set out later in this chapter. Others may believe that they have to focus their incentive schemes on individual rather than group effort.

This chapter starts with a definition of team pay and its aims and continues with a description of how team pay works, an analysis of the arguments for and against team pay and suggestions on how team pay can be introduced. It ends with a summary of a team project in the NHS with mixed results, which illustrates some of the difficulties with the concept.

TEAM PAY DEFINED

Team pay links payments to members of a formally established team to the performance of that team. The rewards are shared among the members of the team in accordance with a published formula or on an ad hoc basis in the case of exceptional achievements. Rewards for individuals may also be influenced by assessments of their contribution to team results. To appreciate how team pay works it is necessary to understand the nature of a team and the various types of teams to which it can apply.

The nature of a team

A team has been defined by Katzenbach and Smith (3) as: 'A small number of people with complementary skills who are committed to a common purpose, performance goals and approach for which they hold themselves mutually accountable.'

Types of teams

There are four types of teams as described below.

Organizational teams

These consist of individuals who are linked together organizationally as members of, for example, the 'top management team', departmental heads in an operational or research division, section heads or team leaders in a department, or even people carrying out distinct and often separate functions, as long as they are all contributing to the achievement of the objectives of their department or section.

Members of organizational teams can be related to one another by the requirement to achieve an overall objective, but this may be loosely defined and the degree to which they act in consort will vary considerably. In a sense, organizations are entirely constructed of such 'teams', but team reward processes may be inappropriate unless their members are strongly united by a common purpose and are clearly interdependent. If such is not the case, some form of bonus related to organizational performance might be preferable.

Work teams

These are self-contained and permanent teams whose members work closely together to achieve results in terms of output, the development of products or processes, or the delivery of services to customers. This type of team will be focused on a common purpose and its members will be interdependent – results are a function of the degree to which they can work well together. It is for this type of team that continuing team pay scheme rewards may be appropriate as long as team targets can be established and team performance can be measured accurately and fairly.

Project teams

These consist of people brought together from different functions to complete a task lasting several months to several years. When the project is completed the team disbands. Examples include product development teams or a team formed to open a new plant. Project teams may be rewarded with cash bonuses payable on satisfactory completion of the project to specification, on time and within the cost budget. Interim 'milestone' payments may be made as predetermined stages of the project are completed satisfactorily.

Ad hoc teams

These are functional or cross-functional teams set up to deal with an immediate problem. They are usually short-lived and operate as a task force. It is unusual to pay bonuses to such teams unless they deliver exceptional results.

AIM OF TEAM PAY

The aim of team pay is to encourage and reinforce the sort of behaviour that leads to and sustains effective team performance by:

- providing incentives and other means of recognizing team achievements;
- clarifying what teams are expected to achieve by relating rewards to the attainment of predetermined and agreed targets and standards of performance or to the satisfactory completion of a project or a stage of a project;
- conveying the message that one of the organization's core values is effective teamwork.

Research conducted by the Institute of Personnel and Development (cited by Armstrong, 4) established that the main reason organizations gave for developing team reward processes was the perceived need to encourage group endeavour and cooperation rather than to concentrate only on individual performance. It was argued that 'pay for individual performance' systems prejudice team performance in two ways. First, they encourage individuals to focus on their own interests rather than on those of the team. Second, they result in managers and team leaders treating their team members only as individuals rather than relating to them in terms of what the team is there to do and what they can do for the team.

HOW TEAM PAY WORKS

The most common method of providing team pay is to distribute a cash sum related to team performance amongst team members. There are a number of formulae and ways of distributing team pay as described below.

The team pay formula

This establishes the relationship between team performance, as measured or assessed in quantitative or qualitative terms, and the reward. It also fixes the size of the bonus pool or fund earned by the team to be distributed among its members, or the scale of payments made to team members in relation to team performance with regard to certain criteria. Bonuses may be related to performance in such specific areas as sales, throughput, achievement of targets in the form of the delivery of results for a project, levels of service or an index of customer satisfaction. Targets are agreed and performance is measured against the targets.

Alternatively bonuses may be related to an overall criterion, which can be a more subjective assessment of the contribution of the team to organizational performance.

Method of distributing bonuses

Bonuses can be distributed to team members in the form of either a percentage of base salary or the same sum for each member, usually based on a scale of payments. Payment of bonus as a percentage of base salary is the most popular method. The assumption behind it is that base salary reflects the value of the individual's contribution to the team. The correctness of this assumption clearly depends on the extent to which base salary truly indicates the level of performance of individuals as team members.

Team pay and individual pay

Some organizations pay team bonuses only. A minority pay individual bonuses as well, which are often related to an assessment of the competence of the person, thus, it is thought, providing encouragement to develop skills and rewarding them for their particular contribution.

Dealing with high and low individual performance in a team

It is sometimes assumed by advocates of team pay that all members of a team contribute equally and should therefore be rewarded equally. In practice the contribution of individual team members will vary and, if this is the case, for example in shop floor groups, team pressure may be forcing everyone to work at the same rate so as to avoid 'rate busting'. (This is an example of how a highly cohesive team can work against the interests of the organization.)

When designing a team pay scheme, decisions have to be made on the likelihood that some people will perform better or worse than others. It may be decided that, even if this happens, it would be invidious and detrimental to single anyone out for different treatment. It could, however, be considered that 'special achievement' or 'sustained high performance' bonuses should be payable to individuals who make an exceptional contribution, while poor performers should receive a lower bonus or no bonus at all.

Project team bonuses

The design considerations described above apply to permanent work teams. Different arrangements are required for project teams specially set up to achieve a task and, usually, disbanded after the task has been completed. Project team bonuses should, wherever possible, be self-financing – they should be related to increases in income or productivity or cost savings arising from the project. Project teams can be set targets and their bonus can be linked with achieving or surpassing targeted results. Alternatively, a fixed bonus can be promised if the project is on time, meets the specification and does not exceed the cost budget. The bonus could be increased for early completion or to reflect cost savings. For lengthy projects, interim payments may be made at defined 'milestones'.

Ad hoc bonuses

Where there are no predetermined arrangements for paying bonuses to teams a retrospective bonus can be paid to a project or ad hoc team in recognition of exceptional achievement.

REQUIREMENTS FOR TEAM PAY

Team pay works best if teams:

- stand alone as performing units for which clear targets and standards can be agreed;
- have a considerable degree of autonomy – team pay is likely to be most effective in self-managed teams;
- are composed of people whose work is interdependent – it is acknowledged by members that the team will deliver the results expected of them only if they work well together and share the responsibility for success;
- are stable – members are used to working with one another, know what is expected of them by fellow team members and know where they stand in the regard of those members;
- are mature – well established, used to working flexibly to meet targets and deadlines, and capable of making good use of the complementary skills of their members.

These are exacting requirements, which helps to explain why the take-up of team pay is low. If the requirements above can be met there may be a good case for team pay.

ADVANTAGES AND DISADVANTAGES OF TEAM PAY

Team pay can:

- encourage team working and cooperative behaviour;
- enhance flexible working within teams and encourage multiskilling;
- clarify team goals and priorities and provide for the integration of organizational and team objectives;
- encourage less effective performers to improve in order to meet team standards;
- serve as a means of developing self-managed or self-directed teams.

But:

- The effectiveness of team pay depends on the existence of well-defined and mature teams. They may be difficult to identify and, even if they can be, do they need to be motivated by a purely financial reward?
- Team pay may seem unfair to individuals who could feel that their own efforts are unrewarded.

- Pressure to conform, which is accentuated by team pay, could result in the team maintaining its output at lowest-common-denominator levels – sufficient to gain what is thought collectively to be a reasonable reward but no more.
- It can be difficult to develop performance measures and methods of rating team performance that are seen to be fair – team pay formulae may well be based on arbitrary assumptions about the correct relationship between effort and reward.
- There may be pressure from employees to migrate from poorly performing teams to high-performing teams, which, if allowed, could cause disruption and stigmatize the teams from which individuals transfer or, if refused, could leave dissatisfied employees in the inadequate teams, making them even worse (this was a serious problem experienced by Pearl Assurance, one of the pioneers of team pay).

To many organizations the disadvantages outweigh the advantages.

DEVELOPING TEAM PAY

If, in spite of the problems that may beset team pay, it is decided to introduce it, the development steps are as follows:

1. *Initial analysis.* This should identify whether there are teams that satisfy the requirements set out above.
2. *Scheme design.* Decisions need to be made on which teams will be eligible for team pay and why, and the team bonus formula (the criteria to be used in judging performance, the amount available for team pay and the method of distributing team pay).
3. *Scheme introduction.* Team pay is likely to be unfamiliar and it should therefore be introduced with care, especially if it is replacing an existing system of individual PRP. The process will be easier if employees have been involved in developing the scheme, but it is still essential to communicate in detail to all employees the reasons for introducing team pay, how it will work and how it will affect them.

   It is easier to introduce team pay into mature teams whose members are used to working together, trust one another and can recognize that team pay will work to their mutual advantage. Although it may seem an attractive proposition to use team pay as a means of welding new work teams together, there are dangers in forcing people who are already having to adapt to a different situation to accept a radical change in their method of remuneration. It should be remembered that it may not be easy to get people in work teams to think of their performance in terms of how it impacts on others. It can take time for employees to adapt to a system in which a proportion of their pay is based on team achievement.

When it comes to launching team pay it may be advisable to pilot it initially in one or two well-established teams. Experience gained from the pilot scheme can then be used to modify the scheme before it is extended elsewhere. If the pilot scheme teams think it has been a success other teams may be more willing to convert to team pay.

NHS CASE STUDY

As reported by Reilly *et al* (5) the UK Department of Health decided to trial team pay in NHS trusts. The 17 teams in the trial were based at a number of sites and were given targets aimed at improving the patient experience through faster response, better service or an improved environment. The team reward was a cash payment, money put into an 'improvement fund' for staff to spend on staff facilities/development or a mixture of the two.

Many positive results were achieved by the trials. These included improvements in the management of the trusts and benefits to patients and staff. The end-of-pilot survey results generally elicited positive responses to questions relating to the operation of team-based pay. But as the researchers involved in the survey observed: 'So far so good, but there are still question marks over the success of the scheme. First, not all sites met their targets… and not every participant was as keen about the benefits of the scheme. Second, even at the better performing sites, did team-based pay drive service improvement, even if the staff thought it did?'

In the opinion of the researchers, the causes of relative failure in some trusts could be attributed to the following three factors:

- *Team structure* – some people were excluded from teams, which they resented, and the teams sometimes cut across natural groupings. But the size of the team and the degree to which it was well established did not make much difference.
- *Targets* – there were a number of difficulties with targets. Some administrators found it hard to specify output, let alone outcome measure. They felt happier with input metrics. It was confirmed that the poorer the 'line of sight' between work actions and the target, the less likely there was to be employee engagement and thereby effort to deliver. In particular, when targets were externally imposed, failure was more probable. The degree of stretch in the targets varied greatly, but it did not always seem easy at the outset to predict what would be hard to achieve and what would be easier.
- *Matters outside the team's control* – these genuinely affected the teams' ability to deliver, producing understandable criticism.

The main conclusions reached by the researchers were that:

- success depends on having a clear purpose, effective leadership, the trust of staff in the integrity and competence of management, good communications and efficient project management;
- the 'right' size of team depended on the objectives of the exercise, eg bigger teams may be necessary to cope with complex processes and multiple targets;
- targets needed to be clear, simple, easy to communicate and evaluate, and relate to the work people do, and people needed to believe the targets were achievable and within their control;
- as with all schemes, team-based pay will only operate successfully for a limited period because employees fear that the performance bar will be continuously raised and the discretionary effort that schemes tap into may not always be there to exploit.

REFERENCES

1   e-reward (2004) *Survey of Contingent Pay*, e-reward.co.uk, Stockport
2   Chartered Institute of Personnel and Development (2006) *Survey of Reward Management*, CIPD, London
3   Katzenbach, J and Smith, D (1993) *The Magic of Teams*, Harvard Business School Press, Boston, MA
4   Armstrong, M (2000) *Rewarding Teams*, Chartered Institute of Personnel and Development, London
5   Reilly, P, Phillipson, J and Smith, P (2005) Team-based pay in the United Kingdom, *Compensation and Benefits Review*, July/August, pp 54–60

22

Paying for organizational performance

Many organizations believe that their financial reward systems should extend beyond individual contingent pay, which does not recognize collective effort, or team pay, which is difficult. They believe that their system should help to enhance commitment and convince employees that they have a stake in the business as well as providing them with additional pay. The response to this belief is to offer financial rewards that are related to organizational performance (sometimes known as company-wide or factory-wide schemes), and the e-reward 2004 survey (1) found that 40 per cent of respondents had one or more of the types of schemes described below.

TYPES OF SCHEMES

The three types of formal organizational schemes are:

1. *profit sharing* – the payment of sums in cash or shares related to the profits of the business; 13 per cent of the respondents to the e-reward survey had such schemes;
2. *share ownership schemes* – employees are given the opportunity to purchase shares in the company; 23 per cent of the respondents to the e-reward survey had such schemes;

3. *gain sharing* – the payment of cash sums to employees related to the financial gains made by the company because of its improved performance; only 4 per cent of the e-reward respondents had such schemes.

Less formally, managements can make decisions on the amount to be paid out in the form of individual performance- or contribution-related increments or individual/team cash bonuses. These decisions are made on the basis of what they believe the organization can afford. This creates what is sometimes called a 'pot' from which payments are funded. The assessment of affordability (a potent word for many managements) can determine pay review budgets on the proportion of the payroll, eg 3 per cent, that can be allocated for increments or bonuses.

Research carried out by IRS in 2003 (2) established that there was a high degree of 'mix and match' amongst the profit-sharing and share ownership schemes offered by companies to their employees. Half of the respondents to the survey with schemes in place ran more than one. Organizations may also provide for payments related to organizational performance in addition to individual contingent pay.

AIMS

The aims of relating rewards to organizational performance are to:

● increase the commitment of employees to the organization;
● enable employees to share in the success of the organization;
● stimulate more interest in the affairs of the organization;
● focus employees' attention on what employees can contribute to organizational success and bring areas for improvement to their attention;
● obtain tax advantages for employees through approved share schemes – such 'tax-efficient' schemes enable the business to get better value for money from its expenditure on employee remuneration.

Perhaps the two most important reasons for organizational schemes are the beliefs that they increase the identification of employees with the company and that the company is morally bound to share its success with its employee stakeholders – those who collectively make a major contribution to it. However, it is generally recognized that they do not provide a direct incentive because the links between individual effort and the collective reward are too remote.

PROFIT SHARING

Profit sharing is a plan under which an employer pays to eligible employees, as an addition to their normal remuneration, special sums related to the profits of the business. The amount shared is determined either by an established formula or entirely at the discretion of management. As a percentage of pay, the value of profit shares varies considerably between companies and within companies from year to year. Between 2 per cent and 5 per cent is a fairly typical range of payments but it can be 20 per cent or more. It is unlikely that profit distributions of less than 5 per cent will make much impact on commitment, never mind motivation. Employees tend to take the smallish sums they receive for granted.

   Profits can be distributed in the form of cash or shares, usually share options. The arrangements for profit sharing are concerned with eligibility, the basis for calculating profit shares and the method of distribution. They vary considerably between companies.

Eligibility

In most schemes all employees except directors are eligible. A period of time, often one year's service, is usually required before profit shares can be received.

Basis of calculation

There are three approaches to calculating profit shares:

1. *A predetermined formula* – a fixed percentage of profits is distributed. This clarifies the relationship of pay-out to profits and demonstrates the good faith of management but it lacks flexibility and the amount available may fluctuate widely.
2. *No predetermined formula* – the board determines profit shares entirely at its own discretion in accordance with its assessment of what the company can afford. This gives it complete control over the amount distributed but, because of the secrecy involved, is at odds with the principle of getting employees more involved with the organization. This is the most typical approach.
3. *A threshold formula* – a profit threshold is set below which no profits will be distributed and a maximum limit is defined. Between these, the board exercises discretion on the amount to be distributed.

Methods of distributing profit shares

There are four methods of distribution:

1. *percentage of pay with no allowance for service* – this is a fairly common method, which recognizes that profit shares should be related to the employee's basic contribution as measured by his or her level of pay, which takes into account service;
2. *percentage of pay with an allowance for service* – this approach is also frequently used on the grounds that it rewards loyalty;
3. *percentage of pay with an allowance for individual performance* – this method is fairly rare below board level because of the difficulty of measuring the relationship between individual performance and profit;
4. *as a fixed sum irrespective of earnings, service or performance* – this is an egalitarian approach but is fairly rare.

SHARE OWNERSHIP SCHEMES

There are two main forms of share ownership plans: share incentive plans (SIPS) and save-as-you-earn (SAYE) schemes. These must be Inland Revenue approved, and produce tax advantages as well as linking financial rewards in the longer term to the prosperity of the company.

Share incentive plans

Share incentive plans must be Inland Revenue approved. They provide employees with a tax-efficient way of purchasing shares in their organization to which the employer can add 'free', 'partnership' or 'matching' shares. There is a limit to the amount of free shares that can be provided. Employees can use up a sum as determined by the Inland Revenue out of pre-tax and pre-national insurance contributions pay to buy partnership shares, and employers can give matching shares in a ratio of up to two matching shares for each partnership share.

Save-as-you-earn schemes

Save-as-you-earn (SAYE) schemes must be Inland Revenue approved. They provide employees with the option to buy shares in the company in three, five or seven years' time at today's price or a discount of up to 20 per cent of that price. Purchases are made from a savings account from which the employee pays an agreed sum each month. The monthly savings must be between £5 and £250. Income tax is not chargeable when the option is granted.

GAIN SHARING

Gain sharing is a formula-based company- or factory-wide bonus plan that provides for employees to share in the financial gains made by a company as a result of its improved performance. The formula determines the share by reference to a performance indicator such as added value or another measure of productivity. In some schemes the formula also incorporates performance measures relating to quality, customer service, delivery or cost reduction.

The most popular performance indicator is value added, which is calculated by deducting expenditure on materials and other purchased services from the income derived from sales of the product. It is, in effect, the wealth created by the people in the business. A manufacturing business 'adds value' by the process of production as carried out by the combined contribution of management and employees.

Gain sharing differs from profit sharing in that the latter is based on more than improved productivity. A number of factors outside the individual employee's control contribute to profit, such as depreciation procedures, bad debt expenses, taxation and economic changes. Gain sharing aims to relate its pay-outs more specifically to productivity and performance improvements within the control of employees.

Although the financial element is obviously a key feature of gain sharing, its strength as a means of improving performance lies equally in its other important features – ownership, involvement and communication. The success of a gain-sharing plan depends on creating a feeling of ownership that first applies to the plan and then extends to the operation. When implementing gain sharing, companies enlist the support of employees in order to increase their commitment to the plan. The involvement aspect of gain sharing means that information generated on the company's results is used as a basis for giving employees the opportunity to make suggestions on ways of improving performance, and for giving them scope to make decisions concerning their implementation.

However, gain sharing has never been popular in the UK, perhaps because its use is mainly limited to the manufacturing sector and it takes time to plan and operate if it is to work well. Conventional profit-sharing and share ownership schemes are much easier to manage.

REFERENCES

1   e-reward (2004) *Survey of Contingent Pay*, e-reward.co.uk, Stockport
2   IRS (2003) Sharing the spoils: profit-share and bonus schemes, *IRS Employment Review*, 784, *Pay and Benefits Bulletin*, 19 September, pp 28–33

23

Recognition schemes

Formal recognition processes acknowledge success. They are based on the belief that taking steps to ensure that people's achievements and contribution are recognized is an effective way of motivating them. This belief is supported by motivation theory (see Chapter 8).

Recognition processes can form an important part of a total reward approach as described in Chapter 3. They complement direct financial rewards and therefore enhance the reward system.

RECOGNITION SCHEMES DEFINED

Recognition schemes enable appreciation to be shown to individuals for their achievements either informally on a day-to-day basis or through formal recognition arrangements. They can take place quietly between managers and individuals in their teams or be visible celebrations of success.

A recognition scheme as defined by Michael Rose (1) typically provides for 'non-cash awards given in recognition of a high level of accomplishment or performance, which is not dependent on achievement against a given target'. A recognition scheme can be formal and organization-wide, providing scope to recognize achievements by gifts or treats or by public applause. Importantly, recognition is also given less formally when managers simply say 'Well done', 'Thank you' or 'Congratulations' face to face or in a brief note of appreciation.

PRINCIPLES OF RECOGNITION

The principles that need to be borne in mind when developing recognition schemes are that recognition:

- should be given for valued behaviours and exceptional effort as well as for special achievements;
- is about valuing people; it should be personalized so that people appreciate that it applies to them;
- should be personal and face to face but can be supported by a handwritten thank-you note;
- needs to be applied equitably, fairly and consistently throughout the organization;
- should take place frequently;
- should be provided in a way that makes everyone feel they have the opportunity to be recognized;
- can be provided simply through being nominated for an award, but be careful about the use of panels to sift nominations – to be rejected by a panel after being nominated can be very demotivating;
- must be genuine, not used as a mechanistic motivating device;
- should not be given formally as part of a scheme if the achievement has been rewarded under another arrangement, for example a bonus scheme;
- needs to be given as soon as possible after the achievement;
- should be available to all – there should be no limits on the numbers who can be recognized;
- should not be predicated on the belief that they are just about rewarding winners – Kohn (2) argues against any such system because, 'for each person who wins, there are many others who have lost';
- should be available for teams as well as individuals to reward collective effort and avoid creating isolated winners;
- should not be limited by the amount available for awards – recognition can indeed be reinforced by awards, but simply saying 'thank you', privately and publicly (applause), can be very effective;
- should not be based on an over-elaborate scheme.

It is also necessary to bear in mind that awards above £100 are subject to income tax.

TYPES OF RECOGNITION

Day-to-day recognition

The most effective form of recognition is that provided by managers to their staff on a day-to-day basis. This is an aspect of good management practice such as getting to know people, monitoring performance (without being oppressive) and providing positive feedback. It is provided orally on the spot or in a short note (preferably hand-written) of appreciation and should take place soon after the event (not delayed until an annual performance review). It must be genuine – people can easily spot insincerity or someone simply going through the motions.

This type of recognition should be a natural part of the daily routine. The organization should aim to develop a recognition culture that is nurtured by the management style of senior managers and permeates the organization through each level of management so that it becomes 'the way we do things around here'. Managers can be encouraged to adopt this style but this should be more by example than by precept, not the subject of a scheme, process or system.

Public recognition

Recognition for particular achievements or continuing effective contributions can be provided by public 'applause' through an 'employee of the month scheme' or some other announcement using an intranet, the house journal or noticeboards.

Formal recognition

Formal recognition schemes provide individuals (and importantly, through them, their partners) with tangible means of recognition in the form of gifts, vouchers, holidays or trips in the UK or abroad, days or weekends away at hotels or health spas, or meals out. Team awards may be through outings, parties and meals. Such schemes may be centrally driven with formal award ceremonies. Managers and employees can nominate individuals for awards. If the awards are substantial, organizations can set up a recognition committee with employee representatives to agree on who should be eligible, thus ensuring that decisions are transparent.

Formal schemes can provide for different levels of recognition and rewards as illustrated in the schedule shown in Table 23.1 developed for a large local authority. This provides for a graduated series of awards that can be made by managers within a budget. At the lowest level, managers may be given quite a lot of autonomy to make immediate small recognition awards. The next-higher-level rewards would have to be approved by a senior manager, and the highest level would be reviewed by a recognition committee for final approval by top management.

Table 23.1   Levels of recognition

Level	Examples
1 Below £25	– Volunteering to help others when the workload is heavy. – Providing extra help to a customer. – Working late or at weekends without extra pay to meet an important deadline. – Taking on a temporary extra task that is not part of normal duties. – Demonstrating valued behaviours.
2 £25 to £150	– Identifying improved work practices. – Providing a sustained level of customer service. – Making or recommending cost savings when not part of the role. – Demonstrating valued behaviours that make a significant short-term impact.
3 £500 to £1,000	– Generating significant extra revenue when not part of the role. – Reducing costs significantly when not part of the role. – Successfully completing a major project that is not part of the normal role. – Demonstrating valued behaviours that make a significant long-term impact.

EXAMPLES OF NON-CASH AWARDS

Some ideas for non-cash awards include:

- basket of fruit;
- books;
- bottle of champagne (with a personalized label);
- cinema or theatre vouchers;
- dinner out for two (include a taxi and a babysitter);
- experience days (eg hot-air balloon ride or a day at a health and beauty spa);
- flowers (delivered to the workplace or home);
- food hamper;
- Fridays off for a month;
- gift certificates;
- handwritten thank-you note – special cards can be printed for managers to use for this purpose;
- jewellery;

- personal letter from the chairman or chief executive;
- plaques or certificates;
- points-based catalogue gifts;
- retail shopping vouchers;
- tickets to a concert, theatre or sports event;
- trip for two to Amsterdam, Barcelona or Paris;
- trophy (passed from one person to another);
- weekend in a hotel for two.

DESIGNING A RECOGNITION SCHEME

The principles set out earlier in this chapter should be borne in mind when designing and implementing a recognition scheme. Line managers and employees should be consulted, guidelines should be prepared and explained to managers and the details of the scheme should be publicized.

The implementation of the scheme should be monitored and steps taken to maintain the impetus – managers can lose interest. Progress reports should be made to employees so that they know that the scheme is working well.

EXAMPLE OF A RECOGNITION SCHEME AT CAMELOT

Camelot has about 950 staff. The company believes that it is important to reward them as near to the event of exceptional performance as possible, so it has put in place a recognition scheme to provide instant rewards. Managers and the staff consultative forum were involved in designing the scheme. Employees can receive pay rises twice a year, once in January (when pay ranges are uplifted in line with the market) and once in April (when they may receive progression pay), but this is not considered frequent enough. And although there are quarterly review meetings and individual ratings, only the annual meeting results in a pay increase. The recognition scheme was also designed to address a staff concern that 'good performance is not being recognized'.

The recognition scheme, called 'Above and Beyond', was launched in September 2005. It rewards 'one off, exceptional, performance that is not part of the normal job'. Managers make their nominations online and they are approved almost immediately. The employee is then informed and can spend the reward, in the form of points, straightaway. The website is supplied by Grass Roots, an organization that provides awards and discounted shopping as an employee benefit. Awards average £50, but range from £10 to £200. The company's recognition budget is £25 per quarter per employee, so there is an expectation that most staff will get at least one award each year.

Staff can 'spend' their awards on goods or retail vouchers or add them to their own money to buy big items such as holidays. The website is also a valued voluntary benefit (ie an arrangement organized by the employer that enables employees to buy discounted goods or services). Camelot uses it to award points in other situations too, such as a prize in the staff magazine, or for long-service awards, given after 5 and 10 years.

Rather than train all the managers, the company used 'champions' to roll out the scheme. These could be employees at any level, who were trained and briefed to explain the scheme to everyone else.

The award scheme is 'well used', with 480 nominations received in the first few months. Its popularity with employees has been confirmed by good ratings in both the staff survey and the *Sunday Times* '100 Best Companies to Work For' questionnaire.

REFERENCES

1   Rose, M (2001) *Recognising Performance: Non-cash rewards*, Chartered Institute of Personnel and Development, London
2   Kohn, A (1993) Why incentive plans cannot work, *Harvard Business Review*, September/October, pp 54–63

24

Performance management and reward

Performance management plays an important part in reward management. This chapter starts with a definition of performance management and its purpose. A summary of the processes involved follows. The chapter ends with a description of how performance management functions as part of total reward with particular reference to motivation and the generation of information to inform contingent pay decisions.

PERFORMANCE MANAGEMENT DEFINED

Performance management is a strategic and integrated process that delivers sustained success to organizations by improving the performance of the people who work in them and by developing the capabilities of individual contributors and teams.

It is strategic in the sense that it is concerned with the broader issues facing the business if it is to function effectively in its environment, and with the general direction in which it intends to go to achieve longer-term goals. It is integrated in two senses: 1) *vertical integration* – linking or aligning business, team and individual objectives and core competences; and 2) *horizontal integration* – linking different aspects of human resource management, especially organizational development, human resource development and reward, to achieve a coherent approach to the management, development and motivation of people.

PURPOSE OF PERFORMANCE MANAGEMENT

The fundamental purpose of performance management is to get better results from the organization, teams and individuals by understanding and managing performance within an agreed framework of planned goals, standards and competence requirements. It is a process for establishing shared understanding about what *is* to be achieved, and an approach to managing and developing people in a way that increases the probability that it *will* be achieved in the short and longer term. It is owned and driven by line management.

Performance management can also make a major contribution to the motivation of people by providing the foundation upon which many non-financial motivation approaches can be built.

Essentially, performance management is concerned with the encouragement of productive discretionary behaviour. As defined by John Purcell and his team at Bath University (1), 'Discretionary behaviour refers to the choices that people make about how they carry out their work and the amount of effort, care, innovation and productive behaviour they display. It is the difference between people just doing a job and people doing a great job.' On the basis of their research into the relationship between HR practice and business performance Purcell and his colleagues noted that 'the experience of success seen in performance outcomes helps to reinforce positive attitudes'. Performance management can help to define what success is and how it can be attained.

PRINCIPLES OF PERFORMANCE MANAGEMENT

The extensive research conducted by the CIPD in 1997 and 2003/04 (Armstrong and Baron, 2 and 3) identified 10 principles of performance management as stated by practitioners:

1. 'A management tool which helps managers to manage.'
2. 'Driven by corporate purpose and values.'
3. 'To obtain solutions that work.'
4. 'Only interested in things you can do something about and get a visible improvement.'
5. 'Focus on changing behaviour rather than paperwork.'
6. 'It's about how we manage people – it's not a system.'
7. 'Performance management is what managers do: a natural process of management.'

8. 'Based on accepted principle but operates flexibly.'
9. 'Focus on development not pay.'
10. 'Success depends on what the organization is and needs to be in its performance culture.'

Egan (4) proposes the following guiding principles for performance management:

> Most employees want direction, freedom to get their work done, and encouragement not control. The performance management system should be a control system only by exception. The solution is to make it a collaborative development system in two ways. First, the entire performance management process – coaching, counselling, feedback, tracking, recognition, and so forth – should encourage development. Ideally, team members grow and develop through these interactions. Second, when managers and team members ask what they need to be able to do to do bigger and better things, they move to strategic development.

THE PERFORMANCE MANAGEMENT CYCLE

Performance management is a natural process of management. It is not an HRM technique or tool. As a natural process of management the performance management cycle as shown in Figure 24.1 corresponds with William Deming's (5) Plan–Do–Check–Act model.

The performance management processes taking place in this cycle are:

● *plan* – agreeing objectives and competence requirements, identifying the required behaviours, producing plans expressed in performance agreements for meeting

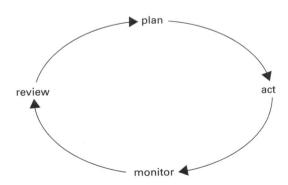

Figure 24.1   The performance management cycle

objectives and improving performance, and preparing personal development plans to enhance knowledge, skills and competence and reinforce the desired behaviours;

● *act* – carrying out the work required to achieve objectives by reference to the plans and in response to new demands;

● *monitor* – checking on progress in achieving objectives and responding to new demands, and treating performance management as a continuous process – 'managing performance all the year round' – rather than an annual appraisal event;

● *review* – a 'stocktaking' discussion of progress and achievements held in a review meeting and identifying where action is required to develop performance as a basis for completing the cycle by moving into the planning stage.

The basis upon which performance management works is further illustrated in Figure 24.2.

KEY FEATURES OF PERFORMANCE MANAGEMENT

The key features of performance management are that:

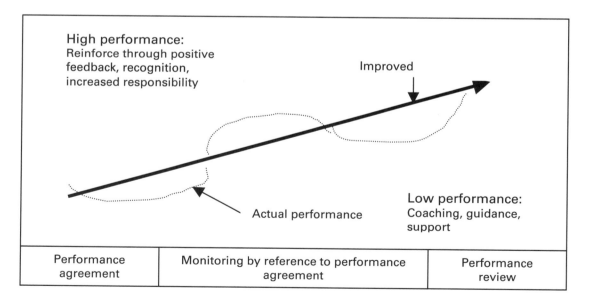

Figure 24.2 Stages of performance management

- at every stage the aim is to obtain agreement between managers and individuals on how well the latter are doing and what can be done *jointly* to develop strengths and deal with any weaknesses;
- discussions between managers and individuals should take the form of a dialogue, managers should not attempt to dominate the process and it should not be perceived as an alternative method of control;
- performance management is largely about managing expectations – both managers and individuals understand and agree what they expect of one another, thus developing a more positive psychological contract;
- positive feedback is used to motivate people by recognizing their achievements and potential;
- the process is forward looking – it does not dwell on the past and the dialogue is about what can be done in the future to give individuals the opportunity to develop and grow (this is an important means of motivation);
- performance management is a continuous process, not an annual event – managers and individuals are there to manage performance throughout the year.

PERFORMANCE MANAGEMENT AS A MOTIVATING PROCESS

Performance management, if carried out properly, can motivate people by functioning as a key component of the total reward process. It provides rewards in the form of recognition through feedback, opportunities to achieve, the scope to develop skills, and guidance on career paths. It can encourage job engagement and promote commitment. All these are non-financial rewards that can make a longer-lasting and more powerful impact than financial rewards such as performance-related pay.

Performance management is, of course, also associated with pay by generating the information required to decide on pay increases or bonuses related to performance, competence or contribution. In some organizations this is its main purpose, but performance management is, or should be, much more about developing people and rewarding them in the broadest sense. Approaches to using performance management to motivate by non-financial means are discussed below. The rest of this chapter then deals with performance management and pay.

PERFORMANCE MANAGEMENT AND NON-FINANCIAL MOTIVATION

Non-financial motivation is provided by performance management through recognition, the provision of opportunities to succeed, skills development and career planning, and by enhancing job engagement and commitment.

Performance management and recognition

Performance management involves recognizing people's achievements and strengths. They can be thanked, formally and informally, for what they have done.

Performance management and the provision of opportunities to achieve

Performance management processes are founded on joint agreements between managers and their people on what the roles of the latter are and how their role can be developed (enriched). It is therefore an essential part of job or role design and development activities.

Performance management and skills development

Performance management can provide a basis for motivating people by enabling them to develop their skills. It provides an agreed framework for coaching and support to enhance and focus learning.

Performance management and career planning

Performance management reviews provide opportunities to discuss the direction in which the careers of individuals are going and what they can do – with the help of the organization – to ensure that they follow the best career path for themselves and the organization.

Performance management and job engagement

People are engaged with their jobs when they have an interest in what they do and a sense of excitement in their work. This can be created by performance management when it concentrates on intrinsic motivating factors such as taking responsibility for job outcomes, job satisfaction and achievement and fulfilment of personal goals and objectives.

Performance management and commitment

One of the prime aims of performance management is to promote commitment to the organization and its goals by integrating individual and organizational objectives.

PERFORMANCE MANAGEMENT AND PAY

Performance management is not inevitably associated with pay, although this is often assumed to be the case. Only 42 per cent of respondents to the CIPD 2003/04 survey (3) with performance management had contingent pay. The proportion in public sector organizations was even less – 29 per cent.

However, those with contingent pay must have a means of deciding on increases, which has to be based on some form of assessment. The most typical approach is performance appraisal, which generates ratings to inform contingent pay decisions, often through a formula (a pay matrix as described in Chapter 19). This may conflict with the developmental purposes of performance management – the performance review meeting is in danger of focusing on the ratings that emerge from it and how much money will be forthcoming. Issues concerning development and the non-financial reward approaches discussed earlier will be subordinated to this preoccupation with pay. Many organizations attempt to get over this problem by holding development and pay review meetings on separate dates, often several months apart (decoupling). Some try to do without formulaic approaches (ratings and pay matrices) altogether although it is impossible to dissociate contingent pay completely from some form of assessment.

Reconciling performance management and pay

The problem of reconciling the developmental aspects of performance management or appraisal and pay has been with us for decades. Armstrong commented as long ago as 1977 (6) that: 'It is undesirable to have a direct link between the performance review and the reward review. The former must aim primarily at improving performance and, possibly, assessing potential. If this is confused with a salary review, everyone becomes over-concerned about the impact of the assessment on the increment. It is better to separate the two.'

Many people since then have accepted this view in principle but have found it difficult to apply in practice. As Kessler and Purcell (7) argue: 'How distinct these processes [performance review and performance-related pay] can ever be or, in managerial terms, should ever be, is perhaps debatable. It is unrealistic to assume that a manager can separate these two processes easily and it could be argued that the evaluations in a broad sense should be congruent.' And Armstrong and Murlis (8) comment that: 'Some organizations separate entirely performance pay ratings from the performance management review. But there will, of course, inevitably be a read-across from the performance management review to the pay-for-performance review.'

The issue is that if you want to pay for performance or competence you have to measure performance or competence. And if you want, as you should do, the process of measurement to be fair, equitable, consistent and transparent, then you cannot make pay decisions, on whatever evidence, behind closed doors. You must convey to individuals or teams how the assessment has been made and how it has been converted into a pay increase. This is a matter of procedural justice, the rules of which were set out in Chapter 1.

Procedural justice demands that there is a system for assessing performance and competence, that the assessment should be based on 'good information and informed opinion', that the person affected should be able to contribute to the process of obtaining evidence to support the assessment, that the person should know how and why the assessment has been made, and that the person should be able to appeal against the assessment.

Rating performance

Traditional performance appraisal schemes almost always included some form of overall rating of performance. There are arguments for the use of rating as a summary of the assessment and to inform performance-related or contribution-related pay decisions. But there are also powerful arguments against. The arguments for rating are that:

- it is useful to sum up judgements about people;
- you cannot have contingent pay without ratings, although this is not actually the case – 52 per cent of the organizations responding to the CIPD 2003/04 survey (3) with contingent pay did not include ratings as part of the performance management process;
- they give people something to strive for along the lines of 'You have given me a "C" rating. What have I to do to get a "B" rating?'

The arguments against ratings are that:

- they are largely subjective and it is difficult to achieve consistency between the ratings given by different managers;

- to sum up the total performance of a person with a single rating is a gross over-simplification of what may be a complex set of factors influencing that performance – to do this after a detailed discussion of strengths and weaknesses suggests that the rating will be a superficial and arbitrary judgement;
- the whole performance review meeting may be dominated by the fact that it will end with a rating, especially if that governs contingent pay increases; this will severely limit the forward-looking and developmental focus of the meeting, which is all-important;
- it *may* be feasible to rate performance against clearly defined quantitative objectives but it becomes much more difficult to rate fairly and consistently when dealing with more qualitative aspects of performance. It is particularly invidious to attempt to rate competency levels because they tend to be generalized statements of behavioural expectations that cannot support precise ratings, even if evidence of actual behaviour is available (which for assessment purposes it must be).

The arguments against ratings are more powerful than the arguments in favour, and more and more organizations have turned against ratings. This is shown by a comparison on the basis of the CIPD surveys of the proportion of organizations that used ratings for any purpose (not just to inform performance pay decisions) in 1992, which was 78 per cent, with the proportion in 2003, which was 59 per cent.

If, in spite of the problems, it is decided that ratings are necessary the following things need to be considered:

1. the basis upon which levels of performance will be defined;
2. the number of rating levels to be used;
3. methods of achieving a reasonable degree of accuracy and consistency in ratings.

Performance level definitions

The rating scale format can be either behavioural, with examples of good, average and inadequate performance, or graphic, which simply presents a number of scale points along a continuum. The scale points or anchors in the latter may be defined alphabetically (a, b, c, etc), numerically (1, 2, 3, etc) or by means of initials (ex for excellent, etc), which purports to disguise the hierarchical nature of the scale. The scale points may be further described adjectivally (eg exceptional, acceptable, unsatisfactory).

The following is a typical example of a five-point rating scale, which progresses downwards from highly positive to negative:

A   Outstanding performance in all respects.

B   Superior performance, significantly above normal job requirements.

C   Good all-round performance, which meets the normal requirements of the job.

D   Performance not fully up to requirements. Clear weaknesses requiring improvement have been identified.

E   Unacceptable; constant guidance is required and performance of many aspects of the job is well below a reasonable standard.

An alternative and increasingly popular approach is to have a rating scale such as the following four-point one, which provides positive reinforcement or at least emphasizes development needs at every level:

Very effective   Consistently performs in a thoroughly proficient manner beyond normal expectations.

Effective   Achieves required objectives and standards of performance and meets the normal expectations of the job.

Developing   A contribution that is stronger in some aspects of the job than others, where most objectives are met but where performance improvements should still take place.

Basic   A contribution that indicates that there is considerable room for improvement in several definable areas.

Note also that, in order to dispel any unfortunate associations with other systems such as school reports, this 'positive' scale does not include alphabetic or numerical ratings.

Number of rating levels

The most common number of rating levels in those respondents to the 2003/04 CIPD survey (3) that used them was four (28 per cent of respondents) or five (47 per cent of respondents). Three levels were used by 5 per cent of respondents. Traditionally, five-level scales have been used on the grounds that raters prefer this degree of fineness in performance definition and can easily recognize the middle grade and distinguish those who fall into higher or lower categories. Four-level scales are used when it is believed that they avoid the problem inherent in five-level scales of taking the easy route of rating in the middle of the scale. Three-level scales are advocated by some organizations because they believe that people are not capable of making any finer distinctions between performance levels. Managers know the really good and poor performers when they see them and have no difficulty in placing the majority where they belong, ie in the middle category.

The number of levels to use is a matter of choice and judgement but there is no evidence that any single approach is superior to the others. It is, however, preferable for level definitions to be positive rather than negative and for them to provide a degree of reliable guidance on the choice of ratings.

Achieving consistency

The problem with rating scales is that it is difficult to ensure that a consistent approach is adopted by managers to rating throughout an organization. There is plenty of room for subjective and biased judgements and this creates difficulties when rating decisions are converted into contingent pay decisions. Performance-related pay schemes have often failed because the people affected do not trust their managers to be fair. The approaches that can be adopted to achieving consistency are:

1. *Forced distribution.* This requires managers to conform to a pattern, which quite often corresponds broadly with the normal curve of distribution. A typical distribution would be:

Rating	%
A	5
B	15
C	60
D	15
E	5

    But the distribution of ability between different departments may vary, and managers rightly dislike being forced to conform to some arbitrary pattern. Only 8 per cent of the respondents to the CIPD survey used forced distribution.
2. *Ranking systems.* An alternative approach is to rank staff in order of merit and then to divide the rank order into segments that define ratings. A forced distribution in a ranking system might involve giving the top 10 per cent an A rating, the next 15 per cent a B rating, the next 60 per cent a C rating and the remaining 15 per cent a D rating. Such distribution systems do ensure a consistent distribution of ratings but still depend on the relative objectivity and accuracy of the rankings.
3. *Training.* Training can take place in the form of 'consistency' workshops for managers who discuss how ratings can be objectively justified and test rating decisions on case study performance review data. This can build a level of common understanding about rating levels.
4. *Calibration (peer reviews).* Groups of managers meet to review the pattern of each other's ratings and challenge unusual decisions or distributions. This process of calibration or moderation is time-consuming but is possibly the best way to

achieve a reasonable degree of consistency, especially when the calibration group members share some knowledge of the performances of each other's staff. Manager workshops to review ratings were held by 16 per cent of the respondents to the CIPD 2003/04 survey.

5. *Monitoring.* The distribution of ratings is monitored by HR, which challenges any unusual patterns and identifies and questions what appear to be unwarrantable differences between departments' ratings. This is the approach favoured by many organizations although there is much to be said for supporting it with training and peer reviews.

Performance matrix

An alternative visual approach to rating is used by Halifax BOS for management appraisals to illustrate managers' performance against the performance of their peers. It is not an 'appraisal rating' – the purpose of the matrix is to help individuals focus on what they do well and also any areas for improvement.

Two dimensions – business performance and behaviour (management style) – are reviewed on the matrix, as illustrated in Figure 24.3, to ensure a rounder discussion of overall contribution against the full role demands rather than a short-term focus on current results.

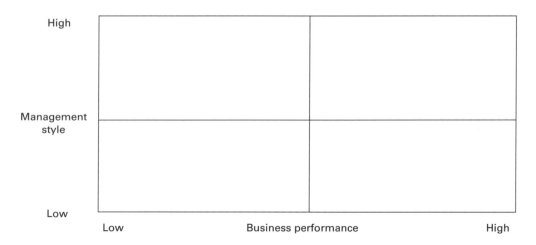

Figure 24.3 Performance matrix at Halifax BOS

This is achieved by visual means – the individual is placed at the relevant position in the matrix by reference to the two dimensions. For example, a strong people manager who is low on the deliverables would be placed somewhere in the top left-hand quadrant but the aim would be movement to a position in the top right-hand quadrant.

REFERENCES

1   Purcell, J *et al* (2003) *People and Performance: How people management impacts on organizational performance*, Chartered Institute of Personnel and Development, London

2   Armstrong, M and Baron, A (1998) *Performance Management: The new realities*, Chartered Institute of Personnel and Development, London

3   Armstrong, M and Baron, A (2004) *Performance Management: Action and impact*, Chartered Institute of Personnel and Development, London

4   Egan, G (1995) A clear path to peak performance, *People Management*, 18 May, pp 34–37

5   Deming, WE (1986) *Out of the Crisis*, Massachusetts Institute of Technology Center for Advanced Engineering Studies, Cambridge, MA

6   Armstrong, M (1977) *A Handbook of Personnel Management Practice*, 1st edn, Kogan Page, London

7   Kessler, I and Purcell, J (1992) Performance-related pay: objectives and application, *Human Resource Management Journal*, **2** (3), Spring, pp 16–32

8   Armstrong, M and Murlis, H (1998) *Reward Management*, 4th edn, Kogan Page, London

Part 6

Reward management for special groups

25

Rewarding directors and senior executives

In this chapter the considerations affecting the rewards of directors (boardroom pay) and senior executives are covered under the following headings:

- the background;
- corporate governance reviews;
- the role of remuneration committees;
- the main elements of the remuneration packages of directors and senior executives: incentives, benefits and service contracts.

THE BACKGROUND

Probably no aspect of remuneration has attracted as much attention in recent years as that of the pay of directors and senior executives. Questions are asked frequently on the level of pay and the basis upon which pay decisions are made.

This is largely a matter of corporate governance. A UK company is owned by its shareholders, but the power and responsibility for running the company are devolved to its board of directors. In the UK (as in the United States) the board of directors is a single or 'unitary' structure, responsible for corporate governance as well as business decision making, including most decisions about pay.

GOVERNANCE REVIEWS AND REMUNERATION

The concern about corporate governance and the belief that directors' pay might be out of control leading to decisions contrary to shareholders' interests led to a series of reviews. The sequence started with the Cadbury Report (1993), was furthered by Greenbury (1985) and tied together by Hampel (1998). In addition the Stock Exchange produced its Listing Requirements Relating to Remuneration in 1997. The main outcomes of these reviews were statements of principle concerning corporate governance, proposals on the role of remuneration committees and requirements for boards to disclose further details of remuneration to shareholders, who were given the right to challenge pay decisions, which in a number of recent cases they have.

Principles of corporate governance relating to remuneration

The key principles of corporate governance as it affects the remuneration of directors that emerged from the various reviews and the Stock Exchange recommendations are as follows:

- Remuneration committees should consist exclusively of non-executive directors and should determine remuneration policy and the reward packages of individual executive directors, which should appear as a section in the annual report. This report should include statements on remuneration policy and the methods used to form that policy and disclose details of the remuneration of individual directors.
- Remuneration committees must provide a remuneration package sufficient to attract, retain and motivate directors but should avoid paying more than is necessary. They should be sensitive to wider issues, eg pay and employment conditions elsewhere in the company.
- Performance-related elements should be designed to align the interests of directors and shareholders.
- Any new longer-term incentive arrangement should, preferably, replace existing executive share option plans or at least form part of an integrated approach, which should be approved by shareholders.
- The pension consequences and associated costs to the company of increases in base salary should be considered.
- Notice or service contract periods should be set at, or reduced to, a year or less. However, in some cases periods of up to two years may be acceptable.
- Remuneration committees should take a robust line on the payment of compensation where performance has been unsatisfactory.

REMUNERATION COMMITTEES

The reports and codes on directors' pay have all emphasized the importance of having a committee with the responsibility for making decisions on the remuneration of chief executives and directors.

Purpose

The purpose of remuneration committees is to provide an independent basis for setting the salary levels and the rules covering incentives, share options, benefit entitlements and contract provisions for executive directors. Such committees are accountable to shareholders for the decisions they take, and the non-executive directors who sit on them should have no personal financial interests at stake. They should be constituted as subcommittees of company boards, and boards should elect both the chairman and the members.

Role

The role of the remuneration committee is to:

- set broad policy for executive remuneration as a whole as well as the remuneration packages of executive directors and, sometimes, other senior executives;
- focus on encouraging corporate performance contribution and ensure that individuals are fairly but responsibly rewarded for their individual contribution;
- comply with the appropriate codes (the Stock Exchange and Hampel);
- report and account to shareholders directly for their decisions on behalf of the board;
- ensure that the relationship between boardroom remuneration and policy for employees below this level remains consistent and sensible;
- ensure that proper and professional advice is obtained to assist in their deliberations.

Remuneration committees should be supported by a senior executive of the company who has suitable expertise in remuneration issues and should seek external help from consultants as required. The committee should obtain information on remuneration levels and practices in comparable companies from an internal or external adviser.

DIRECTORS' AND SENIOR EXECUTIVES' REMUNERATION

The main elements of directors' and senior executives' remuneration are basic pay, short and long-term bonus or incentive schemes, share option and share ownership schemes, benefits and service contracts.

Basic pay

Decisions on the base salary of directors and senior executives are usually founded on largely subjective views about the market worth of the individuals concerned. Remuneration on joining the company is commonly settled by negotiation, often subject to the approval of a remuneration committee. Reviews of base salaries are then undertaken by reference to market movements and success as measured by company performance. Decisions on base salary are important not only in themselves but also because the level may influence decisions on the pay of both senior and middle managers. Bonuses are expressed as a percentage of base salary, share options may be allocated as a declared multiple of basic pay and, commonly, pension will be a proportion of final salary.

Bonus schemes

Virtually all major employers in the UK (90 per cent according to recent surveys by organizations such as Monks and Hay) provide annual incentive (bonus) schemes for senior executives. Bonus schemes provide directors and executives with cash sums based on the measures of company and, frequently, individual performance.

Typically, bonus payments are linked to achievement of profit and/or other financial targets and they are sometimes 'capped', ie a restriction is placed on the maximum amount payable. There may also be elements related to achieving specific goals and to individual performance. Bonuses tend to be high – 70 per cent of base salary or more. Bonuses are ostensibly intended to motivate directors to achieve performance improvements for the business. There is no evidence that this takes place. A more common although not always disclosed reason for bonuses is to ensure that what is believed to be a competitive remuneration package is available: 'Everyone else is doing it so we must too.'

Long-term bonuses

Cash bonus schemes can be extended over periods of more than one year on the grounds that annual bonuses focus too much on short-term results. The most common approach to providing longer-term rewards is through share ownership schemes as described later.

Deferred bonus schemes

Some companies have adopted deferred bonus schemes under which part of the executive's annual bonus is deferred for, say, two years. The deferred element is converted into shares, each of which is matched with an extra, free share on condition the executive remains employed by the company at the end of the deferral period. Such a scheme is designed to reward performance and loyalty to the company.

Scheme effectiveness

In an effective bonus scheme:

- targets will be tough but achievable;
- the reward should be commensurate with the achievement;
- the targets will be quantified and agreed;
- the measures used will refer to the key factors that affect company performance, and these performance areas will be those that can be directly affected by the efforts of those eligible for bonus payments;
- the formula will be simple and clear.

On the evidence of recent bonus pay-outs to failing company directors, it does not seem that these criteria are being applied successfully.

Share option schemes

Many companies have share option schemes, which give directors and executives the right to buy a block of shares on some future date at the share price ruling when the option was granted. They are a form of long-term incentive on the assumption that executives will be motivated to perform more effectively if they can anticipate a substantial capital gain when they sell their shares at a price above that prevailing when they took up the option.

Conditions may be laid down to the effect that the company's earnings per share (EPS) growth should exceed inflation by a set amount over a number of years (often three) and that the executive remains employed by the company at the exercise date.

The arguments advanced in favour of executive share options are that, first, it is right for executives to share in the success of their company, which, it is assumed, they have contributed to, and, second, they encourage executives to align their interests more closely in the longer term with those of the shareholders as a whole (the latter reason is based on agency theory although it is quite possible that those who advance it are unaware that such a thing as agency theory exists). The first point is valid as long as the reward for exercising share options is commensurate with the contribution of the executive to the improved performance of the business. The second point is dubious. The vast majority of shares acquired in this way are sold almost immediately and the gain is pocketed as extra income.

Share options have been severely criticized recently because of the enormous gains made by some executives. There is a strong feeling among some of the major investment institutions that share options do not achieve community of interest between executives and shareholders and are in effect no more than a form of cash bonus in which the pay-out has little or nothing to do with the executive's performance. In spite of this feeling, however, share option schemes may continue because they are well understood and have become an accepted feature of executive remuneration although interest in share ownership as an alternative is increasing.

Performance share schemes

Some companies have performance share schemes under which executives are pro-visionally awarded shares. The release of the shares is subject to the company's per-formance, typically determined on a sliding scale by reference to the company's total shareholder return (a combination of share price growth and dividend yield) ranking against its chosen peer companies over a three-year period. Release is also conditional on the executive remaining employed by the company at the vesting date. Such a scheme rewards loyalty to the company and the value delivered to shareholders in the form of share price performance and dividends but does not link directly to business performance.

Executive restricted share schemes

Under such schemes free shares are provisionally awarded to participants. These shares do not belong to the executive until they are released or vested; hence they are 'restricted'. The number of shares actually released to the executive at the end of a defined period (usually three or, less commonly, five years) will depend on performance over that period against specific targets. Thereafter there may be a further retention period when the shares must be held although no further performance conditions apply.

Benefits

Employee benefits for executives may amount to over 20 per cent of the total reward package. The most important element is the pension scheme, and directors may be provided with a much higher accrual rate in a final salary scheme. This means that, typically, the maximum two-thirds pension can be achieved after 20 years' service rather than the 40 years it takes in a typical one-sixtieth scheme.

Service contracts

Long-term service contracts for directors have been fairly typical, but they are disliked in the City because of the high severance payments to departing chief executives and directors that are made if the contract is two or three years, even when it is suspected or actually the case that they were voted off the board because of inadequate performance. Rolling contracts for directors are now more likely to be restricted to one year.

26

International reward

International reward management is the process of rewarding people in international or multinational organizations. It can involve the worldwide management of rewards not just the management of expatriates. This chapter starts with a review of the international scene, including definitions of what is meant by international and multinational firms and globalization. It continues with a review of international reward strategy before dealing in more detail with the management of rewards for expatriates.

THE INTERNATIONAL SCENE

The international scene is composed of international and multinational firms working in the context of globalization.

International firms are those in which operations take place in subsidiaries overseas that rely on the business expertise or manufacturing capacity of the parent company. They offer products or services that are rationalized and standardized to enable production or provision to be carried out locally in a cost-efficient way. Perkins and Hendry (1) state that international firms seem to be polarizing around two organizational approaches: 1) regionalization, where local customer service is important; and 2) global business streams, which involve setting up centrally controlled business segments that deal with a related range of products worldwide.

Multinational firms are those in which a number of businesses in different countries are managed as a whole from the centre. The degree of autonomy they have will vary and the subsidiaries are not subject to rigid control except over the quality and presentation of the product or service. They rely on the technical know-how of the parent company but usually carry out their own manufacturing, service delivery or distribution activities.

The international scene is linked to the notion of globalization. This is defined by the International Monetary Fund (2) as 'the growing economic interdependence of countries worldwide through increasing volume and variety of cross-border transactions in goods and services, freer international capital flows, and more rapid and widespread diffusion of technology'. Globalization is associated with easily transferable technology and reductions in international trade barriers. As Ulrich (3) has pointed out, it requires organizations to move people, ideas, products and information around the world to meet local needs. New and important ingredients must be added to the mix when making business strategy: volatile political situations, contentious global trade issues, fluctuating exchange rates and unfamiliar cultures.

Firms are being forced to react to these issues in their international resourcing and reward approaches. A survey by Cendant Mobility (4) showed that a majority of international organizations were planning to move more staff between locations to meet their increasingly global business's needs and to transfer relevant knowledge and skills. Yet a growing number also reported increasing difficulty in actually achieving this, with factors such as the growth of dual-career couples and political instability contributing to an apparently greater reluctance to move overseas. All these impact on reward strategy.

Traditionally, discussions of international reward strategies and practices have tended to focus on an elite of expatriate workers, sourced from headquarter locations and rewarded in isolation from local country staff. Today a diverse and complex pattern is emerging, requiring a more strategic approach than simply copying the near-universal practice of other multinationals.

As Stephen Perkins explains (5), achieving an appropriate 'global/local' balance in international staffing and rewards has therefore become a much more strategic and challenging issue for HR and reward managers to address. Major organizations such as BP and the World Bank have overhauled their policies in recent years to better achieve their key strategic reward goals of mobility and affordability in this more demanding global context.

INTERNATIONAL REWARD STRATEGY

International reward strategy is concerned with the development of an integrated approach to building reward policies and practices across international boundaries. It should be integrated in the sense that it takes into account the business goals and drivers of the parent company while at the same time fitting the strategy to the different contexts and cultures across the globe. The issue of the extent to which the reward strategy should be centralized or decentralized (convergence or divergence) needs to be addressed. The strategy should be based on certain guiding principles, which may or may not have been articulated. It should cover all aspects of reward management.

Integration

As White (6) points out, 'Best practice tells us that global rewards must not be considered piecemeal.' He also emphasizes that: 'The development of any reward programme calls for an integrated approach whereby each individual element of reward supports the others to reinforce organizational objectives. A global rewards philosophy and total rewards approach can facilitate alignment of an organization's rewards with business strategy, focus employees on the business goals, and reinforce consistent pay practices.' But he also comments that 'different local market practices, regulations and culture are indicators that a one size fits all system will not be truly effective'.

Convergence or divergence – general considerations

An issue facing all international firms is the extent to which their HR policies, including reward, should either 'converge' worldwide to be basically the same in each location or 'diverge' to be differentiated in response to local requirements. There is a natural tendency for managerial traditions in the parent company to shape the nature of key decisions but there are strong arguments for giving as much local autonomy as possible in order to ensure that local requirements are sufficiently taken into account. These arguments are often expressed in the phrase 'Think globally but act locally.'

As noted by Adler and Ghader (7) organizations have to follow very different HR policies and practices according to the relevant stage of international corporate evolution: domestic, international, multinational and global. Harris and Brewster (8) refer to this as 'the global/local dilemma', the issue being the extent to which operating units across the world are to be differentiated and at the same time integrated, controlled and coordinated. They suggest that the alternative strategies are the global approach, in which the company's culture predominates and HRM is centralized and relatively standardized (an 'ethnocentric' policy), and the decentralized approach, in which HRM responsibility is devolved to subsidiaries. They state that the factors affecting choice are:

- the extent to which there are well-defined local norms;
- the degree to which an operating unit is embedded in the local environment;
- the strength of the flow of resources – finance, information and people – between the parent and the subsidiary;
- the orientation of the parent to control;
- the nature of the industry – the extent to which it is primarily a domestic industry at local level;
- the specific organizational competences including HRM that are critical for achieving competitive advantage in a global environment.

Chris Brewster (9) believes that convergence may be increasing as a result of the power of the markets, the importance of cost, quality and productivity pressures, the emergence of transaction cost economies and the development of like-minded international cadres. The widespread practice of benchmarking 'best practice' may have contributed to convergence.

However, Brewster considers that European firms at least are so locked into their respective national institutional settings that no common model is likely to emerge in the foreseeable future. Since HR systems reflect national institutional contexts and cultures they do not respond readily to the imperatives of technology or the market. Managers in each country operate within a national institutional context and share a set of cultural assumptions. Neither institutions nor cultures change quickly and rarely in ways that are the same as in other countries. As Hofstede (10) emphasizes, it follows that managers in one country behave in a way that is noticeably different from managers in other countries.

Laurent (11) proposes that a truly international approach to human resource management would require the following steps:

1. an explicit recognition by the parent organization that its own peculiar ways of managing human resources reflect some of the assumptions and values of its home culture;
2. an explicit recognition by the parent organization that its peculiar ways are neither universally better nor worse than others but are different and likely to exhibit strengths and weaknesses, particularly abroad;
3. an explicit recognition by the parent organization that its foreign subsidiaries may have other preferred ways of managing people that are neither intrinsically better nor worse but could possibly be more effective locally;

4. a willingness from headquarters not only to acknowledge cultural differences, but also to take active steps in order to make them discussable and therefore usable;
5. the building of a genuine belief by all parties that more creative and effective ways of managing people could be developed as a result of cross-cultural learning.

These principles apply equally well to reward management and are useful criteria to apply when deciding on the degree of centralization (convergence) or decentralization (divergence) that should be adopted.

Convergence or divergence in reward policy and practice

The reward strategy should clarify the extent to which reward policy and practice should converge or diverge internationally. There are four levels as set out in Table 26.1.

Guiding principles for international reward

Guiding principles for international reward can be set out under the following policy headings:

*   the importance attached to a total rewards approach;
*   the use of job evaluation to provide for internal equity;
*   the relationship between levels of pay in the local company and local market rates;
*   the degree of flexibility present in grade and pay structures;
*   the scope for pay progression;
*   the importance attached to paying for contribution;
*   the use of variable pay – short-term, medium-term and long-term incentives;
*   the use of forms of recognition other than pay;
*   the use of flexible benefits;
*   the basis upon which expatriates and third-country nationals should be paid.

The content of international reward strategy

International reward strategy may cover the areas included in the guiding principles, namely: total reward, job evaluation, market pricing grade and pay structures, contingent pay, benefits and remuneration of expatriates and third-country nationals.

Table 26.1 Levels of convergence and divergence of reward policies and practices

Level 1: total convergence	Central reward policies and practices have to be followed by each operating unit. These may include a standard job evaluation scheme, a uniform grade and pay structure (with scope for local market differentiation), a common approach to incentives and a common set of benefits.
Level 2: partial convergence	Central reward policies are applied in some but not all aspects of reward management. Centralization may be limited to senior management or international staff (expatriates or nationals from countries other than the parent company working in the local country – third-country nationals). Reward policies and practices for local nationals are decentralized.
Level 3: partial divergence	Corporate job evaluation schemes and grade structures are recommended but modification is permitted to fit local conditions. However, all locations are expected to comply with the international guiding principles for reward. There may still be centralized policies for senior managers, expatriates and third-country nationals, and some benefits may be standardized. But pay levels and pay progression and incentive arrangements are determined locally.
Level 4: total divergence	Local companies have complete freedom to develop and apply their own reward policies and practices although they may be made aware of the international guiding principles.

REWARDS FOR EXPATRIATES

As businesses expand globally, they tend to send an increasing number of staff abroad as expatriates. The assignment may be a short-term attachment to provide guidance and expertise. Or it may be a secondment to an overseas location that lasts two or three years. Managing expatriates presents a number of problems, for example persuading people to work in possibly unpleasant or even dangerous countries, convincing them that an overseas assignment is a good career move, dealing with the issues raised by the partners of employees who do not want their career or life at home disrupted, and coping with the fact that, on returning to their home country, expatriates often find that real earnings have fallen. A particularly difficult problem is that of remuneration (pay, benefits and allowances) and the approaches available to solving it are considered below.

Expatriate remuneration policies

Expatriate remuneration policies may be based on the following propositions:

- Expatriates should be neither better nor worse off as a result of working abroad.
- Home country living standards should be maintained as far as possible.
- Higher responsibility should be reflected in the salary paid (this may be a notional home salary).
- The remuneration package should be competitive.
- In developing the remuneration package, particular care has to be taken to give proper consideration to the conditions under which the employee will be working abroad.
- Account should be taken of the need to maintain equity as far as possible in remuneration between expatriates, some of whom will be from different countries.
- Account also has to be taken of the problems that may arise when expatriates are paid more than nationals in the country in which they are working who are in similar jobs.
- The package should be cost-effective, ie the contribution made by expatriates should justify the total cost of maintaining them abroad – assignment costs can total three or four times the equivalent package in the home country.

Expatriate pay

There are four approaches to calculating expatriate pay: home country, host country, selected country and hybrid.

Home country basis

The home-based method (sometimes called the balance sheet approach) 'builds up' the salary to be paid to the expatriate in the following steps:

1. Determine the salary that would be paid for the expatriate's job in the home country net of income tax and national insurance contributions.

2. Calculate the 'home country spendable' or 'net disposable' income. This is the portion of income used for day-to-day expenditure at home.

3. Apply a cost-of-living index to the 'host country expendable income' to give the equivalent buying power in the host country. This is used as a measure of expenditure levels in the host country and is an important yardstick that is used to ensure that the expatriate will be no worse off abroad than at home.

4. Add extra allowances for working abroad (see below).

This is the most popular approach.

Host country basis

This involves paying the market rate for the job in the host country. Allowances may be paid for the expenditure incurred by expatriates because they are living abroad, eg second-home costs, children's education.

Selected country basis

The salary structure in a selected country (often where the company's headquarters are sited) provides the base and this is built up as in the home country method.

Hybrid basis

This approach divides the expatriate's salary into two components. One local component is the same for all expatriates working in jobs at the same level irrespective of their country of origin. The other local component is based on a calculation of the spendable income in the host country required to maintain a UK standard of living.

Allowances

Companies add a number of allowances as described below to the expatriate's salary to calculate the total expatriate remuneration package. They are designed to compensate for disruption and to make the assignment attractive to the employee. Most are applied to the notional home salary but one of them, the cost-of-living allowance, is based on spendable income:

● *Cost-of-living-allowance* – the cost-of-living allowance is reached by applying an index to the home country spendable income. The index measures the relative cost, in the host country, of purchasing conventional 'shopping basket' items, such as food and clothing.

- *Incentive premium* – this offers the expatriate a financial inducement to accept the assignment. It may be intended to compensate for disruption to family life. But companies are tending to reduce this premium or do away with it altogether, particularly for intra-European assignments. They are questioning why an employee should receive 10–15 per cent of gross salary for simply moving from one culturally similar country to another when no such allowance would be payable in the case of a relocation within the UK.
- *Hardship allowance* – this compensates for discomfort and difficulty in the host country such as an unpleasant climate, health hazards, poor communications, isolation, language difficulties, risk and poor amenities.
- *Separation allowance* – this may be paid if expatriates cannot take their family abroad.
- *Clothing allowance* – a payment for special clothing and accessories that expatriates need to buy.
- *Relocation allowance* – this covers the cost of expenses arising when moving from one country to another.
- *Housing/utilities* – any additional costs of accommodation or utilities.

Benefits

The benefits provided to expatriates include cars, the costs of educating children, home leave, and rest and recuperation leave if the expatriate is working in a high-hardship territory.

REFERENCES

1 Perkins, S and Hendry, C (1999) *The IPD Guide on International Reward and Recognition*, IPD, London
2 International Monetary Fund (1997) *World Economic Outlook*, IMF, Washington, DC
3 Ulrich, D (1997) *Human Resource Champions*, Harvard Business School Press, Boston, MA
4 Cendant Mobility (2002) *Worldwide Benchmark Study: New approaches to global mobility* (contact: marketing@cendantmobility.com)
5 Perkins, SJ (2006) *Guide to International Reward and Recognition*, Chartered Institute of Personnel and Development, London
6 White, R (2005) A strategic approach to building a consistent global rewards program, *Compensation and Benefits Review*, July/August, pp 23–40

7   Adler, NJ and Ghader, F (1990) Strategic human resource management: a global perspective, in *International Human Resource Management*, ed R Pieper, De Gruyter, Berlin/New York

8   Harris, H and Brewster, C (1999) International human resource management: the European contribution, in *International HRM: Contemporary issues in Europe*, ed C Brewster and H Harris, Routledge, London

9   Brewster, C (2004) European perspectives of human resource management, *Human Resource Management Review*, **14** (4), pp 365–82

10 Hofstede, G (1980) *Cultural Consequences: International differences in work-related values*, Sage, Beverly Hills, CA

11 Laurent, A (1986) The cross-cultural puzzle in international human resource management, *Human Resource Management*, 21, pp 91–102

27

Rewarding sales and customer service staff

Sales and customer service staff make a strong and immediate impact on business results. This has led to an emphasis on financial incentives, especially for sales representatives and sales staff in retailers who are often treated quite differently from other people. The reward system for sales and service staff also has to take account of the fact that they are the people who are in direct contact with customers and this also applies to people in call centres. This chapter deals with the particular features of rewards for sales representatives and customer service staff in turn.

REWARDING SALES REPRESENTATIVES

Sales representatives are more likely to be eligible for commission payments or bonuses than other staff on the grounds that their sales performance will depend on or at least be improved by financial incentives. Many companies believe that the special nature of selling and the type of person they need to attract to their sales force require some form of additional bonus or commission to be paid. The nature of the work of sales representatives means that it is usually easy to specify targets and measure performance against them, and sales incentive schemes are therefore more likely to meet the line-of-sight requirement (ie that there should be a clear link between effort and performance) than schemes for other staff such as managers and administrators. Sales staff, including those in retail establishments, are often paid spot rates with a commission on sales.

Other means of rewarding sales representatives

Financial rewards are usually important for members of the sales force but there are other valuable means of recognizing achievement. These include prizes and non-financial forms of recognition ('sales representative of the month' etc) and other items in the total reward package such as opportunities for growth. As pointed out by Gundy (1):

> In assessing how to motivate the sales force, leading companies view commissions and bonuses as just one tool in the motivational toolbox... Performance management, career pathing and recognition programmes can be powerful ways of producing and managing sales results. Companies that consider the impact of all these programmes in the design process are generally more successful in driving both short- and long-term results.

Overall approach

The following six-point plan for rewarding sales people has been recommended by Zingheim and Schuster (2):

1. Ensure the opportunity for competitive total cash compensation, especially for the top 20 per cent of sales performers.
2. Ensure a proper base–incentive mix based on selling conditions. For example, coordinating a sales team with an emphasis on customer relations may suggest more base pay and less incentive pay, while an emphasis on hard selling may suggest less base pay and more incentive.
3. Update incentive measures and goals consistent with the business plan. For example, the focus in the plan and therefore the criteria for sales commission could be more about getting new customers and retaining existing ones than just sales volume goals.
4. Set realistic goals, given business conditions.
5. Update target customers – broaden the customer base.
6. Reinforce critical selling behaviours and capabilities by rewarding them.

Financial methods of rewarding sales staff

The approaches to rewarding sales staff described below are:
- salary only;
- basic salary plus commission;
- basic salary plus bonus;
- commission only.

Table 27.1 summarizes the different schemes, their advantages and disadvantages and when they may be appropriate.

Salary only

Companies may adopt a salary-only (no commission or bonus) approach when sales staff have little influence over sales volume, when representing the company and generally promoting its products or services are more important than direct selling, and when the company wants to encourage sales staff to build up good and long-term relationships with their customers, the emphasis being on customer service rather than on high-pressure selling.

Basic salary only may also be paid to sales staff who work in highly seasonal industries where sales fluctuate considerably and businesses where regular orders for food and other consumer goods give little opportunity for creative selling.

However, companies that do not pay commission or bonus may have a pay-for-contribution scheme that provides for consolidated increases based on an assessment of performance and competence in such areas as teamwork, customer relations, interpersonal skills and communications. Where sales staff have to work together to achieve results or where it is difficult to apportion a successful sale to individuals, a team pay approach may be adopted. Additionally salary-only sales representatives may be eligible for incentives in the form of prizes as described later.

If no commission or bonus is offered, it is necessary for companies to ensure that the salaries paid to their sales staff are competitive. They have to take account of the total earnings of sales staff in markets from which they recruit people or where their own staff move. If they cannot or do not want at least to match these earnings they may have to offer other inducements to join or stay with the company. These can include opportunities for promotion, learning new skills, more stable pay and greater security.

Table 27.1 Summary of payment and incentive arrangements for sales staff

Method	Features	Advantages	Disadvantages	When Appropriate
Salary only	Straight salary, no commission or bonus	Encourages customer service rather than high-pressure selling; deals with the problem of staff who are working in a new or unproductive sales territory; protects income when sales fluctuate for reasons beyond the individual's control.	No direct motivation through money; may attract underachieving people who are subsidized by high achievers; increases fixed costs of sales because pay costs are not flexed with sales results.	When representing the company is more important than direct selling; when staff have little influence on sales volume (they may simply be 'order takers'); when customer service is all-important.
Salary plus commission	Basic salary plus cash commission calculated as a percentage of sales volume or value	Direct financial motivation is provided related to what sales staff are there to do, ie generate sales; but they are not entirely dependent on commission – they are cushioned by their base salary.	Relating pay to the volume or value of sales is too crude an approach and may result in staff going for volume by concentrating on the easier-to-sell products not those generating high margins; may encourage high-pressure selling as in some financial services firms in the 1980s and 1990s.	When it is believed that the way to get more sales is to link extra money to results but a base salary is still needed to attract the many people who want to be assured of a reasonable basic salary that will not fluctuate but who still aspire to increase that salary by their own efforts.

Table 27.1 *Continued*

Method	Features	Advantages	Disadvantages	When Appropriate
Salary plus bonus	Basic salary plus cash bonus based on achieving and exceeding sales targets or quotas and meeting other selling objectives	Provides financial motivation but targets or objectives can be flexed to ensure that particular sales goals are achieved, eg high-margin sales, customer service.	Does not have a clear line of sight between effort and reward; may be complex to administer; sales representatives may find them hard to understand and resent the use of subjective judgements on performance other than sales.	When flexibility in providing rewards is important; when it is felt that sales staff need to be motivated to focus on aspects of their work other than simply maximizing sales volume.
Commission only	Only commission based on a percentage of sales volume or value is paid, and there is no basic salary	Provides a direct financial incentive; attracts high-performing sales staff; ensures that selling costs vary directly with sales; little direct supervision required.	Leads to high-pressure selling; may attract the wrong sort of people who are interested only in sales and not customer service; focuses attention on high volume rather than profitability.	When sales performance depends mainly on selling ability and can be measured by immediate sales results; when staff are not involved in non-selling activities; when continuing relationships with customers are relatively unimportant.
Additional non-cash rewards	Incentives, prizes, cars, recognition, opportunities to grow	Utilize powerful non-financial motivators.	May be difficult to administer; do not provide a direct incentive.	When it is believed that other methods of payment need to be enhanced by providing additional motivators.

Basic salary plus commission

Salary-plus-commission plans provide for a proportion of total earnings to be paid in commission; the rest is paid in the form of a fixed salary. The commission is calculated as a percentage of the value of sales. The proportion of commission varies widely. As a general rule it is higher when results depend on the ability and effort of individuals or when there is less emphasis on non-selling activities. As a rule of thumb, most sales managers believe that the commission element will not motivate their staff unless they have a reasonable opportunity to earn at least 20 per cent of base pay.

The commission may be a fixed percentage of all sales, possibly with a 'cap' or upper limit on earnings. Alternatively the commission rate can increase at higher levels of sales on a rising scale to encourage sales representatives to make even greater efforts.

Basic salary plus bonus

Cash bonuses may be paid on top of basic salary. They are based on the achievement of targets or quotas for sales volume, profit or sales 'contribution' (sales revenue minus variable expenses). They differ from commission payments in that the latter are based simply on a percentage of whatever sales have been attained. In a bonus scheme, targets or objectives may be set just for sales volume but they can also focus on particular aspects of the results that can be achieved by sales staff that it is felt should be stimulated. These may include the sales of high-margin or more profitable products or services in order to encourage staff to concentrate on them rather than simply aiming to achieve sales volume with low-margin products that are easier to sell. They may also cover reviving moribund accounts, promoting new products and minimizing bad debt. Other criteria may include the level of customer service, the volume of repeat business, the number of productive calls made, product knowledge, teamwork and quality of administration.

There are many ways in which bonuses can be determined. The method used will take into account the following considerations:

● the formula for relating bonuses to sales – a bonus may be triggered when a sales threshold is reached and additions related to increased sales directly or on an accelerated basis;
● the size of bonus payments available at different levels of performance;
● the maximum bonus that will be paid out;
● the bonus criteria – sales revenue is often used, but some companies use profit or contribution to encourage sales representatives to focus on selling high-margin products rather than going for volume;

- any other factors to be included in the bonus plan such as those mentioned above.

Commission only

Sales staff who are at the 'hard' end of selling (eg double glazing) may only receive a straight commission based on a percentage of the value of their sales. No basic salary is paid.

Additional non-cash rewards

While it is possible that the prime motivator for a typical sales representative is cash there are a number of other effective non-cash ways of providing motivation as described below.

Other forms of reward

Gifts and vouchers

Gifts and vouchers provide a tangible means of recognizing achievements. They may be linked to the achievement of specified targets but should not be restricted too much to the 'super sales representatives'; the solid, dependable sales person also needs motivating through the recognition that such incentives provide. Gifts are subject to income tax.

Competitions

Prizes can be awarded to individuals or teams for notable sales achievements, eg bringing in new business. However, competitions can demotivate those who do not win prizes and they should be designed to ensure that all those who are doing well feel that they have a good chance of getting a prize.

Cars as perks

Sales representatives can be motivated by the opportunity to get a bigger and better car if they are particularly successful. The car may be retained for a defined period and made available again if the high performance is maintained.

Non-financial motivators

Sales people typically have high levels of achievement motivation but they still like to be recognized and given the opportunity to make even better use of their talents in more challenging (and remunerative) work. Public applause and private thank-yous are both important.

Effectiveness and use of sales incentives

A survey of the effectiveness of incentive plans by Mercer Human Resource Consulting (3) cited by IDS (4) established that: 'Many organizations feel their plans do not encourage or reward the right performance. Of equal concern is that many staff do not understand the plan.' The survey found that:

- 17 per cent of respondents had between five and eight separate reward criteria;
- 3 per cent used nine or more performance measures;
- volume production targets such as sales revenue, gross profit or units sold were the most used;
- 72 per cent used profit targets for sales directors, along with revenue measures in 64 per cent of organizations and individual objectives in 60 per cent;
- for sales representatives the most widely used measure was sales volume (72 per cent of schemes).

REWARDING CUSTOMER SERVICE STAFF

Customer service staff work mainly in retail establishments and in call or customer contact centres. Their rewards need to reflect the nature of their duties, ie enhancing levels of customer service as well as selling.

Reward practices

The Chartered Institute of Personnel and Development in conjunction with the Institute of Customer Service commissioned Professor Michael West and a team from Aston University to investigate how customer service staff were employed and rewarded (5). The research project took 18 months and encompassed 15 organizations and 22 customer service locations. They represented a variety of industries and sectors – banks, building societies and insurance companies, utilities, telecoms firms, retailers, local and central government departments and services. The service staff employed in each location varied from 37 to over 1,000.

The researchers gathered information on reward and HR policies, interviewed managers and also surveyed employees' views and experiences. The jobs they were carrying out were both face-to-face and telephone-based in a wide range of settings, including: call centre customer service agents and technical support roles; charity workers; financial advisers and branch staff; hotel receptionists, restaurant and bar staff; and employees in leisure centres and libraries.

The 580 staff involved illustrated that front-line customer service workers do not all conform to the young/female/fleeting image. Seventy per cent were women but their average age was 34 years and average length of service six years. Eighty per cent were employed on a full-time basis and just 9 per cent on temporary contracts.

Nor did their typical working environment and conditions reflect the stereotypical 'sweatshop' image. While the HR and reward practices varied, working conditions were generally good and staff rated their supervisors' skills, as well as their colleagues and the level of team working. Staff benefits such as company pension plans and sick pay schemes were the norm, as were various training courses.

The pattern of pay practices used by these 15 organizations for front-line staff and their first-line managers is shown in Table 27.2. Base pay levels were generally competitive for the location and sector, and a number mentioned the effect of the national minimum wage.

Most employees in the researched organizations had the opportunity to progress their base pay on the basis of their performance or competence, either through a range,

Table 27.2 The pattern of pay practices in the Aston research organizations

	Managers	Customer Service Staff
Pay structure:		
Grades	6	6
Broad bands	3	3
Individual ranges	4	4
Pay spine	2	2
Pay progression and bonus:		
Individual performance-related pay	4	5
Skills/competency pay	2	2
Contribution pay	3	3
Individual bonus	5	6
Team bonus	4	6
Commission	0	1
Profit sharing	2	2

or up a pay spine, or between grades/levels of job. Such arrangements have generally supplanted 'spot rate' pay rates for service roles in call centres and retail shops. At Boots the Chemists, for example, shop staff can progress up through a number of pay points according to their level of performance and skill – from entry level, to experienced, to advanced, to expert/specialist. At House of Fraser, employees are allocated to one of four competency bands – training, bronze, silver and gold, with staff assessed for a 'promotion' every six months.

Low base pay/high commission arrangements were rare amongst the 15 organizations, but most of them operated variable performance-related pay schemes of some type, which again has become the norm for service staff today in these contexts, at least in the private sector. Tesco and John Lewis staff, for example, receive company-wide profit-sharing payments. British Gas uses a company-wide balanced scorecard bonus scheme; while Homebase, Asda and Marks and Spencer use team, store-based schemes. A number of the organizations used multiple plans. For example, the Royal Bank of Scotland has a profit-sharing scheme to reward corporate achievement and pays bonuses to reward good and exceptional individual performance.

All forms of performance-related pay and recognition schemes were utilized more frequently and more extensively by the highest-performing organizations in the research than amongst the other participants and by UK organizations as a whole. They were twice as likely as other UK organizations to use individual performance-related pay and various forms of individual and team non-financial recognition schemes, and five times as likely to use some form of team/collective bonus scheme as the remaining organizations in the study.

Reward policies in the research study organizations did not by themselves create high customer service performance. They operated through the medium of staff perceptions and in a general work and management context that encouraged positive perceptions and high levels of staff commitment – see Figure 27.1. The best organizations recognize that, when it comes to delivering outstanding service, staff perceptions and management practice, rather than fancy reward and HR strategy statements, plans and policies, are what matter and make the difference.

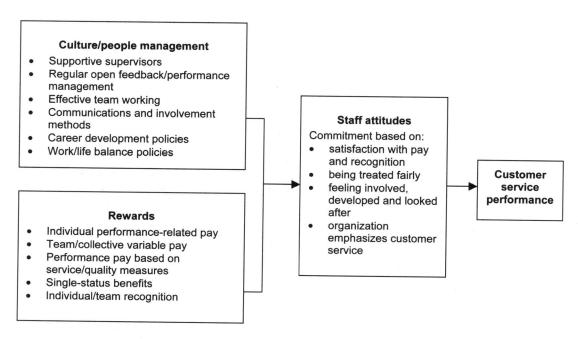

Source: Michael West et al (2005) Rewarding Customer Service? Using reward and recognition to deliver your customer service strategy, CIPD, London

Figure 27.1 A summary of the relationships between HR and reward practices, employee attitudes and customer service performance

REFERENCES

1 Gundy, P (2002) Sales compensation programmes: built to last, *Compensation and Benefits Review*, September/October, pp 21–28

2 Zingheim, PK and Schuster, JR (2004) Sales reward solutions, *Compensation and Benefits Review*, September/October, pp 21–26

3 Mercer Human Resource Consulting (2003/04) *Sales Effectiveness Report*, Mercer, London

4 IDS (2004) How effective are salesforce incentives?, *Management Pay Review*, March, pp 9–10

5 West, M *et al* (2005) *Rewarding Customer Service? Using reward and recognition to deliver your customer service strategy*, Chartered Institute of Personnel and Development, London

28

Rewarding knowledge workers

A knowledge worker was originally defined by Peter Drucker (1) as someone 'who knows more about his or her work than anyone else in the organization'. Today, knowledge workers are generally regarded as people whose work requires a marked degree of expertise. Their work is defined by the knowledge they need to do it. The term therefore embraces such diverse groups as academics, accountants, HR professionals, IT specialists, lawyers, media workers and researchers.

Knowledge workers play a steadily increasing part in organizations. According to the Government's Occupational Employment Trends and Projections, UK 1982–2012, by 2012 knowledge workers will have increased from roughly a quarter of all jobs 20 years ago to almost a half. In the year to March 2005, 90,000 new jobs were created in the UK in both the finance/business services and the education/health/public administration sector.

The importance of the contribution made by knowledge workers means that attention has to be given to how reward policies and practices can be developed to attract, retain and motivate them having taken account of their particular needs. The requirement to consider how knowledge workers should be rewarded is studied in this chapter, which starts with an analysis of what motivates them and then examines the approaches that can be adopted to their rewards.

WHAT MOTIVATES KNOWLEDGE WORKERS?

A study by Tampoe (2) identified four key motivators for knowledge workers:

1. *personal growth* – the opportunity for individuals to fully realize their potential;
2. *occupational autonomy* – a work environment in which knowledge workers can achieve the task assigned to them;
3. *task achievement* – a sense of accomplishment from producing work that is of high quality and relevance to the organization;
4. *money rewards* – an income that is a just reward for their contribution to corporate success and that symbolizes their contribution to that success.

Research carried out by the writer in higher education establishments between 2002 and 2004 (unpublished) broadly confirmed this analysis. Academics, especially those engaged mainly in research, wanted opportunities to achieve (and the support and facilities that enable them to do so) and to grow and develop their expertise. They wanted recognition, within the university and in academic circles elsewhere. Inside, this might include the approval of more senior members of the university and of their peers, and promotion to positions as research team leaders or higher academic posts. Outside, they liked to publish in refereed journals and to speak at major conferences. They wanted to be paid fairly for what they did but generally they were not strongly motivated by money although, as always, there were exceptions.

The motivation factors for scientists working in research-based organizations such as pharmaceutical firms may be similar to academic researchers, perhaps with less emphasis on publications. The motivation for other knowledge workers in businesses, the public sector or not-for-profit organizations is more likely to conform to the pattern described by Tampoe as set out above. But in the words of Reeves and Knell (3) it can be said of all knowledge workers that: 'The brightest and the best want an intellectual challenge and the chance to keep learning.' And Coyle (4) explains that: 'Skilled programmers don't seem to fret about getting enough money. The more highly valued reward, because it is so much harder to come by, is the esteem in which they are held by their peer group.'

MANAGING KNOWLEDGE WORKERS

According to Swart and Kinnie (5) the effective management of knowledge workers presents organizations with a number of dilemmas. Choices have to be made between the retention of knowledge workers and their desire to increase their employability. Tension also exists between the need to develop organizationally specific knowledge and the wish of knowledge workers to develop transferable knowledge. The firm may want to appropriate the value of that knowledge but workers may want to retain their ownership of it.

Swart and Kinnie argue that understanding of these dilemmas is improved by a greater understanding of where professional workers get their primary source of identification – is it from their profession, the organization that employs them, the team or the client? Their loyalty may be to their professional mission rather than their employer. Professional research staff or academics may be committed to achieving professional status and recognition above any forms of performance recognition that the employing organization might be able to offer.

The ways in which knowledge workers are managed and rewarded are affected by the defining characteristics of what they do. They carry out roles. They are less likely than other people to be employed in prescribed jobs. By definition, a role is flexible and it is defined in role profiles by reference to the competencies required to do it as well as the outcomes expected. It is not described as a set of tasks or duties as in a job description. The level of contribution that can be achieved by knowledge workers is a function of the skills and knowledge they can bring to bear and the opportunities they are given to deploy their expertise. Flexibility and autonomy are important aspects of their roles and the reward system applied to them must take account of these.

APPROACHES TO REWARDING KNOWLEDGE WORKERS

Approaches to rewarding knowledge workers are described below under the headings of total reward, pay flexibility, pay related to competency, and career and job family structures. Although these reflect the special needs of knowledge workers, complete differentiation of terms and conditions is being restrained by a number of factors, including most notably: the growing numbers of knowledge and professional workers throughout UK organizations; the drive to encourage innovation in a wide range of cross-functional activities rather than just in the R & D lab; and the increasing pressures to display equitable and consistent pay approaches to comply with equality legislation.

Total reward policies

Taking into account the factors that motivate knowledge workers mentioned above, there is an overwhelming case for adopting a total reward policy. As explained in

Chapter 3, this would mean focusing on non-financial rewards such as recognition, opportunity to grow and achieve and learning and development opportunities as well as financial rewards. Swart, Kinnie and Purcell (6) reported the remarks made by one of the employees in a software company in which they were conducting research: 'It's a great place to work... the people I work with are brilliant, the work is quite challenging. There are plenty of opportunities and the pay is good... people feel valued and there is scope for advancement. They encourage you to make more of your skills.' Flexible working arrangements are also appreciated. Autonomy is another non-financial reward that many knowledge workers value highly. An employee of the company referred to above said to the researchers: 'We organise our own working day. You can organise your own time with nobody looking over your shoulder.'

The following are some examples of the approach used by three firms employing large numbers of knowledge workers.

Bristol-Myers Squibb

The company states that 'reward is much wider than just paying its staff a competitive salary'. It has designed its total reward package knowing that everyone works for the company for different reasons and that everyone places a different emphasis on the importance of each of the elements of total reward – there is no one-size-fits-all. It has also set out to use total reward to 'elevate and differentiate' Bristol-Myers Squibb from other companies, both in the same industry and beyond.

The three elements of total reward are:

1. *Compensation* – salary, performance-based bonus and stock options.
2. *Benefits* – non-contributory pension, life cover, private health care, perks and cars.
3. *Work experience* – defined as: 'All the elements which contribute to providing you with an environment that enables you to optimise your contribution to the company and achieve your full potential, whilst maintaining a balance between your personal and professional life'. These include:
   - acknowledgement, appreciation and recognition;
   - balance of work and life;
   - culture of Bristol-Myers Squibb;
   - employee development;
   - the working environment.

The total reward approach at Bristol-Myers Squibb embraces what they call the 'work experience'. This, says the company to its staff, 'encompasses all the elements which contribute to providing you with an environment that enables you to optimise your contribution to the company and achieve your full potential, whilst maintaining a balance between your personal and professional lives. It recognises that you are an individual with unique needs and offers something for everyone.' Work experience comprises acknowledgement, appreciation and recognition, balance of work and life, organizational culture, employee development and the working environment.

Elan Computers

The company's approach to total reward stresses investment in people, recognition, the quality of life and fair and competitive reward. It is part of Elan's people strategy, the stated aims of which are to:

> Support the group vision, to invest in talented people, and to maintain a people-focused environment that is fun, challenging and rewarding. Starting with our comprehensive induction programme, we aim to secure long term commitment and inspire enthusiasm from day one. And we never stop listening to people. People are given the opportunity every year to take part in a survey to give feedback on every aspect of their life at Elan, and there are open question and answer sessions with board members. And to ensure that we are doing what we can to keep the best people, we study the reasons why people leave, and what retains our most talented people. This strategy allows us to continually improve our position as an employer and as a market force.

GlaxoSmithKline (GSK)

'TotalReward' at GSK consists of three elements:

- *total cash* (base salary and bonus, plus long-term incentives for managers and executives);
- *lifestyle benefits* (health care, employee assistance, family support, dental care);
- *savings choices* (pension plan, ShareSave, ShareReward).

The complete package, the concept of which is based on employees understanding the total value of all the rewards they receive, not just the individual elements, is designed to attract, retain, motivate and develop the best talent. The proposition for employees is that TotalReward gives them the opportunity to share in the company's success, makes it easier to balance home and working life, and helps them to take care of themselves and their families.

Pay flexibility

The overall approach to rewarding knowledge workers advocated by Armstrong and Brown (7) is 'flexibility within a framework'. By this they mean that a common framework of reward arrangements exists across the organization on the grounds that it would be invidious to single out knowledge workers by creating an entirely different reward system. But certain types of flexibility within that framework are still required to vary and tailor arrangements to suit the specific needs of particular groups of knowledge and professional workers and the individuals within those groups. Pay flexibility will include market rate supplements to attract and retain specific categories of staff and the use of selected 'market groups' (separate pay structures for certain types of staff). This is in accord with the view expressed by Lawler (8) that there should be a move away from job-based pay to rewarding on the basis of the market value of a person's skills and knowledge. On a wider scale, career or job families can be installed as described later.

Pay related to competency

If knowledge workers exist to apply their expertise then it seems reasonable to reward them according to the level of expertise (competency) they possess and apply. There are three ways of doing this as described below: 1) by competency-related pay; 2) through structures in which grades or bands are defined in competency terms; and 3) by the incorporation of skills and competencies into job evaluation factor plans.

Competency-related pay

In a competency-related pay scheme, people receive financial rewards in the shape of increases to their base pay by reference to the level of competence they demonstrate in carrying out their roles. It is a method of paying people for the ability to perform now and in the future. This seems to be a highly relevant approach for knowledge workers but the CIPD 2006 annual reward management survey (9) reported that only 6 per cent of technical and professional staff received competency-related pay on its own. As reported in Chapter 19, an explanation of the problem was provided by Sparrow (10), who referred to the complex nature of what is being measured, the relevance of the results to the organization, and the problem of measurement. He concluded that 'we should avoid over-egging our ability to test, measure and reward competencies'.

It has also been noted by Zingheim and Schuster (11) that pay systems built round competencies are:

- complex and over-designed;
- vague and ambiguous;
- laborious and time-consuming;
- disconnected from the labour market; and
- tentatively championed and communicated.

However, while schemes based solely on competencies present difficulties there are arguments in favour of combining competency with performance as in contribution-related pay (described in Chapter 19). The CIPD 2006 survey found that 52 per cent of technical and professional staff were rewarded by a combined performance- and competency-related scheme.

Competency-defined grades or bands

Defining grades or bands in terms of competencies results in what Risher (12) describes as a 'career ladder' structure. He reports the practice of three companies – Dow, IBM and Marriott Hotels – that have defined a set of brief competency factors or criteria that provide a simple and transparent framework based on levels in a career ladder. The criteria consist of the competencies such as knowledge, skills and abilities required at each level.

An example of a UK approach to career ladders is provided by the NHS as part of its Agenda for Change project. Its 'skills escalator' is illustrated in Figure 28.1.

Use of competencies in job evaluation

Traditional job evaluation schemes have always incorporated competencies in their factor plans although they called them knowledge, skill or know-how. Factor plans have recently been developed that deliberately include competencies. This has applied in sectors or organizations such as higher education (the HERA scheme), the senior Civil Service (the JESP system) and the NHS where there are 16 measurement factors but the knowledge, skills and experience factor accounts for almost a quarter of the total points weighting. This scheme acknowledges the explicit bias towards knowledge in an organization with huge numbers of professional workers.

Job and career families

Job and career family structures as described in Chapter 17 consist of separate families of jobs with similar characteristics. Within each family the successive levels of

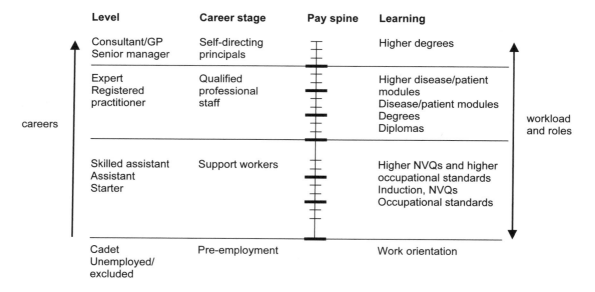

Figure 28.1 The NHS skills escalator

competency required to carry out typical activities are defined, thus indicating career paths. In a job family structure such as that at Canon UK or Norwich Union Insurance each job family has its own pay structure, which takes account of different levels of market rates between families (this is sometimes called 'market grouping'). In a career family structure as at Southampton University, the ranges of pay for each family are the same and the emphasis is on defining career progression rather than market pricing, although market supplements may be paid.

Job and career families are particularly appropriate for knowledge workers because they spell out the career ladders that apply specifically to the different categories employed in an organization.

An example of a job family approach is provided by IMS Health, a global business providing information for pharmaceutical companies, which employs a large proportion of scientists. The aim of the development programme was 'to evolve a system which could be flexible enough to cope with the ever-changing business environment we were in'. The reason for going down the job family route was that it would give IMS Health the flexibility needed, bearing in mind the different functions operating in the organization. Defining career paths was an important consideration affecting the decision to develop job families, as was the need to focus on establishing appropriate pay levels in each job family that were related to market rates. The progression policy was for a personal development plan to be prepared for individuals who were recruited to a role below the reference point, which would enable them to reach the level of competence required. A salary development plan would also be prepared to bring up the individual's rate of pay to the reference point. Progression to the reference point (in effect competence-related pay) is determined by managers within their budgets. Individuals were briefed during induction both on the career opportunities available to them and on the reward associated with their progress.

REFERENCES

1   Drucker, P (1988) The coming of the new organization, *Harvard Business Review*, January/February, pp 45–53

2   Tampoe, M (1993) Motivating knowledge workers: the challenge for the 1990s, *Long-Range Planning*, **26** (2), pp 37–44

3   Reeves, R and Knell, J (2001) All of these futures are yours, in *The Future of Reward*, ed N Page, Chartered Institute of Personnel and Development, London

4   Coyle, D (2001) Power to the people, in *The Future of Reward*, ed N Page, Chartered Institute of Personnel and Development, London

5   Swart, J and Kinnie, N (2004) *Managing the Careers of Professional Knowledge Workers*, Chartered Institute of Personnel and Development, London

6   Swart, J, Kinnie, N and Purcell, J (2003) *People and Performance in Knowledge Intensive Firms*, Chartered Institute of Personnel and Development, London

7   Armstrong, M and Brown, D (2006) *Strategic Reward*, Kogan Page, London

8   Lawler, EE (2002) Pay strategies for the next economy: lessons from the dot-com era, *WorldatWork Journal*, **11** (1), pp 6–10

9   Chartered Institute of Personnel and Development (2006) *Annual Reward Management Survey Report*, CIPD, London

10 Sparrow, P (1996) Too good to be true, *People Management*, 5 December, pp 22–27

11   Zingheim, PK and Schuster, JR (2002) Pay changes going forward, *Compensation and Benefits Review*, **34** (4), pp 48–53
12   Risher, H (2002) Planning a 'next generation' salary system, *Compensation and Benefits Review*, November/December, pp 13–22

29

Shop floor pay

Shop floor payment systems that have not been 'harmonized', ie brought into line with the reward system for staff, frequently differ from the systems described elsewhere in this book in three ways: 1) the use of a time rate basis of payment; 2) the use of spot rates; and 3) the use of incentive schemes. This chapter begins with a brief review of the factors affecting shop floor pay and continues to describe the characteristics of shop floor pay mentioned above. The chapter ends with a discussion of harmonization and single status.

FACTORS AFFECTING SHOP FLOOR PAY

The three main factors affecting shop floor pay are: 1) bargaining arrangements; 2) local labour market rate pressures; and 3) trends in the use of technology on the shop floor.

Bargaining arrangements

Shop floor pay is often influenced strongly by national and local agreements with trade unions, which will determine rates for particular jobs or skill levels. This constitutes an aspect of the effort bargain. The objective of workers and their trade union officials and representatives is to strike a bargain with management about what they consider to be a reasonable amount of pay that should be provided by their employer in return for their contribution. It is, in effect, an agreement between workers and management that lays down the amount of work to be done for an agreed wage, not just the hours to be worked. Explicitly or implicitly, all employers are in a bargaining situation with regard to payment systems. A system will not be effective until it is agreed as being fair and equitable by both sides.

Local labour market pressures

Shop floor workers are usually recruited from the local labour market where the laws of supply and demand can have a marked effect on the rates of pay for particular occupations when there is a skills shortage or reluctance on the part of workers to carry out certain jobs. The local labour market is a fairly perfect market in one of the senses used by economists, ie there is widespread and easily available knowledge on rates of pay (the price of labour) and there may also exist, although not for every occupation, a fair degree of choice by both buyers and sellers of where they obtain labour or where they provide it.

Technology

The increased use of technology on the shop floor, for example in the form of computer-aided manufacture, has meant that the demand for a number of the traditional skills has diminished while the demand for new technical skills has increased. Computer-controlled machines are more likely to be operated by technicians than by members of the old skilled trades. This is one of the factors that has led to pressures to harmonize shop floor and office or laboratory payment systems.

TIME RATES

Time rates, also known as day rates, daywork, flat rates or hourly rates, provide workers with a predetermined rate for the actual hours they work. The rate is fixed by formal or informal negotiations, on the basis of local rates or, less often, by reference to a hierarchy produced by job evaluation. The rate only varies with time, never with performance or output. However, additional payments are made on top of base rates for overtime, shift working, night work, call-outs, adverse working conditions and, sometimes, location.

The situation when time rates are most commonly used is when it is thought that it is impossible or undesirable to use a payment-by-results system, for example in maintenance work. From the viewpoint of employees the advantage of time rates is that their earnings are predictable and steady and they do not have to engage in endless arguments with rate fixers and supervisors about piece rates or time allowances. The argument against them is that they do not provide a direct incentive relating the reward to the effort or the results. Two ways of modifying the basic time rate approach are to adopt high day rates as described below or measured daywork as covered later in this chapter.

Time rates may take the form of what are often called high day rates. These are higher than the minimum time rate and may contain a consolidated bonus rate element. The underlying assumption is that higher base rates will encourage greater effort without the problems created when operating an incentive scheme. This is in line with the theory of the economy of high wages mentioned in Chapter 7. High day rates are usually above the local market rates to attract and retain workers.

INCENTIVE SCHEMES

Incentive or payment-by-result (PBR) schemes relate the pay of workers to the number of items they produce or the time taken to do a certain amount of work. The main types of schemes for individuals are piecework, work-measured schemes, measured daywork and performance-related pay. Team bonus schemes are an alternative to individual schemes, and plant-wide schemes can produce bonuses that are paid instead of individual or team bonuses or in addition to them. Each of these methods is described below and summarized, with an analysis of their advantages and disadvantages and the situations when they may be appropriate, in Table 29.1. First, however, it is necessary to deal with the general considerations affecting the design and use of incentive schemes.

General considerations

The general considerations to be taken into account in developing and maintaining incentive schemes are the criteria of effectiveness and their advantages and disadvantages.

Criteria of effectiveness

Incentive schemes aim to motivate employees to exert greater effort. They will do so effectively only if:

● the link between effort and reward is clear and easily understood;
● the value of the reward is worthwhile in relation to the effort;

Table 29.1 Comparison of shop floor incentive and bonus schemes

Scheme	Main Features	For Employers		For Employees		When Appropriate
		Advantages	Disadvantages	Advantages	Disadvantages	
Piecework	Bonus directly related to output.	Direct motivation; simple and easy to operate.	Lose control over output; quality problems.	Predict and control earnings in the short term; regulate pace of work themselves.	More difficult to predict and control earnings in the longer term; work may be stressful and produce RSI.	Fairly limited application to work involving unit production controlled by the person, eg agriculture, garment manufacture.
Work-measured schemes	Work measurement used to determine standard output levels over a period or standard times for job/tasks; bonus based by reference to performance ratings compared with actual performance or time saved.	Provide what appears to be a 'scientific' method of relating reward to performance; can produce significant increases in productivity, at least in the short term.	Schemes are expensive, time-consuming and difficult to run and can too easily degenerate and cause wage drift because of loose rates.	Appear to provide a more objective method of relating pay to performance; employees can be involved in the rating process to ensure fairness.	Ratings are still prone to subjective judgement and earnings can fluctuate because of changes in work requirements outside the control of employees.	For short-cycle repetitive work where changes in the work mix or design changes are infrequent, down time is restricted, and management and supervision are capable of managing and maintaining the scheme.
Measured daywork	Pay fixed at a high rate on the understanding that a high level of performance against work-measured standards will be maintained.	Employees are under an obligation to work at the specified level of performance.	Performance targets can become easily attained norms and may be difficult to change.	High predictable earnings are provided.	No opportunities for individuals to be rewarded in line with their own efforts.	Everyone must be totally committed to making it work; high standards of work measurement are essential; good control systems to identify shortfalls on targets.

Scheme	Description	Advantages	Disadvantages		When used
Performance-related pay	Payments on top of base rate are made related to individual assessments of performance.	Rewards individual contribution without resource to work measurement; relevant in high-technology manufacturing.	Measuring performance can be difficult; no direct incentive provided.	Opportunity to be rewarded for own efforts without having to submit to a pressured PBR system. Assessment informing performance pay decisions may be biased, inconsistent or unsupported by evidence.	As part of a reward harmonization (shop floor and staff programme; as an alternative to work-measured schemes or an enhancement of a high day rate system.
Group or team basis	Groups or teams are paid bonuses on the basis of their performance as indicated by work measurement ratings or the achievement of targets.	Encourages team cooperation and effort; not too individualized.	Direct incentive may be limited; depends on good work measurement or the availability of clear group output or productivity targets.	Bonuses can be related clearly to the joint efforts of the group; fluctuations in earnings minimized. Depends on effective work measurement, which is not always available; individual effort and contribution not recognized.	When team working is important and team efforts can be accurately measured and assessed; as an alternative to individual PBR if this is not effective.
Factory-wide bonuses	Bonuses related to plant performance – added value or productivity.	Increase commitment by sharing success.	No direct motivation.	Earnings increased without individual pressure. Bonuses often small and unpredictable.	As an addition to other forms of incentive when increasing commitment is important.

- individuals are able to influence their level of effort or behaviour in order to earn a reward;
- rewards closely follow the effort;
- the integrity of the scheme is preserved – it is not allowed to degenerate and cannot be manipulated so that individuals are over-rewarded.

The rationale for incentive schemes

The basic rationale of incentive schemes is the simple proposition that people are motivated by money. It is believed that they will work harder if rewards are tied directly to the results they achieve. This is an expression of 'Taylorism' as described in Chapter 8. Certainly, the experience of most people who have installed a PBR scheme in a workplace where it did not previously exist is that productivity increases substantially when the scheme is new, although the level of increase is not always maintained. Studies in the United States by Lawler (1), Guzzo *et al* (2), Nalbantian (3) and Binder (4) have shown productivity increases of between 15 per cent and 35 per cent when incentive schemes have been put into place.

PBR schemes are used in the belief that they yield increased output, lower the cost of production and provide higher earnings for the workers concerned. It is also commonly believed that less supervision is needed to keep output up. Indeed, when direct supervision is difficult, PBR is often advocated as the only practicable form of payment.

Disadvantages of incentive schemes

The argument that people work harder only when they are paid more is regarded by some people as overwhelming. They do not accept the proposition that intrinsic and non-financial motivators can have an equally, if not more, powerful and longer-lasting impact.

The disadvantages of shop floor incentive schemes are that they can:

- *Be unfair* – earnings may fluctuate through no fault of the individual because of lack of work, shortage of materials, design modifications or the need to learn new skills. It may also be felt that the method of altering rates is unfair.
- *Be ineffective* – workers may have their own ideas about how much they want to earn or how hard they want to work and regulate their output accordingly.
- *Penalize skill* – the more skilled workers may be given the more difficult and often less remunerative jobs.

- *Cause wage drift* – the difficulty of conforming to criteria such as clearly relating pay to effort and the lax approach of some organizations to the management of incentive schemes contribute to increases in earnings at a higher rate than productivity. Degeneration and wage drift are a particular problem with work-measured schemes as discussed later in this chapter.
- *Lead to management escaping its responsibilities* – team leaders and supervisors may rely on the incentive scheme to control output. Instead of taking poor performers to one side and informing them that their work is not up to standard, they are tempted to take the soft option and simply point to the figures.
- *Be costly to maintain* – extra work study engineers, rate fixers and inspectors are often needed to maintain the scheme and exercise quality control.
- *Produce strife in the workplace* – arguments about rates and accusations of unjustified rate cutting are common in workshops where incentive schemes are used.
- *Create reluctance to exert the expected level of effort* – workers may believe that management will progressively increase the performance targets required to trigger the same bonus payment. They may therefore be reluctant to carry on at the incentivized level of performance they have achieved on the grounds that this will only result in higher targets, which will make the bonus more difficult to obtain.
- *Result in poor-quality work* – concentration on output can lead to neglect of quality.
- *Lead to poor teamwork* – individual incentive schemes by definition encourage individual rather than team effort.
- *Result in accidents and health hazards* – workers may be tempted to cut corners and ignore safety precautions to achieve output targets; repetitive strain injury (RSI) may result if they work too hard on tasks requiring repeated small movements.

These are powerful arguments but shop floor incentive schemes persist. The number of workers paid on this basis may have diminished but this is because of structural (the reduction in manufacturing) and technological reasons rather than because managements have turned against it.

Types of incentive schemes

The main types of PBR or incentive schemes are described below. Their characteristics and advantages and disadvantages are summarized in Table 29.1.

Piecework

Piecework is the oldest and simplest form of shop floor incentive scheme. Operators are paid at a specific rate according to their output or the number of 'pieces' they produce. Pay is directly proportional to output, although most piecework schemes provide a fall-back rate at minimum earnings level. The proportion of the minimum rate to average earnings varies. It is typically set at 70 per cent or 80 per cent, although it can be as low as 30 per cent.

Work-measured schemes

Work-measured schemes are the most popular form of incentive plan for shop floor workers. They use work measurement techniques to determine standard output levels over a period or standard times for tasks. The incentive pay is then linked with the output achieved relative to the standard, or to the time saved in performing each task.

The form of work measurement used is time study. Jobs are broken down into their constituent parts or tasks and the time taken by workers to complete each part is measured with a stopwatch by a work study or industrial engineer. A number of measurements will be made of the time taken by different workers on the same task or the same worker carrying out the task at different times of the day and night. Time study is based on objective measurements, but account has to be taken of the fact that there will probably be significant differences between the rate at which operators work – the effort they put into the job. Work study engineers have therefore to assess what that rate is, a process known as effort rating.

Individual effort is rated in terms of 'standard performance'. This is the performance that a qualified and motivated worker should be able to achieve without over-exertion. The effort needed to achieve standard performance is sometimes represented as equivalent to walking at 4 miles an hour (ie quite briskly). All the operators studied are given an effort rating relative to this standard. The raw times observed by the work study are then adjusted by the work study engineer to produce a basic time, which represents a rating of 100, to indicate the performance of an average operator working conscientiously without financial motivation. This involves a large element of subjectivity, although experienced and well-trained engineers should be capable of making reasonably accurate and consistent assessments.

The basic time will be further adjusted to incorporate allowances for relaxation, personal needs, fatigue and any time regularly taken up by other aspects of the work such as cleaning or resetting machines. The result is the standard time for the task, usually expressed as 'standard minutes'.

Work-measured schemes can use performance ratings, which are calculated by a formula as in the following example:

$$\frac{\text{Number of units produced per day (132)} \times \text{standard minutes per unit (4)}}{\text{Actual time taken in minutes per day (480)}} = \frac{528}{480 \times 100} = 110\%$$

In the most common proportionate system of payment, the performance rating is applied directly to the base rate, so that in the above example the incentive payment would be an additional 10 per cent.

The problem with time study is that, although it is based on objective measurements, the standard time that is ultimately obtained is the product of a number of additional subjective judgements. Employees who are being timed may deliberately restrict their performance in order to achieve low standard times and therefore higher bonuses with less effort. It is up to the work study engineer's skill and judgement to detect such restrictions, and this can lead to arguments and even strife. In organizations with trade unions it is common practice to train some representatives in work measurement techniques to promote the achievement of acceptable judgements on standard times.

Alternatively, PBR payments can be based on the time-saved principle. The amount of the bonus depends on the difference between the actual time taken to perform the task and the standard time allowed. If a task is done in less than the standard time, then the percentage of time saved is applied to the base rate to calculate the bonus. The standard times may be determined by work measurement, although traditionally 'rate fixers' were employed to make more subjective and therefore often more controversial judgements.

Measured daywork

Measured daywork schemes were originally developed for large batch or mass-production factories in the 1950s and 1960s, when it became evident that, despite all efforts, it was impossible to control wage drift. They are, however, much less common now. Manufacturing firms often prefer to pay a high day rate.

When they exist, measured daywork schemes provide for the pay of employees to be fixed on the understanding that they will maintain a specified level of performance, but in the short term pay does not fluctuate with their performance. The arrangement depends on work measurement to define the required level of performance and to monitor the actual level. The fundamental principles of measured daywork are that there is an incentive level of performance and that the incentive payment is guaranteed in advance, putting employees under the obligation to perform at the effort level required. In contrast, a conventional work-measured incentive scheme allows employees discretion as to their effort level but relates their pay directly to the results they achieve. Between these two extremes there is a variety of alternatives, including banded incentives, stepped schemes and various forms of high day rate.

Performance-related pay

Performance-related pay systems such as those described in Chapter 19 can be used for manual workers. Employees receive a high base rate and an additional performance-related payment, which is either a lump sum bonus or consolidated into basic pay. The award is governed by assessments of skill and performance ratings under headings such as quality, flexibility, contribution to team working and ability to hit targets. The percentage award is usually small – up to 5 per cent.

Performance-related pay is sometimes introduced for manual workers as part of a programme for harmonizing their conditions of employment with those of salaried staff. It can be appropriate in circumstances where work measurement is difficult or impossible to use, in high-technology manufacturing where operations are computer-controlled or automated and teamwork and multiskilling are important, in organizations where the emphasis is on quality, and in those where just-in-time systems are used.

Group or team incentive schemes

Group or team incentive schemes provide for the payment of a bonus to members of a group or team related to the output achieved by the group in relation to defined targets or to work-measured standards.

Factory- or plant-wide schemes

Factory- or plant-wide schemes pay a bonus to individuals that is related to the performance of the factory as a whole, which may be measured in terms of added value as in a gain-sharing scheme (see Chapter 22) or some other index of productivity (eg units produced, cost per unit of output).

Assessment of schemes

Table 29.1 contains an assessment of the advantages and disadvantages of each type of scheme from the viewpoint of employers and employees and a review of the circumstances when the scheme is more likely to be appropriate.

SINGLE STATUS AND HARMONIZATION

Single status means that shop floor workers on wages are on salaried terms and conditions and are entitled to the same conditions of employment such as sick pay as other members of staff. Harmonization means the reduction of differences in the pay structure and other employment conditions between categories of employee, usually manual and staff employees. It involves the adoption of a common approach and criteria to pay and benefits for all employees.

The pressure for harmonization has occurred because of the belief that status differentials between people in the same employment cannot be justified. Harmonization facilitates the more flexible use of labour, and the impact of technology has enhanced the skills of shop floor workers and made differential treatment harder to defend. Equal pay legislation has been a major challenge to differentiation between staff and manual workers.

ACAS (5) has suggested that organizations, before pursuing a programme of harmonization, should seek answers to the following questions:

- What differences in the treatment of groups of employees are a rational result of differences in the work or the job requirements?
- Is it possible to estimate the direct costs of removing these differences?
- What differences in status are explicitly recognized as part of the 'reward package' for different groups in the labour force?
- What would be the possible repercussive effects of harmonization?
- How do the existing differences affect industrial relations in the organization?

REFERENCES

1   Lawler, EE (1971) *Pay and Organizational Effectiveness*, McGraw-Hill, New York
2   Guzzo, RA, Jette, RD and Katsell, RA (1985) The effect of psychological-based intervention programmes on worker productivity: a meta analysis, *Personnel Psychology*, **38**, pp 275–91
3   Nalbantian, H (1987) *Incentives, Cooperation and Risk Sharing*, Rowman & Littlefield, Totowa, NJ
4   Binder, AS (1990) *Paying for Productivity*, Brookings Institution, Washington, DC
5   Advisory, Conciliation and Arbitration Service (1982) *Developments in Harmonization*, Discussion Paper No. 1, ACAS, London

Part 7

Employee benefits and pension schemes

30

Employee benefits

Employee benefits consist of arrangements made by employers for their employees that enhance the latter's well-being. They are provided in addition to pay and form important parts of the total reward package. As part of total remuneration, they may be deferred or contingent like a pension scheme, insurance cover or sick pay, or they may be immediate like a company car or a loan. Employee benefits also include holidays and leave arrangements, which are not strictly remuneration. Benefits are sometimes referred to dismissively as 'perks' (perquisites) or 'fringe benefits', but when they cater for personal security or personal needs could hardly be described as 'fringe'.

Employee benefits are a costly part of the remuneration package. They can amount to one-third or more of basic pay costs and therefore have to be planned and managed with care.

This chapter covers:

- the rationale for employee benefits;
- employee benefit strategies and policies;
- types of benefit;
- the administration of benefits;
- tax considerations affecting benefits.

Flexible benefit systems are dealt with in Chapter 31 and pensions in Chapter 32.

RATIONALE FOR EMPLOYEE BENEFITS

Employee benefits provide for the personal needs of employees and they are a means of increasing their commitment to the organization and demonstrating that their employers care for their well-being. Not all employers care, but, like the ones that do, they still provide benefits to ensure that the total remuneration package is competitive. And some benefits like maternity leave have to be provided by law.

EMPLOYEE BENEFIT STRATEGIES AND POLICIES

Employee benefit strategies will be concerned in general terms with the direction the organization wants to go with regard to the range and scale of benefits it wants to provide and the costs it is prepared to incur. The strategy forms the foundation for the formulation of employee benefit policies.

Employee benefit policies are concerned with:

- the types of benefits to be provided, taking into account their value to employees, their cost, and the need to make the benefit package competitive;
- the size of the benefits;
- the need to harmonize benefits (harmonization policies were considered in Chapter 29);
- the total costs of benefits provision in relation to the costs of basic pay;
- the use of flexible benefits as described in Chapter 31.

TYPES OF BENEFIT

The main benefits deal with personal security, financial assistance, personal needs, company cars and voluntary benefits as described below. Personal pensions are covered in Chapter 32.

Personal security

Personal security benefits include:

- *Health care* – the provision through medical insurance of private health care to cover the cost of private hospital treatment (permanent health insurance), making periodic health screening available and, sometimes, dental insurance.

- *Insurance cover* for death in service (if not already provided in a pension scheme), personal accident and business travel.
- *Sick pay*, providing full pay for a given period of sickness and a proportion of pay (typically half-pay) for a further period. Sick pay entitlement is usually service-related. Sick pay can be costly unless attendance management and control practices are introduced.
- *Redundancy pay* – additions can be made to the statutory redundancy pay, including extra notice compensation, extra service-related payments (eg one month per year of service) and ex gratia payments to directors and executives in compensation for loss of office (sometimes called golden handshakes).
- *Career counselling* (outplacement advice) can be provided by specialist consultants to employees who have been made redundant.

Financial assistance

Financial assistance can take the following forms:

- *Company loans* – interest-free modest loans, or low interest on more substantial loans, which are usually earmarked for specific purposes such as home improvements.
- *Season ticket loans* – interest-free loans for annual season tickets.
- *Mortgage assistance* – subsidized interest payments on mortgages up to a given price threshold. This benefit is most likely to be provided by financial services companies.
- *Relocation packages* – for staff who are being relocated by the organization or recruited from elsewhere, the costs of removal and legal/estate agent's fees may be refunded.
- *Fees to professional bodies* – eg the CIPD.

Personal needs

Employee benefits satisfying personal needs include:

- maternity and paternity leave and pay above the statutory minimum;
- leave for personal reasons;
- childcare through workplace nurseries or vouchers;
- pre-retirement counselling;
- personal counselling through employee assistance programmes;
- sports and social facilities;

- company discounts – employees can buy the products or services offered by the company at a reduced price;
- retail vouchers to buy goods at chain stores.

Holidays

Before the European Working Time Directive in 1998, there was no statutory obligation to offer any paid holiday except for the standard bank holidays. Employers are now obliged to offer a minimum of 20 days' paid holiday per year, including bank holidays.

In practice, most organizations have always offered annual leave well in excess of this minimum, with few UK companies giving less than four weeks to employees at any level. Basic holiday entitlements are typically five weeks plus bank holidays, with some organizations offering up to six weeks for senior executives (who in practice may rarely have time to take full advantage of the provision) or on a service-related basis to more junior staff. The entitlement for holiday begins to accrue on the first day at work.

Organizations are obliged by statute to provide paid maternal and paternal leave and unpaid family leave.

Company cars

Although the tax liability for individuals with company 'status' cars has increased steadily over the last decade, they still remain one of the most valued perks, perhaps because people do not have to make a capital outlay, do not lose money through depreciation and are spared the worry and expense of maintenance.

Other benefits

Other benefits include free car parking, Christmas parties and tea/coffee/cold drinks.

Voluntary ('affinity') benefits

Voluntary benefit schemes provide opportunities for employees to buy goods or services at discounted prices. The employer negotiates deals with the providers but the scheme does not cost the employer anything.

Popular voluntary benefits include:

- *health* – private medical insurance, dental insurance, health screening.

- *protection* – critical illness insurance, life insurance, income protection insurance, personal accident insurance.
- *leisure* – holidays, days out, travel insurance, computer leasing, bicycle leasing, pet insurance, gym membership.
- *home* – household goods, online shopping.

Concierge services

Concierge services can include dealing with home and car repairs and maintenance, financial services, buying presents, restaurant reservations, theatre tickets and travel arrangements. They originated in the United States in response to the long-hours culture, which limited personal time away from the workplace. Businesses benefit from providing these services because they enable staff to concentrate on their jobs by freeing them from mundane personal tasks such as waiting at home for deliveries or getting their car serviced.

INCIDENCE OF BENEFITS

The 2006 CIPD *Survey of Reward Management* (1) established that the top 10 employee benefits provided by respondents were:

1. occupational sick pay – 83 per cent;
2. 25 days or more of paid leave – 81 per cent;
3. on-site car parking – 74 per cent;
4. tea/coffee/cold drinks – 68 per cent;
5. Christmas party/lunch – 64 per cent;
6. life assurance – 63 per cent;
7. car allowance – 60 per cent;
8. private health care – 60 per cent;
9. enhanced maternity leave – 54 per cent;
10. relocation assistance – 51 per cent.

CHOICE OF BENEFITS

Some benefits such as holidays, maternity leave and redundancy pay have to be provided by statute – there is no choice except on the extent to which statutory provisions may by enhanced. Neither for a responsible employer is there any real choice over the provision of pensions, life insurance or sick pay. Company cars for executives are still popular in spite of the tax penalties because of the felt need to be competitive.

Some optional benefits such as health insurance, childcare and low-interest loans may be selected because they will be appreciated and also because they are frequently offered by other employers.

The factors affecting the choice of provision or scale will be:

- what employees want as established by opinion surveys;
- what other employers are providing as established by market surveys;
- what the organization can afford.

ADMINISTERING EMPLOYEE BENEFITS

Employee benefits can be expensive and it is necessary to monitor the costs of providing them and the extent to which cost/benefit comparison justifies continuing with them on the present scale or at all. There should be a budget for employee benefit costs and expenditure should be monitored against it. Regular surveys should be undertaken of the attitude of employees to the benefits package. They may suggest where benefit expenditure could be redirected to areas where it would be more appreciated. They may also suggest that there is a need to adopt a flexible benefit policy, as described in the next chapter.

TAX CONSIDERATIONS

General principles

Emoluments from employment are subject to income tax under Schedule E. Emoluments are defined by legislation as 'all salaries, fees, wages, perquisites, or profits whatsoever'. In the courts, emoluments have been defined as rewards for 'services rendered, past, present and future' or, more broadly, payments made 'in return for acting as, or being, an employee'.

In general, much of the taxation on benefits applies only to directors and employees earning over £8,500 a year – in most organizations this is likely to be just about all full-time workers. Such employees are sometimes known as P11D employees, P11D being the form on which employers have to report the benefits received by employees to the Inland Revenue. A non-cash benefit such as a gift is taxable on the price it would command if sold. A benefit that cannot be turned into cash by the recipient is taxable on the annual cost incurred by the employer. For employees earning less than £8,500 a year, such 'non-convertible' benefits are not taxed. Regulations on the taxation of benefits are summarized below. They are frequently changed and it is advisable to keep up to date through such publications as the IDS annual guide to taxation for personnel managers.

Taxable benefits

The taxable benefits include:

- Company cars. The tax charged on company cars is based on the 'full cost' of a car for a year. 'Full cost' includes running costs and major fixed costs such as depreciation and financial costs. For income tax purposes, full cost is 35 per cent of the list price of the car. The taxable value of the benefit can, however, be reduced to take business use into account. This amounts to a one-third reduction if between 2,500 and 17,999 business miles are driven a year and two-thirds for 18,000 or more business miles a year. Employers have to pay national insurance contributions on company cars.
- Free fuel is taxed on the basis of fixed scale charges for company cars that are available for private use. The scale charge is applied however much private mileage is driven, so that the free benefit can be a burden if mileage falls below a certain level.
- Car mileage allowances. Under the fixed profit car scheme (FPCS) a scale lays down the size of allowance that will be tax-free according to cylinder capacity and mileage.
- Cheap or interest-free loans. Tax is payable on the taxable benefit of a loan. This is calculated as the difference between the interest, if any, paid by the employee and the interest on the loan, calculated at the 'official rate' of interest set by the Inland Revenue.
- Living accommodation. All employees and directors are liable for tax on the benefit of employer-provided free or cheap housing, unless they are in certain exempt categories such as those required to live on the premises.
- Private medical benefits. Private medical insurance and treatment are taxable on the basis of the cost to the employer.
- Gifts and vouchers are taxed on the full realizable value of the gift, or their full cost if a voucher or credit token is used to obtain them.
- Use of assets. Where assets such as furniture and electrical goods (but not cars or accommodation) are provided as a benefit to employees they are taxed at 20 per cent of the market value of the asset at the time it was first used by the employee.

- Prizes and incentive awards. Cash awards are taxed in the normal way. Awards in the form of goods, vouchers or services such as holidays are taxed on the value of the award. Employers can arrange with the Inland Revenue to pay the tax due on non-cash incentive awards on behalf of their employees so that the awards are 'tax-free'.
- Mobile telephones provided for private use are taxed at the rate of £200 unless the employee refunds the full cost of personal use.

Benefits not usually subject to tax

These include:

- Meals provided for employees, as long as free or subsidized meals are on 'a reasonable scale' and all employees can take advantage of them.
- Subscriptions to approved professional institutions and learned societies.
- Luncheon vouchers of up to 15p a day.
- Christmas parties and other functions. Employees are not liable to tax on the value of a Christmas party or other social function provided by the employer as long as it is open to employees generally and the cost is no more than £50 per head.
- Small gifts and entertainment by third parties. Gifts are tax-free up to the value of £100, as is goodwill entertainment provided by a third party (ie not the employer).
- Relocation expenses. Tax relief is available on relocation packages to a ceiling of £8,000 but this excludes payments by employers to compensate employees for any loss on the sale of their old home.
- Long-service awards. Awards given to mark service of over 20 years are tax-free as long as they are 'tangible articles of reasonable cost' or shares in the employing company. Reasonable cost is defined as no more than £20 per year of service. The employee must not have received a similar award within the previous 10 years.
- Suggestion schemes. Awards made to employees under suggestion schemes are tax-free up to a maximum of £5,000 as long as the suggestion is outside the scope of the employee's normal duties and is implemented. Awards must not exceed either half the net financial benefit expected during the first year of implementation, or 10 per cent of the expected benefit over a period of up to five years. 'Encouragement' awards, given where the suggestion shows merit but is not implemented, are tax-free up to a limit of £25.
- Education and training. Employees are not liable to tax on further education or training paid for by their employers as long as it leads to the acquisition of knowledge and skills that are either necessary for the job or will increase an

employee's effectiveness at work. If the course is of general education employees must be under 21 when it starts.

- Outplacement counselling can be provided free of tax.
- Workplace nurseries. Tax relief is available to employees whose children have a place in an employer-provided workplace nursery.
- Redundancy payments. The first £30,000 of a redundancy payment is tax-free as long as it is a full and final settlement and there is no question of any part of the money being paid to the individual for services rendered. The Inland Revenue has recently been taking a firm line on the latter provision.
- Car parking spaces in or adjacent to the place of work.

NB these tax arrangements are subject to change.

REFERENCE

1 Chartered Institute of Personnel and Development (2006) *Survey of Reward Management*, CIPD, London

31

Flexible benefits

Flexible benefit schemes give employees a choice within limits of the type or scale of benefits offered to them by their employers. A wide variety of approaches is available.

Interest in such schemes has been generated because employee benefits are not all equally wanted or appreciated by the staff who receive them and, from the employer's point of view, some benefits will not therefore provide value for money. However, the number who have introduced formal schemes is relatively small – only 8 per cent of the respondents to the CIPD 2005 *Reward Management Survey* (1) had them. In this chapter the reasons for introducing flexible benefits are set out, the different types of flexible benefit schemes are defined and the steps required to introduce a scheme are explained.

REASONS FOR INTRODUCING FLEXIBLE BENEFITS

Flexible benefit schemes may be introduced in order to:

- meet the diverse needs of employees and increase the perceived value of the package to them – to a degree, they can decide for themselves what benefits they want and the size of particular benefits to suit their own lifestyle rather than being forced to accept what their employers think is good for them;

- enable employers to get better value for money from their benefits expenditure because it meets the needs and wants of employees;
- control costs by providing employees with a fund to spend rather than promising a particular level of benefits;
- aid recruitment and retention – flexible benefits are generally preferred by employees to fixed benefits of equivalent value;
- help to harmonize terms and conditions in a merger.

TYPES OF FLEXIBLE BENEFITS SCHEMES

The are many ways in which benefits can be flexed and the main types of schemes are described below.

Flex individual benefits

Employees are given the opportunity to vary the size of individual benefits, paying extra if they want more or, in effect, being paid cash if they want less. A typical example is a flexible car scheme that enables people to pay more for a better model or, if they decide to downsize, receive the reduction in cost to the company in cash. Choices are made on recruitment or when the car is replaced.

Another common arrangement is to provide scope within limits to buy or sell holiday time over the holiday year; for example, so many extra days could be 'bought' at the daily rate of the employee or so many could be 'sold' and the amount at the daily rate added to pay.

This is a simple approach that is easy to introduce and administer and is therefore the most common method of flexing benefits. The disadvantage is that the impact may be limited.

Flex existing entitlement

Employees may choose to increase, decrease or end their current benefits and select new benefits from the menu provided. The value of the benefits bought and sold is then aggregated and the net amount added to or deducted from pay.

An example of how this might look for an employee whose salary is £30,000 pa is shown in Table 31.1.

This arrangement can be simplified by making only two or three benefits flexible. The rules often stipulate that such essential core benefits as pensions and life insurance cannot be reduced and limits may be placed on the scope for flexing other benefits, for example holidays.

Table 31.1 Example of variation around existing entitlement

Benefit	Standard Entitlement	Selected Entitlement	Monthly Cost Saving or (Extra Cost)
Holidays	25 days	22 days	£35
Car	lease cost £300 per month	£240 per month	£60
Company pension contribution	10% of salary	10% of salary	nil
Private medical insurance	cover for self	cover for self, partner and child	(£45)
Dental insurance	nil	nil	nil
Childcare vouchers	nil	£200 per month	(£200)
Total monthly adjustment			(£150)

Source: Michael Armstrong and Helen Murlis (2004) *Reward Management,* 5th edn, Kogan Page, London

Flex fund

Employees are allocated a fund of money to 'spend' on benefits from a menu. This is therefore sometimes described as the 'cafeteria' approach. Certain 'core' compulsory benefits such as pensions and life insurance have to be maintained. The value of the flex fund is big enough to enable individual employees to 'buy' their existing benefits and thus retain them without additional cost.

A simplified example of a flex fund benefits choice menu for someone with a salary of £30,000 with a flex fund of £12,000 is shown in Table 31.2.

The impact of the choices made is shown in Table 31.3.

The overspend would be funded by salary sacrifice. Had less than £12,000 been spent, the unspent flex fund would be paid as a monthly, non-consolidated cash sum.

Table 31.2 Example of flex fund benefits choice menu

Benefit	Minimum Choice	Maximum Choice	Price
Holidays	20 days	30 days	0.4% of salary per day
Lease car	£300 per month (£3,600 per annum)	£500 per month (£6,000 per annum)	annual lease times 1.25 (to allow for insurance and maintenance)
Company pension contribution	5% of salary	15% of salary	face value less 10%*
Private medical insurance	cover for self only	cover for self, partner and children	£500 each per adult; £200 for one or more children
Dental insurance	n/a	Level 3 cover for self, partner and children	£40, £100 or £180 per individual for Level 1, 2 or 3 cover respectively
Childcare vouchers	n/a	20% of salary	face value less 5%*

* The adjustment reflects the fact that employer NICs are not payable on these benefits. The adjustment for childcare vouchers is lower to allow for the charge payable to the provider.

Source: Michael Armstrong and Helen Murlis (2004) *Reward Management*, 5th edn, Kogan Page, London

Most common flexible benefits

The most common flexible benefits as established in a survey by Hewitt Associates (cited by Daugherty, 2) are:

	% of plans
Private medical cover/insurance	80
Holidays	75
Dental insurance	74
Company car	70
Health screens	59
Critical illness insurance	59

Table 31.3   Example of impact of flex fund choices made (shown in Table 31.2)

Benefit	Choice	Cost
Holidays	25 days	£3,000
Lease car	£350 per month	£5,250
Company pension contribution	10% of salary	£3,000
Private medical insurance	cover for self and partner	£1,000
Dental insurance	Level 2 cover for self and partner	£200
Childcare vouchers	nil	nil
Total		£12,450
Flex fund		£12,000
Over- (under-)spend		£450

Source: Michael Armstrong and Helen Murlis (2004) *Reward Management*, 5th edn, Kogan Page, London

INTRODUCING FLEXIBLE BENEFITS

The steps required to introduce flexible benefits are described below:

1. *Define the business need* – the benefits in terms of meeting the diverse needs of employees, helping recruitment and retention and getting better value for money from expenditure on employee benefits.
2. *Seek views* – conduct an opinion survey of employees on what they think of present benefit arrangements, what they think about flexible benefits and what benefits they would like to be eligible for flex (this could be accompanied by information about how flexible benefits might work and would therefore be the first shot in a communications campaign – communicating about flexible benefits is important).
3. *Decide the strategy* – management should draw up a flexible benefits strategy for approval by top management. This will include broadly the extent to which it is believed that the approach should be to go for a full scheme based either on

flexing existing benefits or on a flex fund, or whether the approach should be to flex individual benefits. There may be something to be said for starting with the latter simpler approach (which will be cheaper to install) with the possibility of extending it at a later stage when experience has shown that it is working well. The strategy should also explore the need for outside advice and, on the basis of initial discussions with potential advisers, how much would need to be spent on developing and maintaining the scheme. One of the common objections to flexible benefits is the costs involved, especially when the proposed scheme is a fairly complex one and outside professional advice and support are required. Preliminary decisions need to be made at this stage on the likelihood that such advice is required so that the costs involved can be estimated. It is also necessary to decide on the need for a project team with employee involvement.

4. *Set up the project team* – this could be a joint management/employee team (involvement is very desirable) with the responsibility of planning and overseeing the development programme.

5. *Decide who is going to carry out the development work* – someone from within the organization should be in charge of the project with help as required and available from flexible benefit, finance, tax and pensions specialists. The development of a scheme requires considerable expertise in these areas in developing and costing schemes, exploring tax considerations and setting up the administration.

6. *Decide finally on the approach* – a choice will need to be made on the basic approach.

7. *Design the scheme* – this involves deciding on core benefits that have to be maintained, identifying benefits that can be flexed, deciding on any limits to the extent to which these benefits can be flexed, costing the benefits as necessary to enable menus to be produced and flex funds set up, if appropriate, and considering how the scheme should be administered. Simple schemes can be administered on paper but there is software available to administer more elaborate ones. An intranet can be used to help with administration – employees can make their choice of benefits from the screen and calculate the financial implications.

8. *Communicate details of the scheme* – employees need to be given detailed but easily understood information about the proposed scheme – how it will work, how it will affect them, its advantages, and how and when it will be introduced.

9. *Pilot-test* – there is much to be said for piloting the scheme in a part of the organization to test reactions and administrative arrangements.

10. *Introduce the scheme* – the earlier communications need to be reinforced generally at this stage and arrangements need to be made to provide individual employees with advice through personal contact, a help line or a help screen on the intranet.

EXAMPLE – LLOYDS TSB

Lloyds TSB decided a flexible benefits programme was the best solution to integrating the huge array of terms and conditions found across the diverse companies acquired by the group. Flex was also seen as a valuable tool to raise staff awareness of the value of their total remuneration package and the value of their benefits in particular.

The company offers a flexible benefits package called 'flavours' that recognizes individual needs and additionally gives employees the opportunity to share in the group's success by becoming Lloyds TSB shareholders.

Flavours is made up of three elements:

- *Flexible benefits* – employees can buy 13 additional benefits from the flex menu such as discounted retail vouchers or up to five extra days' holiday each year. Or they can simply take the cash as an additional monthly allowance.
- *Share incentive plan* – a tax-advantaged plan to encourage employees to hold shares in Lloyds TSB. The company makes use of all three of the main types of plan share provided by the legislation.
- *Sharesave* – offers a regular savings scheme through a savings contract with a guaranteed tax-free bonus, with the option to use your savings plus bonus to buy shares in Lloyds TSB plc.

How flavours works

Employees receive a non-pensionable payment each month with their salary. The company started with a cash allowance that will depend on performance each year. Staff can use the cash sum to purchase benefits from the range on offer or simply take the cash. They can also opt to sacrifice as much as half of their salary, as well as the cash sum, to buy additional benefits and discounted affinity products (resulting in national insurance savings for both the employer and the employee). Alternatively, they can sell some of their benefits back to the organization for cash – for example, up to five days' holiday.

Although employees can sell some of their existing benefits in return for cash, the choice is fairly limited. A key decision made early in the development of flavours was that core benefits such as the basic pensions scheme and death-in-service could not be flexed. Lloyds TSB was nervous about the possibility of employees opting out of these important 'wealth-creating' and security benefits.

Another important principle was to keep the scheme reasonably simple, so most options that can be purchased supplement the existing benefits that were protected.

REFERENCES

1   Chartered Institute of Personnel and Development (2005) *Reward Management Survey*, CIPD, London
2   Daugherty, C (2002) How to introduce flexible benefits, *People Management*, 10 January, pp 42–43

32

Pension schemes

Pensions provide an income to employees when they retire and to their surviving dependant on the death of the employee, and deferred benefits to employees who leave. Schemes offered by organizations (occupational pensions), as distinct from state pensions, are funded by contributions from the organization and usually, but not always, the employee. Pensions are the most significant benefit and are a valuable part of the total reward package. But they are perhaps the most complex part.

The so-called 'pensions crisis' has arisen because many schemes are underfunded and suffering the strain of having to cope with more pensioners who are living longer. But to put that in perspective it should be noted that a huge amount of money in the UK (£1,300 billion) is invested in pension funds, more than the rest of the EU put together.

The aim of this chapter is to present an outline of why pensions are provided, what they provide and the main types of schemes, including the state pension scheme. The reasons for the shift from defined benefit (final salary) schemes to defined contribution (money purchase) schemes are discussed and the chapter continues with a summary of the law relating to providing pensions advice and a discussion of approaches to communicating about pensions. The chapter ends with a summary of the government's proposals about the future of pensions following Lord Turner's Pensions Commission report (1).

WHY PENSIONS ARE PROVIDED

Pensions are provided because they demonstrate that the organization is a good employer concerned about the long-term interests of its employees, who want the security provided by a reasonable pension when they retire. Good pension schemes help to attract and retain high-quality people by maintaining competitive levels of total remuneration. According to the CIPD they are 'a well-perceived and often expected benefit among employees' (2).

WHAT PENSION SCHEMES PROVIDE

The range and level of benefits from pension schemes depend on the type of scheme and the level of contributions. In general, schemes provide:

- *benefits on retirement* – these are related to the final salary of individuals when they retire or the amount that has been paid into a defined contribution scheme while the individuals were members;
- *benefits on death* – the pensions of widows or widowers and children are normally related to the member's anticipated pension (the most common fraction is half);
- *benefits on leaving an employer* – individuals leaving an employer can elect to take one of the following options: a deferred pension from the occupational scheme they are leaving, the transfer of the pension entitlement from the present employer to the new employer (but this is not always possible) or a refund of their contributions, but only if they have completed less than two years' membership of the pension scheme.

THE TWO MAIN TYPES OF SCHEMES

The two main types of schemes are described below. Other types are covered in the next section.

Defined benefit (final salary) schemes

The main features of a defined benefit scheme are as follows:

- *Pension entitlement on retirement:*

- On retiring the employee is entitled to a pension that is calculated as a fraction of his or her final salary (on retirement or an average of the last two or three years) multiplied by the length of pensionable service.
  - The maximum proportion of salary allowed by the Inland Revenue is two-thirds of final salary after 40 years' service.
  - The amount of the pension depends on the final salary, the value of the annuity that provides the pension and the accrual rate. The accrual rate refers to the fraction of final salary that can be earned per year of service. When a pension is described as 1/60th it means that 40 years' service will produce a two-thirds of final salary pension, and 30 years will produce a pension of half the final salary. This is a fairly typical fraction in private sector firms.
- *Employer and employee contributions:*
  - Employer contributions can be a fixed percentage of salary. Alternatively the percentage increases with service or is a multiple of the employee's contribution (eg the employer contributes 15 per cent if the employee contributes 5 per cent). The level of employer contribution is typically around 16 per cent.
  - Employee contribution rates vary considerably, ranging from 3 per cent to 15 per cent with a median of around 8 per cent.
- *Pension fund:*
  - Employee and employer contributions are paid into a combined fund and there is no direct link between fund size and the pensions paid.
  - The money remaining in the fund after any lump sums have been taken out is invested in an annuity to provide a regular income the amount of which may be revised upwards periodically to compensate for inflation.
- *Dependants.* Dependants are entitled to a percentage of the employee's pension entitlement if he or she dies during retirement or in service with the company.
- *Lump sum.* Part of the pension may be exchanged for a tax-free lump sum up to a maximum under Inland Revenue rules of 1/80th per year for up to 40 years' service.

Defined contribution (money purchase) schemes

The main features of defined contribution schemes are as follows:

- *Pension entitlement.* The employee receives a pension on retirement that is related to the size of the fund accumulated by the combined contributions of the employee and employer. The amount of the pension depends on the size of contributions, the rate of return on the investment of the accumulated fund and the rate of return on an annuity purchased by the employer. It is not related to the employee's final salary.

- *Contributions:*
  - The employer contributes a defined percentage of earnings, which may be fixed, age-related or linked to what the employee pays. The level of employer contribution is typically around 6 per cent.
  - The employee also contributes a fixed percentage of salary.
- *Pension fund:*
  - The contributions are invested and the money used at retirement to purchase a regular income, usually via an annuity contract from an insurance company. The retirement pension is therefore whatever annual payment can be purchased with the money accumulated in the fund for a member.
  - Members have individual shares of the fund, which represent their personal entitlements and which will directly determine the pensions they receive.
- *Dependants.* Dependants receive death-in-service and death-in-retirement pensions.
- *Lump sum.* One-quarter of the pension can be taken as a tax-free lump sum on retirement.

Comparison of defined benefit and defined contribution schemes

The main differences are that a defined benefit (final salary) scheme provides a guaranteed pension to the employee but the employer is unable to predict the costs, which can fluctuate unfavourably. Conversely, a defined contribution (money purchase) scheme provides an uncertain pension and the cost to the employer is predictable. The differences are summarized in Table 32.1.

Defined benefit or defined contribution?

Defined benefit scheme costs and risks

Defined benefit schemes are more costly to employers (16 per cent average contribution) than defined contribution schemes (6 per cent average contribution). They are also more risky for employers because the pension is based on a guaranteed formula and the cost of providing this guaranteed benefit may be higher than expected. Typically, employee contributions are fixed and those of the employer vary on the basis of specialist advice from the scheme actuary. Hence, the risk of higher-than-expected costs falls on the employer. Costs might exceed expectations for a number of reasons, for example pensioners are living longer (an important factor in putting up costs), the fund investments perform less well than expected (another important factor recently) or salaries grow faster than expected. Costs have in fact increased significantly in many schemes and as a result some large pension funds are in deficit.

Table 32.1 Comparison of defined benefit and defined contribution schemes

Defined Benefit (Final Salary)	Defined Contribution (Money Purchase)
Benefits defined as a fraction of final pensionable pay	Benefits purchased as an annuity by an accumulation of contributions invested
Benefits do not depend on investment returns or annuity rates	Benefits dependent on investment returns, contributions, and cost of annuities at retirement
Employer contributes necessary costs in excess of employee contributions	Employer contributions are fixed
Employer takes financial risk	Member takes financial risk
Not easily portable to other employers	Easily portable to other employers
Benefits appropriate for long-serving employees with progressive increases in pensionable pay	Benefits appropriate for short-serving employees or those whose pensionable pay fluctuates

Defined contribution scheme costs and risks

In a defined contribution scheme the cost of employer contributions is predictable and generally lower than in defined benefit schemes. However, there is a risk that the resulting pension falls short of expectations because the fund investments perform poorly or because the annuity rate (ie the conversion rate from lump sum to regular pension) is unfavourable. This risk falls on the employee.

The move toward defined contribution schemes

Many leading companies have questioned the financial wisdom of final salary provision. Defined benefit schemes provide much more value to older and longer-serving employees, but greater labour mobility has led many employers to question this emphasis, particularly in newer industries with young, high-turnover workforces.

However, defined benefit schemes are still the most popular. The CIPD 2005 reward management survey (3) established that 56 per cent of employers had such schemes while 26 per cent had defined contribution schemes. But the CIPD 2006 reward management survey (4) found that most new employees in the private sector will be offered a defined contribution scheme. The public sector has so far mostly retained its defined benefit schemes (84 per cent in 2005).

Defined benefit schemes are liked by employees and trade unions because they produce a guaranteed income. Trade unions are therefore always hostile to any move towards defined contribution schemes. Such a move will appear to threaten personal security and be detrimental. Even if the change is restricted to new staff, existing employees may well believe that it will be applied to them sometime. To avoid a major upset in employee relations, employers have to convince their staff that they will not be affected in the future, and they have to mean what they say. If they don't, any trust that exists between them and their employees will be destroyed.

Rather than change to a defined contribution scheme some companies have taken steps to reduce final salary scheme costs. This means retaining final salary provision but with some benefits scaled back. For example, employers have reduced the accrual rate from 1/60th per year of service to 1/80th or, more commonly, have increased employee contributions. Employees and unions are likely to resist such changes but may eventually be persuaded that they are better than a move towards defined contribution provision.

OTHER TYPES OF PENSION SCHEMES

Hybrid schemes

Hybrid schemes aim to split the risk between both parties although only 3 per cent of the CIPD respondents had them. Examples of such schemes include:

- *Combined final salary/defined contribution scheme.* Under this approach, both types of scheme are in operation. A final salary scheme might be provided for staff that meet an age and/or service qualification, with defined contribution provision applying to other staff.
- *Career average revalued earnings (CARE) scheme.* This is a type of defined benefit scheme. Instead of pension being based on final salary, the employee receives a pension proportional to service and career average salary, with salary from earlier years revalued by the Retail Price Index. These produce lower pensions than a final salary scheme.
- *Cash balance scheme.* Employees are provided with a guaranteed individual retirement fund proportional to service and final or average salary. As in a defined contribution scheme, a proportion may be taken as cash with the balance being used to buy an annuity.

- *Schemes with an element of discretion.* Low-level guaranteed benefits are provided, perhaps on a final salary or career average basis. However, there is discretion to provide enhanced pensions as and when the scheme's funding position allows it. A variant of this approach is to operate a defined contribution scheme with a modest final salary (or career average salary) guarantee.
- *Capped final salary.* A self-imposed cap is applied to pensionable salary with defined contribution provision on the excess salary. The logic here is that it is reasonable to transfer some risk to the employee once a basic level of guaranteed retirement income has been built up.

Personal pensions

Employers cannot compel their employees to join their scheme. As an alternative, employees can take out their own personal pension plan from an approved provider, either as an alternative to an occupational scheme provided by the employer or because there is no occupational scheme available. Personal pension schemes can be contracted out of the state pension scheme and may take contributions from an employer. They are defined contribution (ie money purchase) schemes, which means that the pension is based on what has been paid into the scheme and not on final salary.

Group schemes

Group schemes are in effect a bundle of individual personal pensions for which the employer carries out a payroll function by remitting contributions to a pensions provider.

Stakeholder pension

A stakeholder pension is a government-sponsored scheme, primarily designed for individuals earning less than about £20,000. Employers who do not provide a suitable pension scheme for their employees are required by law to offer access to a stakeholder scheme. A suitable pension scheme will be either an occupational pension scheme or a group scheme.

A stakeholder pension is a defined contribution arrangement that satisfies certain conditions, designed to ensure that it provides good value for money and that members' interests are protected. These conditions are:

- *flexible contributions* – members must be free to pay contributions they wish;
- *charges* – the maximum charge is 1.5 per cent of the fund;
- *transfers* – the scheme will be required to accept transfer payments;

- *FSA regulation* – all stakeholder schemes will be regulated by the Financial Services Agency;
- *investments* – the scheme must offer a default investment scheme for members who are unwilling to choose between different funds.

Executive pensions

In the private sector, executive pensions are typically provided for by a defined benefit scheme with an accelerated accrual compared to that for other staff. Instead of providing a maximum two-thirds pension after 40 years of service (an accrual rate of 1/60th per year of service), a full pension may be earned after only 20 or 30 years' service (equivalent to an accrual rate of 1/30th or 1/45th). The two-thirds pension provided is normally inclusive of any pensions from previous employments.

THE STATE PENSION SCHEME

State pension arrangements are subject to change, and this section is based on the current (2007) arrangements. The state pension scheme has two parts, as described below.

The basic state pension

The basic state pension is paid at a standard rate, which may be increased each year as long as the required number of national insurance contributions have been paid.

The state second pension (S2P)

The state second pension (formerly SERPS) pays a pension on earnings for which Class 1 national insurance contributions have been paid over the years that fall between the lower and the upper earnings limit. The lower earnings limit corresponds roughly with the flat-rate pension for a single person while the upper limit is currently about eight times the lower earnings limit. Both limits are adjusted from time to time.

Employers and individuals with a personal pension plan can contract out of S2P. Occupational pension schemes will be able to contract out if they meet an overall quality test. When a scheme is contracted out, both the employer and the employee pay national insurance contributions at a lower rate.

ADVISING EMPLOYEES ON PENSIONS

The Financial Services Act 1986 and the Pensions Act 1995 place restrictions on the provision of financial advice to employees. Only those who are directly authorized by one of the regulatory organizations or professional bodies are permitted to give detailed financial advice on investments. This includes specific advice on the merits or otherwise of a particular personal pension plan – personal pensions are classed as investments by the Financial Services Act. Information can, however, be given to employees:

- on the company's occupational pension scheme, since it is not classed as an investment;
- about the general principles to be borne in mind when comparing an occupational pension scheme with a personal pension; these could include spelling out the benefits of the company's scheme, thus leaving employees in a better position to compare the benefits with whatever an authorized adviser may indicate are the benefits from a personal plan – what should not be done is to tell people categorically that they will be better off with the company's scheme or to advise them to look elsewhere;
- on the rights for staff who are leaving to preserve their pension and the advisability of finding out from their prospective employer whether existing rights can be transferred to the new company's scheme and, if so, what the outcome will be in terms of pension rights at the new company;
- on the general advantages of making additional voluntary contributions.

HR specialists should restrict themselves to giving information. They should never suggest what people should do. If in any doubt as to how to respond to a request for information or advice it is best to refer the matter to the company's own pension specialist or adviser or, if none is available, suggest that the employee should talk to an authorized adviser, for example the individual's own insurance company or bank.

DEVELOPING AND COMMUNICATING PENSIONS POLICIES

The pension benefits provided by employers should be developed as an important part of a coherent total reward package. Good schemes demonstrate that employers care about the future security and well-being of their employees, and pensions are a valuable means of gaining and keeping employee commitment to the organization. Younger and more mobile employees are often indifferent to pensions but the older they get the more they are concerned, and these mature employees contribute largely to organizational success.

Careful consideration needs to be given to telling employees about the scheme. They need to know how it works and how it benefits them – it is too easy for employees to take pensions for granted. It is particularly important to communicate the reasons for any changes, and staff should be involved in discussing the reason for the proposed arrangements and given the opportunity to comment on them. As stated by the CIPD (2), HR professionals have a key role to play 'in being honest about the real picture and its alternatives, and educating their staff'.

GOVERNMENT PROPOSALS ON THE FUTURE OF PENSIONS

The Government's White Paper on pensions reform published in May 2006 made the following proposals:

- A new low-cost savings scheme will be introduced in which employees will be automatically enrolled unless their employer already has an occupational scheme with automatic enrolment. Employers will make matching contributions while the employee chooses to remain in the scheme.
- There will be a higher, fairer state pension re-linked to earnings.
- The state pension age will rise to 66 by 2026, 67 by 2036 and 68 by 2046.
- The number of qualifying years needed to receive a full state pension will be cut to 30.
- Contracting out for defined contribution schemes will be abolished.

REFERENCES

1   Pensions Commission (2004) *Report*, Department for Work and Pensions, London
2   Chartered Institute of Personnel and Development (2002) *Pensions and HR's Role: A guide*, CIPD, London
3   Chartered Institute of Personnel and Development (2005) *Reward Management: A survey of policy and practice*, CIPD, London
4   Chartered Institute of Personnel and Development (2006) *Reward Management: A survey of policy and practice*, CIPD, London

Part 8

Reward management procedures

33

Managing reward

Managing reward systems is a complex and demanding business. This chapter deals with the subject in seven parts:

1. reward procedures for grading jobs, determining levels of pay and hearing appeals;
2. controlling reward: preparation and use of forecasts and budgets, costing, monitoring and evaluating reward policies and practices and obtaining value for money;
3. conducting general pay reviews;
4. conducting individual reviews;
5. communicating to employees, collectively and individually;
6. managing the development of reward systems: the process, involving employees, managing change;
7. the use of computers in reward management.

The responsibilities for reward management are covered in Chapter 34.

REWARD PROCEDURES

Reward procedures deal with grading jobs, fixing rates of pay and handling appeals.

Grading jobs

The procedures for grading jobs set out how job evaluation should be used to grade a new job or regrade an existing one. A point-factor evaluation scheme that has defined grades may be used for all new jobs and to deal with requests for regrading. However, an analytical matching process (see Chapter 11) may be used to compare the role profiles of the jobs to be graded with grade or level profiles or profiles of benchmark jobs. This is likely to be the case in large organizations and for broad-banded structures.

Fixing rates of pay on appointment

The procedure should indicate how much freedom line managers and HR have to pay above the minimum rate for the job. The freedom may be limited to, say, 10 per cent above the minimum or two or three pay points on an incremental scale. More scope is sometimes allowed to respond to market rate pressures or to attract particularly well-qualified staff by paying up to the reference point or target salary in a pay range, subject to HR approval and bearing in mind the need to provide scope for contingent pay increases. If market supplements or recruitment premiums are used the rules for offering them to candidates must be clearly defined.

Promotion increases

The procedure will indicate what is regarded as a meaningful increase on promotion, often 10 per cent or more. To avoid creating anomalies, the level of pay has to take account of what other people are paid who are carrying out work at a similar level and it is usual to lay down a maximum level that does not take the pay of the promoted employee above the reference point for the new range.

Equal pay reviews

The procedure for conducting equal pay reviews (see Chapter 14) should be defined.

Appeals

It is customary to include the right to appeal against gradings as part of a job evaluation procedure (see Chapter 12). Appeals against pay decisions are usually made through the organization's grievance procedure.

CONTROLLING REWARD

The implementation of reward policies and procedures should be monitored and controlled to ensure that value for money is obtained. Control is easier if the grade and pay structure is well defined and clear guidelines exist on how it and the benefits arrangements should be managed. Control should be based on forecasts, budgets and costings, and by monitoring and evaluating the implementation of reward policies as described below.

Reward forecasts

It is necessary to forecast future payroll costs taking into account the number of people employed and the impact of pay reviews and contingent pay awards. The cost implications of developments such as a revised job evaluation scheme, a new grade and pay structure or a flexible benefits scheme also have to be forecast.

Reward budgets

Pay review budgets set out the increase in payroll costs that will result for either general or individual pay reviews and are used for cost forecasts generally and as the basis for the guidelines issued to line managers on conducting individual reviews.

Total payroll budgets are based on the number of people employed in different jobs and their present and forecast rates of pay. In a budgetary control system they are aggregated from the budgets prepared by departmental managers but HR provides guidance on the allowances that should be made for pay increases. The aim is to maintain control over payroll costs and restrain managers from the temptation to overpay their staff.

Costing reward processes

Proposed changes to the reward system need to be costed for approval by senior management. The costs will include development costs such as consultants' fees, software, literature, additional staff and, possibly, the opportunity costs arising when staff are seconded to a development project.

Implementation costs also have to be projected. A new grade and pay structure, for example, can easily result in an increase to the payroll of 3 or 4 per cent. New contingent pay schemes may also cost more although the aim should be to make them self-financing.

Monitoring and evaluating reward policies and practices

The effectiveness of reward policies and practices should be monitored and evaluated against the requirements of the organization. Evaluation should compare outcomes with the objectives set for the new practice (this is why setting objectives for reward initiatives is so important). Twenty aspects of reward policy and practice that need to be monitored and evaluated are set out below:

1. the existence of realistic, innovative and integrated reward strategies;
2. progress towards developing a total reward approach;
3. the practicality and comprehensiveness of reward policies and how well they are applied;
4. the effectiveness of the job evaluation scheme from the point of view of the extent to which it has decayed, how relevant it is to present working arrangements, the degree to which it provides the basis for fair and equitable grading decisions and for preventing grade drift and whether or not it is too bureaucratic or time-consuming;
5. progress towards achieving equal pay for work of equal value (using equal pay review procedures as explained in Chapter 14);
6. the availability of accurate and usable information on market rates;
7. the appropriateness of the grade and pay structure using the criteria set out in Chapter 18 as the basis for evaluation;
8. the distribution of actual salaries and the extent to which it conforms to policy guidelines by mid-point management as described below;
9. the extent to which pay levels are competitive and contribute to the attraction and retention of high-quality staff;
10. whether or not value for money is being obtained from the contingent pay arrangements with reference to their costs and benefits (the latter assessed as far as possible in terms of their impact on motivation and the degree to which they contribute to developing a performance culture);
11. the incidence of attrition to pay costs that takes place when employees enter jobs at lower rates of pay than the previous job holders and the implications for pay policy (large attrition rates may reduce and therefore justify contingent pay costs);
12. the effectiveness of performance management processes with regard to how they function in terms of fairness, equity and consistency, the contribution they make to achieving total reward objectives, and the quality of the outcomes as means of informing contingent pay decisions;

13. the range of employee benefits provided, the extent to which they provide value for money in terms of increasing employee job satisfaction and commitment and the effectiveness of any flexible benefits arrangements;
14. the benefits provided by the pensions scheme and their cost;
15. the quality of the budgetary control arrangements;
16. the cost of the implementation of pay reviews against budget;
17. the degree to which the benefits of reward innovations justify the costs;
18. the opinions of employees about the reward system, which can be obtained by means of regular attitude surveys (an example of a reward opinion survey is given in Figure 5.5);
19. the capacity of line managers to carry out their managing reward duties;
20. the quality of the communications to employees about the reward system and the extent to which they understand how it operates.

Mid-point management

'Mid-point management' techniques analyse and control pay policies by comparing actual pay with the reference point. This is regarded as the policy pay level, ie the competitive rate of pay for a fully qualified, competent and experienced individual. 'Compa-ratios' can be used to measure the relationship between actual and policy rates of pay as a percentage. If the two coincide, the compa-ratio is 100 per cent.

Compa-ratio analysis can cover the pay of all job holders, which, for example, might indicate that if the compa-ratio is less than 100 per cent pay practice is falling behind pay policy and something might have to be done to ensure that pay levels remain competitive. Compa-ratio analysis is also carried out for individuals, so that a compa-ratio of, say, 95 per cent shows that if the individual is fully competent an increase of 5 per cent is required to bring pay into line. Individual compa-ratio analysis is also used as a means of guiding contingent pay increases through a pay matrix as described in Chapter 19.

Obtaining value for money

Assessing the value for money provided by existing practices or by new practices when they are implemented is a major consideration when monitoring and evaluating reward management processes. Evaluating the cost of innovations may lead to the reconsideration of proposals to ensure that they will provide value for money. Evaluating the value for money obtained from existing reward practices leads to the identification of areas for improvement.

Affordability is, or should be, a major issue when examining reward management developments and existing practices. Value for money is achieved when the benefits of a reward practice either exceed its cost or at least justify the cost. At the development stage it is therefore necessary to carry out cost/benefit assessments. The two fundamental questions to be answered are 1): what business needs will this proposal meet? and 2) how will the proposal meet the needs? The costs and benefits of existing practices should also be assessed on the same basis.

CONDUCTING GENERAL PAY REVIEWS

General reviews take place when employees are given an increase in response to general market rate movements, a rise in the cost of living or union negotiations. General reviews are often combined with individual reviews but employees are usually informed of the general and individual components of any increase they receive. Alternatively the general review may be conducted separately to enable better control to be achieved over costs and to focus employees' attention on the performance-related aspect of their remuneration at a later individual review. Employees expect that general reviews will maintain the purchasing power of their pay by compensating for increases in the cost of living. They will want their levels of pay to be competitive with what they could earn outside. And they will want to be rewarded fairly and equitably for the contribution they make.

Some organizations have completely abandoned the use of across-the-board reviews. They argue that the decision on what people should be paid should be an individual matter, taking into account the personal contribution people are making and their 'market worth' – how they as individuals are valued in the marketplace. This enables the organization to adopt a more flexible approach to allocating pay increases in accordance with the perceived value of individuals to the organization.

The steps required to conduct a general review are:

1. Decide on the budget.
2. Analyse data on pay settlements made by comparable organizations and rates of inflation.
3. Conduct negotiations with trade unions as required.
4. Calculate costs.
5. Adjust the pay structure – by either increasing the pay brackets of each grade by the percentage general increase or by increasing pay reference points by the overall percentage and applying different increases to the upper or lower limits of the bracket, thus altering the shape of the structure.
6. Inform employees.

CONDUCTING INDIVIDUAL REVIEWS

Individual pay reviews determine contingent pay increases or bonuses. The e-reward 2004 *Survey of Contingent Pay* (1) found that the average size of the contingent pay awards made by respondents was 3.3 per cent. Individual awards may be based on ratings, an overall assessment that does not depend on ratings, or ranking as discussed below.

Individual pay reviews based on ratings

Managers propose increases on the basis of their performance management ratings within a given pay review budget and in accordance with pay review guidelines. Forty-two per cent of the respondents to the CIPD 2003/04 performance management survey (cited in Armstrong and Baron, 2) used ratings to inform contingent pay decisions. Approaches to rating were discussed in Chapter 24.

There is a choice of methods. Either a pay matrix is used as described in Chapter 19 or there is a direct link between the rating and the pay increase, for example:

Rating	Percentage Increase
A	6
B	4
C	3
D	2
E	0

As mentioned in Chapter 24, many people argue that linking performance management too explicitly to pay prejudices the essential developmental nature of performance management. However, realistically it is accepted that decisions on performance-related or contribution-related increases have to be based on some form of assessment. One solution is to 'decouple' performance management and the pay review by holding them several months apart, and 45 per cent of the respondents to the CIPD 2003/04 survey separated performance management reviews from pay reviews (43 per cent of the respondents to the e-reward 2004 survey (1) separated the review). There is still a read-across but it is not so immediate. Some try to do without formulaic approaches (ratings and pay matrices) altogether although it is impossible to dissociate contingent pay completely from some form of assessment.

Doing without ratings

Of total respondents to the 2004 e-reward survey of contingent pay, 27 per cent did without ratings. The percentage of respondents to the 2003/04 CIPD performance management survey who did not use ratings was 52 per cent (this figure is too high to be fully reliable and may have been inflated by those who treat service-related increments, which do not depend on ratings, as contingent pay). One respondent to the e-reward survey explained that, in the absence of ratings, the approach they used was 'informed subjectivity', which meant considering ongoing performance in the form of overall contribution.

Some companies adopt what might be called a holistic approach. Managers propose where people should be placed in the pay range for their grade, taking into account their contribution and pay relative to others in similar jobs, their potential and the relationship of their current pay to market rates. The decision may be expressed in the form of a statement that an individual is now worth £21,000 rather than £20,000. The increase is 5 per cent, but what counts is the overall view about the value of a person to the organization, not the percentage increase to that person's pay.

Examples of approaches to pay reviews without the use of ratings or a pay matrix are given below.

Aegon UK

The reward system at Aegon UK is designed to recognize three core factors that affect the level of pay that individuals should receive for their 'personal commitment and consistent contribution within their roles'. These are:

1. *internal job value* – the bigger the job, the higher the reward;
2. *external job value* – the level of reward will be influenced by external market rates and the degree to which market forces affect the salaries required to attract and retain quality staff;
3. *value of the person* – individual employees may be rewarded at a higher level because they are making a greater contribution, are performing better, are meeting objectives and have achieved a higher level of skill or competence than their colleagues (measured through the performance management process).

As an internal policy statement explains: 'Whilst the first two factors are the primary responsibility of the compensation and benefits function in group personnel, line managers are best placed to manage the third factor for all staff within their reporting teams.'

GlaxoSmithKline

At GlaxoSmithKline salaries are reviewed annually, usually in April. For individuals on grades A to E, their pay rise is determined by:

- their achievement of objectives;
- their 'behaviours';
- their position in the range;
- their position with regard to their peers;
- their salary in relation to the market;
- the position of the pay ranges with regard to the market;
- the available budget.

Lloyds TSB

To ensure that salary awards are fair and consistent, when making pay decisions for individuals, Lloyds TSB's broad guidelines suggest managers should consider:

- what the individual's current role and pay position is in the salary range;
- what people in the same or similar roles are being paid;
- how they value the individual's skills, competencies and performance in this role, relative to the nearest pay reference point;
- what the function and geographical market rate is for this role;
- what recent pay awards the individual has received;
- expectations – they should conduct a dialogue with their people about where they are and where they could be;
- any other relevant factors such as the degree of challenge of the job, the amount of learning required, and the individual's recent performance history.

Ranking

Ranking is carried out by managers who place staff in a rank order according to an overall assessment of relative contribution or merit and then distribute performance ratings through the rank order. The top 10 per cent could get an A rating, the next 15 per cent a B rating and so on. The ratings determine the size of the reward. But ranking depends on what could be invidious comparisons and only works when there are a number of people in similar jobs to be ranked.

Guidelines to managers on conducting individual pay reviews

Whichever approach is adopted, guidelines have to be issued to managers on how they should conduct reviews. These guidelines will stipulate that they must keep within their budgets and may indicate the maximum and minimum increases that can be awarded with an indication of how awards could be distributed, eg when the budget is 4 per cent overall, it might be suggested that a 3 per cent increase should be given to the majority of their staff and the others given higher or lower increases as long as the total percentage increase does not exceed the budget. Managers in some companies are instructed that they must follow a forced pattern of distribution but only 8 per cent of the respondents to the 2003/04 CIPD survey used this method. To help them to explore alternatives, managers may be provided with a spreadsheet facility in which the spreadsheets contain details of the existing rates of staff and which can be used to model alternative distributions on a 'what if' basis. Managers may also be encouraged to 'fine-tune' their pay recommendations to ensure that individuals are on the right track within their grade according to their level of performance, competence and time in the job compared with their peers. To do this, they need guidelines on typical rates of progression in relation to performance, skill or competence and specific guidance on what they can and should do. They also need information on the relative positions of their staff in the pay structure in relation to the policy guidelines.

Conducting individual pay reviews

The steps required to conduct an individual pay review are:

1. Agree the budget.
2. Prepare and issue guidelines on the size, range and distribution of awards and on the methods of conducting the review.
3. Provide advice and support.
4. Review the proposals against the budget and guidelines and agree modifications to them if necessary.
5. Summarize and cost the proposals and obtain approval.
6. Update the payroll.
7. Inform employees.

It is essential to provide advice, guidance and training to line managers as required. Some managers will be confident and capable from the start. Others will have a lot to learn.

COMMUNICATING TO EMPLOYEES

Transparency is important. Employees need to know how reward policies will affect them and how pay and grading decisions have been made. They need to be convinced that the system is fair.

Communicating to employees collectively

Employees and their representatives should be informed about the guiding principles and policies that underpin the reward system and the reward strategies that drive it. They should understand the grade and pay structure, how grading decisions are made, including the job evaluation system, how their pay can progress within the structure, the basis upon which contingent pay increases are determined and policies on the provision of benefits including details of a flexible benefits scheme if one is available.

Communications at Diageo

Nicki Demby, formerly Performance and Reward Director at Diageo, believes that an essential feature of any implementation programme is the very clear, effective and regular communication of aims, methods of operation and the impact. Transparency is essential. But for Nicki Demby it is imperative not only to explain the planned changes, the rationale behind them, and how they affect the workforce, but also to communicate details of who was involved in the development process so that unnecessary fears are allayed.

Communications at Lloyds TSB

Lloyds TSB feels it is imperative to communicate to staff in advance of launch and at every stage of the process, explaining the planned changes, the rationale behind them, and how they affect the workforce. It is necessary to continue to give progress reports to employees and obtain their input on an ongoing basis thereafter. It requires consistent communication to employees, who must have a clear understanding of why total reward is being introduced and how it will affect them.

However, as Tim Fevyer, Senior Manager, Compensation and Benefits, admits, communicating a wide-ranging change programme is onerous: 'Getting a consistent message across and getting people to understand what the business is trying to achieve is very difficult when rolling out a reward strategy over six, seven and eight years.'

Communicating to individual employees

Individual employees should understand how their grade, present rate of pay and pay increases have been determined and the pay opportunities available to them – the scope for pay progression and how their contribution will be assessed through performance management. They should be informed of the value of the benefits they receive so that they are aware of their total remuneration and, if appropriate, how they can exercise choice over the range or scale of their benefits through a flexible benefits scheme.

MANAGING THE DEVELOPMENT OF REWARD SYSTEMS

The development process is illustrated in Figure 33.1.

Involving employees

Employees should be treated as stakeholders and given every opportunity to contribute to the development of reward policies and practices. This is a matter of involvement in working parties, project teams and panels, not just consultation, although the normal consultative channels have to be used.

Trade unions and their representatives should be involved in the initial stages, to sound out their opinions and reach as much agreement as possible on what needs to be done, especially if this affects job evaluation, pay structures, contingent pay schemes and flexible benefits. The approaches used in three leading organizations to involving people are given below.

Involvement at B&Q

As Will Astill, Reward Manager, B&Q, explains:

> A key challenge is getting the people in all of the different departments involved in the project – recruitment, employment policy, internal communications, human resources and reward – to work together. If change strategies do not carry everyone in the organization willingly forward, the process can be painful and even damaging. So it's vital that the reward manager builds relationships with the right people. You need to get key individuals to work together without them feeling that they are losing control of their initiatives. Never underestimate the value of in-depth employee consultation. It is necessary to spend money on professional research – market research, HR consultants to design and facilitate focus groups – as though you are conducting a market research exercise. Employees are consumers. You need to sell the initiative to them and help them understand why it is taking place.

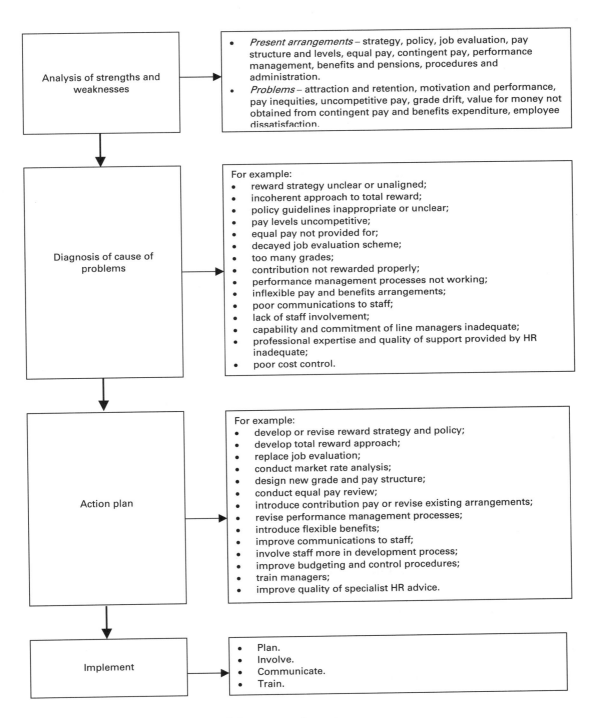

Figure 33.1 Development of the reward system

Involvement at Centrica

At Centrica, employee involvement in designing the new reward package was considered vital. Focus groups were held, attended by some 200 staff. These took the form of structured workshops, which looked at pay, progression, bonuses, holidays, pensions and attitudes to flexibility both in benefit provision and in working time.

The focus groups explained current provision for British Gas Trading and ex-Enron staff and flagged up options for the future. But their most important role was to get an idea of what employees wanted. A union representative attended all the focus groups and played an important part in reassuring staff that the changes were voluntary, and that the function of the workshops was to gain input as to how the pay and benefits spend could be redistributed in a way that suited staff better than the current arrangements.

The outcome of the workshops was that staff believed, correctly, that they were driving the redesign of the reward package, and this helped to dispel any suspicions as to what the company might be planning. What employees wanted was:

- pay in line with the market;
- transparency in pay progression;
- reviews based on performance;
- meaningful bonus potential;
- more frequent bonus payments;
- to be able to retain the final salary pension;
- to keep existing holiday entitlement;
- to be able to trade holidays for other benefits;
- flexibility and choice over benefits.

The next step was to validate these findings. This was done through a series of additional workshops and presentations to the workshop participants, who were asked to confirm that they agreed with them. Once this had happened, work began on designing a reward package that would meet employees' requirements.

Involvement at Lloyds TSB

Tim Fevyer, Senior Manager, Compensation and Benefits, Lloyds TSB, recommends that: 'The success of new reward systems depends heavily on talking to people, and asking what they would like to see. There is much to be said for involving line managers and listening to what employees and their representatives regard as important.' Indeed involvement is seen as a cornerstone of the bank's total reward programme. A range of approaches is used to involve employees, to capture meaningful data and to gain an understanding of employee needs and the rewards that motivate them to deliver results. But Lloyds TSB finds that the best ways are through carefully crafted attitude surveys, focus groups and the like. 'When creating our compelling employment offer, we talked to people and found out what the key trends were. We undertook research about what is really compelling for employees. It is an essential preliminary to any reward strategy.'

Change management

The introduction of new job evaluation schemes, pay structures and contingent pay arrangements concerns employees, who may be alarmed at the possibility that they will be adversely affected. It is therefore necessary to pay particular attention to change management during the development and implementation of reward practices. The following approaches should be adopted:

1. Mobilize commitment to change through the joint analysis of problems.
2. Develop a shared vision of how to organize and manage change to achieve agreed goals.
3. Foster consensus for the new vision, competence to enact it and cohesion to move it along.
4. Institutionalize change through formal policies, processes and practices.
5. Monitor and adjust policies and practices in response to problems emerging during the change process.

The key points emerging from these suggestions are the need for involvement (giving managers and employees a voice) and communications and training as part of a planned approach to implementation.

HR practitioners have an important role in managing change. Lynda Gratton (3) stresses the need for them to: 'Understand the state of the company, the extent of the embedding of processes and structures throughout the organization, and the behaviour and attitudes of individual employees.' She believes that 'The challenge is to implement the ideas' and the solution is to 'build a guiding coalition by involving line managers, which means creating issue-based cross-functional action teams that will initially make recommendations and later move into action'. This approach 'builds the capacity to change'.

Paul Craven, Compensation Director, R & D, GlaxoSmithKline, summed up his approach to change when he said: 'Don't expect people to change overnight and don't try to force change. It is better to reinforce desirable behaviour than to attempt to enforce a particular way of doing things.'

THE USE OF COMPUTERS IN REWARD MANAGEMENT

The ever-evolving world of IT and electronic communications has changed how salary data are reviewed and managed quite radically in the last decade. Applications and data can now be accessed and assessed from almost anywhere in the world; organizations are making increasing use of the internet, data on market rates and pay settlements are published on the internet and users can communicate at speed through e-mail. Computers and software are becoming more and more powerful and sophisticated. HR or reward specialists can analyse the implications of new grade structures, cost pay review matrices and plan salary reviews, and options can rapidly be costed through simple changes on a spreadsheet. 'Self-serve' systems enable line management to carry out a number of reward tasks such as pay reviews. Increasing use is being made of computers to support reward administration and decision making in the areas of:

- providing an employee reward database;
- job evaluation;
- grade and pay structure modelling;
- pay review modelling;
- equal pay reviews.

The employee reward database

The employee reward database stores data on employees' pay, earnings and benefits so that they can be updated, processed and communicated as information to users. The database consists of systematically organized and interrelated sets of files (collections of records serving as the basic unit of data storage) and allows for combinations of data to be selected as required by different users. It contains information imported from the payroll or personnel information system. This information may include personal and job details, job grade, basic pay, position in the pay range (compa-ratio), earnings through variable pay, pay history (progression, and general and individual pay increases), performance management ratings, details of employee benefits, pension contributions, contributions to save-as-you-earn schemes and the choices made under a flexible benefits system, including pension contributions.

The database can be used to:

- produce listings of employees by job category, job grade, rate of pay, position in range and size in actual or percentage terms of the last increase and, if required, previous individual performance pay increases;

- generate reports analysing distributions of pay by grade, including compa-ratios for each grade and the organization as a whole – extracts from these reports can be downloaded to the personal computers of managers responsible for pay decisions to assist them in conducting pay reviews;
- initiate and print notifications of pay increases and update the payroll database;
- use electronic mail facilities to transmit data.

In using the database it is necessary that the provisions of the Data Protection Act 1998 are met. This requires *inter alia* that personal data held for any purpose should not be used or disclosed in any manner incompatible with that purpose, and appropriate security measures must be taken against unauthorized access to or disclosure of those data. If data are going to be downloaded it will be essential to control who gets what. The importance of data protection will also have to be spelt out to managers.

Computer-assisted job evaluation

Computers can be used to help directly with job evaluation processes as described in Chapter 11.

Software packages

Micro-based software packages have been developed to carry out the various processes referred to above. Proprietary software is usually designed as a standard software shell within which there are a number of functions that allow users to customize the system to meet their own needs.

Grade and pay structure modelling

Software packages available from firms such as Link Consultants and Pilat UK use the output from a computerized job evaluation exercise contained in the database to model alternative grade structures by reference to the distribution of points scores against the existing pay rates for the jobs covered by job evaluation. The computer produces a scattergram and a trend line showing the relationship between pay and the job evaluation scores. The program will then enable a proposed grade structure to he superimposed on the scattergram, which identifies those jobs above or below the new grade boundaries. The cost of bringing the pay of those below the new boundaries to the minimum rate for their new grades is then calculated by the computer.

Alternative grade configurations can then be superimposed on the scattergram to find out if the number of jobs below the lower limits of their new grades will be reduced. The computer then calculates the lower costs of bringing the fewer jobs up to the minimum. This modelling process can continue until the optimum configuration of grades from the point of view of costs is achieved. A decision can then be made if this grade structure or one of the others should be selected. The lowest-cost option will not necessarily be chosen as it might produce an unmanageable grade structure, eg too few grades with too much scope for pay progression within them.

Pay review modelling

General reviews

The computer can use the database to provide information on the total cost of a proposed general pay review and the effect this will have on other costs, for example pensions. It can then model alternative levels. Computers can model the effect on costs of alternative increases.

Individual reviews

It is now increasingly typical to manage pay reviews for an organization on an Excel or Lotus 1-2-3 spreadsheet, through which a number of alternative options can be tested. This provides line managers with a worksheet, divided into cells, into which can be inserted text, numbers or formulae. This allows the user to carry out complex 'what if' analyses of the impact on the pay review budget of alternative distributions of awards to staff. Analyses can be saved as a separate file for future recall when the proposals are approved. Spreadsheets can be printed out in report or graphical form. In some organizations line managers carry out the modelling themselves using a spreadsheet with data provided by HR, and their conclusions can be reviewed and approved and aggregated into an overall cost of the review analysed by departments. In others HR and reward specialists carry out salary reviews for each function or department with the relevant line managers on-site using a laptop.

The problem with spreadsheets is that they can be quite complex and do not always work well in larger applications. Software such as the Pay Modeller marketed by Link Consultants may be the answer to these problems.

Equal pay reviews

Software is available to support equal pay reviews and analyses. These range from database tools that enable data to be imported from a range of sources to generate pay gap analyses, such as the e-reward equal pay toolkit, to more sophisticated tools that allow for a broader range of analysis possibilities using different data cuts, including the tool developed by Link.

REFERENCES

1   e-reward (2004) *Survey of Contingent Pay*, e-reward.co.uk, Stockport
2   Armstrong, M and Baron, A (2004) *Performance Management: Action and impact*, Chartered Institute of Personnel and Development, London
3   Gratton, LA (2000) Real step change, *People Management*, 16 March, pp 27–30

34

Responsibility for reward

Reward strategy is formulated and actioned by people. Top management is in charge but HR professionals, especially reward specialists, are actively involved. Increasingly, however, it is line managers who have the responsibility for implementing reward policies and practices. This chapter deals with the roles of the reward professional and line managers. The chapter concludes with a brief note on the use of management consultants.

THE ROLE OF THE REWARD SPECIALIST

HR and reward specialists develop and implement reward strategies, policies and processes, administer and audit existing systems and provide advice and guidance to line managers. They deal with employee relations issues such as involvement, communications, negotiations, appeals and grievances.

The 2005 CIPD reward survey (1) asked reward specialists to indicate what they felt were their most important activities and which were the most time-consuming. The survey results are shown in Figure 34.1.

The most valuable activities are clearly in developing reward arrangements that support the business strategy and working with line managers as consultants to support this: 'Shifting our culture to a more performance-oriented business and aligning reward policies accordingly', as one head of reward in the survey put it. Yet significant portions of the function's time are still being absorbed in routine administrative activities and responding to immediate queries and crises.

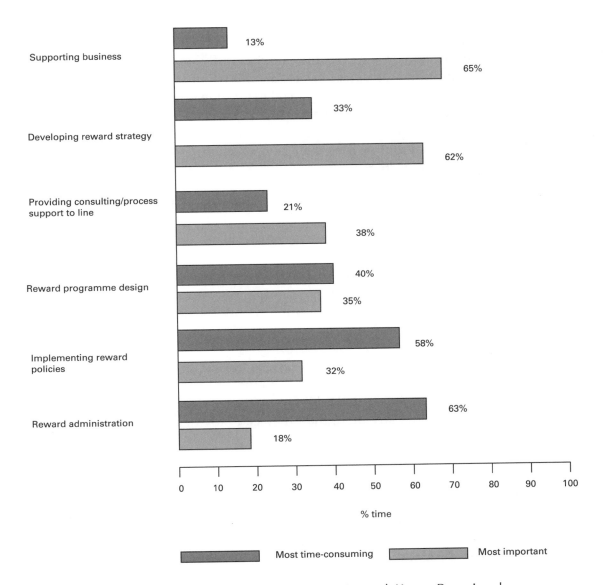

Source: M Armstrong and D Brown (2006) Strategic Reward, Kogan Page, London

Figure 34.1 The strategic work of reward professionals? Contrasting their most important and most time-consuming activities

Qualities required

As cited by Armstrong and Brown (2), John Campbell, HR Vice President for Citigroup, emphasizes the multiple, octopus-like requirements of the European regional compensation roles that he manages. They need to provide line managers with reliable external market data, set guidelines for and help to administer and monitor the merit review and annual bonus processes, design new bonus schemes and so on. Technical design skills are essential. But he sees their key contribution being to act as internal consultants and business partners:

- bringing parties together to facilitate and make sustainable and effective decisions;
- sharing experiences and transferring successes, while tailoring and adapting to local needs;
- encouraging a focus on long-term sustainability and future development;
- managing and coordinating communications;
- having the cultural sensitivity successfully to build relationships and teamwork based on trust and respect.

Above all, as he describes it, he needs in these jobs 'confident, bright people who can inform thinking, gain credibility, understand change, and move the business agenda along in a collaborative but influential role'. It is no use reward professionals just being 'strategic' in their thinking, any more than they can only design schemes on paper. They are equally concerned with service delivery.

Technical expertise

At the 2005 e-reward/CIPD Reward Symposium, Helen Murlis (3) characterized the role of the reward professional as that of the technical design craftsman, expert in all the techniques of pay and reward, knowing all the possibilities and the potential of the craft, and then designing something unique to meet the exact needs of the user, rather than 'banging out' standard products on the performance pay or broad-banding production line.

Change management

New reward policies can have a major effect on terms and conditions of employment. Inevitably, people will resist changes that they believe will have an adverse effect on them financially or conflict with their views on fairness and distributive justice. It is therefore essential for reward specialists to have change management skills.

ROLE OF THE FRONT-LINE MANAGER IN MANAGING REWARD

In the 2005 e-reward/CIPD Reward Symposium, the importance of line management capability was stressed by participants throughout the day. It was generally agreed that employees experience HR policies through the way their managers interpret them, and through the management skills they apply. Problems with understanding, conviction, capability and consistency were raised, and it was a more or less universal opinion that line managers needed more training and support if they were to carry out their reward duties such as performance management or recognition effectively. Line managers have to both commit to the reward strategy and be capable of implementing it.

Devolution of reward responsibilities to line managers

Many HR and reward professionals believe that more responsibility for managing reward should be devolved to line managers. But as the CIPD 2006 reward survey (4) revealed, the amount of discretion given to line managers to determine pay rises was limited on a scale of 1 to 5 to 2.21. This compares with 3.13 for training and development. And the survey confirmed a lack of confidence in the reward decision-making skills of line managers (2.02) and even less confidence in their reward communication skills (1.92).

Be that as it may, it can be argued that the whole implementation programme for any reward initiative should be the responsibility of the line management concerned, on the grounds that it is their system and they should own it. But HR and reward specialists can play a vital part in giving guidance and help in monitoring progress.

The main areas in which line managers have responsibility for reward are pay decisions, total reward, performance management and communicating to staff on reward matters. These are discussed below.

Pay decisions

When devolution of reward responsibilities to line managers does take place, it is often mainly concerned with pay decisions, as in the following examples.

Aegon UK

At Aegon UK department managers make pay recommendations for all their staff within the budgets agreed for each individual business unit, which is further devolved down to line managers in some areas of the organization. The recommendations are based upon the individual's actual performance over the previous year, as evidenced by the performance management review system. In cases where the target rate has moved, the affected individual's existing salary in relation to the target rate and performance zone is also taken into consideration.

Guidance is provided to line managers on the pay review process taking into consideration the individual's performance against the job description and required competences. Managers are able to make larger or smaller awards, providing there is a sound basis for their decision, so that the reward system is responsive to the individual performance of each member of staff.

As each department has different reward needs – dependent upon the profile of staff within the area – there is scope for flexibility in the guideline budget at departmental level. So a department with a high number of staff developing into their roles but under their relevant performance zone threshold may require a higher level of pay funding than a similar department where the majority of staff are already competent and continue to perform at a competent level.

Friends Provident

The rationale behind the new approach to salary management at Friends Provident was the need to match salaries directly to the market and to give line managers greater accountability for staff salaries and career progression. Providing line managers with the means to reward the best performers was a top priority at a time when the organization was trying to change the culture from paternalism to high performance.

Lloyds TSB

Lloyds TSB has increasingly devolved pay decisions to line managers, who are given more freedom to manage the pay of their staff using relevant policy and budgetary guidelines. The HR function at Lloyds TSB had traditionally controlled the implementation of pay policies and practices. Line managers had tended to do what they were told. During the 1990s, the company gradually replaced these centralized, command-and-control arrangements with a system of devolved pay management. It was felt that managers who were on the spot were best equipped with the information to manage pay and rewards.

As Tim Fevyer, Senior Manager, Compensation and Benefits, explained:

> Lloyds TSB considered that the best place for making decisions about people's basic pay is where the majority of information is. Most of the information, skills and knowledge is held at the local level with the line manager. Rather than dictate pay adjustments from

the centre or set pay matrices, which to a slightly lesser degree dictated adjustments from the centre, pay management decisions were devolved. Line managers were given a pot of money and were free to allocate it where the need was greatest and where circumstances dictate.

As part of this process, Lloyds TSB pursued a 'progressive phasing' policy, moving from a fixed merit matrix, via a variable matrix the following year with more flexibility for managers in the level of award they could allocate, and finally to a position where salary decisions were made and budgets held locally. The final stage in the devolution of pay decisions to line managers was the scrapping of the variable pay matrix. Line managers were given freedom to manage the pay of their staff within pay budgets held locally, following policy guidelines and referring to information on market rates and relativities within their departments supplied by HR. The system was designed to provide greater scope for progressing individual pay according to a line manager's judgement about an employee's performance, competence and contribution in relation to market trends.

Tesco

Richard Sullivan, Group Reward Manager, explained to the e-reward researcher that:

> Now our line managers have the freedom to reward performance, contribution and potential, we are going to see that they use this to produce the top-class staff we need to enable Tesco to continue to succeed. With just six work levels, the new Tesco structure provides line managers with much greater flexibility to manage the career development and pay of their teams. Detailed guidelines have been issued to all line and human resource managers to help them manage pay within the new work levels.

Implementing total reward

Line managers have a key role in implementing total reward policies as described in Chapter 3. They are the people on the spot who can recognize achievement, provide scope for individuals to develop, increase autonomy, enhance skills through coaching, create a rewarding work environment, influence the design of jobs and deal with work/life balance issues. HR and reward specialists may define what total reward means but line managers put it into effect. Involving line managers in the development of total reward strategies, training managers in the operation of total reward schemes, giving them appropriate online support and using them to communicate schemes to their staff are all ways in which reward professionals can partner with line managers to deliver total reward strategies into practice.

Performance management

The only people who can make performance management work are line managers. It stands or falls on their commitment, efforts and skills. It is line managers who discuss role requirements with their staff in terms of objectives, skills and competencies, agree performance improvement programmes and take part in dialogues with individuals about their performance and learning and development needs. But they don't always do it very well or even want to do it. In the e-reward 2005 *Survey of Performance Management* (5) the issues most frequently mentioned by respondents were:

- Line managers do not have the skills required – 88 per cent.
- Line managers do not discriminate sufficiently when assessing performance – 84 per cent.
- Line managers are not committed to performance management – 75 per cent.
- Line managers are reluctant to conduct performance management reviews – 74 per cent.

Gaining the commitment of line managers takes a lot of time, effort and persistence but it has to be done. Here are some of the approaches that can be used:

- *Provide leadership from the top.* Top management has a crucial role to play in implementing performance management. They have to communicate and act on the belief that performance management is an integral part of the fabric of the managerial practices of the organization. They should demonstrate their conviction that this is what good management is about and this is how managers are expected to play their part.
- *Communicate.* Simply telling line managers that performance management is a good thing will not get you very far. But somehow the message has to reach them that managing performance is what managers are expected to do. The message should come from the top and be cascaded down through the organization. It should not come from HR except, incidentally, as part of a training or induction programme. The message should be built into management development programmes, especially for potential managers. It should be understood by them from the outset that performance management is an important part of their responsibilities and that these are the skills they must acquire and use. The significance of performance management can also be conveyed by including the effectiveness with which managers carry out their performance management responsibilities as one of the criteria used when assessing their performance. In addition, 360-degree appraisal systems can help to indicate how well line managers, in reality and the eyes of their staff, are carrying out their performance management and reward responsibilities.

- *Keep it simple.* Willing participation in performance management activities is more likely to be achieved if managers do not see it as a bureaucratic chore. Forms should be as simple as possible, no more than two sides of one piece of paper. It should be emphasized that performance management is not a form-filling exercise and that the important thing is the dialogue between managers and individuals that continues throughout the year and is not just an annual event.

- *Reduce the pressure.* Line managers can feel pressurized and exposed if they perceive that performance management is just about carrying out an annual appraisal meeting in which they have to tell employees where they have gone wrong, rate their performance and decide on the pay increase they should be given. This pressure can be reduced if the emphasis is on performance management throughout the year, as a continuous process. It should be regarded as part of normal good management practice that involves recognizing good work as it happens, dealing with performance problems as they arise and revising roles and objectives as required. The annual review meeting takes the form of a stocktaking exercise – no surprises – but, more importantly, becomes a forward-looking exercise: where do we go from here?

  Pressure can also be reduced if managers do not have to make and defend ratings, although they still have to reach agreement on areas for development and improvement and what needs to be done about them. A further reduction of pressure can be achieved if the emphasis in performance management is primarily forward-looking and developmental, rather than purely about performance rating and the resulting pay award.

- *Involve.* Involve line managers in the design and development of performance management processes as members of project teams or by taking part in pilot studies. This can be extended by the use of focus groups and general surveys of opinions and reactions. They can also be involved in reviewing the effectiveness of performance management. Commitment can be enhanced by getting line managers to act as sponsors and as coaches in developing performance management skills and as mentors to managers unfamiliar with the process. The more performance management is owned by line managers the better.

- *Encourage.* Line managers can be encouraged to believe in performance management through communities of practice – gatherings of managers during which information is exchanged on good practice. They are more likely to take notice of their peers than of someone from HR. But HR can still play a useful role in encouraging managers.

An example of dealing with the line management issue

One of the respondents to the e-reward 2005 *Survey of Performance Management* explained that they were dealing with this problem by:

- generating leadership from the top of the hierarchy to support/encourage the need for managers to tackle poor performance head on in a fair and positive manner;
- getting senior management to lead by example;
- tackling the negative connotations associated with performance management through cultural mindset change;
- providing education and training on how to do this effectively;
- ensuring that people see the link between individual performance and overall organizational performance.

Explaining reward policies and decisions

As has been mentioned frequently in this book, it is vital to ensure that employees understand reward management policies in general and the reward decisions that affect them in particular. This can be done centrally by senior management and HR but it is the face-to-face contact that matters most. Line managers must be capable of providing clear explanations of policies and giving people information on their pay and benefits. Following a major revision of the reward system, BT's line managers received letters from their HR business partner for each member of their team, containing their role mapping, on-target bonus level and benefits package. Each line manager was asked to ensure that the role and job family details for each individual were correct. They then printed and presented the letter to the employee in a one-to-one session, to ensure that there was an opportunity to answer any questions that the individual may have had. The responsibility was clearly with the line manager, with background HR function support.

USING REWARD CONSULTANTS

Reward consultants are used frequently to help with major development projects by providing expertise and additional resources (an extra pair of hands). They can conduct diagnostic reviews and employee attitude surveys, and provide disinterested advice. Effective consultants add credibility and value because they have the knowledge of good practice and project management that may not be available in the organization. To make good use of consultants it is necessary to:

- spell out terms of reference, deliverables and the timetable;
- take great care when selecting them to ensure that they have the expertise and experience required and will 'fit' into the organization, and that they produce realistic and acceptable indications of the cost of their fees and expenses;
- meet and vet the consultant who is going to carry out the work, not just the senior consultant who presents the proposal;
- agree up front how they will work alongside line management, HR and trade unions and the basis upon which the project will be monitored and controlled;
- ask for regular reports and hold 'milestone' meetings in order to review progress and costs.

REFERENCES

1 Chartered Institute of Personnel and Development (2005) *Reward Management Survey*, CIPD, London
2 Armstrong, M and Brown, D (2006) *Strategic Reward*, Kogan Page, London
3 Murlis, H (2005) Diverse engagement factors, Unpublished, e-reward/CIPD Reward Symposium
4 Chartered Institute of Personnel and Development (2006) *Reward Management Survey*, CIPD, London
5 e-reward (2005) *Survey of Performance Management*, e-reward.co.uk, Stockport

Appendix A

Reward bibliography

REWARD MANAGEMENT GENERAL

Books

Advisory, Conciliation and Arbitration Service (ACAS) (1994) *Introduction to Payment Systems*, ACAS, London

Armstrong, M (1999) *Rewards and Benefits Audit*, Cambridge Strategy Publications, Cambridge

Armstrong M (2002) *Employee Reward*, 3rd edn, Chartered Institute of Personnel and Development, London

Armstrong, M and Brown, D (2001) *New Dimensions in Pay Management*, Chartered Institute of Personnel and Development, London

Armstrong, M and Brown, D (2006) *Strategic Reward*, Kogan Page, London

Armstrong, M and Murlis, H (2004) *Reward Management*, 5th edn, Kogan Page, London

Beer, M (1984) Reward systems, in *Managing Human Assets*, ed M Beer *et al*, Free Press, New York

Berger, LA and Berger, DR (eds) (1999) *The Compensation Handbook*, 4th edn, McGraw-Hill, New York

Chartered Institute of Personnel and Development (2001) *Reward Determination in the UK*, CIPD, London

Chartered Institute of Personnel and Development (2001) *The Future of Reward*, CIPD, London

Chartered Institute of Personnel and Development (2003) *Reward Management 2003: A survey of policy and practice*, CIPD, London

Chartered Institute of Personnel and Development (2004) *Reward Management 2004: A survey of policy and practice*, CIPD, London

Chartered Institute of Personnel and Development (2005) *Reward Management 2005: A survey of policy and practice*, CIPD, London

Chartered Institute of Personnel and Development (2005) *Reward Management Manual*, CIPD, London

Chartered Institute of Personnel and Development (2006) *Reward Management 2006: A survey of policy and practice*, CIPD, London

Cox, A and Purcell, J (1998) Searching for leverage: pay systems, trust, motivation and commitment in SMEs, in *Trust, Motivation and Commitment*, ed SJ Perkins and St J Sandringham, Strategic Remuneration Centre, Faringdon

Druker, J and White, G (2000) *Reward Management: A critical text*, Routledge, London

e-reward (2003–06) *Reward Case Studies*, e-reward.co.uk, Stockport

Flannery, TP, Hofrichter, DA and Platten, PE (1996) *People, Performance, and Pay*, Free Press, New York

Gomez-Mejia, LR and Balkin, DB (1992) *Compensation, Organizational Strategy, and Firm Performance*, Southwestern Publishing, Cincinnati, OH

Haymarket Business Publications (1997) *Reward Strategy*, Haymarket Business Publications, London

Heneman, RL (ed) (2002) *Strategic Reward Management: Design, implementation, and evaluation*, Information Age Publishing, New York

Homans, G and Thorpe, R (2000) *Strategic Reward Systems*, FT Prentice Hall, London

Incomes Data Services (1990) *Putting Pay Philosophies into Practice*, IDS, London

Kanter, RM and Wilson, TB (2002) *Innovative Reward Systems for the Changing Workplace*, 2nd edn, McGraw-Hill, New York

Lawler, EE (1971) *Pay and Organizational Effectiveness*, McGraw-Hill, New York

Lawler, EE (1990) *Strategic Pay*, Jossey-Bass, San Francisco

Lawler, EE (1994) Effective reward systems, in *Diagnosis for Organizational Change: Methods and models*, ed A Howard, Guilford Press, New York

Lawler, EE (2000) *Rewarding Excellence: Pay strategies for the new economy*, Jossey-Bass, San Francisco

Lawler, EE (2003) *Treat People Right! How organisations and individuals can propel each other into a virtuous spiral of success*, Jossey-Bass, San Francisco

Leventhal, GS (1980) What should be done with equity theory?, in *Social Exchange: Advances in theory and research*, ed GK Gergen, MS Greenberg and RH Willis, Plenum, New York

Martocchio, J (2003) *Strategic Compensation: A human resource*, 3rd edn, Prentice Hall, New York

Murlis, H (1996) *Pay at the Crossroads*, Institute of Personnel and Development, London

Pfeffer, J (1998) *The Human Equation: Building profits by putting people first*, Harvard Business School Press, Boston, MA

Purcell, J *et al* (2003) *Inside the Black Box: How people management impacts on organisational performance*, Chartered Institute of Personnel and Development, London

Stredwick, J (1997) *Case Studies in Reward Management*, Kogan Page, London

Suff, P (2001) *The New Reward Agenda*, IRS Management Review 22, Industrial Relations Service – Eclipse Group, London

Thompson, M (1998) Trust and reward, in *Trust, Motivation and Commitment: A reader*, ed SJ Perkins and St J Sandringham, pp 66–71, Strategic Remuneration Research Centre, Faringdon

Tyler, TR and Bies, RJ (1990) Beyond formal procedures: the interpersonal context of procedural justice, in *Applied Social Psychology and Organizational Settings*, ed JS Carrol, Lawrence Erlbaum, Hillsdale, NJ

Wright, A (2003) *Reward Management in Context*, Chartered Institute of Personnel and Development, London

Zingheim, P and Schuster, JR (2000) *Pay People Right! Breakthrough strategies to create great companies*, Jossey-Bass, San Francisco

Journal articles

Armstrong, M and Brown, D (2005) Reward strategies and trends in the United Kingdom: the land of diverse and pragmatic dreams, *Compensation and Benefits Review*, July, pp 155–63

Case, J (2001) When salaries aren't secret, *Harvard Business Review*, **79** (5), May, pp 37–49

Gherson, DJ (2000) Getting the pay thing right, *Workspan*, **43** (6), June, pp 47–51

Giles, P (2001) Building a foundation for effective pay programs, *Workspan*, **44** (9), pp 28–32

IRS (2006) Making the most of reward, *IRS Pay and Benefits Bulletin*, 19 May, pp 27–31

Lawler, EE (2002) Pay strategies for the next economy: lessons from the dot-com era, in *WorldatWork Journal*, **11** (1), pp 6–10

Pfeffer, J (1998) Six dangerous myths about pay, *Harvard Business Review*, May/June, pp 42–51

Risher, H (2002) Planning a 'next generation' salary system, *Compensation and Benefits Review*, November/December, pp 13–23

Watson, S (2002) Heart stoppers: creating change with harming performance, *Workspan*, **45** (5), pp 58–62

Zingheim, PK and Schuster, JR (2002) Pay changes going forward, *Compensation and Benefits Review*, **34** (4), pp 48–53

INTERNATIONAL REWARD

Books

Perkins, SJ (2006) *Guide to International Reward and Recognition*, Chartered Institute of Personnel and Development, London

Perkins, S and Shortland, SM (2006) *Strategic International Human Resource Management*, Chapter 5, Kogan Page, London

Journal article

White, R (2005) A strategic approach to building a consistent global rewards program, *Compensation and Benefits Review*, July/August, pp 23–40

REWARD STRATEGY

Books

Armstrong, M and Brown, D (2006) *Strategic Reward*, Kogan Page, London

Ashton, C (1999) *Strategic Compensation*, Business Intelligence, London

Boxall, P and Purcell, J (2003) *Strategic Human Resource Management*, Palgrave Macmillan, Basingstoke

Brown, D (2001) *Reward Strategies: From intent to impact*, Chartered Institute of Personnel and Development, London

Mintzberg, H, Quinn, JB and James, RM (1988) *The Strategy Process: Concepts, contexts and cases*, Prentice-Hall, Englewood Cliffs, NJ

Schuster, JR and Zingheim, PK (2000) *Pay People Right! Breakthrough reward strategies to create great companies*, Jossey-Bass, San Francisco

Journal article

Lawler, EE (2000) Pay strategy: new thinking for the new millennium, *Compensation and Benefits Review*, **32** (1), January/February, pp 7–12

TOTAL REWARD

Books and reports

Bowen, RB (2000) *Recognizing and Rewarding Employees*, McGraw-Hill, New York

Chartered Institute of Personnel and Development (2002) *Total Reward*, CIPD, London

Graham, MD and Manus, TM (2002) *Creating a Total Rewards Strategy: A toolkit for designing business-based plans*, Amacom, New York

Herriot, P (2000) *The Employment Relationship: A psychological perspective*, Routledge, London

Manus, TM and Graham, MD (2003) *Creating a Total Rewards Strategy*, American Management Association, New York

Mintzberg, H, Quinn, JB and James, RM (1988) *The Strategy Process: Concepts, contexts and cases*, Prentice-Hall, Englewood Cliffs, NJ

Towers Perrin (2005) *Reconnecting with Employees: Quantifying the value of engaging your workforce*, Towers Perrin, London

WorldatWork (2000) *Total Rewards: From strategy to implementation*, WorldatWork, Scottsdale, AZ

Journal articles

Ben-Ora, D and Lyons, FH (2002) Total rewards strategy: the best foundation of pay for performance, *Compensation and Benefits Review*, **34** (2), April, pp 34–40

O'Neal, S (1998) The phenomenon of total rewards, *ACA Journal*, **7** (3), pp 18–23

MOTIVATION, ENGAGEMENT AND COMMITMENT

Books

Adams, J (1965) Injustice in social exchange, in *Advances in Experimental Psychology*, ed L Berkowitz, Academic Press, New York

Alderfer, C (1972) *Existence, Relatedness and Growth*, Free Press, New York

Goleman, D, Boyatzis, R and McKee, A (2002) *Primal Leadership: The hidden driver of great performance*, Harvard Business School Press, Boston, MA

Gratton, L (2004) *The Democratic Enterprise: Liberating your business with freedom, flexibility and commitment*, FT Prentice Hall, London

Hay Group (2002) *Engage Employees and Boost Performance*, Hay Group, London

Herzberg, F, Mausner, B and Snyderman, B (1957) *The Motivation to Work*, Wiley, New York

Katzenbach, JR (2000) *Peak Performance: Aligning the hearts and minds of your employees*, Harvard Business School Press, Cambridge, MA

Maslow, A (1954) *Motivation and Personality*, Harper & Row, New York

Porter, L and Lawler, EE (1968) *Management Attitudes and Behaviour*, Irwin-Dorsey, Homewood, IL

Thomas, KW (2003) *Intrinsic Motivation at Work: Building energy and commitment*, Berrett-Koehler, San Francisco

Vroom, V (1964) *Work and Motivation*, Wiley, New York

Wallace, MJ and Szilagyi, L (1982) *Managing Behaviour in Organizations*, Scott, Glenview, IL

Journal articles

Gupta, N and Shaw, JD (1998) Financial incentives *are* effective!, *Compensation and Benefits Review*, March/April, pp 26, 28–32

Herzberg, F (2003) One more time: how do you motivate employees?, *Harvard Business Review*, **81** (1), pp 87–96

Hollyforde, S and Whiddett, S (2002) How to nurture motivation, *People Management*, **8** (14), 11 July, pp 52–53

Kessler, I and Purcell, J (1992) Performance-related pay: objectives and applications, *Human Resource Management Journal*, **2** (3), Spring, pp 16–32

Kohn, A (1993) Why incentive plans cannot work, *Harvard Business Review*, September/October, pp 54–63

Latham, G and Locke, EA (1979) Goal setting: a motivational technique that works, *Organisational Dynamics*, Autumn, pp 68–80

Lawler, EE (1969) Job design and employee motivation, *Personnel Psychology*, 22, pp 426–35

Murlis, H and Watson, S (2001) Creating employee engagement: transforming the employment deal, *Benefits and Compensation International*, **30** (8), pp 25–29

Watson, S (2003) Total rewards: building a better employment deal, *Workspan*, **46** (12), pp 48–51

JOB EVALUATION

Books and reports

Advisory, Conciliation and Arbitration Service (2003) *Job Evaluation: An introduction*, ACAS, London

Armstrong, M *et al* (2003) *Job Evaluation: A guide to achieving equal pay*, Kogan Page, London

Grayson, D (1987) *Job Evaluation in Transition*, ACAS, London

Incomes Data Services (2003) *IDS Studies Plus: Job evaluation*, IDS, London

International Labour Office (1986) *Job Evaluation*, International Labour Office, Geneva

Jaques, E (1961) *Equitable Payment*, Heinemann, London

Pritchard, D and Murlis, H (1992) *Jobs, Roles and People*, Nicholas Brealey, London

Quaid, M (1993) *Job Evaluation: The myth of equitable settlement*, University of Toronto Press, Toronto

Journal articles

Arvey, RD (1986) Sex bias in job evaluation procedures, *Personnel Psychology*, **39**, pp 35–48

Emerson, SM (1991) Job evaluation: a barrier to excellence, *Compensation and Benefits Review*, January/February, pp 4–17

Heneman, RL (2001) Work evaluation: current state of the art and future prospects, *WorldatWork Journal*, **10** (3), pp 65–70

Heneman, RL and LeBlanc, PV (2002) Developing a more relevant and competitive approach for valuing knowledge work, *Compensation and Benefits Review*, **34** (4), pp 43–47

Lawler, EE (1986) What's wrong with point-factor job evaluation?, *Compensation and Benefits Review*, March/April, pp 20–28

Research

e-reward (2002) *Survey of Job Evaluation*, e-reward.co.uk, Stockport

EQUAL PAY

Books

Chartered Institute of Personnel and Development (2001) *Equal Pay Guide*, CIPD, London

Equal Opportunities Commission (2003) *Good Practice Guide: Job evaluation schemes free of sex bias*, EOC, Manchester

Equal Pay Task Force (2001) *Just Pay*, Report of the Equal Pay Task Force to the Equal Opportunities Commission, EOC, Manchester

Falconer, H (2003) *One Stop Guide: Equal pay reviews*, Personnel Today Management Resources – Reed Business Information, London

Hastings, S (1989) *Identifying Discrimination in Job Evaluation Schemes*, Trade Union Research Unit, Oxford

Hastings, S (1991) *Developing a Less Discriminatory Job Evaluation Scheme*, Trade Union Research Unit, Oxford

Kingsmill, D (2001) *Review of Women's Employment and Pay*, HMSO, Norwich

National Institute of Economic and Social Research (2001) *The Gender Pay Gap*, Women and Equality Unit, Department of Trade and Industry, London

Journal articles

Arvey, RD (1986) Sex bias in job evaluation procedures, *Personnel Psychology*, **39**, pp 315–35

IRS Employment Review (2003) Chasing progress on equal pay, *IRS Employment Review*, 774, 18 April, pp 19–22

Paddison, L (2001) How to conduct an equal pay review, *People Management*, 14 June, pp 58–59

GRADE AND PAY STRUCTURES

Books and reports

Armstrong, M and Brown, D (2001) *New Dimensions in Pay Management*, Chartered Institute of Personnel and Development, London

Gilbert, D and Abosch, KS (1996) *Improving Organizational Effectiveness through Broad-Banding*, American Compensation Association, Scottsdale, IL

Incomes Data Services (2006) *IDS HR Studies: Job families*, IDS, London

Journal articles

Armstrong, M (2000) Feel the width, *People Management*, 3 February, pp 34–38

Armstrong, M (2004) What's happening to broad-banding?, *IDS Executive Compensation Review*, June, pp 7–8

Braddick, CA, Jones, MB and Shafer, PM (1992) A look at broad-banding in practice, *Compensation and Benefits Review*, July/August, pp 24–28

Fay, CH *et al* (2004) Broadbanding, pay ranges and labour costs: an empirical test, *WorldatWork Journal*, **13** (2), pp 32–39

LeBlanc, PV and Ellkis, ME (1995) The many faces of broad-banding, *ACA Journal*, Winter, pp 52–56

Richter, AS (1998) Paying the people in black at the big blue, *Compensation and Benefits Review*, May/June, pp 51–59

Risher, H (2002) Planning a 'next generation' salary system, *Compensation and Benefits Review*, November/December, pp 13–22

PERFORMANCE MANAGEMENT

Books and reports

Armstrong, M (2006) *Performance Management*, 3rd edn, Kogan Page, London

Armstrong, M and Baron, A (1998) *Performance Management: The new realities*, Chartered Institute of Personnel and Development, London

Armstrong, M and Baron, A (2004) *Performance Management: Action and impact*, Chartered Institute of Personnel and Development, London

Baguley, P (2002) *Performance Management in a Week*, 2nd edn, Hodder Arnold, London

e-reward (2005) *Survey of Performance Management*, e-reward.co.uk, Stockport

Incomes Data Services (2003) *IDS Studies: Performance management*, IDS, London

Personnel Today and PeopleSoft (2004) *Performance Management Survey*, Personnel Today Management Resources – Reed Business Information, London

Suff, P (2001) *Performance Management – Revisited*, IRS Management Review 21, Industrial Relations Service – Eclipse Group, London

Journal articles

Egan, G (1995) A clear path to peak performance, *People Management*, 18 May, pp 34–37

Grint, K (1993) What's wrong with performance appraisal? A critique and a suggestion, *Human Resource Management Journal*, Spring, pp 61–77

Lawler, EE and McDermott, M (2003) Current performance management practices: examining the varying impacts, *WorldatWork Journal*, Second quarter, pp 49–60

McGregor, D (1957) An uneasy look at performance appraisal, *Harvard Business Review*, May/June, pp 89–94

Morris, E and Sparrow, T (2001) Transforming appraisals with emotional intelligence, *Competency and Emotional Intelligence Quarterly*, **9** (1), pp 8–32

Peiperl, MA (2001) Getting 360 degree feedback right, *Harvard Business Review*, January/February, pp 142–47

Stiles, P, Gratton, L and Truss, C (2001) Performance management and the psychological contract, *Human Resource Management Journal*, **7** (1), pp 57–66

Williams, V (2001) Making performance management relevant, *Compensation and Benefits Review*, July/August, pp 47–51

Winstanley, D and Stuart-Smith, K (1996) Policing performance: the ethics of performance management, *Personnel Review*, **25** (6), pp 66–84

CONTINGENT PAY

Books and reports

Armstrong, M (2000) *Rewarding Teams*, Chartered Institute of Personnel and Development, London

Brown, D and Armstrong, M (1999) *Paying for Contribution: Real performance-related pay strategies*, Kogan Page, London

Cannell, M and Wood, S (1992) *Incentive Pay*, IPM, London

Chartered Institute of Personnel and Development (2002) *Guide to Bonus and Incentive Plans*, CIPD, London

Cross, M (1992) *Skill-based Pay*, IPM, London

Crystal, G (1970) *Financial Motivation for Executives*, AMA, New York

e-reward (2004) *Survey of Contingent Pay*, e-reward.co.uk, Stockport

Geldman, A, Holroyd, K and Suff, P (eds) (2003) *Restructuring Performance-related Pay*, Managing Best Practice 105, Work Foundation, London

Incomes Data Services (2003) *IDS Studies Plus: Employee recognition schemes*, IDS, London

Marsden, D and French, S (1998) *What a Performance: Performance-related pay in the public services*, Centre for Economic Performance, London

Parker, G, McAdams, J and Zielinski, D (2000) *Rewarding Teams: Lessons from the trenches*, Jossey-Bass, San Francisco

Reilly, P (ed) (2003) *New Reward: Team, skill and competency based pay*, Institute for Employment Studies, Brighton

Rose, M (2001) *Recognising Performance: Non-cash rewards*, Chartered Institute of Personnel and Development, London

Thompson, M (1992) *Pay and Performance: The employer experience*, Report No. 218, Institute of Manpower Studies, Brighton

WorldatWork (2001) *The Best of Variable Pay: Incentives, recognition and rewards*, WorldatWork, Scottsdale, AZ

Journal articles

Fisher, J (2001) How to design incentive schemes, *People Management*, 11 January, pp 38–39

Freeman, R (2001) Upping the stakes, Employee share ownership feature, *People Management*, 8 February, pp 25–29

IRS (2003) Sharing the spoils: profit-share and bonus schemes, *IRS Employment Review*, 784, *Pay and Benefits Bulletin*, 19 September, pp 28–33

Keegan, BP (2002) Incentive programs boost employee morale and productivity, *Workspan*, **45** (3), March, pp 30–33

Reilly, P, Phillipson, J and Smith, P (2005) Team-based pay in the United Kingdom, *Compensation and Benefits Review*, July/August, pp 54–60

Ryan, R (1983) The relation of reward contingency and interpersonal context to intrinsic motivation, *Journal of Personality and Social Psychology*, **45** (4), pp 56–71

REWARDING SALES AND SERVICE STAFF

Books

Holmes, SG and Smith, N (1987) *Sales Force Incentives*, Heinemann, London

Langley, M (1987) *Rewarding the Sales Force*, IPM, London

Moynahan, JK (1991) *Sales Compensation Handbook*, American Management Association, New York

West, M *et al* (2005) *Rewarding Customer Service? Using reward and recognition to deliver your customer service strategy*, Chartered Institute of Personnel and Development, London

Journal articles

Gundy, P (2002) Sales compensation programmes: built to last, *Compensation and Benefits Review*, September/October, pp 21–28

Luo, S (2003) Does your sales incentive plan pay for performance?, *Compensation and Benefits Review*, **35** (1), January/February, pp 18–24

Zingheim, PK and Schuster, JR (2004) Sales reward solutions, *Compensation and Benefits Review*, September/October, pp 21–26

EMPLOYEE BENEFITS

Books and reports

Chartered Institute of Personnel and Development (2002) *Pensions and HR's Role: A guide*, Chartered Institute of Personnel and Development, London

Chartered Institute of Personnel and Development (2004) *Flexible Benefits*, CIPD, London

House of Commons Work and Pensions Committee (2003) *The Future of UK Pensions, Third Report of Session 2002–03*, Stationery Office, Norwich

Hutchinson, P (2002) *Flexible Benefits: A practical guide*, Butterworths Tolley, Croydon

Journal articles

Daugherty, C (2002) How to introduce flexible benefits, *People Management*, 10 January, pp 42–43

IRS Employment Review (2003) Benefits and allowances, Annual survey, Part 1, *IRS Employment Review*, 776, 23 May, pp 29–34

IRS Employment Review (2003) Benefits and allowances, Annual survey, Part 2, *IRS Employment Review*, 777, 6 June, pp 30–35

IRS Employment Review (2003) Benefits and allowances, Annual survey, Part 3, *IRS Employment Review*, 778, 20 June, pp 28–34

Lewin, C (2003) Pension developments in the UK, *Benefits and Compensation International*, **32** (9), pp 19–21

Appendix B

Alignment of CIPD Professional Standards for Employee Reward to text

This appendix links the CIPD Professional Standards for Employee Reward with page references to where each part of the Standards is covered in the text of this book.

Index